SECOND EDITION

STRATEGIC MANAGEMENT
• PRINCIPLES • AND PRACTICE

BARRY J. WITCHER
VINH SUM CHAU

CENGAGE
Learning®

Australia • Brazil • Japan • Korea • Mexico • Singapore • Spain • United Kingdom • United States

Strategic Management: Principles and Practice, 2nd edition
Barry J. Witcher and Vinh Sum Chau

Publishing Director: Linden Harris

Publisher: Andrew Ashwin

Development Editor: Felix Rowe

Senior Production Editor: Alison Cooke

Senior Manufacturing Buyer: Eyvett Davis

Typesetter: Cenveo Publisher Services

Cover design: Adam Renvoize

For product information and technology assistance, contact **emea.info@cengage.com**.

For permission to use material from this text or product, and for permission queries, email **emea.permissions@cengage.com**.

British Library Cataloguing-in-Publication Data
A catalogue record for this book is available from the British Library.

ISBN: 978-1-4080-6395-8

Cengage Learning EMEA
Cheriton House, North Way, Andover, Hampshire, SP10 5BE United Kingdom

Cengage Learning products are represented in Canada by Nelson Education Ltd.

For your lifelong learning solutions, visit
www.cengage.co.uk

Purchase your next print book, e-book or e-chapter at
www.cengagebrain.com

Printed in China By RR Donnelley
1 2 3 4 5 6 7 8 9 10 – 16 15 14

Dedications

Per Kate, *mia moglie, Che è la mia vita*
– B. J. Witcher

For my wife and daughter
– V. S. Chau

Brief contents

Contents

I Strategic management and its purpose 3

II Strategic objectives and analysis 61

3 Objectives 62

4 The external environment 90

5 The internal environment 122

III Strategy 155

 Managing strategy in action 247

List of cases

Acknowledgements

We wish to express our appreciation of the editorial and production team at Cengage Learning EMEA for the excellent and patient support given to us in the writing of this book. In particular, we thank Felix Rowe for his inspiration (and sometimes patience!) without which you would not be reading this book. Many people supported us beyond the call of duty, including our families. And not least, of course, we appreciate the help of tutors and contribution of our students.

We wish to thank the following colleagues who supplied advice and insights during the writing process:

Neil Wellard, Cardiff Business School (UK)
Piotr Zmuda, Cologne Business School (Germany)
Stephen Henderson, Leeds Metropolitan University (UK)

The publisher also thanks the various copyright holders for granting permission to reproduce material throughout the text. A credits page is provided at the back of the book.

About the book

The purpose of *Strategic Management: Principles and Practice* is twofold: to provide a comprehensive and concise study of the basic principles and essentials for the strategic management of organizations, and to provide an account of developing practice as internal and external organizational environments change. The term, 'organizations', includes a wide range of different types including, for example, private, public and non-profit, together with a comprehensive range of sizes and structures of organizations. The scope of the book is international, going beyond examples of American and European experience to the emerging global economies, such as those of the BRICS countries. We have used many examples drawn from our own research.

Strategic management is the direction and management of an organization in its entirety, subject to the strategic requirements of long-term purpose, overall objectives, and strategy. The basic principle is that an organization should build its strengths around its resources in ways to help it proactively adapt to change, so that it is able to influence its environment and over the long period be able to control its own destiny subject to the needs of its stakeholders. The *management* part of strategic management is every bit as important as the strategic or strategy part of strategic management. We have written this book in a way that we hope we have been true to our belief that management matters.

The strategic management of organizations should be understood as an entire or whole process, not just as a collection of functional parts. In this sense, strategic management is the most challenging and arguably the most important function in an organization. The book introduces essential theory in ways to engage readers who have little or no business and management experience. Strategy and policy concepts are presented to help understand concisely, and easily, the prescriptive and emergent perspectives current in the subject area.

The book has 11 chapters. The first provides a model and overview of the subject area and distinguishes clearly between strategic management and strategy.

The next chapter explains the meaning of strategic purpose, which provides the basis for the nature of an organization's strategic management.

The third chapter covers strategic objectives: the translation of purpose into benchmarks for strategy.

Chapters 4 and 5, explain the important environmental influences, external and internal, on exploring and choosing strategy.

The development of strategy at three levels is considered in the next three chapters about business, corporate and global strategy. These explain strategy for the single business, strategy for more than one business, and the special circumstances that are important to international strategy.

Chapter 9 explains putting strategy in place through organizing, while Chapter 10 considers the strategic management of performance following strategy implementation.

The book concludes with an examination of strategic leadership in relation to management.

About the authors

Barry Witcher

Dr Barry Witcher is Emeritus Reader in Strategic Management at the Norwich Business School, University of East Anglia (UEA). He teaches and researches in strategic management. His experience includes directorships of the school's undergraduate, masters' and research programmes. Barry has held three major ESRC grants in the subject areas of strategy, including videotext and Japanese *hoshin kanri*. Before joining the university sector he worked as an economist in the City of London, and various other jobs have included fish farming and the developing of community cooperatives in the Hebrides. Barry has worked at Strathclyde, Stirling, Teesside, and Durham Universities and is a visiting professor at several overseas universities. He has published widely in strategic management.

Vinh Sum Chau

Dr Vinh Sum Chau is Senior Lecturer in Strategy at the Kent Business School, University of Kent (UK). Vinh teaches and researches in strategic management. He has given major keynote addresses at internationally acclaimed management symposia and presented original research in Europe, the Americas and China. His consultation includes major UK energy companies and advice to UK public sector emergency services. He is an Associate Editor of the *British Journal of Management* and holds the Chair of the British Academy of Management's special interest group and annual conference track in Performance Management. Vinh has published his research widely in areas of strategic performance management, strategy implementation, service quality, Asia-Pacific management, public sector management, and customer satisfaction.

Walk through tour

Learning Objectives Appear at the start of every chapter to help you monitor your understanding and progress.

Business Vignette Appear at the start of each chapter to show how issues are applied in real-life business situations.

Quotes Quotes are used throughout the text to illustrate a spectrum of opinions; these are ideal for provoking class discussion and examination questions.

Principles in Practice Examples of key principles in real-life scenarios.

Key Debates Discussions of different perspectives on key issues.

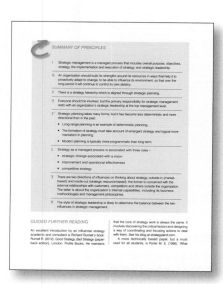

Summary Each chapter ends with a comprehensive summary that provides a thorough re-cap of the key issues, helping you to assess your understanding and revise key content.

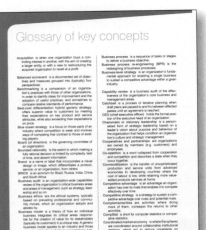

Glossary and Key Terms Key terms are listed at the beginning of each chapter, highlighted in colour throughout and explained in full at the end of the book, enabling you to find explanations of key terms quickly.

End of Chapter Cases Long cases discuss in depth the issues and principles encountered during the chapter.

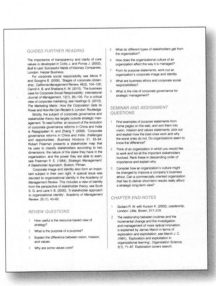

Further Reading At the end of each chapter allows you to explore the subject further, and acts as a starting point for projects and assignments.

DIGITAL RESOURCES

Dedicated Instructor Resources

To discover the dedicated instructor online
support resources accompanying this textbook,
instructors should register here for access:
http://login.cengage.com

Resources include:

- Instructor's Manual
- ExamView Testbank
- PowerPoint slides

Instructor access

Instructors can access the online student platform by registering
at http://login.cengage.com or by speaking to their local
Cengage Learning EMEA representative.

Instructor resources

Instructors can use the integrated Engagement Tracker to track students' preparation and
engagement. The tracking tool can be used to monitor progress of the class as a whole, or for
individual students.

Student access

Students can access the online platform using the unique personal access card included in the
front of the book.

Student resources

The platform offers a range of interactive learning tools tailored to the second edition of
Strategic Management: Principles and Practice, Second Edition, including:

- Quizzes and self-test questions
- Interactive eBook
- Games
- Glossary
- Flashcards
- Links to useful websites

CO CON

'THE PRIMARY RESPONSIBILITY FOR CARRYING OUT STRATEGIC MANAGEMENT BELONGS TO AN ORGANIZATION'S SENIOR MANAGERS. EVERYBODY IN THE ORGANIZATION IS INVOLVED IN THIS ACTIVITY TO SOME EXTENT, BUT ONLY A SENIOR LEVEL WILL HAVE THE REQUIRED BREADTH OF KNOWLEDGE AND OVERSIGHT TO BE ABLE TO SEE THE ORGANIZATION AS A WHOLE.'

Strategic management and its purpose

Part 1 is an introduction to thinking about strategic management (Chapter 1) and the role of purpose as a starting point for strategy as a managed business-wide process (Chapter 2).

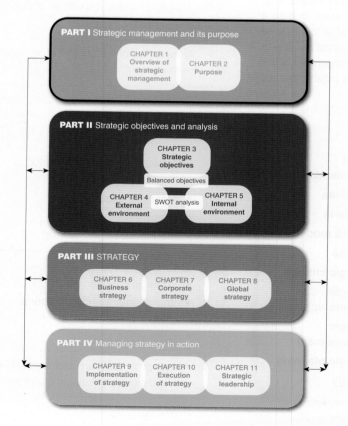

Chapter 1
OVERVIEW OF STRATEGIC MANAGEMENT

Strategic management

Strategic management is the direction and management of an organization in its entirety subject to the strategic requirements of long-term purpose, overall objectives and strategy.[1] A basic principle is that an organization should build its strengths around its resources in ways to help it proactively adapt to change, to be able to influence its environment, and so over a long period be able to control its own destiny. Strategic management is the most challenging and arguably the most important function in an organization.

KEY TERMS

- bounded rationality
- competitive advantage
- deliberate strategy
- emergent strategy
- execution
- implementation
- improvement change
- inside-out
- logical incrementalism
- objectives
- outside-in
- POSIES model
- purpose
- strategic change
- strategic leadership
- strategic management
- strategic planning
- strategy

LEARNING OBJECTIVES

This chapter provides you with an understanding of the following:

1 An overview of the subject of strategic management

2 The basic model of strategic management

3 Strategy perspectives

4 Strategic planning in relation to
   - long-range planning
   - emergent strategy
   - logical incrementalism
   - modern strategic planning

5 The meaning of
   - strategic change
   - improvement and operational effectiveness
   - competitive strategy

6 A distinction between outside-in and inside-out influences on strategic management

Business vignette
Look at any two organizations and you will see differences based on strategy.

Strategy is fundamental to why a customer continues to buy and experience a product and service over time, and it should differentiate an organization's value from that offered by its competitors. Value is the satisfaction and benefits customers (and other stakeholders) receive in return for buying and using products and services.

The secret of success is not to excel equally in everything, but – and especially – in those things that are vital to the *unique* value that an organization creates for its customers. This is important to nearly all organizations. Take for example the difference in service offered by retail banks by the UK brands, NatWest and HSBC.

NatWest has a locally pitched strategy based on 'helpful banking' and the 'local bank', and the importance of its branches is paramount for an attentive service based on a Customer Charter prominently displayed at every branch outlet. At HSBC strategy is linked to 'celebrating global diversity', which emphasizes the importance of customer convenience, and the importance to this of flexible, internationally organized but cost saving online processes.[2] This difference has been characterized as 'bricks versus clicks' competition.

Of course, all retail banks provide a basic universal banking service and have also encouraged the convenience of internet-based services, which in turn has encouraged some banks to reduce costs by closing branches. However, HSBC has followed this path more than most and has gone further to automate service at its remaining branches.

At NatWest, strategy is all about personal service, while at HSBC strategy is about product based on convenience and cost.

NatWest and HSBC operate different service strategies

> # Strategic management is the direction and management of an organization in its entirety subject to the strategic requirements of long-term purpose, overall objectives, and strategy.

What is strategic management?

Paul Robinson, a speech writer for President Reagan, wrote a book about his time as a student at Stanford University in California, in which he said he thought strategic management gave:

… a sense of a subject that didn't know what it was. One article, entitled Crafting Strategy, argued executives should develop their business strategy the way potters crafted clay, abandoning conscious, analytical thought in favour of feel and intuition. … This Mintzberg was the author who had compared running big companies to making clay pots.[3]

It is true the titles of strategy textbooks and college programmes display a bewildering variety of names. These include 'business policy', 'corporate strategy', 'competitive strategy' or just 'strategy'. They emphasize strategic thinking and leadership, rather than strategic management.

These differences stem, at least partly, from the variety that exists in the range of different social science and business management perspectives. For example, Mintzberg and others[4] compare strategy to an elephant and suggest there are ten different schools of strategy, which are different from each other because they each look at a different part of the strategy elephant. There is a degree of irony about this, because if strategy is about anything it is about seeing the whole picture, even if it is as big as an elephant.

A relatively new European-based field of scholarship, strategy-as-practice, has emerged, which takes a micro-view of how people strategize at a detailed level of practice. On the official website, it is stated that the approach focuses on the processes and practices constituting the everyday activities of organizational life and relating to strategic outcomes.[5]

Generally, strategy is defined in many ways in the business and management literature. In a much cited typology, Mintzberg and Quinn identify five meanings, which are discussed later.[6]

1. Strategy as a plan
2. Strategy as a pattern
3. Strategy as a position
4. Strategy as a perspective
5. Strategy as a ploy

In a recent *Harvard Business Review article,* the editor argues that science must be brought to the art of strategy, 'to marry', as the journal puts it, 'empirical rigour with creative thinking'.[7] Perhaps the time for making clay pots is coming to an end.

Question: How would you define strategic management as a subject for study?

The strategic management model

The basic components of the strategic management process are as follows: Purpose – Objectives – Strategy – Implementation – Evaluation – Strategic leadership (**POSIES model**; Figure 1.1).

Purpose is the primary and basic reason for the existence of an organization and it properly represents the starting point for understanding an organization in its entirety. It is articulated at the top level of an organization and is communicated from there through purpose statements about vision, mission, and values (see Chapter 2).

Objectives are an organization's desired strategic outcomes. The responsibility for these lies with top management and they are used to help guide an organization's management of its strategy (see Chapter 3).

FIGURE 1.1 The POSIES model of the strategic management process

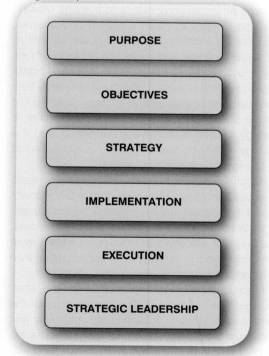

Strategy is an approach for directing an organization's operations over time. It is a long-term approach or policy for accomplishing an organization's purpose and objectives. Its nature differs for many reasons. Notably it can be based on an organization's needs associated with its external environment (see Chapter 4) or with its internal environment (see Chapter 5). Strategy is also likely to differ in terms of an organization's scale, industry and markets: for a single business (see Chapter 6), a multi-business organization (Chapter 7) and at the global-level (Chapter 8).

Implementation involves putting in place the appropriate organizational structure to carry out an organization's strategy (Chapter 9). **Execution** is the management of delivery of strategy in daily management (see Chapter 10). Finally, **strategic leadership** is the style and general approach used by leaders for strategically managing an organization. A leadership's style and level of expectation are important influences on how other organizational levels work strategically (see Chapter 11).

The responsibilities for strategic management

The responsibility for strategic management belongs to the top of an organization. It is the job of an organization's leaders and senior managers to take charge of purpose, objectives and strategy. While everybody is involved to some extent, it is the senior level of management that spends most of its time on strategic management (see Figure 1.2). Other organizational levels spend most of their time on daily management, which is typically routine work of an operational and functional character. However, while strategic management is essentially a top-down directed process, it needs to facilitate bottom-up decision-making and feedback about the feasibility and progress of objectives and strategy at operational and functional levels.

FIGURE 1.2 Involvement in strategic management

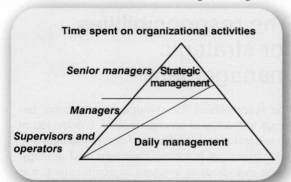

Strategy and strategic management

Modern ideas of strategy as a business management concept developed during the second half of the 20th century. Two notable contributions to scholarship came from Alfred Chandler, a business historian, and Igor Ansoff, a senior executive who worked at Lockheed Electronics. Chandler developed strategy as a concept for understanding the structures used by large American corporations to manage growth.[9] He used strategy to mean a pattern of objectives; this included overall purpose and goals, as well as the major policies and plans for achieving them. Igor Ansoff produced one of the first general books about corporate strategy.[10] He argued, differently from Chandler, that objectives and strategy (which could include policies and plans) act upon each other: a strategy is used to achieve an objective, and if a strategy cannot be found, then the objective has to be changed to make it more realistic.

Ansoff's more narrow use of strategy as the means to achieve an objective is essentially a practitioner's view of the concept and it is probably the more useful for understanding the strategic management process. The view that strategy is broader is associated more with understanding 'strategy' as a subject rather than as a part of the strategic management process.[11]

Practitioners often distinguish between the 'what' and the 'how' of strategy. The former is about the content of a strategy, including its objectives and what must be achieved, and the latter is about the process for managing strategy to achieve its objectives. Scholars sometimes add a third dimension, context: that is, the reason for the strategy.

Strategy perspectives

More generally strategy is used in many ways. Much depends upon the background of who is using the word. It is possible to distinguish between two general categories of meanings for strategy: there are technical meanings about what strategy does, and subject meanings about how the subject of strategy is thought about. An example of the former is the five meanings of strategy[12], and of the latter, the ten schools of strategy. The five meanings involve:

- A plan is a consciously intended course of action to achieve an objective.
- A pattern is a consistent pattern of behaviour emerging deliberately and unintentionally.
- A position is a place in an environment relative to a rival and potential rivals.
- A perspective is a shared organization-wide sense of purpose in the world.
- A ploy is a manoeuvre to achieve a particular aim (such as to outwit a rival).

Seeing strategy in these terms helps clarify thinking about what kind of job a strategy should do. Of course they should not constrain thinking, but understanding how a strategy might be used makes their management easier.

Mintzberg and others[13] identify ten schools of strategy. They describe the strategic management beast as an elephant, and argue that each school is focused on, and sees only, a part of the whole animal. The first three schools are prescriptive in that they focus on how strategy should be formulated and implemented. Prescription typically involves using an organizational hierarchy to instruct and control middle management, a level of management which in turn instructs lower-level subordinates. The rest are descriptive, where the primary focus is on how strategy formation is shaped in character depending upon the nature of organizational actors and the relations between them.

1. The design school: this sees strategy formation as a process of conception, often to attain a fit between an organization's internal capabilities and its external opportunities.

2. The planning school: strategy formation is a formal process; typically involving strategic planning, its implementation is a series of sequential steps.

3. The positioning school: strategy formation as an analytical process, involving generic strategy to sustain a competitive position within an industry.

4. The entrepreneurial school: strategy formation is a visionary and intuitive process, typically embodied in the outward character of a leader.

5. The cognitive school: strategy formation as a mental process in the minds of strategists.

6. The learning school: strategy formation as an emergent process involving, for example, logical incrementalism; the resource-based view of strategy.

7. The power school: strategy formation as a process of negotiation, including power games.

8. The cultural school: strategy formation as a collective process, involving social and cultural processes.

9. The environmental school: strategy formation as a reaction to events, where the environment is the central actor in the strategy-making process.

10. The configuration school: strategy is a process of transformation from one state (an organizational configuration) to another.

The idea that views of strategic management are partial seems to belie the notion that its processes should be understood holistically. The debates surrounding 'what is strategy' are perhaps philosophical. Of course, in practice there is no one right answer that favours one view over another. Indeed the likelihood of achieving a consensus about what is strategy is problematic. The lesson of the ten schools is that it is possible to define strategy in different ways and probably there are as many views as there are people. One implication of the five definitions and ten schools is that strategy will be deployed in many different ways depending on context for decisions at the time and the functional area of the business concerned. This is especially so in different parts and levels of an organization.

Strategy in China

Beijing State-owned Assets Management Co., Ltd (BSAM) was established in April 2001 by the Chinese government. It is a wholly-owned state enterprise funded by the Beijing Municipal Government.

Its purpose is to manage the operations of state-owned assets and to grow financial capital through (1) the disposal of non-core assets; (2) attracting financial and industrial investors; and (3) the expansion into profitable and high-tech areas. China is going through fundamental economic change; many state-owned enterprises need financial restructuring, a clean-up of their non-performing loans and improvement of the overall quality of their assets.

In the words of BSAM's Chairman, Li Qiqing, the role of the company is:

As a company, we are dedicated to hastening the pace of modernization in accordance with the highest international standards. To achieve our targets, we will further expand our highly qualified staff and seek technological and financial cooperation with reputed international companies to expand and diversify our business ventures. We will pay attention to corporate governance and we are confident that our new management system coupled with a company culture dedicated to the spirit of creativity, loyalty, hard work and team spirit will be a model to be emulated overall in China. With the cooperation of all we are convinced that BSAM is a key link to a better future for Beijing, our business partners and our staff and that we can jointly face the challenges of tomorrow with confidence.[14]

There are five strategies:

1. Develop as a large scale holding company through equity management in diverse financial institutions, to be able to act quickly to provide investment capital through one-to-one financial services.

2. Strengthen international co-operation and establish strategic alliances with foreign companies, to act as investors, or are able to provide advanced technology, management expertise or international networking.

3. Engage in state-owned capital operations of large-scale enterprises, to obtain the best advantages for investment.

4. Employ international and professional competences.

5. Develop corporate values and culture generally, in terms of corporate governance to emphasize the accountability and conduct of board members and managers, which enhance internal control reforms and transparency.

Question: How will the five strategies help the company achieve its role?

The strategy hierarchy

'Strategy' in the POSIES model is defined in an overall sense for the organization as a whole, but strategy also occurs as a strategy hierarchy across different organizational levels. This is illustrated in the case of a corporation with several businesses in Figure 1.3: this depicts corporate strategy as an influence on business strategy, which in turn influences departmental strategy, and so on through operational levels to influence the strategies of teams and individuals.

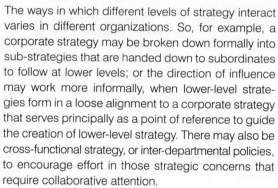

The ways in which different levels of strategy interact varies in different organizations. So, for example, a corporate strategy may be broken down formally into sub-strategies that are handed down to subordinates to follow at lower levels; or the direction of influence may work more informally, when lower-level strategies form in a loose alignment to a corporate strategy that serves principally as a point of reference to guide the creation of lower-level strategy. There may also be cross-functional strategy, or inter-departmental policies, to encourage effort in those strategic concerns that require collaborative attention.

So, be warned, the term 'strategy' can apply anywhere in an organization. Functional strategy, such as marketing or financial strategy, is used only within the specialist area concerned. It is context that actually defines what it is, how it is used, where and who uses it. The most important consideration for strategic management, however, is *overall* strategy, as this should influence all other strategies. The direction of the influence of overall strategy to lower organizational levels is organized by senior managers through strategic planning.

Strategic planning

Strategic planning is a management process of sequencing activities in terms of responsibilities and resources within a given time frame to progress an organization's purpose, objectives and strategy. Planning, of course, can be applied to almost any function and course of action, but the word 'strategic' means that this form of planning applies to the organization as a whole and not just to a part of the organization, such as a functional area like finance, human resources, marketing or operations. An example that is fairly typical of the sequence is a process carried out at a business level for Honeywell[16]:

1 Review the business foundations to question basic assumptions to see if the vision, values, mission, and core competencies of the organization continue to remain appropriate, and check behaviour against values.

2 Conduct a situation analysis.

3 Conduct a current condition analysis.

4 Develop issues to identify the critical areas to derive action statements.

5 Create strategic initiatives from the action statements, order them according to priority, and examine these against the business foundations, situation, and current conditions.

These steps used at Honeywell are similar to the POSIES strategic management model presented above. The sequence of POSIES may suggest strategic management to be a compartmentalized process of separated steps. In practice these elements of strategic management intertwine and interconnect.

FIGURE 1.3 Strategy hierarchy

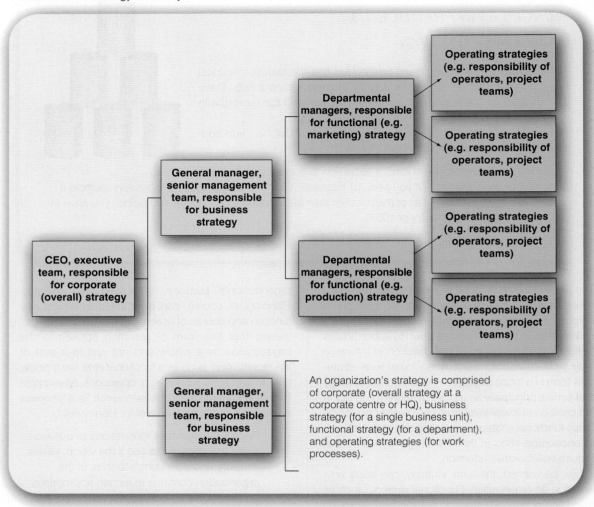

An organization's strategy is comprised of corporate (overall strategy at a corporate centre or HQ), business strategy (for a single business unit), functional strategy (for a department), and operating strategies (for work processes).

Purpose – Objectives – Strategy are by nature relatively stable and together they work to guide the organization strategically over time and while long-term they are constantly monitored and reviewed. In contrast the Implementation – Evaluation – Strategic leadership components are shorter term, since they are action-centred and concerned with the detail of action plans; these are managed organization-wide normally as part of an annual planning cycle, when long-term objectives and strategies are tested in the light of experience at operational levels.

The development of Purpose – Objectives – Strategy is the strategy development process. It involves the leaders of the organization taking responsibility for the analysis and diagnosis of the conditions that influence and determine the critical success factors. This will include understanding both an organization's external and internal environments (see Chapters 4 and 5). The strategy development process is the starting point for strategic planning and the sequencing of a programme to allocate resources and responsibilities.[17]

The basic reason for strategic planning is to provide a capacity to manage change. Peter Lorange's classic work, *Corporate Planning,* describes strategic planning as a strategic decision-making tool designed to motivate and support strategic change.[18] He identified four roles:

- To allocate a company's scarce resources, such as funds available for discretionary use, critical management talent that can be transferred from one use to another, and sustainable technological knowledge.

- To help adapt to environment opportunities and threats, to identify relevant options, and to provide an effective strategic fit with the environment.

- To co-ordinate strategic activities to reflect internal strengths and weaknesses to achieve efficient internal operations.

- To instil systematic management development by building an organization that is learning from the outcomes of its strategic decisions so it can improve on its strategic direction.

Long-range planning

Strategic planning has changed over the years from a deterministic form of long-range planning, to a looser form more focused on the medium term, where strategy is shaped over time rather than prescriptively driven.[19] Writing in the 1960s Ansoff gave a major role in corporate strategy to strategic planners.[20] These were specialists who analyzed the elements of strategy and detailed a plan's sequence of tasks: their primary role was to 'plan the plan'. Another important part was to examine trends in order to predict or forecast events, sometimes far into the future, and this feature came to characterize long-range planning. It involved long-term goal-setting and budgeting that was typically based on extrapolative forecasts as a set of predictions made on the basis of the historical growth of the organization. Strategic objectives thus degenerate into little more than a mechanically fixed set of percentage improvements based on the organization's previous performance. As a process it is typically optimistic and fails to adjust easily when unforeseen changes arise.

Making long-term forecasts is always difficult. During the mid-1980s few expected the rapid rise of the

mobile (cellular) phone. A major management consultancy firm, McKinsey, in a report for the American telephone company, AT&T, forecast in 1984 that a million mobiles would be in use by 2000, when the actual figure turned out to be 741 million.[21]

However uncertain long-term planning is, it is still, perhaps because of its very uncertainty, necessary if an organization is investing for the future; such as when it needs to build plants or develop new markets or technologies, as these and many other things normally take years to bring into commercial use. Alongside the technical difficulties of producing a reliable long-term plan are other issues associated with its effective management. Planning for change is inevitability influenced by organizational politics, which often are likely to serve vested interests rather than the collective future needs of the wider organization. For example, powerful individuals can use plans to reinforce their status or the autonomy of their group, such as to guarantee salaries, jobs and a share of a budget. If this happens then plans are unlikely to be taken seriously as guides to action, and feelings of 'going-through-the-motions' or a 'tick-the-boxes' mentality can take over the planning process. The result is that a strategy can turn out very differently from what a senior level of management had expected.

Emergent strategy

Taking the idea that an organization's intended strategy is changed during its implementation, Henry Mintzberg and Jim Waters[22] argue that new strategy

FIGURE 1.4 Intended strategy becomes realized strategy

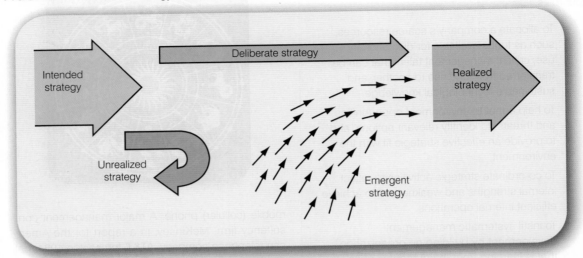

emerges to modify and change the planned strategy; over time the actual realized strategy is one that is different from the original intended by senior managers. Thus in practice strategy is really a pragmatic mixture of senior management's deliberate strategy and the organization's emergent strategy. **Deliberate strategy** is a planned strategy designed at a senior level of management for implementation at other organizational levels. **Emergent strategy** is strategy not foreseen by a senior level that arises during the implementation of deliberate strategy (see Figure 1.4).

Henry Mintzberg is especially critical of conventional wisdom that implies strategy formulation comes first in planning, before implementation.

Virtually everything that has been written about strategy-making depicts it as a deliberate process. First we think, then we act. We formulate, then we implement. The progression seems so perfectly sensible. Why would anybody wish to proceed differently?

Our potter is in the studio, rolling the clay to make a wafer like sculpture. The clay sticks to the rolling pin, and a round form appears. Why not make a cylindrical vase? One idea leads to another, until a new pattern forms. Action has driven thinking; a strategy has emerged.

Out in the field, salesman visits a customer. The product isn't quite right, and together they work out some modifications. The salesman returns to the

company and puts the changes through; after two or three more rounds, they finally get it right. A new product emerges, which eventually opens up a new market. The company has changed strategic course.[23]

The idea that in planning, strategy comes first and implementation second is associated by Mintzberg and many other scholars with a classical or design school of strategy. An alternative perspective is that of the processual or learning school of strategy comprising scholars who believe strategy forms as a learning process involving a concurrent intertwining of both formulation and implementation so that a pattern emerges over time. The strategy process is more in its nature like a craft than a science (see the Honda Effect, Key Debate 1.2).

In his influential book, *The Rise and Fall of Strategic Planning*,[24] Mintzberg argues there are three fundamental fallacies about strategic planning:

1 Predetermination – planners believe they can predict accurately, but this only leads to a false sense of security.

2 Detachment – planners believe they are professionals, which encourages them to think they are objective and can offer a valuable expertise, but this only distances planners from the customer and creates an indifference to products.

3 Fallacy of formalization – planners believe innovation and difference are generated by analysis and structure, but this only squeezes out passion and intuition.

In the administrative science literature there are other long-standing doubts about how deliberate and rational a manager can ever be in making a decision. In an attempt to bring a more realistic perspective, Herbert Simon[25] suggests managers are subject to **bounded rationality**, when making a fully rational decision is limited by the complexity of problems, time constraints, and the absence of necessary information. Decision-making is never perfect. A manager should be satisfied that a decision is sufficient to give a good enough result. Simon called this 'satisficing' – a combination of satisfied and sufficient. Thus strategic planning should be flexible to allow for the limited cognitive capacity of managers: an approach to strategic planning that is incremental and more explorative than one which is deliberately predetermined and follows a strategy first, implementation second, process.

Logical incrementalism

For many organizations the implementation of a strategy can happen by default and accident. This may be because of bad strategic management, but it may be a pragmatic and incremental response to the problems managers face at a local level. Early literature about public sector strategy in the United States suggests, rather darkly, that strategy is a garbage can mixture of unrelated problems, solutions, and resources; or, more hopefully, that strategy is the result of a process of muddling through successive incremental decisions.[26]

Brian Quinn, in his book *Strategies for Change*,[27] introduced a concept, **logical incrementalism**: when strategy is formed as a result of small steps implemented by managers at lower levels as a logical response to local circumstances, and which add up for the organization as a whole as a substantial change to the strategy introduced originally by a senior level. A corporate level deploys its intended strategy through its business divisions (see Figure 1.5),

FIGURE 1.5 The deployment of strategy and its incremental modification

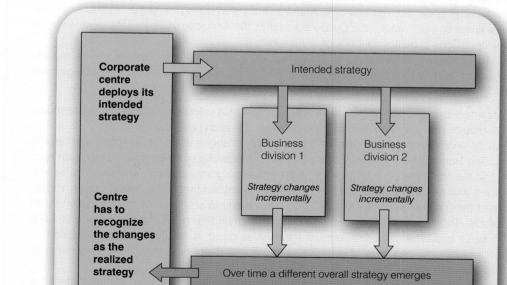

where managers, responding to their local circumstances and conditions, implement the corporate strategy incrementally as opportunities arise. It may be necessary, for example, to explore what is actually possible in terms of resources and people, especially to take into account existing strategies and plans at the local level. It may be necessary to win over or reach compromises with key personnel. The practical consequence for corporate management is that its strategy is likely to change, and it must recognize and work with this realized strategy. To be able to do this effectively requires good organization-wide feedback and review systems for the senior level to understand how the organization is implementing and changing its strategy.

KEY DEBATE 1.2

Rational strategic planning in the too-difficult box

I n September 2012 it was the *Harvard Business Review*'s 90th birthday and the journal looked back on what it called the 'management century'.[28] In a series of articles asking about strategic planning, a quartet of authors writes that the challenge is to bring science to the art of strategy, to marry empirical rigour with creative thinking. This is unlikely to be easy.

Robert McNamara was a pioneer in the adoption of strategic planning ideas in Ford, the American government, and the World Bank. He believed in human rationality, but towards the end of his life in 2009, he began to have his doubts. This is taken from Errol Morris' documentary[29] about McNamara, and featuring him in an interview:

> A nuclear policy of mutually assured destruction depends on the critical assumption that leaders of all nations will always prefer life over death. McNamara discovered during the Cuban missile crisis that there were some on both sides – the Cuban leadership, the American military – who were willing to countenance millions of deaths for ideological reasons.
>
> 'That's how close we came', a tearful McNamara confessed to Morris' camera, measuring the space of an inch with his thumb and finger, an inch that confounded his own faith in the saving power of reason.[30]

The most perfect strategic plan, in the sense of it being the most rational, and based on the best data and analysis, may be useless in the face of the irrationality of human behaviour.

Plans may be only statements of intent, which are quickly changed when it suits those who have to follow them. 'The Honda Effect' is a term that concerns the capacity of an organization to learn from experience and the accidents of strategy, rather than stick too rigorously to predetermined objectives and planning. It was the title of an article by Pascale[31] who argued that in the United States, Honda executives had experienced setbacks to their intended strategy to sell large motorbikes when these proved unreliable. The Japanese sensed an unanticipated demand for small bikes and a new strategy emerged to sell these. The Japanese proved themselves good at 'strategic accommodation … adaptive persistence … underscoring their belief that corporate direction evolves from an incremental adjustment to unfolding events.'[32]

Mair, however, concludes that such studies are partial representations of more complex situations and that many of the presented 'facts' were wrong, while other evidence more supportive of planning was ignored.[33]

Question: Is it really possible to successfully plan strategically?

The popularity of strategic planning

According to management consultants, Bain and Company, the findings of its annual survey of management practices show consistently that 80–90 per cent of large international organizations have used strategic planning and that they are generally satisfied with how it works:

> Practitioners usually say that strategic planning is their most frequently utilized and highly satisfying management technique. One of our survey participants commented, 'it's so easy to get absorbed in daily operating urgencies that we need the strategy process to challenge traditional thinking and redirect where we spend our time and money'. [34]

From our research we think that the nature of strategic planning has changed from what it was 20 or so years ago. In general it is now less based on long-range planning and more on strategic management. A documented example of how it has changed is the example of General Electric; this is an organization that over the years has played an important part in the evolution of ideas in strategic management. [35] The role of formal plans as a part of the strategic management process is to programme overall objectives and strategy as sub-objectives and local strategies for implementation and evaluation.

Mintzberg has expressed it in a similar way. For him, the role of formal planning is to elaborate and operationalize the overall strategy an organization already has. He gave an example of a supermarket chain:

> Planning did not give this company an intended strategy. It already had one, in the head of its entrepreneur, as his vision of its future. . . . Rather, planning was the articulation, justification, and elaboration of the intended strategy the company already had. Planning for it was not deciding to expand into shopping centres, but what schedule, etc. In other words, planning was programming: it was used not to conceive an intended strategy, but to elaborate the consequences of an intended strategy already conceived. [36]

Nevertheless, according to Mintzberg there remains a disconnect between leaders and their grand strategies, and operational levels which have to make sense of them. [37] A form of strategic planning is required that keeps a senior level in touch with how the organization is managing strategy.

Best practice strategic planning

The influential Malcolm Baldrige Performance Excellence Framework [38] defines best practice strategic planning in terms of a set of management principles and components. The management principles consist of:

1 All tasks must be planned properly.
2 Plans must be implemented so that people are working to these plans.
3 Work must be monitored and progress reviewed.
4 Necessary action must be taken to account for any deviation from plan.
5 Organizations must have structures and management systems to ensure the above work in practice.
6 Everybody must be involved in these structures and systems.

The sequence of principles 1 to 4 follows the PDCA (plan-do-check-act) cycle (itself a more general principle of how to manage, explained in Chapter 5), while principle 5 is about the necessary organizational support, principle 6 is about establishing a favourable corporate culture. In addition to the implementation of these principles, Baldrige specifies that to be effective a strategic plan must have six components:

- A defined strategy.
- Action plans that are derived from this strategy.
- A recognition and understanding of the differences between short and longer-term plans.
- An approach for developing company strategy that takes into account external environment and internal strategic resources.

- An approach for implementing action plans that takes into consideration the organization's key processes and performance measures.
- An approach for monitoring and evaluating organizational performance in relation to the strategic plan.

Baldrige does not lay down a specific way for carrying out strategic planning; only a set of principles and what a plan should have. Strategic planning takes many forms in practice, and there is often confusion about what a strategic plan should do. Broadly, there are three possibilities: strategic change, improvement and operational effectiveness, and competitive advantage.

Strategic change

Strategic change is transformational change. This is done to progress the organization to a higher level of performance. It may require new approaches, such as change to existing purpose, objectives and strategy. Strategy for change works by focusing energy and resources on a few critical success factors or priorities, their accomplishment will lead to a new desired state for the organization. Typically, the direction of change is guided by a strategy that is designed to achieve a vision, when the number of objectives in a plan can be kept to a small number that top managers can realistically manage. Jack Welch, formerly chief executive of General Electric, stressed the importance of keeping it simple:

> Strategy is actually very straightforward. You pick a general direction and implement like hell ... you just should not make strategy too complex. The more you think about it, and the more you grind down into the data and details, the more you tie yourself into knots about what to do ... strategy is an approximate course of action that you frequently revisit and redefine, according to shifting market conditions. It is an iterative process . . .[39]

This view from a practitioner accords with Mintzberg's view that:

> strategy is simply putting things in one's head, making sense of things in a meaningful way. . . .

> Strategy is a sense of where you are going, what direction you and your organization are taking. Strategy in a sense is to move an organization forward.[40]

The need to make substantial strategic change is episodic. It normally occurs when threats and opportunities in the external and sometimes the internal environment call for radical change. A visionary strategy is thus dynamic and likely to involve making a fundamental change to the organization's existing strategy and business model.[41] Most organizational strategy, however, is designed to be relatively stable over time to provide a frame of reference for the organization as a whole. This guides decision-making that is consistent with the need to sustain and improve the effectiveness of an established strategy over time.

Improvement and operational effectiveness

Improvement change is incremental and is typically driven by the need to sustain and improve productivity and customer value in daily management.[42] The difference between visionary change and improvement change is a cause of confusion for strategic planning. A college we know has recently introduced a five-year strategic plan. This is divided into nine core areas that are typical for an educational institute and which represent a business model for education generally as a way to create value for education's range of stakeholders.[43] These include the student educational experience, research, employability, enterprise and entrepreneurship, engagement with community, internationalization, staff development, finance, and estate management. Improvements are sought in all of these areas so each has objectives, up to 15 from most of the areas, along with a similar number of strategies, and targets. Altogether the plan has around 800 objectives, strategies and targets. The overall purpose of the plan is to move the college to a new position of strength and the plan is considered by its managers as visionary.

While many of these objectives will be passed down to operational levels, the overall total is a big number for any organization to manage effectively, and for senior managers to understand and oversee. It is unclear from the plan how particular objectives fit to the list of strategies and the targets to strategies and their usefulness to help implementation is questionable. It resembles a dog's dinner of things to accomplish.[44] Many strategic plans at the present time, especially in non-profit sectors of the economy, are like this. It has merit as an impressive list of potential best practice improvements and if successful the institution will become more operationally effective, perhaps more so than rival colleges. However, this may not be enough to sustain a competitive advantage. Important change has to be proactively managed by senior managers, who focus effort and leverage resources on those few activities that will make a significant impact on moving the organization to a new position.

Competitive advantage

The meaning of **competitive advantage** is that it gives to a particular organization a basis for earning above average profits and a level of customer value that is superior to that offered by rivals. To do this effectively it is necessary to have a strategy that is unique to the organization and which is sustainable over time. The purpose of a competitive strategy is to coordinate and integrate all those hundreds of differences in an organization's activities that make an organization different. Difference is not simply a case of doing similar activities better than rivals, say, by following best practice, such as in customer care or the efficient use of technology to reduce costs. These are important considerations but they constitute operational effectiveness, which is not competitive strategy because rivals can also do these things.

Competitive strategy is about performing activities that are different from those of rival organizations, or performing similar activities in ways that are different.[45] This is the real question for strategic planning. It is not simply how marketing can be used to design a marketing mix to satisfy a target market segment, but how to do this in ways that are different from rivals and in ways that rivals will find it difficult and too costly to emulate over time. The management question is about how activities can be made different and a strategy used as an overall approach to manage actively those activities important to sustaining competitive difference.

However, both competitive strategy and operational effectiveness are necessary for successful strategic management and strategy may fail if organizations lack an overarching management system that integrates and aligns them.[46] This dichotomy is partly a reflection of two traditions that dominate thinking in strategic management. One of these is focused around the importance of the direction of external influence on making strategic decisions – a market-based view; and the other is focused on the importance of internal influence – a resource-based view.

Outside-in thinking

The most significant strategy scholar of the last 30 years has been Michael Porter of the Harvard Business School. His ideas about how strategy should sustain an organization's competitive position in its chosen industry classically define strategic management as the management of competitive difference. Porter's thinking belongs to a well-established industrial organization tradition, which dates back at least to the 1960s and places an importance on the external environment as a determining influence for successful strategy. The direction of this influence is **outside-in**, from the external, especially the competitive, environment (see Figure 1.6). Outside-in is also sometimes referred to as market-based thinking.

The principal order of areas given prominence include starting with the external environment, the determination of an industry's attractiveness, the design and formulation of a strategy to achieve above average returns in the chosen industry, and a value chain to manage organizational activities to sustain the chosen strategy. The purpose of outside-in is to identify and address the opportunities and threats in the external environment and classically a SWOT analysis is used to fit and position the organization within its environment so that it will be able to sustain above-average returns over time and withstand competition from rivals.

FIGURE 1.6 Outside-in and inside-out influences on strategy

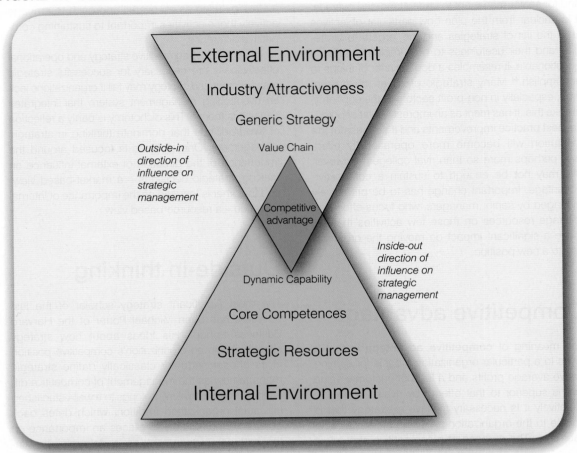

Inside-out thinking

A second, and contrasting, strand of thinking in strategic management is centred on the internal, especially an individual organization's strategic resources – the resource-based view of strategy. This is the **inside-out** approach to strategy thinking. Its origins go back in economics at least to Edith Penrose,[47] and many scholars now claim it is 'arguably the dominant theoretical foundation in strategic management today'.[48] At its heart is the idea that strategic resources are firm-specific which makes them difficult for rivals to understand and emulate; so the emphasis is on the internal rather than the external environment and the direction of influence on forming strategy is inside-out.

The influence (see Figure 1.6) begins with the internal environment and the configuration and development of strategic resources, the integration and alignment of core processes and core competences, and development of dynamic capabilities. The purpose of inside-out thinking is essentially to build a framework for marshalling the learning abilities of an organization around those core business areas that are of highest importance to the creation of value for its customers. The aim is to achieve an internal fit of strategic resources so that they sustain above average returns.[49]

Strategic leadership

How top management designs the means for leadership style and how this exerts its influence on thinking about strategy reflect to some extent its background and experience (see Chapter 11). There is evidence that individuals and teams favour either outside-in or inside-out approaches. To some extent this reflects whether a leader sees their role as either a big-picture strategist or a hands-on manager; the former taking an outside-in view, and the latter the inside-out. We think that both are necessary. For example, consider the views of Chanda Kochhar, manager director and chief executive of India's ICICI Bank:

> In today's world, leaders must have one eye on the broad trends – what is happening in the world ... and at the same time have a very clear view of day-to-day operations. ... I have to be very close to reality while at the same time keeping the big picture in mind. Getting that mix right – thinking

Chanda Kochhar (far left) at a press conference

> strategically and staying close to execution – is the essence of the CEO's [Chief Executive Officer] job. You don't want to micromanage every little thing and constrain people in your team. But at the same time, you can't get so preoccupied with a vision or dream ... It's essential that I get right into the nitty-gritty of how decisions are being executed and make sure things are moving as fast as I want.[50]

KEY DEBATE 1.3

The purpose and scope of strategic management

The subject of strategic management has been criticized by Clegg and others on the grounds that it should be more inclusive and include issues such as its role in civil society, the involvement of trade unions, or its neglect of the dispossessed.[51] The purpose of strategic management as a subject discipline is to understand and improve managerial practices and on the face of things, this is more concerned with strategic change than social change.

The late strategy scholar, Sumatra Ghoshal, argued that the fundamental issue was how a single ideology had captured thinking over the last 50 years. He observed that management research has made truth-claims which are based on only partial analysis that is unrealistic and biased. Unlike theory in the physical sciences, theory in management is self-fulfilling: when a management idea gains sufficient attention it then changes the behaviour of managers who start to act in accordance with the theory. Yet research is centred on a so-called 'scientific' approach, which attempts to discover patterns and laws, and has ignored the importance of human intentionality for explaining corporate performance.[52]

Gibson Burrell and Gareth Morgan argue that research in business and management is either interpretivist and subjective, or functionalist and objective, and is concerned primarily to preserve a view of organizational reality that is profoundly conservative.[53]

Question: Is strategic management as a managerial discipline too narrow?

1   Strategic management is a managed process that includes overall purpose, objectives, strategy, the implementation and execution of strategy, and strategic leadership.

2   An organization should build its strengths around its resources in ways that help it to proactively adapt to change, to be able to influence its environment, so that over the long period it will continue to control its own destiny.

3   There is a strategy hierarchy which is aligned through strategic planning.

4   Everyone should be involved, but the primary responsibility for strategic management rests with an organization's strategic leadership at the top management level.

5   Strategic planning takes many forms, but it has become less deterministic and more directional than in the past:

   - Long-range planning is an example of deterministic planning.

   - The formation of strategy must take account of emergent strategy and logical incrementalism in planning.

   - Modern planning is typically more programmatic than long term.

6   Strategy as a managed process is associated with three roles:

   - strategic change associated with a vision

   - improvement and operational effectiveness

   - competitive strategy.

7   There are two directions of influences on thinking about strategy, outside-in (market-based) and inside-out (strategic resource-based). The former is concerned with the external relationships with customers, competitors and others outside the organization. The latter is about the organization's internal capabilities, including its business methodologies and management philosophies.

8   The style of strategic leadership is likely to determine the balance between the two influences in strategic management.

GUIDED FURTHER READING

An excellent introduction by an influential strategy academic and consultant is Richard Rumelt's book: Rumelt, R. (2012), *Good Strategy, Bad Strategy* (paperback edition), London: Profile Books. He maintains that the core of strategy work is always the same. It involves discovering the critical factors and designing a way of coordinating and focusing actions to deal with them. See his blog at strategyland.com.

A more technically based paper, but a must read for all students, is Porter, M. E. (1996), 'What is Strategy?' *Harvard Business Review,* November-December, 61–78.

A very different type of book by scholars, but as its long title suggests, fairly interesting and inexpensive (and perhaps left-field in its thinking) is Carter, C., Clegg, S. R. and Kornberger, M. (2008), *A Very Short, and Fairly Interesting and Reasonably Cheap Book about Studying Strategy,* London: Sage.

For a good oversight of the history and the ideas of the major contributors to strategic management see Moore, J. I. (2001), *Writers on Strategy and Strategic Management* (2nd edit. 2 edn), London: Penguin Business.

REVIEW QUESTIONS

1   What does strategic management do?

2   What are the main components of strategic management?

3   Whose job is strategic management?

4   Why is emergent strategy important to planning?

5   What are the strengths and weaknesses of an incremental approach?

6   How is strategy for visionary change, a business model, and competitive strategy, different?

7   What is the importance of the external environment to outside-in and the inside-out ways of thinking?

8   Why is joined-up management important to leaders in their strategic management?

SEMINAR AND ASSIGNMENT QUESTIONS

1   Discuss with anyone known to you who works in an organization what strategy means to them. Ask them how 'strategy' helps them do their work. What are your conclusions? In doing this, consider how an ordinary job is different from a strategically oriented one of a leader.

2   John Lennon sings, 'life is what happens to you while you're busy making other plans'. Do *you* believe in planning?

Consider strategic planning and how useful it is to organizations. Compare examples from distinctly different contexts, for example:

- small and medium-sized business;
- a service organization;
- multinational corporations;
- public sector organizations.

Consider how practice might vary for organizations with different purposes, scope and size of operations, and the administrative nature of the organizations.

3   Compare and consider how shops known to you, such as supermarkets, differ in terms of products and service. Identify and compare the overall approaches being followed in these outlets, and discuss the reasons. What are the main features of the strategy being used by these organizations?

To help your discussion, see what you can find on company websites and the blogs of industry observers, such as industry pundits. It is also useful to think about how the profile of a retailer's customers differs from those of the competition.

CHAPTER END-NOTES

1   Many definitions emphasize the importance of competitive advantage in order, for instance, to earn above average returns. Our definition here, however, is designed to cover all organizations including ones which may not be in competitive environments.

2   Baxter, A. (2010), 'Rebound is on the cards in banking', *Financial Times,* special report on Global Brands, 28 April, 1–3.

3   Robinson, P. (1994), *Snapshots from Hell: The Making of an MBA,* London: Nicholas Brearley. The Mintzberg reference is Mintzberg, H. (1987), Crafting strategy, *Harvard Business Review,* July-August, 66–71.

4 Mintzberg, H., Ahlstrand, B. and Lampel, J. (2008), *Strategy Safari* (2 edn), London: Prentice Hall.

5 Strategy-as-Practice website, www.strategy-as-practice.org. For a critique, see Carter, C., Clegg, S. R. and Kornberger, M. (2008), 'Strategy as practice?', *Strategic Organization*, 6(1):83–99.

6 Mintzberg, H. (1987), 'Five Ps for strategy', *California Management Review*, 30(1):11–24; Quinn, J. B. (1980), *Strategies for Change: Logical Incrementalism*, Homewood, IL: Irwin.

7 Ignatius, A. (2012), 'Toward a "Proper Theory of Business"', *Harvard Business Review,* an editorial, September, 12.

8 Dye, R. (2008), 'How chief strategy officers think about their role: a roundtable', *The McKinsey Quarterly,* May, mckinseyquarterly.com.

9 Chandler Jr., A. D. (1962), *Strategy and Structure: Chapters in the History of the Industrial Enterprise*, Cambridge MA: MIT Press, p. 13.

10 Ansoff, H. I. (1965), *Corporate Strategy: An Analytic Approach to Business Policy for Growth and Expansion*, London: Pelican edition (published 1968), Chapter 6.

11 The two concepts are contrasted and compared in Hofer, C. W. and Schendel, D. (1978), *Strategy Formulation: Analytical Concepts,* St. Paul, MN: West Publishing.

12 Adapted from Mintzberg, H. (1987), 'Fives Ps for strategy', *California Management Review,* 30(1):11–24.

13 Mintzberg, H., Lampel, J. and Ahlstrand, B. (2005), *Strategy Safari: a Guided Tour through the Wilds of Strategic Management* (2 edn), London: Prentice Hall.

14 Adapted from Beijing Global Strategy Consulting (2004*), Beijing State-Owned Management Company,* corporate presentation, April 2004, www.Strategy4china.com/SAMintro.pdf.

15 Baer, J. and Guerra, F. (2007), The man who reinvented the wheel, *Financial Times,* December 3:18.

16 Jones, R. D. (1998), 'The new management accounting system at Honeywell's Micro Switch Division', in Christopher, W. F. (ed.) (1998), *New Management Accounting,* Crisp Publications, 1–17.

17 For the balanced scorecard Kaplan and Norton suggest that building a strategic plan involves four stages: clarifying the vision, developing the strategy, translating strategy to derive a scorecard, and developing the plan by determining initiatives, funding, and accountability. See Kaplan, R. S. and Norton, D. P. (2008), *The Execution Premium: Linking Strategy to Operations for Competitive Advantage,* Boston MA: Harvard Business Press, Ch. 2.

18 Lorange, P. (1980), *Corporate Planning: An Executive Viewpoint,* Englewood Cliffs, NJ: Prentice-Hall.

19 Since the late 1960 a transition has occurred at places like the Harvard Business School from talking about long-range planning to thinking about strategy, its principles and conceptual frameworks. See Gilmartin, R. (2011), 'How we do it: strategic tests from four senior executives', *McKinsey Quarterly,* January, www.mckinseyquarterly.com.

20 Ansoff, H.I. (1965) *op cit., Corporate Strategy: An Analytic Approach to Business Policy for Growth and Expansion,* London: Pelican edition (published 1968). Ansoff (1976) later played down the role for specialists and took a more multi-disciplinary view of planning, see Ansoff, H. I., Declerck, R. P. and Hayes, R. L. (1976), *From Strategic Planning to Strategic Management*, London: Wiley.

21 Cited in Hopper, K. and Hopper, W. (2009). *The Puritan Gift, Reclaiming the American Dream amidst Global Financial Chaos,* London: I. B. Taursis, p. 151. The Hoppers use this example to criticize the use of consultants to determine strategy. They argue that strategy is the job of leaders and consultants cannot be expected to understand a client's business. This is true. However, detachment can also be an advantage and is a common justification for consultants; they can be used to bring into an organization knowledge and skills that are otherwise unavailable.

22 Mintzberg, H. and Waters, J. A. (1985), 'Of strategies, deliberate and emergent', *Strategic Management Journal*, 6:257–272.

23 Mintzberg, H. (1989), *Mintzberg on Management: Inside Our Strange World of Organizations*, New York: The Free Press, pp. 29–30.

24 Mintzberg, H. (1994), *The Rise and Fall of Strategic Planning*, London: Prentice-Hall.

25 Simon, H. A. (1947) (1997, 4th edn), *Administrative Behaviour: A Study of Decision-Making Processes in Administrative Organizations*, New York: Free Press, p. 67.

26 See Cohen, M. D., March, J. G. and Olsen, J. P. (1972), 'A garbage can model of organizational choice', *Administrative Science Quarterly*, 17(1): 1–26, and Lindblom, C. E. (1959), 'The science of muddling through', *Public Administration Review*, 19, Spring, 79–88.

27 Quinn, J. B. (1980), *Strategies for Change – Logical Incrementalism*, Homewood, IL: Irwin.

28 Ignatius, A. (2012), 'Toward a "proper theory of business"', *Harvard Business Review*, September, 12.

29 Morris, E. (2003), *The Fog of War*, film.

30 Borins, S. (2010), 'Strategic planning from Robert McNamara to Gov 2.0', *Public Administration Review*, Special Issue, December.

31 Pascale, R. T. (1996), The Honda effect, *California Management Review*, 38(4):80–93 (a shortened version of a 1984 paper).

32 Pascale, R. T. (1984), Perspectives on strategy: the real story behind the Honda success, *California Management Review*, 26(3):47–72.

33 Mair, A. (1999), Learning from Honda, *Journal of Management Studies*, 36(1):25–44.

34 Rigby, D. and Bilodeau, B. (2007), 'Selecting management tools wisely', *Harvard Business Review*, December, 20–22.

35 See Ocasio, W. and Joseph, J. (2008), 'Rise and fall – or transformation? The evolution of strategic planning at the General Electric Company, 1940–2006', *Long Range Planning*, 41: 248–272.

36 Mintzberg, H. (1981), 'What is planning anyway?' *Strategic Management Journal*, 1:319–24.

37 De Holan, P. M. and Mintzberg, H. (2004), 'Management as life's essence: 30 years of the Nature of Managerial Work', *Strategic Organization*, 2(2):205–12.

38 National Institute of Science & Technology (2008), *Malcolm Baldrige National Quality Program*, www.quality.nist.gov.

39 Welch, J. (with Welch, S.) (2005), *Winning*, London: HarperCollins.

40 De Holan, P.M. and Mintzberg, H. (2004), 'Management as life's essence: 30 years of the Nature of Managerial Work', *Strategic Organization*, 2(2):205–12.

41 Yip, G. S. (2004), Using strategy to change your business model, *Business Strategy Review*, 15(2):17–24; Delbridge, R. Gratton, L. and Johnson, G. (2006), *The Exceptional Manager*, Oxford: Oxford University Press.

42 This meaning for incremental change should not be confused with 'incrementalism' as previously discussed in this chapter. The ideas of Quinn and others relate to small changes made during the implementation and formation of overall strategy. Incremental change as used here refers to the integration of activities and improvements made in organizational routines that sustain a strategy already in place.

43 A 'generic' business model is one that is not unique to the organization using it, but is a model used generally within an industry by organizations to create value.

44 These colourful words are borrowed from Richard Rumelt: Rumelt, R. (2011), *Good Strategy/Bad Strategy: the difference and why it works*, New York: Crown Business. p. 53.

45 See Porter, M. E. (1996), 'What is strategy?' *Harvard Business Review*, November-December:61–78. He argues that the Japanese aim for best practice and operational effectiveness rather than competitive strategy.

46 Hodgetts, R. M. (1999), 'A conversation with Michael E. Porter: A significant extension towards operational improvement and positioning', *Organizational Dynamics,* 28(1):24–33.

47 Penrose, E. T. (1959), *The Theory of the Growth of the Firm,* Oxford: Basil Blackwell.

48 Stieglitz, N. and Heine, K. (2007), 'Innovations and the role of complementarities in a strategic theory of the firm', *Strategic Management Journal,* 28:1–15.

49 Helfat, C. E., Finkelstein, S., Mitchell, W., Peteraf, M. A., Singh, H., Teece, D. J. and Winter, S. G. (2007), *Dynamic Capabilities: Understanding Strategic Change in Organizations,* Oxford: Blackwell Publishing.

50 McKinsey & Company (2012), Leading in the 21st century: an interview with ICICI's Chanda Kochhar, The *McKinsey Quarterly,* mckinseyquarterly.com

51 Carter, C., Clegg, S. R. and Kornberger, M. (2008), 'So!apbox: editorial essays: Strategy as practice?' *Strategic Organization*, 6:83–99.

52 Ghoshal, S. (2005), 'Bad management theories are destroying good management practices', *Academy of Management Learning and Education,* 4(1):75–91.

53 Burrell, G. and Morgan, G. (1979), *Sociological Paradigms and Organizational Analysis,* London: Glover.

CASE 1.1 The Nelson Touch

While it was during the 20th century that strategy was developed as a business and management concept its origins belong in military history.[1] The British admiral, Lord Nelson, is still remembered for his strategy and leadership in the defeat of the combined fleets of Spain and France at the Battle of Trafalgar in 1805. The French emperor Napoleon had fought a series of battles and dominated most of Europe, and he now hoped to use his ships to conquer Britain.

Nelson's Column, a monument in Trafalgar Square, London

Conventionally sea battles were fought in two parallel lines of opposing ships sailing alongside and firing broadsides at each other. The strategic challenge for Nelson, however, was that he was facing superior numbers; his ships numbered 27, compared with the 33 of the enemy. So he decided to concentrate his forces into two columns and sailed them at a right-angle to and across the enemy's line of ships. His ships could then turn and cut off the slower of the enemy's ships, outnumbering them as they did so. However this had the risk of exposing Nelson's leading ships in the early part of the battle to heavy fire as they crossed the enemy's line and leaving them unable to return fire because of the angle of the British ships to the enemy.

The strategy worked very well and the French and Spanish lost 22 ships, about two-thirds of the combined fleet. Nelson was killed, but he lived long enough to learn that no British ship had been lost. Nelson's strategy was original and he needed his captains to understand his strategy, so they would work together to apply their power where it would have the most effect in the battle. Once the battle started there would be no chance for the admiral to direct operations.

Thus Nelson had patiently instilled the strategy in his own commanders during tactical discussions in the days before the battle. He indoctrinated his subordinate captains so that once the battle started they would be able to act independently on their own initiative, but in accordance with Nelson's overall strategy to win the battle. In writing home to Emma Hamilton, he described his strategy as the 'Nelson Touch':

> I believe my arrival was most welcome, not only to the Commander of the Fleet, but also to every individual in it; and, when I came to explain to them the 'Nelson Touch', it was like an electric shock. Some shed tears, all approved: 'It was new – it was singular – it was simple'; and, from Admirals downwards, it was repeated.[2]

The Nelson Touch is today regarded as the inspiration of a natural leader. Through his example and actions he inspired and motivated others, notably his captains and the people they commanded. However, the success of Nelson's strategy at the battle involved a longer-term and greater strategy.

The British Admiralty had ensured its sailors were highly trained, organized, and more disciplined and able to out-fire the French and Spanish gunners. The British fleet had more seasoned sailors and marines. It is likely that without these factors, the risk of cutting through the enemy's line would not have been worth taking.

In the event there were also favourable environmental factors. The combined fleet had to pull out of harbour, which gave time for the British to organize and position. When the British began to come within range of enemy guns, a heavy sea swell was hitting the combined fleet more or less side-on and this made it difficult to aim at the rigging of the British ships. The French and Spanish tradition was to aim high rather than at the hull of a ship.

Discussion questions

1 What was 'strategy' and what were 'tactics'?

2 How did competitive strategy and operational effectiveness play their parts?

3 Is there an important role for strategic planning when fighting battles and winning wars?

Case end-notes

1 This goes back to ancient times. The oldest source most often cited is from China, see Sun Tzu (1963), *The Art of War*, translated by Griffith, S. B., Oxford: Oxford University Press (written around 500 BC).

2 Adkins, R. (2004), *Trafalgar: The Biography of a Battle*, London: Little, Brown, p. 54.

Chapter 2
PURPOSE

Purpose

There is no sensible management at any level of any organization without purpose. This is especially important if everybody is to work effectively together. Thus senior managers spend considerable time clarifying and making it meaningful to the rest of the organization. Not only should purpose inspire and motivate everybody, it should also be used strategically to help everybody in the organization to develop their priorities and roles, and to understand the priorities and roles of others they work with.

Business vignette Starting with purpose sorts out the things that matter

Rudy Giuliani, ex-mayor of New York City, points out in his book, *Leadership*, that purpose is fundamental to how a leader manages an organization.

He writes, that when considering a public agency:

I tried to look at its core purpose and direct every decision based on how well it helped advance that purpose ... aligning the resources and focus along with that purpose ... finding the right organizational structure starts with a mission. Then you have to identify your aims, and what you should do to achieve them; find the right people for the job; and constantly follow up to make sure everyone is sticking to the original purpose, that no one's taken over your team and sidetracked them. My interest in avoiding the pitfalls of organizational confusion began years ago, when I was the US Attorney for the Southern District of New York. The first question is always, 'What's the mission?' Ask yourself what you'd like to achieve − not day-to-day, but your overarching goal. Then assess and analyze your resources ... think about the job thematically ... means just not making use of my own resources, but thinking how best to integrate them with outside resources. Consider organized crime. Checking it against our mission statement reveals that prosecuting its leaders was obviously worthwhile. The goal was not to tot up a number of arrests and score convictions, but to eliminate some of the [crime] organizations − a far broader purpose ... Any complex system will inevitably evolve in ways that no longer make sense when circumstances change ... A leader has to be aware of mismatches ... The organization of systems was a top priority for me ... Anyone leading a large organization risks losing a feel for the forest while managing the trees. I deliberated on the purpose not only of individual agencies, but of government itself. I'd go through the questions: What are we here for? What are the available resources? ... The reality is that there's only so much a city government can do − or should do

Rudy Giuliani, Ex-Mayor of New York City, addressing a press audience on crime fighting

... One of my immediate goals was to streamline the government to allow us to focus on our major priorities ... The organization chart is not simply a cold management contrivance. It's a living, evolving tool a leader uses to send a message – to those that work for him, and even to remind himself – regarding the organization's goals and priorities ... I always strive to determine the purpose of an organization, then to set it up so that everything else flows from there.[1]

> # There is no sensible management at any level of any organization without purpose.

An organization's purpose is the primary and basic reason for its existence. Ultimately, a basic purpose for being in existence is founded on belief. People have to believe that the organization serves a useful purpose. This requires some sort of belief system to make sense of what an organization does; in everyday work much has to go unquestioned. The conventional view is that organizations are purely instrumental in the sense that they exist to serve their stakeholders, particularly their customers. In this, there are three dimensions that are important to how the organization manages itself as a collective entity:

1 **Vision** – a view of some desired future state or ideal for the organization.
2 **Mission** – a statement of an organization's present main activities.
3 **Values** – the expected collective norms and behaviour of everybody in an organization.

Each is relevant to a primary concern for strategic management (see Figure 2.1).

Visionary purpose concerns strategic change or transformational change, which is focused on a strategy for changing an existing overall strategy or

FIGURE 2.1 Three dimensions of organizational purpose

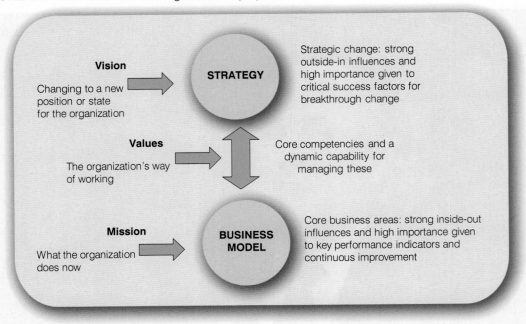

business model. Missionary purpose is associated with improvement change that is focused on sustaining an existing strategy or a business model. Strategic change defined in this way is primarily associated with an outside-in or market-based perspective, while improvement change is more centred on an inside-out or resource-based view.

The management of change within these perspectives requires different approaches for organizational learning. Visionary purpose concerns strategic change that is radically innovative and organizational learning is centred more on a need to explore new sources of knowledge to understand the opportunities and threats for the organization in its external environment. Change is transformational and focused on a strategy for moving the organization forward to an extent that is likely to require fundamental changes to its existing overall strategy and business model.

Missionary purpose, on the other hand, involves sustaining an existing strategy through incremental improvement that is primarily associated with the exploitation of knowledge of the organization's existing routines that are presently central to the delivery of customer value, and which will sustain competitive advantage.[2]

Values relate to the principal way of working that an organization follows. Conventionally in the business management literature this relates to ethical behaviour and corporate culture. Increasingly within strategic management it also includes how an organization uses common management philosophies and business methodologies to produce a unique way of organization-wide working, or a common set of core competences.

Vision statements

When a vision is drawn up in a document to serve as a statement of purpose, it typically represents a statement of intent to move to an improved condition or towards a desired state of being. In this form it provides everybody with a sense of purpose in terms of the direction the organization is heading and how it is going to make the organization a better one.

A vision statement is typically short and to-the-point. It should be memorably different from the ordinary, and for a competitive organization, the difference should be relatively outstanding compared with rivals, as well as ambitious but not over-blown. A vision provides the basic rationale for change, so the reasons for change and the broad implications for action should be made obvious to the organization as a whole. Vision should adequately excite and motivate to encourage people to rethink their work and to stretch them. It should appear to everybody as realistic, but senior managers need to walk a narrow line between distant ambition and the possibilities of getting there carefully.

While not explicitly described as a vision statement, a good example of a visionary purpose is the Hangzhou Wahaha Group's public statement of its future vision. Wahaha, which translates as laughing child, is the largest beverage company in China, and its ambition is to become of the world's largest companies.

In the coming 3 to 5 years, Wahaha would [be] 'Going out of China' on the basis of focusing on the beverage industry as our main task, catching more opportunities. Meanwhile we would also enter the high-tech industry by progress. Currently, Wahaha set its goal of reaching the operation revenue of 100 billion RMB in the next 3 to 5 years, striving for the World Top 500 enterprises, making Wahaha of China become Wahaha of the world.[3]

The development of a new vision requires an organization-wide communications programme to explain the reasons for change. This sometimes involves an organizational envisioning process that includes the participation of the organization's important stakeholders. This dialogue should include ordinary employees since they will be involved in using it to help develop the plans, which will help to close gaps between the present and the desired future goals.

A particular kind of vision statement is a simple 'big idea' – something very different that will change the organization. This is used as a memorable catch-phrase that can be easily communicated as a slogan to spur people on to make exceptional efforts to achieve an ambition. Jim Collins and Jerry Porras[4] write about a Big Hairy Audacious Goal or

BHAG – pronounced as 'bee-hag'. This is so daring in its ambition that it seems impossible. The nature of the goal is that it should be appropriate for the long term, perhaps taking decades to achieve. Sony had a 25-year-old vision to become 'the company most known for changing the worldwide image of Japanese products as poor quality'.[6] At the time, in the 1960s, Japanese products had a reputation for poor quality. Many Japanese companies used similar slogans and some of these focused specifically on their much larger Western rivals, such as Komatsu's declared intent to 'encircle Caterpillar', and Canon's to 'beat Xerox' (see strategic intent in Chapter 3). The point about longevity is important. Purpose statements are for the longer term and should not be confused with slogans that are used to drive medium-term programmes or business plans designed for three or five years.

Mission statements

A mission statement explains why an organiza- tion exists. This is normally short and concise and should only consist of a few sentences. However, it is generally longer than a vision statement, since it should explain the scope of what the organization does now, with a rationale that explains how it adds value for its main stakeholders. The style and form of statements vary considerably in practice since organizations use them in different ways.[7]

It may be used for public relations to influence important publics, or for marketing to include claims, or aspirations, to provide a quality service that is dis- tinctive, and sets what the organization does uniquely apart from its competitors. Care is necessary to ensure that the organization is able to live up to its claims. The statement may claim excellence and quality, but if it actually fails to deliver these then reputation will suffer. Platitudes like 'we make your life better' can leave both customers and employees feeling cynical.

The use of mission as part of strategic management is about how an organization identifies those main things it is working to achieve and how it defines its purpose in terms of its business areas. Used in this way a mission statement summarizes its overall purpose and its value to its key stakeholders.

Stakeholders

Stakeholders are individuals and groups who benefit directly by receiving value from what an organization does and provides. The relationship with stakeholders is typically reciprocal since the organization will to some extent depend on the support of its stakeholders. These include the groups shown in Figure 2.2. Some will be more important than others, such as owners who can remove senior managers from the organization and change the strategic management of their organization.

Peter Drucker, in an often-quoted piece from his classic book, *The Practice of Management*, puts the customer first:

> *If we want to know what a business is we have to start with its purpose. And its purpose must lie outside of the business itself. In fact, it must lie in society since a business enterprise is an organ of society. There is only one valid definition of business purpose: to create a customer.*[8]

The primacy of the customer for commercial organizations should be obvious in everything they do.

FIGURE 2.2 Stakeholders in an organization

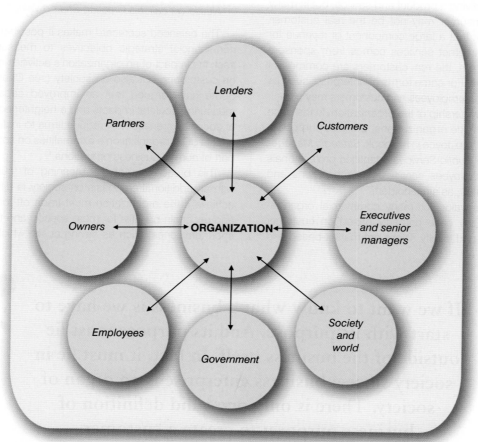

Customer value is the satisfaction from the benefits customers receive from buying and using a product or service. (The term 'value' is also sometimes used to refer more generally to the aggregate value that all stakeholders receive from the organization's activities.) A related idea is a customer value proposition (CVP), which is a purpose statement to identify the sum of benefits important to a particular group of customers. It is fundamental to why a customer should continue to buy and experience a product over time, and it should differentiate an individual organization's market offers from those of its competitors. The secret of success is not to excel equally across all capabilities, but to be absolutely clear about those that are vital to the needs of target customers. The articulation of value is central to lean working, when the importance of how processes can focus on value is at least as important as measuring production and service costs (see Chapter 5).

However, customer can be a hard term to define for some organizations. Conventionally, a **customer** pays for receiving a product and service, but in many cases a consumer may not be the real customer. To the extent that a large component of revenue for media and internet services comes from sponsors and advertisers, the real customers are commercial organizations. For some forms of enterprise, such as a cooperative, employees and customers may participate in the ownership of the organization. In the case of public service organizations, political purpose is important. Philip Joyce in his book, *Strategic Management for the Public Services,* identifies professionals and other employees, service users and citizens, and other providers, as stakeholders.[9]

Customer value for many commercial organizations is in any case primarily based on customer satisfaction and loyalty. These are market-based and may not relate very well to longer-term value for the customer (or society) of tomorrow. A major question asked, especially since the global financial crisis of 2008, has been about how the wider community can be treated as a customer. Michael Porter and Mark Kramer argue for **shared value**, when policies and operating practices work to enhance the competitiveness of a company while simultaneously advancing the economic and social conditions in the communities in which it operates.[10] In other words, organizations should create value in ways that also address society's needs. The concept is used by Peter Brabeck-Letmathe and Paul Bulcke, respectively chairman and chief executive, of the Swiss food multinational, Nestlé:

> We have built our business on the fundamental principle to have long-term success for our shareholders. We not only have to comply with all applicable legal requirements and ensure that all our activities are sustainable, but additionally we have to create significant value for society. At Nestlé we call this Creating Shared Value.[11]

The balanced scorecard makes it possible to use non-financial strategic objectives to measure and track the impact of an organization's activities not only on customers, but also on society (see Chapter 3). Some have argued that an improved capacity of measuring societal impacts and a heightened sense of social awareness now require firms to include the effects of an organization's externalities on society as part of normal business operations.[12]

This broadening of the meaning of 'customer' with an additional emphasis on society is difficult to achieve if the organization must trade off long-term and uncertain benefits for more specific and tangible short-term ones, such as saving costs, which many

 If we want to know what a business is we have to start with its purpose. And its purpose must lie outside of the business itself. In fact, it must lie in society since a business enterprise is an organ of society. There is only one valid definition of business purpose: to create a customer.

shareholders seem to expect. If the task for top management is to align *all* stakeholder interests and to work to ensure these interests support the direction the organization is taking, then it is necessary to identify stakeholder priorities to establish what they have in common so that it becomes possible to build on joint interest.[17] The type and range of stakeholders are an important influence on an organization's values.

Values statements

A values statement documents the expected collective norms and standards of behaviour for an organization's managers and workforce. It may also include expectations about how an organization's people should manage their work and work together; this is often expressed in a values statement as a way of working – for instance the HP Way, or the Nissan Way. This meaning of values is different of course to stakeholder value. Values are the standards by which people work, while value is an outcome produced by that work.

A good statement is designed to reinforce trust, fairness, support, and honesty – values on which most working relations depend. Values statements have become more important with the rise in the importance of global organizations and a requirement to integrate corporate management philosophies and business methodologies across global workforces that comprise contrasting national cultures. More specifically, large organizations have to harmonize cross-functional activity with functional ones; this needs a general context in which individuals can work consistently in relation to each other, so that they are able to develop and sustain organization-wide competences.

An organization's general context for working must be stable over a long period. Jim Collins in his book, *Good to Great*, argues that the best companies sustain their position by preserving their **core values** and purpose, while their business strategies and operating practices continuously adapt to a change.[18] It does not matter what these core values are, so much that to be successful companies must have them, and that senior managers are aware of them, can build them explicitly into the organization and preserve them over time.

An organization's core values are its basic strategic understanding on which it operates, and Collins emphasizes the importance of a culture of self-disciplined people who adhere to a consistent system, within which they have the freedom and responsibility to take action. This discipline is felt as much intuitively as it is consciously. It may not be possible to write down a set of core values exactly, but it should be communicated through a common organizational culture which is shared by key managers and, to some extent, by employees.

Virgin, a UK-based conglomerate, gives what it calls its vision, which is about creating happy and fulfilling lives, when the Virgin brand is always about having fun in a unique Virgin way. This is really a statement of brand values, which according to Virgin have remained the same for 40 years (see branding, Chapter 8). Values are core to its idea of competing in established industries, to give customers new ways to enjoy their products and services, which otherwise they would have to get from long-serving, though perhaps typically complacent and stuffy, organizations.

PRINCIPLES IN PRACTICE 2.2
Two examples of purpose statements

Alibaba Group[19]

Culture and Values

Company Overview
Executive Team
Culture and Values
› Integrity and Compliance
Alibaba in the Community
Press Center
› Press Releases
› Alibaba Group in the News
› Media Resources
› Media Relations Contacts
Contact Us
We Are Hiring

▣ Our Culture

We have established a strong company culture based on a shared mission, vision and value system as the cornerstone of Alibaba Group and its subsidiaries. Our business success and rapid growth is built on the spirit of entrepreneurship, innovation, and an unwavering focus on meeting the needs of our customers.

When new employees join Alibaba Group, they attend an extensive orientation and team-building program at the company's headquarters in Hangzhou, China. This program includes a strong focus on the company's mission, vision and values; reinforced in our regular training programs, team-building exercises and company events. Strong shared values have enabled us to maintain a common company culture and community, no matter how large we grow.

▣ Our Mission and Vision

Mission

To make it easy to do business anywhere

Vision

- *To become the first platform of choice for sharing data*
- *To be an enterprise that has the happiest employees*
- *To last at least 102 years*

Because of the nature of our businesses, Alibaba Group subsidiaries are repositories of massive amounts of market information and statistical data. As part of our commitment to SMEs, we are working to be the first company to make this market data available free to all of our users, enabling them to adjust their strategies to suit fast-changing market conditions and to expand the reach of their businesses. In addition, we strive to be the company with the highest employee satisfaction and to build a company that flourishes for at least 102 years, spanning three centuries (Alibaba was founded in 1999).

◪ Our Values

We work every day to uphold the following tenets: "customer first, employee second and shareholder third."

Our six core values that guide our operations and are fundamental to our corporate culture and an integral component of Alibaba Group's DNA are:

Customer First	The interests of our community of users and paying members must be our first priority.
Teamwork	We expect our employees to collaborate as a team in pursuit of our shared mission. We believe teamwork enables ordinary people to achieve extraordinary things.
Embrace Change	We operate in a fast-evolving industry. We ask our employees to maintain flexibility, continue to innovate and adapt to new business conditions and practice.
Integrity	Integrity is at the heart of our business. We expect our employees to uphold the highest standards of integrity and to deliver on their commitments.
Passion	Our employees are encouraged to maintain a positive attitude towards their work and never give up doing what they believe is right.
Commitment	We expect our employees to demonstrate professionalism and continuously strive for excellence.

Bank Islam (Malaysia)[20]

Our Vision: To be the Global Leader in Islamic Banking

'Global Leader' is defined as being the ultimate guidance and source of reference for innovative Shariah-based products and services.

Our Core Values

Leader: Our Islamic products are the benchmark.
Reputed as the pioneer in Islamic banking, we helped to build the Islamic banking industry.
Dynamic: Progressive and innovative.
We are constantly moving ahead as we offer new and technologically advanced products and services.
Professional: Fast, efficient and responsive service.
We are knowledgeable and equipped to handle global business challenges.
Caring: Approachable and supportive partner.
We help to fulfil every customer's financial needs.
Trustworthy: Dependable and Reliable.
Fully Shariah-compliant products, services and corporate values.

Our Mission Statement

To continually develop and innovate universally accepted financial solutions in line with Syariah Principles.
To provide a reasonable and sustainable return to shareholders.
To provide for a conducive working environment and to become an Employer of Choice for top talents in the market.
To deliver comprehensive financial solutions of global standards using state-of-the-art technology.
To be a responsible and prudent corporate citizen.
In the performance of this corporate mission, Bank Islam shall be guided by its corporate brand values of being: A LEADER; DYNAMIC; PROFESSIONAL; CARING AND TRUSTWORTHY.

Question: How are these statements of purpose likely to influence the organization's overall approach to business?

Speaking about banking, Jayne-Anne Gadhia, chief executive of Virgin Money, notes, 'if we feel there is a market that we can come into where we can give the customer a better deal, we would like to be in it. I think there is no better market at the moment [than retail banking] where you can see how to give customers a better deal.'[21] At the time of writing, the local retail branch to us is full of red balloons and mulled red wine, cushions and comfortable easy-chairs that you can sit in and read free newspapers. Virgin is all about hullabaloo.

Organizational culture

The anthropologist, Clifford Geertz explained culture as a historically transmitted pattern of meanings, which is embodied in symbolic forms that people use to communicate, perpetuate, and develop their knowledge and attitudes about life.[22] In the context of business organizations the terms corporate and organizational culture are used (for the influence of national cultures, see Chapter 8). Edgar Schein, in his influential book, *Organizational*

Culture and Leadership, explains **organizational culture** as the shared basic assumptions and beliefs learned from experience.[23] These operate unconsciously and determine the taken-for-granted perceptions everybody in an organization has of their environment. Assumptions and beliefs are forged over time as people learn from dealing with the organization's problems, and they become embedded in behaviour, which reliably and repeatedly proves itself over time.

It is important not to think of organizational culture superficially as artefacts and espoused values, which are really only manifestations of something deeper. Schein explains that there are three levels of culture (see Figure 2.3); these should be understood for how they influence each other. Artefacts are visible as work places and processes and constitute how people appear and visibly interact with each other. Espoused values are the conscious reasons for the organization and its action, such as documental purpose statements and slogans and commentary published in communication media, such as newsletters, emails, and so on. The basic underlying assumptions are felt consciously and determine how people carry out their work.

FIGURE 2.3 Three levels of culture

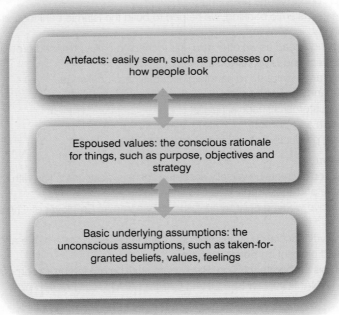

Artefacts: easily seen, such as processes or how people look

Espoused values: the conscious rationale for things, such as purpose, objectives and strategy

Basic underlying assumptions: the unconscious assumptions, such as taken-for-granted beliefs, values, feelings

KEY DEBATE 2.2

Was Enron a bad case of disconnected values?

Organizations do not always use purpose statements accurately. Perhaps the most notorious instance is Enron, a company that failed amid scandal in 2002, which led to suicide and jail sentences for some of its executives.

At the turn of the century Enron was the world's largest energy company and it aspired to become the blue-chip electricity and gas company of the 21st century. The company won praise and was used as an illustrative example of a 'uniquely entrepreneurial culture' by Gary Hamel.[24] In a leading strategic management textbook Enron was described as a good example of how a company's values, beliefs, and philosophy connect closely to its strategy.

According to Enron's website and its annual report (1998), the company believed (among other good things) in 'integrity: We work with customers and prospects openly, honestly, and sincerely. When we say we will do something, we will do it; when we say we cannot do something, then we won't do it'.[25]

In his book about leadership, Jack Welch, suggests Enron's problems came about because its organizational culture became disconnected from its values.

> In its prior [life] ... energy company. Everyone was
> focused on [a] mission they accomplished very
> well by hiri[ng] ... the company changed missions.
> Someone g[ot] ... [goal] was faster growth ... figuratively
> speaking – [with] MBAs in suspenders. Enron's
> new missio[n] ... [t]rading anything and everything.
> That change [no] one stopped to figure out and
> explicitly bro[ught] ... [su]pport such a heady goal. The
> trading desk [generation] businesses got shoved
> to the backgr[ound] ... [th]e checks and balances for the
> suspenders c[ulture] ... [Enr]on's collapse occurred.[26]

Question: What r[ole] ...

Handwritten note: See pg 317–319.
See also pg 227 for national cultures

Organizational cultur[e] ... [about] changes, especially in large, complex its influence. So senior [managers should] be aware and manage its effects, or else they are likely to find that culture will manage them. Culture is expressed in an everyday sense, as 'the way we do things', and because individuals find it practical to work with the system rather than change it, it is likely that in the end everybody becomes part of the culture. This happens without managers fully realizing the strength of its influence. To an outsider it is sometimes called 'going native' and is dangerous if managers are trying to

organizations where there are likely to be subcultures or, as Schein called them, clans. These can comprise specialists and professionals, or semi-independent groups such as geographically removed departments and units. While managers may find it difficult to change something as fundamental as organizational culture, they should be aware of how it influences the effectiveness of decisions and their implementation.

Jim Collins argues that organizations should not change their core values and purpose. In writing about

> ## Senior managers should be conscious of culture, or they are likely to find that culture manages them.

visionary companies, he emphasizes the importance of building an organization over time. Visionary companies should not be mistaken for companies that have grown through visionary leaders, but they are characterized by having in place mechanisms that preserve core values, tight cultures and a top level management that has risen within the corporation. These companies are ambitious, but change is managed through purposeful evolution and continuous improvement. If a new chief executive is appointed to a company from outside, and tries to impose a new vision that is not aligned with the company's historic core values, then the organization is unlikely to buy into the change.

If Collins is right about the importance of core values, changing an organizational culture may not be a good thing. The 'way we do things' is typically an organization-specific quality that gives an organization its unique competitive advantage and a reason why its customers prefer the organization to others (see Chapter 5). These should be understood, especially by anyone who comes from another organization to a senior position and has to take responsibility for strategic management.

Many of the corporate failures of recent years came about in part because top management lost sight of organizational culture. For example, an appropriate organizational culture for retail banking is one based on a personal service, while one for investment banking it is more transactional and market-based. However up to 2008, many banks seemed to favour the latter approach for both types of business.

Stephen Hester, group chief executive of the Royal Bank of Scotland (RBS), is on record as saying:

I think that, at the heart of the mistakes that the banking industry has made, was not 'serving customers well' as the purpose of the existence for the institution, from which all prosperity should derive. In my observation, the best companies in the world in any industry achieve that. In other words, they understand that serving customers

well leads customers to do business with them, and leads to the possibility for a good business model.

Sadly, companies in lots of industries, but the banking industry fairly comprehensively, took a short-cut, a rather crucially flawed short-cut in this thinking and came to a point of behaviour when too many people saw the customer as the thing from which you make money, and making money for your shareholders and elsewhere as being the primary purpose. We have to reverse that.[27]

Changing organizational culture is a slow process but, typically, a crisis like the collapse of some banks, is a wake-up call to get everybody to agree and bring about change. There is an old adage that you should never let a good crisis go to waste, but use it to do something more fundamental than you could before.[28]

An organization may impose and sustain a culture that embodies a set of values that stakeholders, especially customers, can easily understand, identify with, and see clearly the organization's purpose. Starbucks is a good example, and its founders and its senior management team have built a culture, summed up by the phrase, 'the Third Place: a place where customers want to spend time between home and the workplace'. The coffee is good (at least some think it is), the staff do not hassle you to hurry up, and there is a friendly ambience conducive to getting out the laptop or smart phone. This is supported by training that helps mould a distinctive service that is much the same worldwide. The organizational culture is imposed and does not allow much adaptation at a country level.

In general, people want to feel they belong and work in an organization that has a clear common purpose which is recognized beyond the organization. This is a powerful altruistic force that helps to reinforce a positive corporate image held of the organization by stakeholders, such as customers and investors. An involving culture and the sense of identity it brings help to make people feel good about themselves and what they do. When, for example, an employee says they work for Apple, and the response is, 'Oh, that's an exciting company', they feel they belong to something worthwhile, and the next time they may go a little bit further in pleasing a customer. A management can provide an organization with a strong culture by establishing a clear set of values to guide the way it operates; how things are done will influence the image that customers and other stakeholders have of the organization and the benefits it provides.

Corporate image and identity

A **corporate image** is a general perception of an organization held by the public and its stakeholders, especially its customers. A positive image works to enhance an organization's competitive advantage and is also likely to facilitate support from stakeholders, and reassure customers about the value offered to them through the organization's products and services. It provides an important support for an organization's brand. An associated concept is **corporate identity**: this is an organization's managed self-image that can serve as a communicable expression of an organization's purpose.[29] Over the long term this can be used to build and sustain the organization's corporate reputation, and trust in the organization's offers and activities.[30]

Public relations (PR) is a functional area used to explain organizational purpose to external stakeholder groups and to influence corporate image so it can be aligned to corporate identity. PR also has an internal proactive role in moulding and sustaining identity to influence organizational culture and create communication strategies that convey purpose and meaning, which define success and offer valuable lessons from experience. Managers should be willing to come out from behind their desks to create a feeling of trust and to show that employees are cared about. Tom Peters called this 'walking the talk', a form of management conducted by walking about.[31] The interactivity of managers, especially the senior level, with employees generally in an organization is central to understanding the organization and controlling it as a strategic entity (see Chapter 10).

Public relations and communication strategies are prone to short-term promotions of themes currently important to an organization. This raises the dangers of faddism. The management of an organization's identity and image should be strategic and be seen by everyone to involve senior managers for the long term. However, variety is necessary since employees need to be kept interested and feeling involved. Ray Kroc, who as chief executive presided over the global expansion of McDonald's, said that a 'thousand communication techniques [are needed] to keep morale high and instil an atmosphere of trust and cooperation. These [include] Hamburger University and the All-American Hamburger Maker competition among employees.'[32]

A harmonious organization and workforce, however, is not without dangers if it promotes a narrow approach for decision-making. There can be a view that if the senior level thinks something should be done, then it is going be good for the rest of the organization.

Groupthink

Groupthink is a phenomenon that occurs when a team or group avoids disagreement among itself and seeks consensus that is tendentious, biased or superficial, which acts to exclude any real discussion of alternatives. Strategic management works to create conditions that will enable everybody in the organization to work to a common cause and within a shared organizational culture, but this must not work in ways that limit critical thinking, the evaluation of ideas and alternatives, and stifle creativity.

The first use of the term seems to have been by William H. Whyte[33] when he explained it as a rationalized conformity, not an instinctive conformity, but one that consciously holds that a group's values are not only expedient but right and good as well. Groupthink may result from an overly dominating leadership and a culture of fear, where employees (and even dissenters at board level) may fear reprisals or reputations for negative and obstructive thinking. Groupthink is probably at its most destructive when the organization encourages a culture that is unethical.

Business ethics

Business ethics are the ethical systems, typically based on prevailing professional and community morals, which an organization adopts and abides by. Organizations may document these formally as codes to give an explicit set of guidelines for everybody to follow; or they may be written as a values statement and articulated for key stakeholders, such as employees, a community or society. An industry's, or a profession's, ethics are understood as those commercial practices and behaviours that are generally accepted by participants as essential to trust and stable business relationships. Ethics are important to many non-profit organizations that serve the wider community; however, commercial organizations may use ethics to drive corporate strategy. One of the best known examples is The Body Shop:

> Activism has been part of the DNA of the Body Shop. The Company's campaigns against human rights abuses, in favour of animal and environmental protection and its commitment to challenge the stereotypes of beauty perpetuated by the cosmetics industry, have won the support of generations of consumers. The unique blend of product, passion and partnership that characterizes the story of The Body Shop will continue to evolve. It is a shared vision. The company continues to lead the way for businesses to use their voice for social and environmental change.[34]

The Body Shop was founded by Anita Roddick, an activist and campaigner for environmental and social

issues, and the shops closely reflected her concerns. However, in 2006 the company was acquired by the large French fashion multinational, L'Oreal. The Body Shop was against using animal testing for cosmetics, but L'Oreal may not have pursued the same aim. Details of their stance can be found on their website.

In recent years other multinationals have shown an interest in smaller ethically-driven companies. Ben and Jerry's Holdings, a company which has a social mission and makes 'natural homemade' ice cream, was taken over by the giant, Unilever, in 2000. Coca-Cola in 2009 bought a financial stake in Innocent, the maker of 'real fruit' smoothies. While these big companies are diversifying as they have always done into new and growing markets, it is questionable if ethical brands will be able to hold on to the values that were originally a major part of their success.

Ben Cohen, co-founder of Ben and Jerry's, has said he thinks this is not possible and he regrets the sale to Unilever.[35] Jostein Solheim, who became the Unilever's divisional head of Ben and Jerry's in 2010, disagrees and thinks its values can continue:

> My mantra that I've repeated a hundred times since starting at Ben & Jerry's is: Change is a wonderful thing. The world needs dramatic change to address the social and environmental challenges we are facing. Values led businesses can play a critical role in driving that positive change. We need to lead by example, and prove to the world that this is the best way to run a business. Historically, this company has been and must continue to be a pioneer to continually challenge how business can be a force for good and address inequities inherent in global business.[36]

A major problem for multinational companies is that the nature of ethics and sense of what is right vary between countries. These differences are reflected in the norms and behaviours of their business cultures. A good example is a practice used in Chinese communities called **guanxi**, which means relationships, but more meaningfully, connections: 'guan' and 'xi' approximate to 'a closed up door' and 'a joined-up chain' respectively.[37] This is the practice of building a network of interpersonal relationships and connections through a process of reciprocal manners or, as it seems sometimes through suspicious Western eyes, favours. The key to getting things done is who you know and in how a person views his or her obligations to you. If you don't have guanxi it can mean many doors will be closed to you, and as a result there may be many administrative and bureaucratic delays. As Chinese entrepreneur, Wu Fangfang laments, getting bank loans is hard: 'It's almost impossible for small, private businesses to get a loan in China, unless you have guanxi'.[38]

Of course there are similar practices in Russia (called blat) and in Arab countries (wasta). The importance of national culture for global strategy is discussed in Chapter 8, but the wider constituency of corporate social responsibility and its associated issues of sustainability have become more important with globalization and, in general, multinationals see social responsibility as a vital part of their purpose.

Corporate social responsibility

Corporate social responsibility (CSR) is the view that large (especially international) organizations should fulfil a corporate (and world) citizen role. This involves the pursuit of profits going hand-in-hand with good citizenship. Organizations should also set a good example by achieving high standards of business morality, especially in relation to their practices in the developing world. On 26 July 2000, the United Nations introduced The Global Reporting Initiative to encourage organizations to adopt socially responsive policies and to report on their implementation; this saw the introduction of a ten-principles framework, covering human rights, labour standards, environment, and anti-corruption.[39]

Good practice, however, does not necessarily lead to enhanced value for stakeholders.[40] However, in corporate image terms, especially for a global brand, CSR is more important than ever. For example, Walmart is known for its single-minded insistence that its suppliers produce the lowest prices. In 2008 it publicized how it was moving to create a greener supply chain, when it introduced a scorecard for its Chinese suppliers. This is written in simplified Chinese and evaluates suppliers for how they reduce packaging waste. Walmart will no doubt ask for lower prices if this does lead to lower supplier costs.

A related term to CSR is **corporate sustainability**; this puts an emphasis on the longer-term and the need to take into account the implications of an organization's activities for the welfare of future generations. It therefore includes consideration of the creation of long-term customer and employee

value, as well as a regard for the natural, social, cultural, and economic, environments. The most challenging aspect is how to incorporate sustainability as manageable objectives into strategic plans. The tendency is to regard such objectives as constraints on normal working rather than as fully integrated components of daily management that increase value. For sustainability to become strategic and workable at an operational level, the senior management level has to understand how issues such as climate change, regulation of waste, energy and water scarcity, natural resource depletion, human rights, population growth, poverty and health, and economic development, may impact on their strategy and stakeholders.

While it is good practice management to take these things into account, taking a moral long-term view is difficult if it somehow threatens the purpose of the organization. One thinks of the slow response of tobacco firms to the mounting evidence of the damage cigarettes were causing to health. At the present time there is some evidence to suggest that young people today will be the first generation expected to live shorter lives than their parents due to obesity and related diseases.[41] The calls to reduce the number of marketing messages toward young people may not be easy for the large beverage companies to embrace. Enormous profits are made and companies must compete against other companies that are less responsible.

In 2011, Pepsi fell to number three in soda sales behind Coca-Cola and Diet Coke. The company was criticized by investors for focusing more on its new healthier products than its core soda business. In response Pepsi pledged to spend over 30 per cent more on soda marketing in 2011, focusing on its cola products. PepsiCo also signed a $60 million deal for placement in the popular TV show, The X Factor, in order to compete more effectively with rival Cola-Cola, which had a deal with American Idol. The short-term imperatives of marketing seem to make corporate sustainability a strategic goal too far.[42]

The responsibilities of business

Two contrasting views of the responsibilities of business organizations come from Milton Friedman and

Archie Carroll. Friedman argues that social responsibilities are likely to involve the organization in social costs, which will lower its longer-term efficiency. A business should pursue profits as long as it engages in open and free competition without deception or fraud.[43] The role of a moral actor in a business context is always uncertain since the ethical problem is often one of realism, about effectiveness and getting things done.

Carroll in contrast notes four responsibilities: economic, legal, ethical, and discretionary.[44] He recognizes that business organizations must look first to economics and produce products and services that society wants at a profit. In doing this they should comply with laws. An organization's social responsibilities come next, first to follow the generally held beliefs about behaviour in society, such as notions of fairness and justice, and then discretionary responsibilities, which are the purely voluntary obligations an organization adopts, such as philanthropic activities. Ethical responsibilities are typically expected, but discretionary responsibilities are not. Turning Friedman's contention about efficiency on its head, Carroll argues that if organizations ignore social responsibilities then government must intervene, which will then reduce the efficiency of organizations.

The 2008 global financial crash and the following economic uncertainty have led some leading observers to advocate changes that favour a form of responsible capitalism, which jettisons a short-term orientation in favour of a longer-term focus that serves all of a firm's stakeholders, rather than just shareholders. In the view of McKinsey's global managing director, Dominic Barton, the financial crash was as much a result of how organizations are governed as it was an economic phenomenon.[45]

Corporate governance

Corporate governance is the governing of the organization by a board or committee made up of executives who lead and manage the organization, and non-executives who are outsiders appointed or elected to advise and oversee the work of the executives. For example, publicly quoted companies are owned by shareholders who elect boards of directors, who appoint (and can remove) executives as their agents to manage day-to-day activities. The need to oversee agents is important because the interests of the owners and managers may not always coincide.[46] For example, executives and managers may favour a growth strategy if this maximizes revenue in ways that lead to higher bonuses, rather than a strategy to maximize the rate of company earnings on assets which support dividends and raise stock prices for shareholders. On the other hand, a preoccupation on the part of non-executives with short-term performance on stock markets could lead to an undue pressure on executives to neglect the longer-term health of a business.

Boards should work to ensure the following:

- The purpose and policies of the organization are clarified and understood (typically in terms of vision, mission and values).
- Ethical, legal and regulatory standards are fully adhered to.
- Executives pursue objectives and strategy that are appropriate and fit for purpose.
- Executives in practice act and perform in the interests of the owners and if necessary other stakeholders in the organization.

There are two contrasting theories in corporate governance: agency theory and stewardship theory. **Agency theory** sees executives as agents who act on the behalf of owners called principals. It is based on the assumption that unless agents are given the appropriate incentives they are likely to follow their own interests rather than those of their principals, such as shareholders. This is important when a company's stock is widely distributed and the knowledge of an organization held by the non-executives is limited.[47] A bias that favours the agents is sometimes present when a significant proportion of the board comprises personal friends of top management and when the number of executives is relatively large. **Agency theory** argues that agents should be given a strong stake in the long-term performance of their companies, typically through substantial stock holdings and bonuses based on long-term performance.

Stewardship theory argues for a relationship that is principal-and-steward. Executives are motivated by achievement and self-actualization and feel their organization is an extension of themselves. In this instance it is possible for executives to take a longer-term view of performance when the rest of the board might favour shorter-term interests such as keeping stock prices and dividends high.[48]

The extent to which a board influences or makes overall strategy varies between organizations. A board is often active in challenging strategy during its formulation and will be involved in approving its final form, but only a minority of boards is active in developing the content of a strategy. Research has suggested that nearly a quarter of a board's time is spent on strategy and that this proportion of time has changed little over the years.[49]

The personality of the leader is often critical. If it is dominating then this is often enough to deter critical questions from other board members. In Europe, publicly quoted companies typically separate the roles of board chairman and chief executive, to give a chairman the freedom to act independently of the executive. In some countries though, notably in the United States, the roles can be combined and the chief executive acts as chairman of the board often in the position of a company president.

Non-executives should be able and willing to replace executives and, if it seems necessary, overturn a strategy. An example occurred at the Ford Motor Company when non-executive directors removed Jac Nasser from his position as chief executive in 2001. Nasser's strength as a chief executive had seemed to be based on a visionary view of the future. He thought that only small growth would come in the future from assembling cars and selling them in showrooms. Nasser believed Ford should develop ancillary services from personal finance to recycling, which would give the company revenues over the entire life of a

---

KEY DEBATE 2.3

Do boards control their executives?

I n their book, *The Puritan Gift,* Kenneth and William Hopper argue that present day corporate boards are composed of financially oriented directors, who identify with the shareholders rather with the organization and its employees.[50] This is made worse by the cult of the professional manager and the belief that leaders can manage any kind of business without the domain knowledge that would give them an understanding of how the organization they are running works. The rot set in during the 1970s, when the large corporations began to finance growth through borrowing rather than reinvested revenue. The focus of boards changed from the long term to a shorter-term one focused on satisfying shareholders.

John Kay suggests that sometimes boards and executives lose control of the basic purpose of the business. General Electric Company (GEC) was a successful United Kingdom-based conglomerate, which employed around 40 000 people in 1995, when it came under new management. The company had successfully fought off competition from the Japanese and had accumulated a 'cash mountain', which its chief executive refused to spend on new businesses, and was often criticized by investors as too conservative.

The company's new management changed its name to Marconi; sold off most of the old core businesses, such as those in heavy engineering and domestic electronics, and reinvested the proceeds in telecommunication companies. This was done at the height of the dot.com boom, and by 2005 Marconi was bankrupted and reduced to a rump of about 4500 employees.

In Kay's view, it was not a case simply of the Marconi board doing its job badly, but that the job itself was wrong: 'senior executives [should] understand that managing companies is not about mergers, acquisitions and disposals but about running operations businesses well; and that corporate strategy is about matching the capabilities of the business to the needs of its customers'.[51]

Question: Could the global financial crisis, as the Hopper brothers suggest, be another story of boards not understanding the businesses they are supposed to oversee and manage?

> **The sorry tale of corporate scandals and failures over the last few years, down to the unfortunate strategies of the banks, has raised questions about how effectively boards, and in particular the non-executives, do their job.**

Ford vehicle: for example, Ford purchased Kwikfit, a profitable UK-based tyre and exhaust service company. Ford's non-executives, however, thought the purpose of Ford was to make cars. Nasser's departure represented a back-to-basics move and companies like Kwikfit were sold off. [52]

However the sorry history of corporate scandals and failures over the last few years, especially the collapse of the financial sector in 2008, has intensified questions about how effectively boards work. Not all organizations are owned by shareholders, and for these purpose is defined differently.

Cooperatives and partnerships

Many organizations are owned by members and employees. The UK-based Co-operative Group comprises 80 independent cooperative societies, which are owned by 7.2 million individual members.[53] The purpose of the group is to serve its membership, by carrying on business as a cooperative, subject to its values of self-help, self-responsibility, democracy, equality, equity and solidarity. Members elect representatives to oversee the business, and the Group board of 20 directors is elected by the cooperative societies. Profits are shared between members in proportion of the trade they have with the cooperative.

The John Lewis Partnership is owned by its partners made up of 81 000 permanent staff who work in 30 John Lewis department stores and 286 Waitrose supermarkets, and other allied businesses. The Partnership's purpose is 'the happiness of all our members, through their worthwhile, satisfying employment in a successful business'.[54] As a partnership John Lewis is

a democracy and shares its profits and the company claims there 'is a true sense of pride in belonging to something so unique and highly regarded'.

Both organizations have weathered the economic recession following the global financial crisis and because their purpose is based on the customers and employees respectively, they offer an alternative form of profit making enterprise that is different from those owned by shareholders. Another perhaps more recent form is social enterprise.

Social entrepreneurs, and the social economy or third sector

Social entrepreneurs lead organizations that trade for social and environmental purposes, when surpluses are reinvested rather than used to maximize returns to owners and shareholders. A social enterprise seeks to proactively create social value, whereas an ethical business might only seek to minimize its negative impact (see Principles in Practice 2.3).[55]

The social economy is the space between the private and public sectors, and because of this it is sometimes referred to as the third sector. It includes organizations such as non-government organizations (NGOs) and charities. A distinction can be made between a community organization that is active at a local level involving small groups that rely on unpaid effort, and a voluntary organization, which involves formally constituted organizations. These involve organizations such as housing associations, large charities and national campaign associations, which are self-governing and independent of government, and their purpose is primarily to provide a not-for-profit public service.[57]

A mission, not just for profit

A social business is a profit-making company driven by a larger mission. Like a conventional company it has to recover its full costs and make as much money as possible, subject to its mission, which is driven by a cause, rather than profit. The phrase, 'make as much money as possible' is the thing that differentiates the social business from a non-profit organization. Investors typically receive an annual dividend, but the social mission takes priority and most of the profits are returned to build the business.

The Grameen Bank[56] was founded in Bangladesh by Muhammad Yunus in 1976. Ten years later Yunus received the Nobel Peace Prize for his bank's work in helping to alleviate poverty. This was achieved through the provision of very small (micro) loans to community entrepreneurs, and work involving joint ventures with large Western companies, such as the Norwegian telecoms business, Telenor, and Groupe Danone, the French yogurt maker.

The banking industry had believed it difficult to make money through the provision of micro-loans to the poor. In 2006, when Yunus received his Nobel Prize, Grameen reported $725 million in disbursed loans, and $20 million profits. The bank's example has been followed in other places, notably in Mexico, where the Compartamos Banco has reported returns on investment as high as 40 per cent.

The idea for the yogurt began in 2005, when Franck Riboud, the chief executive of Groupe Danone, told Yunus the company wished to find ways to help the poor. The result was Grameen Danone Foods; its mission is to bring affordable food nutrition to malnourished children in Bangladesh with a fortified yogurt. The brand name is Shokti Doi, which in Bengali means 'yogurt for power'.

The idea of a hybrid enterprise with longer-term aims, rather than a purely shorter-term profit driven company, has been attracting wider attention, notably from Bill Gates, the former chief executive of Microsoft, who has been advocating a new form of creative capitalism.

However, there are already good examples of hybrid profit-making organizations, notably the cooperative. These are of many kinds, including community cooperatives in Ireland, which involve rural communities in the management of small local enterprises. A cooperative is owned by and controlled by the members they serve; these may be customers, producers, employees, or another group of stakeholders.

Question: Consider how a social business might differentiate its vision, mission and values.

Muhammad Yunus

The public sector

Proactive forms of strategic management by which managers guide their organizations towards strategic objectives can be as important in the public as in the private sector, although according to some scholars it may be extremely rare.[58] This is due to a highly politicized environment that has changing policy and programmes, and typically a complex list of beneficiaries. It is likely also that rule-bound administrative systems work to limit managerial discretion. Much of private sector strategy thinking is rooted in competitive strategy and has little to offer organizations whose purpose is often to seek collaborations and social partnerships. Public organizations may be intrinsically conservative if their concern is to achieve a legitimacy to conform to the expectations of key stakeholders, which is likely to encourage a tendency to conformity rather than to work differently.[59]

However, over the last 20 years the new public management movement has brought a hands-on and entrepreneurial approach that is different from traditional bureaucratic public administration.[60] Of particular importance has been strategic performance management, which has put a greater emphasis on the importance of strategy execution (see, for example, CitiStat and Delivery Units in Chapter 10) and brought about some change to thinking.

We have emphasized in this chapter the central importance of purpose. In the discussion and arguments about responsible management, purpose is central – what an organization is for. This is often thought about in terms of owners, managers, customers and other stakeholders, including the wider community. However, while the creation of value to a purpose is all important, how this is accomplished goes well beyond the ownership of the organization and its financial and physical assets. For effective strategic management once purpose is clear, it is the identification of critical success factors, many of them intangible, which mould competitive advantage and make an organization different.

SUMMARY OF PRINCIPLES

1   The overall purpose of an organization decides the nature of an organization's overall objectives and strategy. If objectives and strategy are to be managed, the process of strategic management must start with purpose.

2   Vision, mission, and values have different roles in strategic management and should be managed strategically as an integrated set.

3   Organizations create value for all their stakeholders, but the primacy of the customer is central to strategic management.

4   Organizations have distinctive organizational cultures, which purpose must take full account of, if strategic management is to be effective.

5   Business ethics, sustainability, and business responsibility, are central to the creation of public value, and should be managed strategically.

6   Corporate governance is an ownership function that oversees an executive's strategic management.

GUIDED FURTHER READING

The importance of transparency and clarity of core values is developed in Collis, J. and Porras, J. (2002), *Built to Last: Successful Habits of Visionary Companies,* London: Harper Business.

For corporate social responsibility see Mirvis, P. and Googins, B. (2006), 'Stages of corporate citizenship', *California Management Review,* 48(2):104–126; Carroll, A. B. and Shabana, K. M. (2010), 'The business case for Corporate Social Responsibility', *International Journal of Management,* 12(1):85–105. For a critical view of corporate marketing, see Hastings, G. (2012), *The Marketing Matrix: How the Corporation Gets its Power and How We Can Reclaim it,* London: Routledge.

Strictly, the subject of corporate governance and stakeholder theory lies largely outside strategic management. To read further, an account of the evolution of corporate governance reforms in China and India is Rajagopalan, N. and Zhang, Y. (2008), 'Corporate governance reforms in China and India: challenges and opportunities', *Business Horizons* 51:55–64. Robert Freeman presents a stakeholder map that he uses to classify stakeholders according to two dimensions: the nature of the stake they have in the organization, and the power they are able to exert, see Freeman, R. E. (1984), *Strategic Management: A Stakeholder Approach,* Boston: Pitman.

Corporate image and identity also form an important subject in their own right. A special issue was devoted to organizational identity in the *Academy of Management Review.* This includes a view of identity from the perspective of stakeholder theory, see Scott, S. G. and Lane, V. B. (2000), 'A stakeholder approach to organizational identity', *Academy of Management Review,* 25 (1):43–62.

REVIEW QUESTIONS

1   What is the purpose of a purpose?

2   Explain the difference between vision, mission, and values.

3   Why are some values core?

4   What do different types of stakeholders get from the organization?

5   How does the organizational culture of an organization affect the way it is managed?

6   From its purpose statements, work out an organization's corporate image and identity.

7   What are business ethics and corporate social responsibilities?

8   What is the role of corporate governance for strategic management?

SEMINAR AND ASSIGNMENT QUESTIONS

1   Find examples of purpose statements from home pages on the web, and sort them into vision, mission and values statements: pick out and explain how the best ones work and why the worst ones do not. Do organizations seem to know the difference?

2   Think of an organization in which you would like to work and list all the important stakeholders involved. Rank these in descending order of importance and explain why.

3   Consider how an organization's culture might be changed to improve a company's business ethics. Can a commercially-oriented organization that has to deliver short-term results really afford a strategic long-term view?

CHAPTER END-NOTES

1   Giuliani, R. W. with Kurson, K. (2002), *Leadership,* London: Little, Brown, 317–319.

2   The relationship between routines and the incremental change and the investigation and management of more radical innovation, is explained by James March in terms of exploration and exploitation; see March, J. C. (1991), 'Exploration and exploitation in organizational learning', *Organization Science,* 2(1):71–87. Expressed succinctly, exploration is the pursuit of new knowledge of things that might come to be known, while exploitation

is the use and development of things already known.

3 Wahaha Group's home page, 'About Us', en.wahaha.com.cn/about us/future.

4 Collins, J. C. and Porras, J. I. (1994), *Built To Last: Successful Habits of Visionary Companies*, New York: Harper Business.

5 Lester, T. (2011), 'Managing customers in the age of big data', FT.com Reports, *Financial Times,* www.ft.com/cms.

6 Collins, J. C. (2001), *Good to Great: Why Some Companies Make the Leap … and Others Don't,* London: HarperCollins.

7 Campbell, A., Devine, M. and Young, D. (1990), *A Sense of Mission*, London: Economist Publications.

8 Drucker, P. F. (1955), *The Practice of Management*, London: Heinemann Butterworth. (1954, American edit.), New York: Harper Row, 34–35.

9 See Joyce, P. (1999), *Strategic Management for the Public Services,* Buckingham: Open University Press. The differences between private and public sectors are identified in a seminal paper: Murray, M. A. (1975), 'Comparing public and private management: an exploratory essay', *Public Administration Review,* 34(4):364–371.

10 Porter, M. E. and Kramer, M. R. (2011), 'Creating shared value', *Harvard Business Review,* January-February, 63–77.

11 Nestlé (2010), *The Nestlé Corporate Business Principles,* June, p. 3 www.nestle.com.

12 Meyer, C. and Kirby, J. (2010), 'Leadership in the age of transparency', *Harvard Business Review,* April.

13 Rigby, D. and Bilodeau, B. (2007), 'Selecting management tools wisely', *Harvard Business Review,* December, 20–22.

14 Campbell, A. and Yeung, S. (1991), 'Creating a sense of mission', *Long Range Planning,* 24(4):10–20.

15 Bartlett, C. A. and Ghoshal, S. (1994), 'Changing role of senior management: beyond strategy to purpose', *Harvard Business Review*, November-December, 79–88.

16 Waterman, R. H., Peters, T. and Phillips, J. R. (1980), 'Structure is not organization', *Business Horizons*, June, 14–26; Hamel, G. and Prahalad, C. K. (1994), *Competing for the Future*, Boston MA: Harvard Business School Press, and Christensen, C. M. (1997), *The Innovator's Dilemma: When New Technologies Cause Great Firms to Fail,* Boston MA: Harvard Business School Press.

17 One of the most influential texts is by Ed Freeman, see Freeman, R. E. (1984), *Strategic Management: A Stakeholder Approach,* London: Pitman. The main concern of stakeholder theory has been to suggest ways for working out the relative importance and levels of interest for different stakeholders; for example, by applying stakeholder mapping, and power/interest grids: see Mitchell, R. K., Agle, B. R. and Wood, D. J. (1997), 'Toward a theory of stakeholder identification and salience: defining the principle of who and what really counts', *Academy of Management Review,* 22(4):853–888.

18 Collins J. (2001), *Good to Great: Why Some Companies Make the Leap … and Others Don't,* London: HarperCollins.

19 Alibaba Group (2013), http://news.alibaba.com/specials/aboutalibaba/aligroup/culture_values.html

20 Bank Islam (2008), www.bankislam.com.

21 Evidence to the UK Parliamentary Commission on Banking Standards, sub-committee panel on retail competition, (2012) 13 November.

22 Geertz, C. (1973), *The Interpretation of Cultures,* New York: Basic Books.

23 Schein, E. H. (1985), *Organizational Culture and Leadership,* London: Jossey-Bass.

24 Hamel, G. (2008), 'Quest for innovation, motivation inspires the gurus', interview by Erin White, *The Wall Street Journal,* 5 May.

25 Enron (1998), *Annual Report.*

26 Welch, J. (with Welch, S.) (2005), *Winning,* New York: Collins.

27 Evidence taken before the UK Parliamentary Commission on Banking Standards, (2012) 13 November: evidence to public question 864, www.parliament.uk.

28 Kurt Lewin asserted that change requires a three-stage process of unfreeze–change–freeze: an organization must unlearn or reformulate its basic assumptions; followed by change and a period of uncertainty; finally there is an institutionalization of a new corporate culture for the business. Lewin, K. (1952), 'Group decision and social change', in Swanson, G. E., Newcomb, T. N. and Hartley, E. L. *Readings in Social Psychology* (revised edn) New York: Holt, Rinehart & Winston. See also Burgelman, R. A. and Grove, A. S. (2007), 'Let chaos reign, the rein in chaos – repeatedly: managing strategic dynamics for corporate longevity', *Strategic Management Journal,* 49(3):6–26.

29 This external and internal distinction is made in Scott, S. G. and Lane, V. R. (2000), 'A stakeholder approach to organizational identity', *Academy of Management Review,* 25(1):43–62.

30 Gray, E. R. and Balmer, J. M. T. (1998), 'Managing corporate image and corporate reputation', *Long Range Planning,* 31(5):695–702.

31 Peters, T. J. and Waterman, R. H. (1982), *In Search of Excellence*, London: Harper and Row.

32 Miller, G. J. (1990), 'Managerial dilemmas: political leadership in hierarchies', in Cook, K. S. and Levi M. (eds) *The Limits of Rationality,* London: The University of Chicago Press, 324–348.

33 Whyte, W. H. (1952), 'Groupthink', *Fortune,* March. Janis found that senior management was prone to defective strategic decisions, especially in crisis situations, unless precautions had been made to avoid groupthink: see Janis, I. L. (1982), *Groupthink: Psychological Studies of Political Decisions and Fiascos,* (revised edn. of *Victims of Groupthink,* 1970) Boston MA: Houghton Mifflin.

34 The Body Shop (2003), www.thebodyshop.com.

35 Ben Cohen (2009), interviewed on BBC news, Radio 4, 7 April.

36 Quoted in *Food Processing,* (2010), 'Division President: Jostein Solheim, Ben and Jerry's Homemade' www.foodprocessing.com.

37 Ai, J. (2006), 'Guanxi networks in China: its importance and future trends', *China and the World Economy,* 14(5):105–118. A chapter about how to manage guanxi strategically is included in Tian, X. (2007), *Managing International Business in China,* Cambridge: Cambridge University Press, ch 3.

38 Hanbury-Tenison, M. (2011), 'Web offers a comfortable fit', *Financial Times,* 24 November.

39 The framework is continuously improved and the core. Guidelines are in their third generation, and were released in October 2006, see: The Global Reporting Initiative, www.globalreporting.org.

40 Vogel, D. (2005), *The Market for Virtue: The Potential and Limits of Corporate Social Responsibility,* Brookings: Institution Press.

41 Yale Rudd Center (2011), *Sugary Drink FACTS; Evaluating Sugary Drink Nutrition and Marketing to Youth,* report, November, Rudd Center for Food Policy and Obesity.

42 For a full account of nefarious marketing practice from a viewpoint of social marketing, see Hastings, G. (2012), *The Marketing Matrix: How the Corporation Gets its Power and How We Can Reclaim it,* London: Routledge.

43 Friedman, M. (1970), 'The social responsibility of business is to increase its profits', *New York Times Magazine,* 13 September, 126–127.

44 Carroll, A. B. (1979), 'A three dimensional conceptual model of corporate performance', *Academy of Management Review,* October, 496–505.

45 Barton, D. (2011), 'Capitalism for the long term', *Harvard Business Review,* March, 84–91.

46 The clash of interests between owners and managers as a subject for study goes back to the 1930s, see the classic Berle, A. and Means, G. (1932), *The Modern Corporation and Private Property,* (2 edn 1967, New York, Harcourt, Brace and World). The rise

of the large American corporation and the emergence of a new managerial class has suggested a new stage in capitalism, where the ownership of the means of production is secondary to management, see Burnham, J. (1942) (American edn, 1941), *The Managerial Revolution or What is Happening in the World Now,* London, Wyman & Sons. Alfred Sloan chronicled the early emergence of a cadre of professional managers who effectively controlled General Motors: see Sloan, A. P. (1963), *My Years with General Motors,* London: Sedgewick & Jackson.

47 This might also apply to the executives! The Hopper brothers cite Jeff Immelt, chief executive of GE, who has criticized the mobility of leaders as professional managers who can manage any type of firm, but who lack a deep (or domain) knowledge and understanding about their industries. In our view this may have been a contributory cause of the failure of some banks in 2008. See: Hopper, K. and Hopper, W. (2009), *The Puritan Gift: Reclaiming the American Dream Amidst Global Financial Chaos,* New York: I. B. Tauris & Co, p. 266.

48 The view that stewardship may have declined over the last 50 years with the rise of the professional manager for large corporations in the USA is a central thesis of Hopper, K and Hopper, W (2009) *The Puritan Gift: Reclaiming the American Dream Amidst Global Financial Chaos,* New York: I. B. Tauris & Co.

49 Bhagat, C., Hirt, M. and Kehoe, C. (2011), 'Governance since the economic crisis: McKinsey Global Survey results', *McKinsey Quarterly,* July.

50 Hopper, K. and Hopper, W. (2009), *The Puritan Gift: Reclaiming the American Dream Amidst Global Financial Chaos,* New York: I. B. Tauris & Co,

51 Kay, J. (2002), 'A vital item is missing', *Financial Times,* 29 January, p. 13.

52 Kwitfit was sold back to its original owner at a substantial loss. Ford ran into serious problems around 2005 and Nasser's vision may have been a correct one to aim for.

53 The Co-operative Group (2012), *Sustainability Report 2011,* www.co-operative.co.uk/ sustainabilityreport.

54 John Lewis (2012), *About us,* www. johnlewispartnership.co.uk/about.html.

55 This distinction was offered by Social Enterprise UK: Garrett, A. (2012), 'Crash course in … creating a social enterprise', *Management Today,* July/August, p. 20. There is a social enterprise mark for organizations that dedicate at least half of profits to social purposes. See Ashton, R. (2010), *How to be a Social Entrepreneur,* London: Wiley.

56 Seelos, C. (2009), 'New models for the future', *Financial Times,* 12 February; and Kelly, M. (2009), 'Not just for profit', *Strategy+Business,* February, www.strategy-business.com.

57 For a review of the non-profit sector, see Salamon, L. A. and Anheier, H. K. (1997), *Defining the Nonprofit Sector: A Cross-National Analysis,* Manchester: Manchester University Press.

58 The differences between private and public organizations were identified in a seminal paper: Murray, M. A. (1975), 'Comparing public and private management: an exploratory essay', *Public Administration Review,* 34(4): 364–371. See also, Nutt, P. C. and Backoff, R. W. (1995), 'Strategy for public and third sector organizations', *Journal of Public Administration Research and Theory,* 5(2):189–211; Brown, T. L. (2010), 'The evolution of public sector strategy', *Public Administration Review,* special issue, December, S212–S214.

59 Ashworth and others found for 101 public sector organizations in England between 2001 and 2004 evidence of isomorphic pressures on strategies and cultures. See Ashworth, R., Boyne, G. and Delbridge, R. (2007), Escape from the iron cage? Organizational change and isomorphic pressures in the public sector, *Journal of Public Administration Research and Theory,* 19:165–187.

60 New public sector management was coined from UK experience: see Hood, G. (1991),

'A new public management for all seasons?' *Public Administration,* 69(1):3–19. Although parallel work in the USA was published around the same period: see Osbourne, D. and Gaebler, D. (1992), *Reinventing Government,* New York: Addison-Wesley. New public sector management has been criticized as a managerial paradigm, which, because it seems to endorse a neo-liberal philosophy, works against joined-up government as it has encouraged more fragmentation: for example, see Bogdanor, V. (2005), 'Introduction', in Bogdanor, V. (ed.) (2005), *Joined-Up Government,* Oxford: Oxford University Press.

CASE 2.1 Trying to change core values at HP

Hewlett Packard (HP), one of the world's largest information technology multinationals, was founded in a small garage in Palo Alto, California, by Bill Hewlett and Dave Packard. They followed a collegiate engineering culture from the start that became known as the HP Way and defined the 'sort of people we are, like working with'. It became a set of deeply held beliefs that were at the heart of the company's purpose and activities. According to Dave Packard, the HP Way had distinguished the company more than its products had done (see Exhibit 2.1).[1]

In 2005 the company's public statement of the HP Way disappeared to be replaced with a 'vision and a strategy' that emphasized diversity and inclusion:

At HP, we believe diversity is a key driver of our success. Putting all our differences to work across the world is a continuous journey fuelled by personal leadership from everyone in our company. Our aspiration is that the behaviours and actions that support diversity and inclusion will come from the conviction of every HP employee – making diversity and inclusion a conscious part of how we run our business throughout the world. Diversity and inclusion are woven into the fabric of our company. They are an intrinsic part of our nature and key to fulfilling our vision for HP: to be 'a winning e-company with a shining soul'.[3]

This was supported by an additional list of policies and practices designed to support diversity. The HP Way seemed to have gone.

With the rise of Silicon Valley and the ongoing revolution in information technology, the HP board had begun to feel the company had grown conservative

EXHIBIT 2.1 The HP Way[2]

HP's organizational values (The HP Way)

I feel that in general terms it is the policies and actions that flow from belief that men and women want to do a good job, a creative job, and if they are provided the proper environment they will do so.

Bill Hewlett

HP's organizational values and our commitment to meeting our corporate objectives shape our strategies and policies.

- We have trust and respect for individuals.
- We focus on a high level of achievement and contribution.
- We conduct our business with uncompromising integrity.
- We achieve our common objectives through teamwork.
- We encourage flexibility and innovation.

Traditional practices as management by wandering around, hoshin planning and the open door policy, are supported by others, including a ten-step business planning process, and total quality control.

and complacent. So in 1999, a new chief executive was appointed for the first time from outside HP. She was Carly Fiorina and came from a sales background with no experience of the HP Way. She had worked her way up at AT&T to become a vice-president. She took a leading part in divesting that company's telephone equipment business, Lucent Technologies, in 1995. Until her appointment, growth at HP was largely organic, but in 2002 she masterminded a friendly merger with the struggling computer giant, Compaq. The aim was to create a new company to challenge IBM as an end-to-end solutions provider for HP customers.

The leading shareholders at this time were Walter Hewlett, son of the founder, and the Packard family, and these were opposed to the merger. They worried that the new company would find it difficult to compete with Dell in the personal computer (PC) market. Walter Hewlett thought that HP should reduce its emphasis on PCs and increase investment in areas such as digital photography and commercial printing equipment. He felt that HP should restructure

to improve shareholder value rather than attempt to grow market share. As one observer put it, there was a potential culture clash between the hard-driving Compaq and egalitarian HP.[4]

The merger was only just approved by a bare 51 per cent of HP shareholders, and the board appointed Carly Fiorina as chairman and chief executive of the enlarged company, which retained the Hewlett Packard name. The company started to do better than expected. HP continued to rely heavily on its very profitable and growing printer business, and the losses on personal computers were cut dramatically. The new company seemed to be sorting out its product range and sales forces, which had overlapped significantly.[5]

Carly Fiorina and the HP Way

Interviewed by the *Financial Times* in 2003, a successful Fiorina offered insights into her leadership style. Her reputation as an aggressive leader followed her from AT&T where she had gone on stage to address an audience of salespeople with three socks stuffed down the front of her trousers:

You have to speak to people in the language they understand,' she said, 'these were guys who, to be direct, thought a lot about the size of their balls. They were sales guys. It was a very macho culture. They thought they had been taken over by a bunch of wimps and that they were going to run the place, and I needed to tell them who was in charge.

I tell people inside HP that leadership requires a strong internal compass ... So you have to learn to ignore a lot of conventional wisdom and a lot of talk that isn't core to the purpose of what you're doing ... No change programme is unanimously supported. ... HP was such a great company, but it was almost frozen in time... [in some ways it had] lost its ambition. Its rate of innovation had declined rapidly. It was growing in single digits in the middle of the biggest technology boom in history... But this was a company that had not ever brought in an outsider at the top... 50 per cent of our employees had been there less than five years, but not in the senior ranks, which were genuinely built from within ... Because I was an outsider I couldn't dictate, knowing this was a strong and deep culture and I was only one person. I know that big companies can thwart a CEO. The organization had to decide its own vision, its goal and its willingness to change. Then I could lead ...

If you looked at our company values today, you would find they are the exact same values that have guided HP for 60 years, except we have added "speed and agility". We don't want to change the fact that trust and respect are part of our value system, that contribution is important and that passion for customers is important ... Those basic values originally were referred to as the HP Way. Over time, the phrase came to mean any defence against any change. I would go into meetings where somebody would bring up a new idea and someone would say: "We don't do it that way, that's not the HP way".

Especially for a technology company, it is death if you stop trying new things. HP tended to be very process intensive, which is really important when you're dealing with big complex systems and problems. The downside is that sometimes HP processed endlessly and never decided. Compaq tended to be fast and aggressive, which is good in a fast moving market. The downside was sometimes

Compaq lacked judgement. Sometimes they had to do things over and over because they hadn't thought it through ... We said: "The goal is to be fast and thorough".[6]

Subsequent problems

Carly Fiorina was fired in February 2005 after HP shares had fallen to around 15 per cent of what they been over the previous year. This was largely due to concerns about HP's ability to execute its strategy profitably. Waters and London summarized the reasons in the *Financial Times*:

Dell is fast becoming to technology what Walmart is to retailing: an operator that by virtue of its scale and business model is impossible to beat on price ... The PC market is structurally unattractive if you aren't a Dell. A lot of well-managed companies, well-resourced companies have tried and failed ... Standardization and commoditization are sucking profits out of the business ... it is harder for companies to differentiate their products and demand premium prices ... HP's purchase of Compaq was partly designed to make it the leader in low-cost servers – products that are replacing the corporate computers that used to account for much of its profits. The company has been left with little choice but to cannibalize its own business.

[Last year] Ms Fiorina proudly trumpeted 200 new consumer technology products from HP, yet none of those has caught the consumer imagination ... perhaps HP should sell its PC operation, which requires a business approach rather than one of technology innovation. Michael Porter ... wrote that there are only two basic types of strategy: high value and low cost ... Arguably, Ms Fiorina lost her job this week because her 'high-tech, low cost' notion ignored that stricture.[7]

The abandonment of the HP Way may have been important if, as one observer notes, the 'new practices have been nothing short of trampling of company's heart and soul'.[8] Fiorina said 'we didn't involve middle and first-line supervisors in the process enough ... I had underestimated in many ways the people of the company, their appetite for change and their ability to do hard things. And I learned that sometimes you have to go slow to go fast'.[9]

Back to basics or a continuing identity crisis?

HP has since overtaken IBM in revenue and Dell has stumbled in the PC market. Mark Hurd, the chief executive who replaced Fiorina, observed that 'to become "great" companies eventually have to accept the organization they have and turn to the hard task of honing their processes to perfection. The way you get good at this stuff is you do it for years. You do it for years. And at the end of the day, when you've done it for years, this stuff rolls off people's tongues.'[10]

Here is an echo of Jim Collins about how core values make an organization great. With Hurd processes seemed to be back in favour at HP. While not changing the strategic logic that drove the Compaq merger, HP was organized back to a more decentralized model that was more consistent with HP's original culture, and which refocused HP on its strengths as a technology company, but with services in a more supporting role.[11] In 2007 HP overtook Dell as the world's largest PC maker by sales, and its operating margins rose from 4 to 6 per cent. In 2012 it had maintained its position and sold more PCs than its rivals.

However, successful Silicon Valley companies exhibit rapid growth and high margins and when growth is relatively slow, executives and boards start to worry. There may still be cultural problems at the top at HP. The temptation indulged by HP's various chief executives over the past few years to restore growth by buying high-growth companies at inflated prices to tack on to mature operations remains.[12] For example, HP acquired Autonomy, a UK software company, in 2011 for $11 billion in 2011, only to write down its value the following year by $8.8 billion!

Discussion questions

1 Jim Collins used HP as an example of a visionary company with core values. He argued in his book, *Good to Great,* that great companies do not change their core values. Is HP an exception to the general rule?

2 Fiorina may well have been right all along to merge with Compaq since HP has become the largest producer of PCs. However, after her departure some things were put into reverse. If you had been Carly Fiorina how would you have done things differently?

3 Search for information on the web about how Dell and HP compare, and the importance of growing competition from companies such as the Chinese manufacturer, Lenovo. How do the purpose statements of these companies compare, and do they suggest different approaches in their strategic management?

Case end-notes

1 Packard, D. (1995), *The HP Way: How Bill Hewlett and I Built the Company,* New York: Harper Business.

2 Hewlett-Packard (2002), home page, December, www.hp.com.

3 Hewlett-Packard (2005), 'Our vision and strategy', February, www.hp.com.

4 Morrison, S. (2002), 'Investors weigh up merger outcomes', *Financial Times,* 15 March, p. 26.

5 Waters, R. and London, S. (2002), 'Resilient HP rebounds from Capellas exit', *Financial Times,* 22 November, p. 32.

6 Maitland, A. (2003) 'I have learnt from my mistakes', *Financial Times*, 20 November, p. 14.

7 Waters, R. and London, S. (2005), 'A struggle over strategy: HP counts the cost of playing the other guy's game', *Financial Times,* 11 February, p. 15.

8 Dong, J. (2002), 'The rise and fall of the HP Way', *Palo Alto Weekly,* Online edn, 10 April, www.paloaltoonline.com.

9 Maitland, A. (2003) 'I have learnt from my mistakes', *Financial Times,* 20 November.

10 Allison, K. and Waters, R. (2007), 'Hewlett-Packard comes back fighting', *Financial Times,* 30 April, p. 27.

11 Burgelman, R. A. and McKinney, W. (2006), 'Managing the strategic dynamics of acquisition integration: lessons from HP and Compaq', *California Management Review,* 48(3): 6–27.

12 Gapper, J. (2012), 'HP should have known all about Autonomy', *Financial Times,* 22 November.

· 2 · 4 · 5 · 1 · 3 · 6 · 4 · 3 · 2 ·

'MANAGEMENT IS, ABOVE ALL, A PRACTICE
WHERE ART, SCIENCE, AND CRAFT MEET.'
HENRY MINTZBERG

Strategic objectives and analysis

Part 2 is an introduction to strategic objectives and the analysis of the external and internal environments. These three come together as opportunities and threats, and strengths and weaknesses, within a joint SWOT framework.

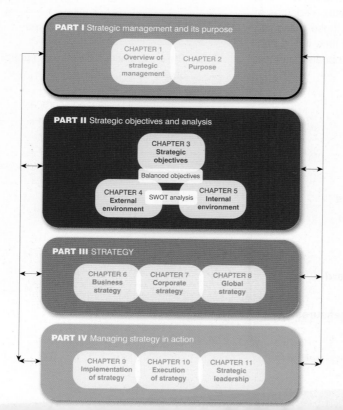

Chapter 3
OBJECTIVES

The nature of objectives

An objective is a statement of a specific outcome that is to be achieved. Objectives must be meaningful and clear to the people who devise and use them, including the people who must manage the objectives. Thus, objectives have to be linked to realistic measures of progress and achievement so that those managing the objectives will know in enough time if it is necessary to intervene and make appropriate changes.

LEARNING OBJECTIVES

This chapter provides you with an understanding of the following:

1	The nature and use of objectives
2	The importance of balance in managing objectives
3	The strategic balanced scorecard
4	The nature of a strategy map
5	The management of a balanced scorecard

KEY TERMS

balanced scorecard

critical success factors

key performance indicators

performance measurement

perspectives

SMART objectives

strategic balanced scorecard

strategy map

strategic objectives and measures

Business vignette Aims and objectives provide purpose

One of the most famous wartime speeches was given around the time of the start of World War Two by Winston Churchill to the British parliament. It clearly got across the war strategy but above all else, its overall objective – victory:

I have nothing to offer but blood, toil, tears and sweat. We have before us an ordeal of the most grievous kind ...

You ask, what is our policy? I will say: it is to wage war, by sea, land and air, with all our might and with all the strength that God can give us: to wage war against a monstrous tyranny, never surpassed in the dark, lamentable catalogue of human crime. That is our policy.

You ask, what is our aim? I can answer in one word: It is victory, victory at all costs, victory in spite of all terror, victory, however long and hard the road may be; for without victory there is no survival.[1]

Sir Winston Churchill, former British Prime Minister

Objectives form the basis of a common language for understanding the wider context for any part of work, particularly for identifying the inevitable knock-on effects of change, since agreement with others is usually needed to implement change successfully. This requires common ways of working that are based on dialogue and consensus, and the determination and management of objectives, in ways that are transparent and can be clearly understood by all.

Peter Drucker, who has deservedly been called the 'father of modern management' and who wrote extensively about the use of objectives, argues persuasively that their role is to liberate managers by making things clearer about what has to be done and that this makes work easier.

> Each manager, from the 'big boss' down to the production foreman, or the chief clerk, needs clearly spelled-out objectives. These objectives should lay out what contribution he and his unit are expected to make to help other units obtain their objectives. Finally, they should spell out what contribution the manager can expect from other units towards the attainment of his own objectives. Right from the start, in other words, emphasis should be on teamwork and team results.[2]

It is generally observed in the management literature that objectives should be practical, and therefore, **SMART objectives**:

- **S**pecific
- **M**easurable
- **A**ction oriented (some might use Agreed upon)
- **R**ealistic
- **T**ime-bound

In practice, strategic objectives *can* be usefully open, general, and intangible. These objectives are often ambitious perhaps to a degree that can seem unrealistic. This happens when the objective is used as a spur to creative thinking about having to do things differently, and to encourage a diversity of solutions for open-ended problems.

It is our view that these kinds of objectives must be grounded if they are to be managed strategically. So, for example, Gary Hamel and C. K. Prahalad argue

that the competitive success of the Japanese during the 1980s was due to the simplicity of their long-term vision statements, which Hamel and Prahalad call statements of strategic intent.[3] Examples are Komatsu's declared intent to 'Encircle Caterpillar', and Canon's to 'Beat Xerox'. The aim of these was to create an organization-wide obsession with a level of achievement that was at the time, out of all proportion to a firm's existing resources and capabilities. This type of strategic objective is an open objective, but the nature of its translation into mid-term objectives for implementation is SMART.

> Strategic intent is like a marathon run in 400-metre sprints. No one knows what mile 26 will look like, so the role of top management is to focus the organization on the ground to be covered in the near 400 metres, and it does this by setting corporate challenges that specify the next 400 metres … top management is specific about the ends (reducing product development times by 75 per cent, for example) but less prescriptive about the means.[4]

The 'challenges' are medium-term plans, and the 'ends' are the targets associated with the plan's objectives: the objective referred to here is 'reducing development times' and its associated target is 75 per cent. The 'means' are the actions that have to be developed to achieve the plan's objectives. The principle is that the closer strategically-related objectives come to execution at an operational level, the more detailed and specific they must become. The development and the deployment of strategically related objectives in daily management are subjects that belong to managing implementation, which are discussed in Chapter 10.

It was Nobel Prize winner, Herbert Simon, who first wrote that organizational goals should be set by senior management and then broken down into sub-goals for use at each level of the organization.[5] In this way each lower-order goal becomes a means to a higher-order goal. In this sense there is a hierarchy of objectives (which is analogous to the strategy hierarchy; see Chapter 1, Figure 1.2). An organization's overall objectives, such as corporate objectives, are translated and used to deploy lower-level sub-objectives; typically through management by objectives (MBO) (see Chapter 10). At an operational level, objectives are often referred to as targets, and corporate objectives are sometimes called goals. However, there is no clear consensus about the use of such terms: goals, targets, aims and objectives, are often used interchangeably. In understanding their meaning, it is important you should carefully note how the particular context in which they are being used defines what they exactly mean.

The general management of objectives

Whatever the context for objectives, the woes that beset objective management are numerous. We summarize these as the 'ten deadly sins of objective management' in Table 3.1: any of these can kill or maim progress. Senior managers should actively manage organization-wide review to ensure that there are owners for objectives who take responsibility for their progress. This should involve an open and a transparent approach that makes sure owners and others are not too cautious because they fear failure, or too optimistic, because of unrealistic assumptions and estimates of outcomes and progress. Objectives are central to both organizational learning and motivation; so objective owners should be involved in setting their own objectives.

Realism and practicality are important. Objectives should clarify what should be achieved, but it has to be recognized that they are often subjective and rely on personal judgement. They should not be plucked from out of the air as a nice thing to have. If a desired outcome is essential for management success, then whatever it takes should be used to produce it, and this may mean changing the nature of an objective as work progresses. Although, if this is a higher level objective and likely to affect many people, changes should be made very rarely and instead the focus should be placed on finding alternative means. As a working principle, higher level objectives should be managed by senior managers in ways to keep them relatively stable over time.

There is no reliable method for setting objectives, but their management should be flexible and based upon an open understanding of the organization's current way of doing things. In other words, how things are done now is the starting point for doing things differently. It is important to manage objectives actively so that different things can be attempted as necessary to achieve a desired result.

TABLE 3.1 The ten deadly sins of objective management

In general the following should be avoided in the management of objectives:

1 Too many objectives – they can breed like rabbits and mushroom out of control

2 Meaningless objectives – to motivate people they must be relevant

3 Useless objectives – must be able to use them to review and learn

4 Old objectives – must be relevant to today's challenges

5 Myopic objectives – must be far-seeing and relevant to the bigger picture

6 Insular objectives – should not be selfish or easy to do, to the detriment of others

7 Inconsistent objectives – all objectives must work synergistically

8 Pet objectives – should not be the favourites of powerful individuals

9 Non-agreed objectives – all affected parties must be consulted

10 Complex objectives – must never be elaborate, but always understandable

Objectives and strategic management

Purpose must be translated into a set of primary objectives, which are called 'strategic objectives'. These serve as the indicators and measures of a firm's or an organization's long-term effectiveness in managing purpose. They cover the most important areas of the enterprise and are used to help determine the priorities for the implementation and execution of objectives. There is a natural tendency for managers to react more positively to short-term, rather than longer-term, objectives; and as Drucker powerfully points out:

> There are few things that distinguish competent from incompetent management quite as sharply as the performance in balancing objectives [to] obtain

balanced efforts, the objectives of all managers on all levels and in all areas should be keyed to both short-range and long-range considerations … Anything else is short-sighted and impractical.[6]

This is basic for effective strategic management (see Figure 3.1).

Determining the balance is not easy; this is clear from remarks of senior managers who have had responsibility for strategy. Consider the respective remarks from Ed Arditte, a senior vice-president of strategy and investor relations at Tyco International, and Stuart Grief, vice president of strategy and business development at Textron:

> The responsibility is both in the short and long-term results. There has to be a balance, but there's never a perfect answer for how you balance them. You need a dialogue that aligns resource

KEY DEBATE 3.1

What is wrong with objectives?

Much of the early work in economics assumed that firms would have to follow profit-maximizing objectives. Dissident economists, notably Cyert and March, saw firms as satisficing collections of coalitions which are motivated by their own objectives. As Simon observed, 'the goals that actually underlie the decisions made in an organization do not coincide with the goals of the owners or of top management but have been modified by[7] managers and employees at all echelons.'[8]

The early pioneers of management theory pointed to the inadequacy of a single profit objective. Drucker identified eight core business areas where objectives should be set: these included market standing, innovation, productivity, physical and financial resources, profitability, manager performance and development, worker performance and attitude, and public responsibility.[9] The problem is that this is a loosely related, or even unrelated, group of lagged and lead objectives. At least with financial objectives a manager could be certain the objective means something. Also if the non-financial objectives are wrong it may be better to have no objectives at all (although the very act of managing objectives can make managers aware that they ought to be doing something else).

The answer for Ansoff is to distinguish clearly between financial and strategic objectives.[10] The strategic objectives are those organizational characteristics that enable a successful longer-term performance. This is very similar to Rockart's CSFs, but it is probably difficult to be sure about what an organization's CSFs are. The answer would seem to be to make a constant review of the basic assumptions underlying an organization's purpose and its strategic objectives.

Question: According to Kaplan and Norton the strategy map is the answer: how?

FIGURE 3.1 Striking a balance in strategic objectives

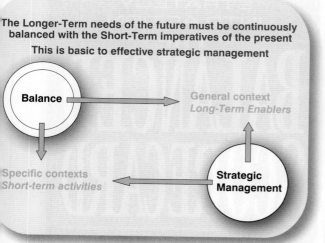

The Longer-Term needs of the future must be continuously balanced with the Short-Term imperatives of the present

This is basic to effective strategic management

Balance

General context
Long-Term Enablers

Specific contexts
Short-term activities

Strategic
Management

The Massachusetts Institute of Technology – home of CSFs

allocation, people, and money with both the short and long-term.

Balancing the short versus long term is the biggest challenge we have. How do you balance the trade-off between the short-term compensation lift from near-term performance and the investments – and therefore the depressed economics, shorter-term – that make the long-term strategies pay off?[11]

Critical success factors

In pioneering work that addressed the importance of balance, John Rockart popularized the concept of **critical success factors (CSFs)**. These are the factors that primarily account for an organization's success in achieving its strategic purpose. He based his ideas on research at the Massachusetts Institute of Technology.[12] Ronald Daniel had earlier observed that critical success factors were likely to be different in different industries. For example, in the automobile industry, styling, an efficient dealer network and the tight control of manufacturing costs are paramount; in food processing, new product development, good distribution and effective advertising, are major success factors.[13] Rockart went further than Daniel and argued that CSFs are a function of four things:

1 the structure of a particular industry;

2 competitive strategy, industry position and geography;

3 environmental factors (Rockart gives the example of the abrupt rise in world oil prices in the 1970s);

4 temporal factors (which are internal concerns, which require special attention at different times).

Rockart suggests CSFs can be applied to monitor current results, and to build for the future. CSFs make an organization's key activities explicit and offer up strategic insights that go beyond a mere shared understanding of purpose. He uses an example of CSFs and its associated measures for a communications company active in the development of microwave technology:

- Image in financial markets: measure is P/E ratio.

- Technological reputation with customers: measures are order/bid ratio, customer perception interviews.

- Market success: measure is change in market share (all products).

- Risk recognition in major bids/contracts: measures are company experience with similar new or old customer, prior customer relationship.

- Profit margin on jobs: measure is profit margin as ratio on profit on similar jobs in this product line.

- Company morale: measures are employee turnover, absenteeism etc., informal feedback.
- Performance to budget on job: measures are job cost budgets/activities.

CSFs are often confused with **key performance indicators (KPIs)**. However, there is an explicit distinction between them. KPIs are those strategically related targets used at lower levels in the organization, such as in daily management. They are derived or aligned with the overall strategic objectives but in themselves they are not longer-term, being concerned with the execution of strategy at an operational level (this is discussed in Chapter 10). Because Rockart drew a distinction between a CSF and its measures, he heralded the balanced scorecard's important distinction between a strategic objective and its measures.

The balanced scorecard

A **balanced scorecard** is a documented set of objectives and measures grouped into four perspectives. The concept was first introduced by Robert Kaplan and David Norton in a *Harvard Business Review* article in 1992.[14] It has been widely adopted. It is perhaps the most widely adopted management methodology of recent times and is used by every kind of organization.[15] Its role is to help organizations take a fuller account not only of their essential financial objectives, but also of the strategic objectives that identify and measure those core activities that enable and lead to desired financial and other outcome objectives.

Lagged and lead measures

Kaplan and Norton distinguish between outcome measures, which they call lagged measures of past progress, and process measures of performance that is leading to future outcomes, which they call lead measures. Lagged measures include taking account of present financial performance and

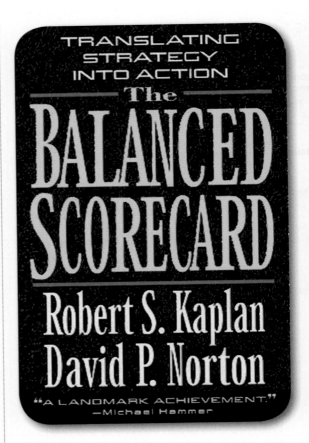

productivity, while lead measures include taking account of changing perceptions such as customer satisfaction and retention, and the development and management of employees. The modern woes of General Motors are put down to the corporation's focus in the United States on the financial (and market) attractiveness of large rather than small cars. The organization did not want or was unable to foresee the implications of changing consumer preferences from gas guzzlers to economy cars.

Objectives and measures

A balanced scorecard comprises a limited number of **strategic objectives and measures**. Each objective has its own set of **measures**. These are formulated to enable senior management to move an organization strategically towards the achievement of an overall vision. The objectives and measures are decided in terms of four different scorecard **perspectives**.

These are shown in Figure 3.2 and some examples of an objective for each of the four perspectives, along with examples of possible measures, are given in Table 3.2 (for simplicity only one objective per perspective is shown; an ideal number is three or fewer, see below). Kaplan and Norton advise that the chosen objectives and measures should answer four fundamental questions (Figure 3.2).

The perspectives cover areas of concern which are of importance to different stakeholders. The financial perspective will matter more to people who have a financial stake in the organization, such as owners and leaders to the business. The customer perspective is of a more direct concern to the buyers and users of the organization's products and services. The other two perspectives are more directly relevant to the employees of the organization. It is important in the design of the scorecard that the questions shown in Figure 3.2 should as far as possible reflect the perspectives and the voices of the relevant stakeholders. For example, if shareholders think that a given rate of profit is a necessary return to justify their investment, then senior managers should reflect this in a financial objective.

Organizations may change the number of the perspectives to suit their own circumstances. Perspectives could be added to include broader stakeholder interests including CSR responsibilities, such as environment issues.[16] The Canadian firm, Novacor Chemicals, has added a fifth perspective, 'society', 'to reflect the fact that the governments and local communities where we operate are important to us as stakeholders. In this perspective we have incorporated measures on our environmental performance, safety record, community opinion rating, and product stewardship.'[17]

FIGURE 3.2 The four perspectives of the balanced scorecard[18]

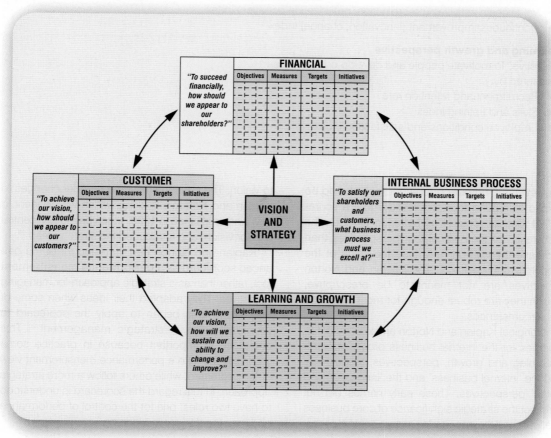

TABLE 3.2 Four perspectives as a framework for objectives and measures

Financial perspective

Objective: To maximize financial returns to the owners of an organization's capital

Measured by:
- Return on capital employed
- Payments (e.g. dividends) to owners
- Cash flow

Customer perspective

Objective: To sustain customer relationships

Measured by:
- Customer satisfaction and delight index
- Repeat purchase patterns
- Brand awareness in target segments

Internal business processes perspective

Objective: To create and maximize value in the customer-vendor relationship

Measured by:
- Value streams analysis (to minimize non-value creation activities) index
- Value chain activities (co-ordination, optimization activities) index
- Continuous improvement (innovation, change) index

Learning and growth perspective

Objective: To motivate people and develop competences

Measured by:
- Recruitment and retention rate
- Skills and training index
- Employee conditions and satisfaction index

However, the number of perspectives should be restricted to around four or it is likely that a scorecard will lose its focus. It is better to broaden the interpretation of the original four perspectives than to increase the number and lose the value of the scorecard's compactness. The Kaplan and Norton perspectives are not meant to be prescriptive, although they are robust enough for most organizational circumstances.

The original Kaplan and Norton article used different names for the internal business processes, and the learning and growth, perspectives, respectively called the 'internal business' and the 'innovation and learning' perspectives. These early names did not fully reflect the strategic significance of core business processes, and the importance of core competences,

to vision. The changes reflected broader changes to Kaplan and Norton's thinking, which was evident in new work published in 1996, which provides a central role for vision, and introduced the strategy map.[19]

Kaplan and Norton had first thought of the balanced scorecard as a **performance measurement** tool, rather than as a strategic approach for managing objectives. They adapted their ideas when some of their client firms began to apply the scorecard to progress vision in strategic management.[20] This difference is important because in practice some organizations take a performance measurement view of the scorecard, while others follow a more strategic approach. In this regard the scorecard is understood to have two roles: one for the control of performance and the other for use in planning.

PRINCIPLES IN PRACTICE 3.1

Ambitions as objectives to define a way of working

'By simply choosing a particular set of criteria for judging business success or failure, you are immediately defining a set of values and a particular way of working', says Mark Bromley, Director of Business Objectives and Performance at EDF Energy. 'Conversely, as soon as you exclude particular business factors from the measurement process, you will almost certainly find that those factors have little or no bearing on the directions you set for yourself and those around you. It's necessary to make the choice between what is really strategic and important, and other performance management objectives and measures.'

Électricité de France S.A. (Electricity of France), or EDF, employs over 158 000 people, and earned more than $83 billion in revenue in 2010; the company produces electricity in Europe, Latin America, Asia, the Middle-East and Africa. The corporate group's senior managers use a balanced scorecard approach to link overall objectives to continuous improvement. By so doing EDF aims to instil a strategy-linked culture throughout all of its divisions.

The Group's strategic vision is expressed in the form of five ambitions, each with a group-level measure, see the figure below (the star symbol signifies good progress, diamonds indicate satisfactory performance, circles mean that performance is below expectations, and squares that performance is well below expectations).

The EDF balanced scorecard

Ambition to:	Measures:	status	forecast
Meet shareholders' expectations	Net income	★	◆
	Capital expenditure	★	◆
	Working capital (free cash flow)	■	◆
Care for our customers	Mass market customers	●	◆
	Major business customers	●	◆
Be a positive point of reference (corporate image)	Corporate responsibility index	●	◆
Be safe and responsible	Health, Safety and Environment management index	★	◆
Maximize employee satisfaction	Employee opinion survey	●	◆

The ambitions are used across the organization to create a working knowledge of performance and a cultural alignment around its corporate purpose.[21]

Question: How do strategic objectives influence the way everybody works?

A performance management scorecard – Tesco's steering wheel[23]

The UK-based supermarket group, Tesco, uses a balanced scorecard to keep local store managers and employees engaged in satisfying consumers in ways that are consistent with the Tesco shopping experience and which differentiates it from the shopping experience at other rival supermarkets. Tesco based their approach on Kaplan and Norton's original article.[24] The steering wheel (see Figure 3.3) is used by corporate executives to focus stores on the delivery of Tesco's core purpose, which is 'to create value for customers to earn their lifetime loyalty'.

The company regularly asks its customers and staff what the company can do to make shopping and working a little bit better: this is the 'Every Little Helps' strategy, and the steering wheel is used to link every member of staff's work to this strategy. The performances of the stores on the wheel's objectives are reviewed quarterly at board level, and a summary report is prepared for the top 2000 managers to cascade to staff in the stores. The remuneration of senior management is shaped by the

FIGURE 3.3 The Tesco steering wheel

wheel's objectives with bonuses varying according to the level of their overall achievement. The wheel is considered annually for changes depending on circumstances, and to check that the objectives remain consistent with the Every Little Helps strategy. The most significant change since its introduction has been the addition of a fifth perspective based on community values. At store level, every member of staff uses a 'plan and review' document at their bi-annual appraisal to agree with a superior their contribution to the wheel's objectives.

The steering wheel is not a strategic scorecard in the Kaplan and Norton sense of being based on a strategic vision, but rather it is a strategic performance measurement framework that uses KPIs to drive the performance of employees and align their daily activities with core purpose. In this sense the steering wheel gives to senior management a dynamic capability for strategically managing the core competences of Tesco's staff (see Chapter 5).

What makes a scorecard 'strategic'?

The basic scorecard idea is straightforward, but confusion easily occurs when practitioners lose sight of its importance as a strategic approach that aims to give the organization its overall priorities. The biggest problem is that objectives and measures become too numerous to manage, especially if newcomers to the approach try to create their measures from a larger number of existing measures. Owen Berkeley-Hill, a manager at Ford, found the scorecard became unwieldy if it involved too many objectives and measures:

> ... the first scorecards at Ford. Unrelated to any strategic planning, these were developed because scorecards were the fashionable management accessory. The main driver appeared to be the now

often quoted Kaplan and Norton expression – 'If you can't measure it, you can't manage it'. Every conceivable measure for the particular operation was added to the card that was then reduced so it could fit a shirt pocket. What was not taken into consideration for this monthly exercise was the effort involved in collecting and verifying the measures before publication. To no one's surprise the second edition was never published.[25]

The over-abundance of objectives and measures is typically down to confusion about which objectives and measures are strategic and which are operational. This applies particularly to measures. Measures provide the essential handle for understanding and reviewing progress on an objective. However, it is often easier to measure known and alike activities than uncertain and different ones, and measures are typically more reliable for tracking specific indicators for diagnostic control, rather than for broader and more general strategic matters.

Kaplan and Norton make a distinction between strategic objectives and measures, and diagnostic objectives and measures. The former deal with the CSFs for an organization's vision and a strategic scorecard is limited to strategic objectives only. The diagnostic objectives monitor the health of the organization to ensure it remains fit for purpose; they indicate whether the organization remains in control and can signal up the unusual events that require attention. Senior managers are proactively involved with strategic objectives, and become involved with diagnostic objectives by exception, when their intervention is required. This is important because a scorecard's focus on vision keeps the number of scorecard objectives and measures to a manageable number.

There is no absolute rule about what this should be, but effective scorecards typically have no more than about 8 objectives and 24 measures. An organization's diagnostic objectives and measures, on the other hand, can run into many dozens. Some of these will be strategically linked KPIs, which are in place to monitor and drive improvement in the key areas of the business. Of course, the needs of scorecard's objectives may require adjustments to the diagnostic objectives, but diagnostic objectives should not be on a strategic balanced scorecard. According to Kaplan and Norton, the aim of vision-linked objectives and measures is to drive competi-

tive breakthroughs. However, there is no reason why scorecard objectives and measures should only be used to achieve this type of breakthrough.

Strategy maps

A **strategy map** is a reference framework drawn out to help strategists think about a scorecard's perspectives, objectives and measures – to explore possible cause-and-effect relationships and pressing issues. While the balanced scorecard is a powerful reference framework for object representation, the strategy map is a methodology to support and examine the scorecard, and to evaluate the basic assumptions for choosing objectives and measures. Kaplan and Norton write about 'cause-and-effect hypotheses', which sounds scientific if not deterministic and operationally focused. However the idea is not to think up definite answers to specific issues, but rather to think strategically to explore any possible connections and evaluate them as an inter-related whole.

In their early work, Kaplan and Norton, had originally thought a consensus on the choice of objectives and measures would emerge among senior managers through a discussion based around the answers to the four perspectives' questions (see Figure 3.2 above), and they believed this would be good enough to provide a workable framework for thinking about performance measurement. Later on, however, they argue that a strategy map is a more comprehensive and strategic approach that allows senior managers to explore and develop the organization's CSFs for the achievement of a strategic vision.

The strategy map is used to document the CSFs in terms of the possible cause and effect linkages between the perspectives and the objectives. It enables managers to explore strategically the relationships to understand how the scorecard objectives relate both to vision and the mission of the organization and how to select and check the appropriate measures for the scorecard's objectives. Figure 3.4 illustrates this idea for a university: the arrows show directional links between areas of core activities that contribute to the two strategic themes of organizational growth and influence, and knowledge contribution.

FIGURE 3.4 A strategy map for a university

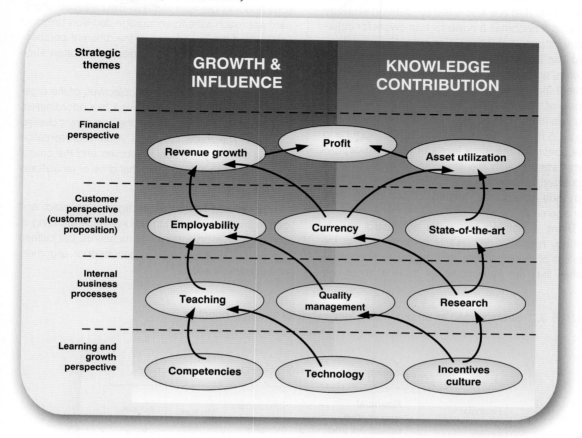

The strategy map retains a focus on financial results, but it also recognizes the importance of the enablers of those results. It is a principle of score-card management that no perspectives are favoured to the detriment of the others. The position of the financial perspective at the top of the cause-and-effect hierarchy shown in the figure does not imply an order of priority; only the direction of cause-and-effect influences. So, for example, the learning and growth perspective takes into account that growth and influence require particular learning skills, which are necessary to manage the key processes that create the value to students and sponsors, who provide the necessary income to meet the financial objectives of the university.

There cannot be any known definitive and deterministic quantitative linkage between the non-financial and financial perspectives. The financial perspective is dependent, but working out a definite causal link is difficult as the influences generated by the external environment dominate over internal improvement. For example, when a prototype of the scorecard was used to improve non-financial performance at Analog Devices, an American semi-conductor company, its stock prices fell due to the vagaries of the business cycle and lag effects.[26]

The important thing is for the senior and other levels of management to use the strategy map continuously, as one senior manager has put it:

It is important to use this as a strategic tool and ask, 'why are we off on that particular measure? Are we measuring the right thing? Is it what we are doing is never going to deliver a good result, or is there something else going on here?' ... and using it to inform and have an informal discussion about where we should be putting resource going forwards.[27]

If the scorecard is used with other analytical techniques that are also used for crafting strategy choices, it becomes a powerful framework for determining strategic priorities. For example, a strategy map can be readily used to order evidence about external and internal environmental conditions (see Table 3.3). The left-hand column indicates the evidence of factors taken into account for strategic analysis (these can be used for SWOT analysis, see Figure 5.6). The three columns to the right-hand side constitute the three levels of objective deployment: starting with the strategic objectives in the scorecard, followed by objectives in a medium-term plan and strategically-related objectives in daily management.

There is nothing about the scorecard and its strategy map that necessarily determines what the content of the objectives and measures should be. Rather, they are frameworks for thinking about and monitoring decisions and for working out the assumptions about longer-term strategy. The balanced scorecard approach aims to encourage decision-takers to understand the importance of the different perspectives as related elements. Kaplan and Norton state that strategy maps:

> ... are linked to the overall objectives of the organization, enabling them to work in a coordinated, collaborative fashion toward the company's desired goals. The maps provide a visual representation of a company's critical objectives and the crucial relationships among them that drive organizational performance.[28]

Kaplan and Norton argue against an exact and deterministic-based organizational understanding of corporate level objectives and measures, but instead stress the importance of organizational alignment and communication.

TABLE 3.3 Strategy map as an organizing framework for strategic priorities

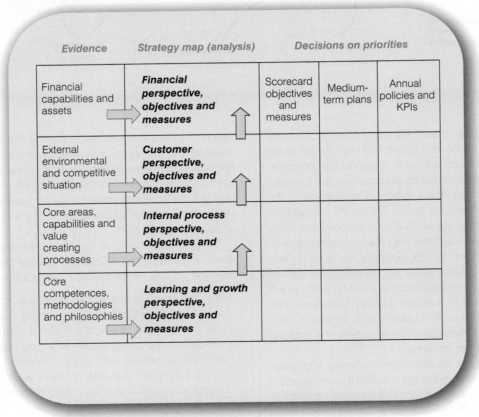

Managing the balanced scorecard

If a balanced scorecard is to work effectively as an integral part of strategic management, then it is necessary to have in place high-level supports. Kaplan and Norton propose a four-part process (see Figure 3.5). This starts with senior level agreement on the appropriate strategic objectives and measures, which are chosen to achieve the organization's vision. The scorecard is then communicated to the rest of the organization, so that performance management systems generally, such as incentives and rewards, can be aligned to the scorecard. After this, the scorecard is used as a basis for deciding on policies, mid-term plans and other strategic initiatives. The final part provides feedback on the implementation and execution of these, but in ways that enable senior managers to evaluate and learn how the scorecard's objectives and measures are working, and to test the assumptions against the CSFs. Kaplan and Norton emphasize the importance of the senior management team taking full charge and responsibility for managing the scorecard. This requires the chief

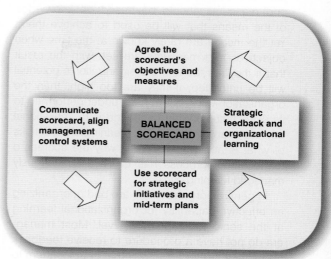

FIGURE 3.5 The process for managing the balanced scorecard[29]

executive to take responsibility for the whole process, while each of the four parts should be the responsibility of an individual executive.

The non-financial variables on the scorecard are difficult to identify correctly and in principle the

---

KEY DEBATE 3.2

Is the balanced scorecard hard to manage?

Kaplan and Norton, in their recent work, have emphasized the importance of administrative supports for the scorecard, such as a strategy office.[30] A lot of this looks like the old corporate planning office that used to administer and plan the strategic plan.

David Otley has made the point that effectiveness may depend upon how other management control systems are managed in relation to the scorecard.[31]

If the influence of the strategic objectives and measures are to reach down to operational levels, where the actual improvement activities reside, the organization's deployment system is important. Arthur Schneiderman, the inventor of the balanced scorecard, used *hoshin kanri*[32] and argues that a state-of-the-art business methodology, such as PDCA-based continuous improvement (see Chapter 5), is necessary for the management of objectives.

It is important to measure the right things, improve analytical skills, and ensure that a disciplined focus is maintained (as an acronym it spells out MAD).[33]

Question: How would you as a senior manager manage MAD?

wider organization should be involved in their formation (the first part of the model). The objectives and measures should be based on knowledge of the means that will be used to achieve them. Yet the means are rarely known at the time when objectives and measures are set, with the result that if they are too low, the organization's potential will be unfulfilled; if they are too high, then the organization will seem to have under-performed to its expectations. What is needed is to set rational objectives and measures as meaningful yardsticks of what is achievable. This is why the scorecard management process has to be a continuously managed learning cycle.

In general, organizations are bad at organizing an effective capability for organizational learning at the senior management level. Most managers do not have a procedure to receive feedback about their strategy in a way that enables them to examine the assumptions on which their objectives and measures are based. The scorecard and its accompanying strategy map should give to the senior level a greater capacity for strategic learning, which, Kaplan and Norton say makes the balanced scorecard the cornerstone of a stra-tegic management system.[34] They suggest that a formal administrative function could be used to support the management of the scorecard,[35] and its role would be to manage implementation (see Chapter 10).

Non-profit and public sector balanced scorecards

A non-profit or a public sector organization is likely to have a very different vision to an organization active in a competitive environment. To some extent, of course, there are always alternatives for an organi-zation's products and services, and an organization must manage financial along with other enabler objectives. However, this types of organization may change the content of the four perspectives, de-pending upon their strategic purpose, but the nature of the scorecard remains essentially the same (see Figure 3.6).

FIGURE 3.6 The public sector scorecard[36]

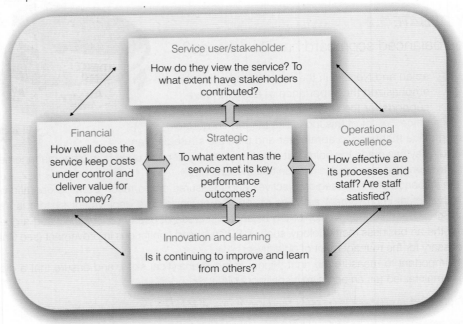

Figure 3.6 above, shows a suggested template for the public sector and how the perspective may be modified. One of the problems is defining a customer or user requirement: when a sponsor is involved, it is likely to prescribe what 'use' means, and it is not always the same as the user thinks it should be. Another is the nature of the strategic box in the centre, where a vision would sit for a commercial organization, but for a public service organization this might be a public policy priority.[37]

PRINCIPLES IN PRACTICE 3.3

A balanced scorecard at the non-profit making University of Virginia Library

The University of Virginia Library adopted the balanced scorecard in 2001. The reason was to make the library accountable to purpose, and to identify and develop indicators of purpose, which could be used to strategically manage those CSFs that would actually produce a difference in performance. The balanced scorecard is shown below. This shows only objectives and not measures (the number of measures will be at least twice the number of objectives). The library has defined its purpose as a set of core values, shown in the centre of the figure.[38]

User perspective

Provide excellent service to our users

Educate users to fulfil their information needs

Build, maintain, and preserve high quality collections

Provide convenient and timely access to collections

Learning/growth perspective

Foster learning among employees

Recruit, develop, retain productive, highly qualified staff

Provide facilities that promote productivity. Encourage library use, and ensure top quality services

Maintain a cutting-edge information technology infrastructure

CORE VALUES

We respond to the needs of our customers

We use our resources wisely

We continuously improve our processes

We enable and develop our people and our systems

Finance perspective

Increase financial base through private donations and increased external and institutional support

Provide resources and services with a high ratio of value to cost

Internal process perspective

Deliver high quality information resources in a timely manner

Use resources in the most innovative, efficient, and effective way possible

Develop a culture of assessment

Continuously review and improve high impact processes

Question: Values are different to vision: is this scorecard about control or change?

The relation of a strategic balanced scorecard to other scorecards

The success of the scorecard has meant that many organizations, especially non-profit ones, call any list of objectives and measures a scorecard. It is important to distinguish these from the real **strategic balanced scorecard**. The translation of strategic objectives for implementation and daily management are discussed in Chapter 10. However, note at this point that a large and complex organization may have several levels of scorecards, just as they have a hierarchy of strategy (Chapter 1). So a strategic scorecard may be translated into scorecards for different parts of an organization. A business division may have its own scorecard, and at an operational level departments and units may document their KPIs and other daily management objectives in the style of a balanced scorecard. These may be derived from, or aligned with, a corporate level scorecard.

In their example of practice at Mobil Oil, Kaplan and Norton show how Mobil's division allowed their business units to develop their own scorecard in light of local circumstances.[39] The objectives and measures they used did not have to add up a higher level divisional scorecard, but rather managers chose local measures that would influence the measures on the divisional scorecard. In other words it was not a simple decomposition of the higher-level scorecard. Also at lower levels, scorecards were interrelated to some extent, for example, where a unit was an internal supplier to another, then the customer perspective on its scorecard was likely to reflect the scorecard requirements of that internal customer.

KEY DEBATE 3.3

Do balanced scorecards really work?

At least one theorist thinks that Kaplan and Norton's work does not contribute any new and convincing theory, but rather it is only 'persuasive rhetoric'.[40] On the whole, research that links the scorecard to value creation is positive.[41]

However, many theorists continue to question its ideas. So, for instance, Kaplan and Norton argue that the strategy map should be used pragmatically, but observers, such as Ittner and Larcker, and Jensen, suggest the map is used superficially, since they find that managers do not really question the underlying assumptions of the objectives and measures.[42]

There is also confusion about its role: whether it should be used for controlling performance, or more strategically for planning and learning approach: Zingales *et al.*, suggest it is used for control, while Mooraj *et al.* find that European-based organizations use it for planning – but Antarkar and Cobbold argue it is equally effective for both.[43]

The scorecard may be unsuitable for organizations that have a large number of stakeholders, and alternative approaches have been suggested, notably for performance management, see, for example, Neely A., Adams, C. and Kennerley, M., who argue their own framework for linking stakeholder value to strategic objectives is superior.[44] However, as one study of German organizations points out, the balanced scorecard is not meant to integrate the needs of stakeholders into strategic objectives.[45]

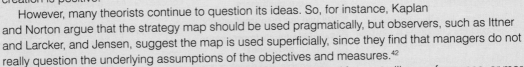

Question: What are the strengths and weaknesses of the balanced scorecard approach?

Some organizations continue to use versions of Kaplan and Norton's original performance measurement scorecard rather than the later strategic scorecard. Some textbooks and journal articles present the balanced scorecard as an implementation tool. While Kaplan and Norton address how to link strategic objectives to operations in one of their most recent books, their work makes it plain that the development of an organization's overall objectives is an integrated part of the development and continuous review of an overall strategy.[46] The purpose of this chapter is to explain the use of the *strategic* balanced scorecard within the context of strategic management of objectives. This part of the book considers strategic analysis and in the next chapters the importance of situational analysis to strategic objectives and strategy is examined and discussed.

SUMMARY OF PRINCIPLES

1   An objective is a statement of a specific outcome to be achieved. A strategic objective and its measures are used to sustain and progress an organization's purpose. Every level of objectives in an organization should be aligned with the organization's overall strategic objectives and measures.

2   The closer strategically related objectives come to execution at an operational level, the more specific and detailed they must become (SMART).

3   The balance of objectives to meet the needs of today must be balanced with the needs of the future – this is central to strategic management.

4   The balanced scorecard aims to balance objectives (each objective must have its own measures) from the point of view of four perspectives, which are managed as an integrated set.

5   Critical success factors (CSFs) should be identified to account for factors that are primarily responsible for the success of the scorecard's objectives. These must not be confused with key performance indicators (KPIs), as they are measures of progress. KPIs may be considered objectives only as lower-level objectives that are derived from and aligned with the higher level strategic scorecard objectives.

6   To keep scorecard objectives and measures to a manageable number, it should be focused on the achievement of a vision. This type of scorecard is a strategic scorecard and differs from a performance measurement one, which may be used at lower levels of the organization and has more operational detail.

7   A strategy map is used creatively to explore cause-and-effect hypotheses to think about and review objectives and measures.

8   The balanced scorecard must be managed by the chief executive and the senior management team.

GUIDED FURTHER READING

This chapter follows mainly the Kaplan and Norton balanced scorecard cannon. Despite a huge extant literature on the subject, the work of Kaplan and Norton remains paramount and they continue to publish widely. The most useful for further reading include their first two books on the subject, see Kaplan, R. S. and Norton, D. P. (2001), *The Strategy-Focused Organization: How Balanced Scorecard Companies Thrive in the New Business Environment*, Boston MA: Harvard Business School Press; Kaplan, R. S. and Norton, D. P. (1996), *The Balanced Scorecard: Translating Strategy into Action*, Boston MA: Harvard Business School Press.

Many of the ideas have antecedents in Japanese organizational management. The prototype balanced scorecard was developed as part of hoshin kanri (see Chapter 10) at Analog Devices, see Stata, R. (1989), 'Organizational learning – the key to management innovation', *Sloan Management Review*, Spring, 63–74. The relationship between the two is explained in Witcher, B. J. and Chau, V. S. (2007), 'Balanced scorecard and hoshin kanri: dynamic capabilities for managing strategic fit', *Management Decision*, 45(3): 518–537.

REVIEW QUESTIONS

1   Why are objectives important to the process of managing work?

2   How do strategic objectives achieve purpose?

3   Should strategic objectives be SMART?

4   What does balance mean in the context of strategic management?

5   Why does balance matter?

6   How are strategic objectives different from objectives used for implementation and execution?

7   What is the difference between strategic and diagnostic objectives?

8   How is strategic management different from performance management?

9   What is the nature of the link between the financial perspective and the others?

10   What is the difference between a CSF and a KPI?

11   How do senior managers take responsibility for a balanced scorecard?

SEMINAR AND ASSIGNMENT QUESTIONS

1   Using Kaplan and Norton's four perspectives, design a balanced scorecard for your own (or group's) career aspirations.

2   With your group draw a strategy map to show the main CSFs involved in achieving a successful career.

3   Compare and contrast Kaplan and Norton's 1992 performance measurement balanced scorecard with their 1996 strategic balanced scorecard. In regard to particular organizations of your own choice discuss how scorecards differ and consider the possible reasons.

CHAPTER END-NOTES

1   Jenkins, R. (2001), *Churchill,* London: Pan Books, p. 591.

2   Drucker, P. F. (1955), *The Practice of Management,* London: Heinemann Butterworth, p. 124. (1954, American edn, New York: Harper & Row).

3   Hamel, G. and Prahalad, C. K. (1989), 'Strategic intent', *Harvard Business Review*, May-June, 63–76.

4   Hamel, G. and Prahalad, C. K. (1989), 'Strategic intent', *Harvard Business Review*, May-June, 63–76.

5   Simon, H. A. (1947), *Administrative Behaviour: A Study of Decision-Making Processes in Administrative Organizations*, New York: Free Press.

6   Drucker, P. F. (1955) *The Practice of Management*, London: Heinemann Butterworth, p. 67. (1954, American edn, New York: Harper & Row).

7   Cyert, R. M. and March, J. G. (1963), *A Behavioural Theory of the Firm,* Englewood Cliffs, NJ: Prentice-Hall.

8   Simon, H. A. (1976), *Administrative Behaviour* (3rd edn), London: Free Press.

9   Drucker, P. F. (1955), *The Practice of Management,* London: Heinemann Butterworth. (1954, American edn. New York: Harper Row.), p. 60.

10 Ansoff, H. I. (1965), *Corporate Strategy: An Analytic Approach to Business Policy for Growth and Expansion*, London: Pelican edn (published 1968).

11 Dye, R. (2008), 'How chief strategy officers think about their role: a roundtable', *McKinsey Quarterly,* May. www.mckinseyquarterly.com.

12 Rockart, J. F. (1979), 'Chief executives define their own data needs', *Harvard Business Review,* 57(March-April), 81–93.

13 Daniel, D. R. (1961), 'Management information crisis', *Harvard Business Review,* September-October, 111.

14 Kaplan, R. S. and Norton, D. P. (1992), 'The balanced scorecard: measures that drive performance', *Harvard Business Review,* January-February, 71–79.

15 2GC Limited (2011), *Balanced Scorecard Usage Survey 2011: Summary of Findings,* www.2gc.co.uk.

16 See Lansiluoto, A. and Jarvenpaa, M. (2010), 'Greening the balanced scorecard', *Business Horizons,* 53:385–396.

17 Boivin, D. W. (1996), 'Using the Balanced Scorecard', letter to the editor, *Harvard Business Review,* March-April, p. 168.

18 Adapted from Kaplan and Norton (1992) 'The balanced scorecard: measures that drive performance', *Harvard Business Review,* January-February, 71–79 and, Kaplan, R. S. and Norton, D. P. (1996), *The Balanced Scorecard: Translating Strategy into Action*, Boston MA: Harvard Business School Press.

19 Kaplan, R. S. and Norton, D. P. (1996), 'Using the balanced scorecard as a strategic management system', *Harvard Business Review*, January-February, 78–85; and Kaplan and Norton (1996), *The Balanced Scorecard: Translating Strategy into Action,* Boston MA: Harvard Business School Press.

20 Kaplan, R. S. and Norton, D. P. (2001), 'Transforming the balanced scorecard from performance measurement to strategic management: part 1', *Accounting Horizons,* 15(1):87–104.

21 Witcher, B. J. and Chau, V. S. (2008), 'Contrasting uses of balanced scorecards: case studies at two UK companies', *Strategic Change,* 17:101–114.

22 Gumbus, A. and Lyons, B. (2002), 'The balanced scorecard at Philips Electronics', *Strategic Finance*, November.

23 Witcher, B. J. and Chau, V. S. (2008) 'Contrasting uses of balanced scorecards: case studies at two UK companies', *Strategic Change, 17.*

24 Kaplan, R. S. (2008), 'Tesco's Approach to Strategy Communication', *HBR Blog Network,* September 2. blogs.hbr.org/kaplan-norton

25 Berkeley-Hill, O. (2002), *Is the balanced scorecard concept compatible with Policy Deployment?* unpublished paper, Cardiff Business School, January, p. 10.

26 Gumbus, A. and Lyons, B. (2002), 'The balanced scorecard at Philips Electronics', *Strategic Finance*, November.

27 Schneiderman, A. (1999), 'Why balanced scorecards fail', *Journal of Strategic Performance Management,* January, 6–11.

28 Kaplan, R. S. and Norton, D. P. (2000), 'Having trouble with your strategy? Then map it', *Harvard Business Review,* September-October, 167–176.

29 Adapted from Kaplan, R. S. and Norton, D. P. (1996), *The Balanced Scorecard: Translating Strategy into Action,* Boston MA: Harvard Business School Press.

30 Kaplan, R. S. and Norton, D. P. (2005), 'The office of strategy management', *Harvard Business Review,* October, 72–80.

31 Otley, D. (1999), 'Performance management: a framework for management control systems

research', *Management Accounting Research,* 10:363–382.

32 Schneiderman, A. (1999), 'Why balanced scorecards fail', *Journal of Strategic Performance Management,* January, 6–11:9.

33 Scopes, J. (2006), 'Balanced scorecards in the UK', *PMA Forum,* email, February, 23.

34 Kaplan, R. S. and Norton, D. P. (1996), *The Balanced Scorecard: Translating Strategy into Action,* Boston MA: Harvard Business School Press p. 269.

35 Kaplan, R. and Norton, D. P. (2005), 'The office of strategy management', *Harvard Business Review,* October, 72–80.

36 Adapted from the Public Balanced Scorecard, Sheffield Hallam University.

37 Jennings Jr., E. T. (2010), 'Strategic planning and balanced scorecards: charting the course to policy destinations, *Public Administration Review,* December, S224–226.

38 University of Virginia Library, www2.lib.virginia.edu/bsc.

39 Kaplan, R. S. and Norton, D. P. (2001), *The Strategy-Focused Organization: How Balanced Scorecard Companies Thrive in the New Business Environment,* Boston MA: Harvard Business School Press.

40 Norreklit, H. (2003), 'The balanced scorecard: what is the score? A rhetorical analysis of the balanced scorecard', *Accounting, Organizations and Society,* 28:591–619.

41 For example, see De Geuser, F., Mooraj, S. and Oyon, D. (2009), 'Does the balanced scorecard add value? Empirical evidence on its effect on performance', *European Accounting Review,* 18(1), 93–122.

42 Ittnerm C. D. and Larckerm D. E. (2003), 'Coming up short on non-financial performance measurement', *Harvard Business Review,* November, 88–95; Jensen, M. C. (2001), 'Value maximisation, stakeholder theory, and the corporate objective function', *European Management Journal,* 7, 3:297–317.

43 Zingales, F., O'Rourke, A. and Hockerts, K. (2002), *Balanced Scorecard and Sustainability: State of the Art,* working paper 65, Centre for the Management of Environmental Resources, INSEAD; Mooraj, S., Oyon, D. and Hostettler, D. (1999), 'The balanced scorecard: a necessary good or an unnecessary evil?', *European Management Journal,* 17, 5:481–491; Antarkar, N. and Cobbold, I. (2001), *Implementing the Balanced Scorecard – Lessons and Insights from a Multi-Divisional Oil Company,* working paper, Maidenhead: 2GC Limited.

44 Neely, A., Adams, C., and Kennerley, M. (2002), *The Performance Prism: The* Scorecard for Measuring and Managing Business Success, London, Prentice-Hall.

45 Speckbacher, G., Bischof, J. and Pfeiffer, T. (2003), 'A descriptive analysis on the implementation of balanced scorecards in German-speaking countries', *Management Accounting Research,* 14 (4):361–388.

46 Kaplan, R. S. and Norton, D.P. (2008), *The Execution Premium,* Boston MA: Harvard Business School Press.

CASE 3.1 Constructing a balanced scorecard for the Namibian National Sanitation Strategy[1]

Since independence access to safe water for the rural population of Namibia was raised from just over 40 per cent in 1991 to 80 per cent in 2001. However, sanitation coverage has not progressed to expectations: by 2009 only 13 per cent of the rural population and 61 per cent of the urban population had access to improved sanitation. New policies were brought in by government during 2008, and the balanced scorecard was adopted the following year to achieve the new policy's vision:

A healthy environment and improved quality of life for 66 per cent of the population having

adequate sanitation services with a high level of hygiene by 2015.

There are two other purpose statements: mission and core values statements. The mission is:

To provide, with minimal impact on the environment, acceptable, affordable and sustainable sanitation services for urban and rural; households, informal settlements and institutions through inter-sectoral coordination, integrated development and community based management with a Sector-wide Approach in financial resource allocation.

Namibian water pumps

The core values:

Represent the non-negotiable style in which the Sanitation Sector will provide services,

thus the:

sector cherishes good governance through the following core values:

- *Integrity comprising honesty, trust and transparency of the service providers.*
- *Commitment to a shared responsibility to improve quality of life.*
- *Collaboration and communication at all levels for effective services delivery.*

The development of a strategy map

Key strategic concerns were identified by using a situational analysis, involving an external and internal analysis, which revealed the major threats, opportunities, strengths and weaknesses. Areas of important strategic considerations were identified. These included social, economic and environmental outcomes; the capability of management, enforcement, and performance management; resources; community involvement, and community education; and capacity. Their relative importance was discussed in terms of the impact for the desired socio-economic and environmental outcomes required for reaching the vision. They formed the basis of the creation of the six strategic themes, below, to build the Sanitation House (see Exhibit 3.1).

1 Water and sanitation coordination (good partnerships, especially in terms of relational resources).
2 Institutional capacity building (people development and resources in all levels of government).
3 Community education and participation (hygiene and sanitation education).
4 Construction (development of physical resources).
5 Operation and management, performance management and enforcement (core competencies and systems).

6 Socio-economic, environmental outputs and outcomes (end-outcomes of the other themes).

Each of the six strategic themes is listed to the left-hand side of the exhibit to form a building block, beginning with water sanitation sector coordination, and progressing upwards to the roof – the socio-economic–environmental outputs and outcomes theme. Each theme has a number of identified critical success factors (CSFs) and these are shown within the different levels of the blocks of the 'house'. They are arranged from bottom to top in the order of their lead–lag time relationships, shown by the direction of the arrows. The exhibit forms a strategy map that shows how the 20 CSF objectives (or essential building blocks) are dependent on each other.

The balanced scorecard's components

The six themes approximate to the four perspectives of the balanced scorecard:

- The customer/community perspective, which is the roof of the sanitation house, covers the socio-economic–environmental outcomes and outcomes theme.
- The internal process perspective is relevant to the next three themes; the walls and rooms of the house.
- The learning and growth perspective corresponds to the bottom two themes, and provide the foundation for the house.
- The financial perspective is the very bottom of this foundation, and applies to the water sanitation coordination theme.

The strategy map summarizes the strategy, but the scorecard gives the strategy more detail for planning. While the CSFs shown in Exhibit 3.1 are open-ended, the scorecard is used to turn these into SMART objectives: when the scorecard objectives are given measures that are Specific, Measurable, Agreed upon, Realistic, and Time-bound. So, for example, taking the customer/community perspective, there are three objectives to cover the three parts of the socio-economic-environmental theme.

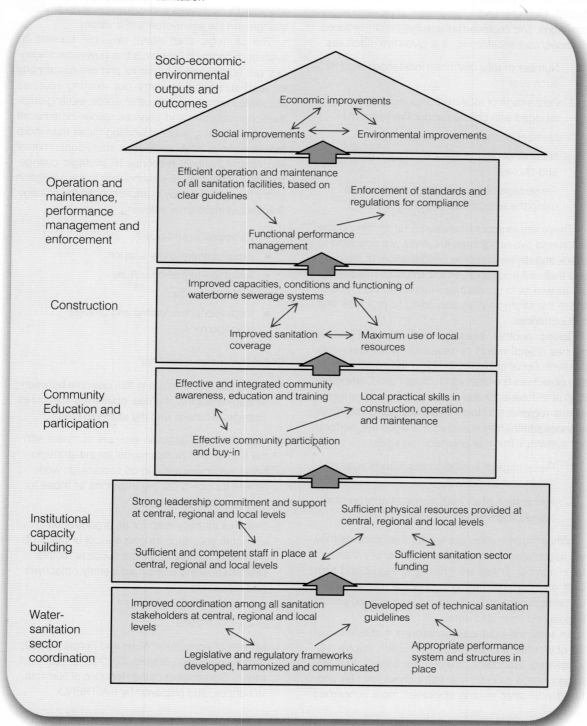

Taking the first (social) one, its objective is written as 'Social Outputs and Outcomes: Improved social conditions, and improved knowledge, health, reduced diseases, user satisfaction', It is given five measures:

1 Number of total diarrhoea incidences reported each year.

2 Percentage of total diarrhoea incidences reported with children under five years old.

3 Number of cholera cases reported.

4 Number of deaths associated with diarrhoea and cholera.

5 Percentage of households accepting and using the selected sanitation systems.

These are outcome measures for achieving the vision and two associated initiatives are specified to check and review outcome performance: to measure and evaluate and report on the statistics used annually as well as to conduct satisfaction surveys; and to revise the strategic plan according to progress and circumstances.

Taking another example, but this time for an enabler objective and its measures, which belong to the institutional capability building theme. One of its four objectives is written as 'Sufficient and Competent Staff at all Levels: Skilled in sanitation related areas at central regional and local levels; including technical, financial administration, project management, perform ant systems'. This has only two measures:

1 Percentage of sanitation positions filled at all levels and all regions.

2 Percentage of all institution staff appropriately trained in sanitation.

While the measures are few for this objective they are associated with the highest number of initiatives – 21 in number. These are (mainly) to recruit and train staff, each initiative having its specified ownership for its management and review, along with agreed annual targets and estimated costs.

In total the balanced scorecard is made up of 20 objectives and 69 measures, which involve 162 initiatives or associated projects. This adds up to a very large change programme, but it should not be confused with other existing objectives more concerned with mission and core values. The focus on this scorecard's objectives and measures is on strategic change and the achievement of a vision.

The strategic plan notes possible barriers to success. A particular concern is that government agencies are administrative in nature and are functionally focused designed to carry out existing routines associated with mission. In other words, existing organizational structure and services favour incremental change to existing ways of working rather than more radical change that involves a multi-departmental and cross-functional response to strategic change. The plan notes that all stakeholders in the sanitation sector have roles to play in implementing the strategy. This should involve the following:

- Participation and buy-in.
- External stakeholder support.
- A high performance culture.
- Sufficient funds.
- Inspirational leadership and change management.

Discussion questions

1 Clarify the relationships in this example between strategy mapping, themes, objectives, measures, strategic initiatives and the strategic plan.

2 How does the Namibian example compare with the Kaplan and Norton model for the strategic balanced scorecard and do scorecards work as well for non-profit organizations as those for commercial organizations?

3 Sketch a strategy map for an organization known to you, such as your school or place of work, and identify its critical success factors. Discuss how the CSFs help identify objectives and measures.

Case end-notes

1 Ministry of Agriculture, Water and Forestry (2009) *Namibia Sanitation Strategy 2010/2011 – 2014/15*, report, Government of the Republic of Namibia, Windhoek, and prepared by ITALTREND.

Chapter 4

THE EXTERNAL
ENVIRONMENT

The external
environment

n organisation's 'external' environment
consists of the conditions outside the
organisation, including people and organisations, which influence the external changes
on the organisation's enquiry, especially those that
influence the enquiry of competition. External conditions are constantly changing and organisations
need to monitor and review strategy continually to
effectively manage any emerging threats and to be
able to exploit advantageous opportunities. Many
changes are difficult to identify and their consequences
are often uncertain and even unknowable.

KEY TERMS

blue ocean strategy	industry life cycle
black swans	PESTEL
BRICS	strategic fit
disruptive innovation	strategic groups
external environment	strategic map
first mover	strategic risk management
five competitive forces	structural break
hypercompetition	value curve

LEARNING OBJECTIVES

These topics provide you with an understanding
of the following:

1. The nature of competitive environment

2. Industry life cycles

3. The major competitive forces in an industry

4. Strategic analysis

5. Blue ocean strategy

Chapter 4

THE EXTERNAL ENVIRONMENT

The external environment

An organization's **external environment** consists of the conditions outside the organization, including people and organizations, which influence the external changes in the organization's industry, especially those that influence the intensity of competition. External conditions are constantly changing and organizations need to monitor and review strategy continually to effectively manage any emerging threats and to be able to exploit advantageous opportunities. Many changes are difficult to identify and their consequences are often uncertain and even unknowable.

KEY TERMS

blue ocean strategy	industry life cycle
black swans	PESTEL
BRICS	strategic fit
disruptive innovation	strategic groups
external environment	strategic map
first mover	strategic risk management
five competitive forces	structural break
hypercompetition	value curve

Business vignette   See the bigger whole picture …

The most significant trend in the world economy is the rise of the **BRICS** economies. This is an acronym for the growing importance of the economies of Brazil, Russia, India, China and South Africa.[1] Since 2008 these countries have met annually to discuss mutual economic interests. Since the 2008 global economic crisis the growth of BRICS economies have slowed down; however, by 2025 they could together account for over half of the size of the combined economies

Russia

China

South Africa

of today's richest countries: the United States, Japan, Germany, the United Kingdom, France and Italy. By 2050 their economies could be even larger.

The BRICS countries have important advantages in the supply of primary commodities (from Brazil, Russia and South Africa), services (India), and manufactured products (China). These advantages seem likely to continue, but much depends on how the BRICS continue to manage their economies. The following seem important:

1 to pursue sound macroeconomic policies and create a stable economic infrastructure;

2 to develop strong and stable political institutions;

3 to continue to open their economies to trade and foreign direct investment;

4 to maintain high levels of secondary education.

These are long-term factors, but they provide the context that organizations, no matter where they are in the world, will have to use in the immediate term to inform strategy and make sure that everybody has identified the right issues. On this basis an organization can prioritize the opportunities and provide a strategic framework for that prioritization.

The BRICS countries represent a growing opportunity for Western organizations, but they will need to continue to adapt their products and service to suit tastes in these countries. For example, box office takings for the BRICS countries for Hollywood films doubled to over $6 billion between 2008 and 2012, and these are expected to equal takings in the United States itself in five years. It seems likely that BRICS' own film industries, such as India's well-established Bollywood, will grow dramatically. If Hollywood is to continue to compete effectively then it seems it will need to make films that are more appropriate to the growing emerging markets: Hollywood will need to make Bollywood films!

The PESTEL framework

The **PESTEL** framework is a mnemonic used in strategic management to group macro-environmental factors to help strategists look for sources of general opportunity and risk. PESTEL stands for political, economic, social, technological, environment and legal factors.[2] The framework is shown in Figure 4.1. These factors have the potential to be fundamental and changes in them can lead to the transformation of industries, especially over the longer term. The assumption is that if an organization monitors and audits its external environment it will be better able to respond to change, and perhaps change more quickly than its competitors. As an old adage goes, 'the early bird catches the worm'.

While the framework comprises six categories it is important to use it as an integrated, not compartmentalized, view of trends and changes. Strategic management is about seeing and understanding connections, it is not just concerned with isolated trends, nor is it only oriented to marketing and a single market, but the longer-term management of the big picture. While many trends may look familiar it is important to understand how they come together

FIGURE 4.1 The PESTEL framework

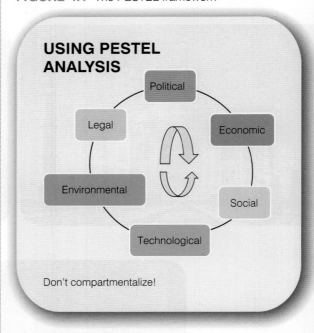

to drive change and innovation. Some trends will carry risk and others opportunities. A regular PESTEL review will challenge an organization to think about long-term trends and raise questions such as 'Will our strategy give us enough flexibility to deal with new competition?'

Political

Political factors include trends in the actions of local, national and international governments and agencies, but also thinking and activities of influential groups and individuals.

China's twelfth five-year plan characterizes several industries as emerging battlegrounds where countries will be competing for leadership during the coming decades.[3] These include industries associated with new energy sources and biotechnology. The policy is to incubate national and global champions by helping them gain leading technologies and expand their commercial capabilities. Competition in many of these fields will be shaped by regulatory decisions. Two Chinese companies, Sinovel and Xinjiang Goldwind, now rank among the world's three largest wind turbine manufacturers. Those organizations from other countries, such as Denmark's Vestas, will have to take account of these developments.

Economic

Economic factors include trends about resource use and prices, policies, such as taxation, interest rates and more general trends such as disposal income, economic growth, inflation and productivity.

In China, sales of premium cars have risen from something just short of 100 000 to over 500 000 in the past five years. However, according to Carlos Ghosn, chief executive of Renault and Nissan, much of the auto industry's growth over the next decade will come in the sales of small and cheap cars bought by first-time customers in emerging markets generally.[4] While the trend in China has so far shown little reaction to the recessionary effects of the global financial crisis, markets for small cars have not been strong. The economic troubles of 2008 may be short term, but the prospects for sales of cars, for example, in all the BRICS countries over the next 20 years seem exciting.

During the last century the developed economies became consumer societies, when markets became

the dominant economic systems for distributing resources and creating wealth. This is continuing as the emerging economies bring perhaps an extra billion consumers, as annual household incomes rise above $5000; a level when family spending seems to extend to discretionary buying. Consumer spending power in emerging economies is expected to increase from $4 trillion to more than $9 trillion in 2015, which is nearly the current spending power of Western Europe. This trend will be linked increasingly to the development of more sophisticated sources of information, and consumers are likely to have access to the same or similar products and brands. While globalization *has* slowed down in the wake of the global financial crisis, it still shows every sign of continuing.

Social

Social factors include demographic, social and lifestyle trends, national cultures, ethics, morality and expectations.

The post-Second World War baby boom, from 1945 to around 1960 in developed countries, brought into existence a sizeable and distinct group of consumers. These are now aged between 50 and 65 years and constitute the largest and wealthiest group of consumers in history. Their spending is likely to take a disproportionate share of consumption in markets in industries that have not previously seen older customer profile markets as profitable areas.

Baby boomers are likely to spend more on health and leisure as they become older, and they will continue to influence consumer electronics, clothing and home-furnishings, which are areas that have not been associated with the older consumer before.

Technology

Technology includes change and the impact of new and developing technological change on resources, organizational behaviours, products and services and operations.

The prevalence of smart phones and price scanning applications is transforming the nature of shopping. Organizations can manipulate the information they get from shoppers so that some argue that the idea of an informed consumer is an illusion. Facebook introduced an advertising system called Beacon, which broadcasts users' purchases on other sites to friends on the social network without permission. It caused an outcry and Facebook eventually closed the system down. Nevertheless the prospect that everybody's histories are being opened up and 'colonized and stored by the very people who want to sell us things' could be evidence that 'online shopping is becoming a master of these technologies of simultaneous coercion and seduction'.[5]

Environmental

Environmental factors include the quality of life, sustainability and recycling of resources, but also logistical possibilities, infrastructure and facilitators.

Tetra Pak is a Swedish multinational food packaging and processing company that has gained recognition for its sustainability work in designing cartons that are technologically superior to cans for their economies in transportation, storage and retailing. However they are more difficult than glass bottles and tin cans to recycle because of their multiple layers of paper and plastic, and consequently they end up in landfill sites. While very successful, Tetra Pak's future is at risk since its cartons increasingly encounter criticism, especially from local councils. Realizing this, Tetra Pak is working on joint ventures with local councils across the world to change and increase carton recycling.

TABLE 4.1 Managing PESTEL

- Someone should be in charge of the process, including meetings and discussions.
- Before starting the PESTEL process think through the process and be clear what the objectives of the PESTEL analysis are.
- Keep it simple and do not get bogged down in detail so the wood gets lost in the trees.
- Discussion should involve a balance of pessimists and optimists, and include outsiders with different perspectives. Beware of vested interests and groupthink.
- Agree appropriate sources. Check inside the organization first for information.
- Use visual tools and discussion aids. Manage the process.
- Identify the most critical factor issues, especially for strategy and its CSFs.
- Produce a discussion document for wider circulation.
- Use feedback, follow-up checks on actions; keep all PESTEL participants informed on follow-up to encourage continuous dialogue.
- Decide which issues to monitor on an ongoing basis. Link to existing processes for monitoring and reviewing change, especially for planning.

Legal

Legal factors include laws and regulatory action, standards, border requirements, labour regulations, and so on. This may also include globalization issues dealing with international trade and competition law.

National legal frameworks vary considerably and their consequences for individual industries are profound. One of the most significant trends has been the tightening of regulatory accounting standards following the large corporate failures, such as Enron, Tyco International, Peregrine Systems and WorldCom, and the bursting of the dot.com bubble. In July 2002, the Public Company Accounting Reform and Investor Protection Act (otherwise known as the Sarbanes–Oxley Act) became law in the United States. Similar regulatory measures were introduced throughout the world.

The PESTEL process

All the examples used above overlap and influence each other. The picture can get complex and seem uncertain, so the process of thinking through a framework of PESTEL factors should be kept as simple as possible. They should not always be thought about as a simple list of unrelated bullet points, however, but as an interrelated set that should be used to scan continuously and review regularly the general environment as a whole. The process for carrying out a PESTEL analysis should follow sound management principles (see Table 4.1 above).

PRINCIPLES IN PRACTICE 4.1

The metropolitans

Around the present time a historical point is being reached when city dwellers will outnumber people who live in the countryside. Across the world new global groups are emerging which will have profound implications for everybody, but especially advertisers. Many of these are affluent, especially those who belong to the growing urban middle class in the emergent economies. This is more than an economic phenomenon; it is also a change in lifestyle to more post-materialistic values.

Metro International is a Swedish media company based in Luxembourg. It is the leading global distributor of free newspapers with 56 newspapers in 53 countries.[6] The newspaper distributes seven million copies daily and its sales from advertising have increased about 40 per cent per annum since its foundation in 1995.

An important method of distribution is to commuters on trains during the rush hour. While the company aims to consolidate its hold on mature markets, expansion is sought in Latin America, Asia and Russia; advertisers will be global brands. It seeks to entertain young affluent audiences in cities around the world. Subjects of celebrity gossip, lurid stories and political slants are avoided. However, the papers do use celebrity and in 2011 Lady Gaga was used to bring to the forefront issues concerned with equality and individuality in the news that day. She selected stories and provided comments on the breaking news that reflected aspects of her personality: creative, inspiring and exciting. Street promoters dressed as Lady Gaga lookalikes.

The company is remarkable since its growth in international markets has come at a time when traditional newspapers have been facing competition from the Internet, where many papers have elected to charge for their news content.

Question: Metro is a good example of outside-in influences on strategy; free newspapers have a long history, so why has Metro become so successful as a global organization?

PESTEL factors may interact negatively as well as positively. It is a useful framework to check and determine strategic priorities. Managers are encouraged to look beyond their organization and industry, to be less insular. However, there are weaknesses in that it can be too easy to scan data and a lazy tick box mentality can take over. A good PESTEL analysis should go deep enough to consider root causes. The analysis should not merely highlight the obvious and strategists should avoid information overload. Issues should be strategic not operational. For example, there should be a concentration on those factors and issues of most relevance to driving change. Of course, it is a question of judgement. In this the importance of PESTEL factors must be relevant to the purpose and nature of the organization.

Black swans and structural breaks

PESTEL analysis is primarily about monitoring and reviewing longer-term trends, but a global financial crisis is a **structural break** that subverts trends and changes existing behavioural patterns. It is a fundamental and unpredictable event in the general environment, which is likely to require organizations to suddenly rethink their purpose and strategy. Some unpredictable events are potentially so very catastrophic that a societal, or even a world response, is required. The World Health Organization's projected impact of an influenza A/H5N1 pandemic (avian flu) is 7 to 350 million deaths.

Nassim Nicholas Taleb is the author of *The Black Swan*.[12] In 1698, Dutch explorers discovered black swans in a river inlet in what later became known as Western Australia. Before then Europeans had no reason to believe that swans were any colour other than white. David Hume, the philosopher, used the discovery to illustrate that no matter how many times something can be proved, it only takes a single event to prove it untrue.

Taleb takes the idea to describe events like the Internet and the September 11 terrorist attacks as **black swans** because they cannot be predicted and when they occur they take everyone by surprise. He states that such events have three properties: when they happen it has a massive impact; people do not see it coming (low probability), but afterwards everybody think they saw it coming. While many claim that the global financial crisis was a black swan event, Taleb disagrees. In his first edition of the book, in fact, he is critical of banking and can claim to have foretold the crash. However, it is certainly true that its effects did constitute a structural break.

According to Richard Rumelt, a structural break is the best time to be a strategist because old sources of competitive advantage weaken and new ones appear.[13] He argues that a break occurred in the 1980s because of changes in technology.

The development of microprocessors led to cheaper computing, personal and desktop computers and the rise of a new kind of software industry. These changes brought about the Internet and electronic commerce that enabled Silicon Valley's small team culture to overtake Japan's advantages in structural engineering and organizational management: it 'changed the wealth of nations'.

There seems to be no obvious and useful way to see structural breaks coming. Taleb writes about turning black swans into white ones. For instance, downturns in the world economy occur in cycles, or at least very regularly, and there have been four global recessions over the last 50 years. While the timing of a future downturn is uncertain, it is possible to learn something from these. Some industries, for instance, seem able to weather recessions better than others, such as utilities, telecommunication services, health care and consumer staples, but these are less likely to grow significantly during an upturn.

Alerting executives and managers to possible scenarios and the discussion of hypotheses, to look around corners and not be taken by surprise should new trends emerge and the unexpected happen is important.[14] If executives are paying attention it is possible to see when things are turning. Herbert Henkel, chief executive of the Irish-based Ingersoll-Rand, in the summer of 2008 noticed that European orders in the company's transport refrigeration business had slumped, even though in the rest of the organization business seemed to be doing well. A decrease in the sales of perishable foods indicated trouble in the supply chain. 'I couldn't help thinking, what if that figure really is indicative of what's out ahead? What are we going to do about it?' Ingersoll Rand quickly put contingency plans in place that involved restructuring and reducing inventory. 'Of course, we still had to go back and do more. But by not ignoring that one indicator, we did get a head start.'[15]

Strategic risk management

Strategic risk management is a systematic and overall approach for managing those external events and trends that could seriously harm an organization's effectiveness for achieving its longer-term purpose. According to Richard Waterer, a senior vice president at Marsh & McLennan Companies, risk management is a central part of any organization's strategic management. It involves methodically addressing the risks attached to the management of an organization's core business areas or, in other words, those that are important to the effective strategic management of an organization's purpose. Sharman and Smith[16] suggest it should have the following key aspects:

- statement on the value proposition for risk management (specific to the organization in relation to business objectives and the risk environment);
- definition of agreed risks; definition of the objectives for risk management based on the organizational objectives and supporting business strategy;
- statements on the required corporate culture and behavioural expectations with regard to risk taking;
- definition of organizational ownership of risk management strategy at all levels;
- reference to the risk management framework or system being employed to deliver the above requirements;
- definition of the performance criteria employed for reviewing the effectiveness of

the risk management framework in delivering the risk management objectives.

Compliance requirements have helped to drive the documentation of strategic risks in organizations. The US Securities and Exchange Commission (SEC) now requires publicly listed companies to document the key business areas and the underlying assumptions that are core to strategic success.[17]

Industry life cycle

The concept of the **industry life cycle** likens the life of an industry to a living organism, which goes through stages of introduction, growth, maturity and decline, with each stage exhibiting distinct characteristics. The shape of the cycle is shown in Figure 4.2 where the vertical axis indicates rising output and the horizontal one the passage of time. Thus, the curved line traces how as time passes output rises, stabilizes and eventually declines. The competitive conditions of the industry change as the stages change.

Introduction stage

The introduction stage is when production is low, costs are high and demand is very low. There may

FIGURE 4.2 Industry life cycle stages

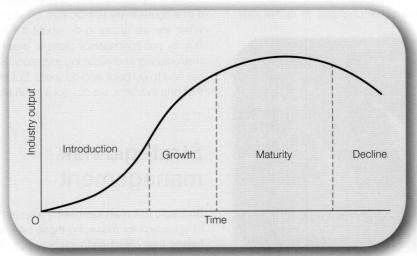

be a large variety of products and services involving different sizes of enterprise, including small entrepreneurial organizations to ones that are well-established in other industries but are diversifying. An important barrier to entry may be knowledge of a developing technology and large organizations may acquire this by taking over small specialist firms. Competition may be based on opening up distribution channels and perfecting the design of products and services. The first to perfect a robust design and applications may be able to capture a significant part of the future market. This is the advantage of being a first mover. As personal computing developed, Apple was able to create a loyal pool of innovative users, which the company used to develop a distinctive approach to design that was to influence all its later products including the iPod, iPhone and iPad, and which was to give it a dominant industry position. Success is not necessarily based on either the best functionality or lowest cost. This often depends upon how first users, who often buy for reasons of novelty, accept and use a new product and service.

Growth stage

First-time demand expands as customers and others facilitating promotion and distribution, become familiar with the product and services, and prices can fall significantly as the industry climbs the experience curve and exploits scale economies (see Chapter 7). Growth is strong and at some point there may come a tipping point when a moment of critical mass is reached and takes sales over a threshold so that a bandwagon effect on sales takes over.[18] The number of competing organizations reduces to a handful and a dominant design establishes itself. A point is reached when the industry becomes too crowded for demand to support and excess capacity builds up. A shakeout then ensues when perhaps only a very few of the largest organizations will stay in profit – this is Bruce Henderson's (the founder of the Boston Consulting Group) Rule of Three and Four, that a stable market will not have more than three rivals, and the largest will have no more than four times the market share of the smallest.[19]

This is the time when **first movers** become well established and take dominant positions in their industries. The term 'category killer' is sometimes used by observers to describe an organization that has been able to eliminate most of the competition for a category of product or service. For example, eBay, a pioneer in developing Internet services was a first mover to offer online auctions and it has since created a near-monopoly to an extent that similar me-too auction sites at the present time have only a very small portion of the market.

Whereas it is the general external environment that is important to an embryonic industry and the introduction stage of a new industry, the growth stage is more influenced by the competitive environment. Here is another important lesson from the biological sciences – Charles Darwin's notion of the survival of the fittest:

> Some make the deep-seated error of considering the physical conditions of a country as the most important for its inhabitants; whereas it cannot, I think, be disputed that the nature of the other inhabitants with which each has to compete is generally a far more important element of success.[20]

Maturity stage

Eventually an industry's growth must slow and enter a maturity stage, when competing organizations can no longer maintain growth rates without capturing market share from each other. This may drive down prices encouraging rivals to bring down costs and build brand loyalty. The maturity stage is also a time when large rivals have developed their core competences and those other strategic resources that are specific to an individual organization and to the industry more generally. These factors constitute significant barriers to entry and the small number of surviving companies if they are able to build oligopoly positions and avoid price wars, may be able to take advantage of high prices and earn high profits. It is also possible in the case of large corporations to take revenue from mature stage businesses (milk cows) to re-invest in the introduction and cash hungry growth stages of new and growing industries (see Chapter 8 and strategic portfolio analysis). The maturity stage is the most likely to have within it product life cycles, when the basic product or service is developed into a range of different but related marketing offers to different target market segments. Each offer is subject to its own lifecycle and the marketing mix is changed to suit the needs of the lifecycle's stages.[21]

Decline stage

Industries may decline for many reasons, from technological substitution, such as television for the cinema, or social changes, such as an increased awareness of health issues and the decline of the tobacco industry. The reasons may lie embedded in the general environment and PESTEL factors. Sometimes industries rally sales through innovation. When steam technology threatened sailing ships, sailing improved significantly and for a time became more efficient than steam.[22]

In recent times the most notable change has been the convergence of the computing, telecommunications, entertainment and media industries. Companies which had favoured positions in television manufacturing, for example, such as Sony and Philips, have found themselves with obsolete products, and have given ground to Samsung and Panasonic. Changes in new technology and global trends that have seen the transfer of much manufacturing to China and other countries has meant that the television manufacturing industry life cycle has effectively started over.

Do industry life cycle models work?

An industry life cycle model helps strategists identify the opportunities and threats that characterize different industry environments. Managers need to design their strategy to take account of changing conditions. However, it is often difficult to identify a stage precisely, and even more difficult to forecast since there is no universally recognized standard length of cycles, and competitors typically organize to influence the length of the cycle. However, the value of the concept lies in its use as a powerful tool for clarifying strategic options. Industries and markets do seem to develop broadly along trajectories from uncertain beginnings through typically chaotic and intensely competitive growth, and afterwards reach more mature and relatively stable states.[23]

The industry life cycle focuses on the characteristics of an industry's stages of development. A different approach is offered by Michael Porter, who argues an industry's profitability, and therefore its attractiveness, is determined by its competitive forces and their relative strengths.

Industry profitability and the five competitive forces

Arguably the most influential contribution to thinking about competitive strategy has come from Michael Porter who introduced the industry profitability and **five competitive forces** framework (see Figure 4.3).[24] The forces determine an industry's intensity of competition and the longer-term profitability of all the organizations that make up an industry. The central force is the intensity of the rivalry between existing competitors. This force is influenced by four other forces: the threat of new business, the bargaining power of customers, the bargaining power of suppliers and the threat of substitute products and services. The strength of these forces and the way they influence each other determine an industry's profitability and shape its structure.

On the surface, industries seem to differ, but the underlying driving forces will be the same. Porter contrasts the global automotive industry, the international art market, and the regulated health-care industry in Europe, and observes that while each is different on the surface, the profitability of each is conditioned by the underlying structure of the five forces.[26] The principle is the same: to sustain an advantageous position, an organization has to compete in a way that takes account of its industry's five forces.

If the forces are intense, an organization is likely to be unable to earn attractive returns on its investment. If they are weak then above-average returns are possible. Many factors have an influence on short-term profitability, but it is important to realize that the five competitive forces are factors that apply to the longer-term. For example, while the price of food moves up and down depending upon the weather and the cost of fuel for storage and transport, the

FIGURE 4.3 The five competitive forces[25]

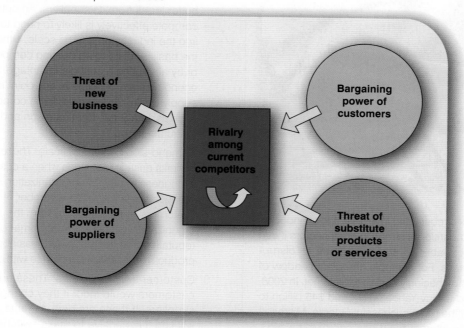

general and longer-term profitability of supermarkets rests favourably on the bargaining power of the retail chains in relation to their suppliers and to their customers (albeit to a lesser extent). The threat of new entrants is low, and the scope for substitutes for groceries is very limited.

An individual organization must consider the health of its industry structure, as well as its own strategic position within the industry, if it is going to defend itself and shape an industry's forces in its favour. The nature of the forces differs by industry, and the strongest force may not be obvious. Traditionally, the value created for customers of supermarkets lies in their convenience and low costs,

which critically depends for the customer on the location of the outlets. However, dealing with the substitute, Internet shopping, may over the longer-term favour those companies that are first to build up a critical mass of customers and a reputation for a quality service.

The threat of new entrants (new business)

New competition from outside brings additional capacity pressures on existing market shares that

An individual organization must consider the health of its industry structure, as well as its own strategic position within the industry, if it is going to defend itself and shape an industry's forces in its favour. The nature of the forces differs by industry, and the strongest force may not be obvious.

influence prices, costs and investment in an industry. If the new competition is strong in other sectors it can leverage its capabilities and cash flows to disrupt existing business. For example, the giant shadow of Microsoft falls menacingly across the Internet. In 2008, Microsoft tried to buy Yahoo for around $45 billion to compete with the more successful Google. Microsoft was late to the Internet but it has one of the world's largest R&D budgets. While its key software products like Windows and Office are still very profitable, its personal computing business is becoming less important, and although it lost heavily on broadband and cable television in the late 1990s, it has enough cash and marketable securities to afford moves in other directions.

It is the threat or possibility of entry that holds down profitability in an industry. This is because when entry barriers are low enough for an outside rival, and profitability in the industry is high, then new business can enter the industry and drive down prices and raise costs for the existing competitors, or the existing organizations must spend more to raise entry barriers. There are eight sources of barriers to entry:

1   Supply-side economies of scale (see Chapter 7): These are economies that result when an organization is able to reduce its fixed costs per unit of an increasing output. It is probable that a larger organization is able to lower its costs and therefore offer lower prices and increase its market share still further, than a smaller organization. This will in turn enable more investment to be made in improved technology and negotiate better terms from its suppliers. An outsider to compete effectively is likely to need to come into the industry on a large scale, either on the basis of dislodging existing competitors, or by accepting a cost disadvantage. Scale economies are possible at any point in the supply chain; for example, large corporations, such as Tata Steel, dominate iron and steel manufacturing.

2   Demand-side benefits of scale: These benefits arise in industries when a customer's willingness to pay for an organization's product increases with the number of customers who already buy from the organization. An organization's image, its reputation and general awareness about its products and services, increase with size.

3   Customer-switching costs: These are costs customers would incur if they change suppliers. If these are high entrants will find it expensive to make switching worthwhile to customers. For example, in many industrial markets, a supplier's input or service is important to the quality of a large customer's own products; changes in supply are likely to increase uncertainty and require modified working and extra investment.

4   Capital requirements: Where the cost of entry is high, access to large financial resources is necessary. If the values of capital, or the expectations of the owners of capital, are influenced by uncertain financial markets and interest rates, then the associated costs may reduce the viability of any investment. An important consideration is the potential resale value of assets.

5   Incumbency advantages independent of size: The existing organizations in an industry may have other advantages that potential entrants may not be able to match. Many of these are associated with early advantage, such as proprietary technology, preferential access to established materials and labour, perhaps because of favourable geographical locations, especially for

existing customers, and a history, with established brands and an accumulated experience that is important to a particular organization's competitive advantage. Entrants may attempt to bypass such advantages.

6 Unequal access to distribution channels: The fewer the wholesale and retail channels, the more likely it is that existing competitors will have them tied up and the harder it will be for entrants to break in and replace existing customers. Sometimes new competitors have had to bypass existing distribution channels, even develop new markets, altogether.

7 Restrictive government policy: Government policy and regulation, licensing and other controls that favour national interest, or even facilitate trading agreements, can work to limit or even foreclose entry to industries.

8 Expected retaliation: The ability and history of competitors to retaliate when faced with new competition will influence how potential entrants see the attractiveness of an industry. Incumbents often use public statements and responses to one entrant to send an aggressive message to others. Considerations concern the abilities of competitors to manage all the above barriers to entry, and to consider the possibility of new growth and customers, the power of competitors to weather or lower prices, and the underlying health of their balance sheets.

The challenge 'is to find ways to surmount the entry barriers without nullifying, through heavy investment, the profitability of participating in the industry'.[27]

The bargaining power of customers

Powerful customers, or groups of customers, can force down suppliers in an industry to lower prices, demand more customized features and force up service and quality levels. This activity drives down an industry's profitability and shifts the balance of power and value in favour of the buyers. Customers have an advantage if the following conditions apply:

1 Customers are few and buy in quantities that are large in relation to the size of suppliers. If suppliers' fixed costs are high and marginal costs are low there are likely to be attempts to keep capacity filled through discounting.

2 The industry's products are standardized or undifferentiated. If buyers can find equivalent products elsewhere, then it is possible to play suppliers of against each other.

3 Customers have low switching costs in changing suppliers.

4 Customers are able to threaten backward integration and can produce the product themselves if a supplier is too costly.

Buyers are likely to be sensitive to suppliers' prices if the cost of the product or service is a major concern to a buyer if it is a significant portion of its costs or available funds. A buyer is likely to search for best deals and negotiate hard in this situation, but the opposite is true when price is a low percentage of a buyer's costs. Price is less important when the quality of the supplied product and its influence on the buyer's own products are vital considerations; the importance of service, especially when quick response and advice are involved, can be much more important to the buyer. In general, cash rich and profitable customers with healthy enterprises may be likely less sensitive to levels of price.

Intermediate customers and customers who are not the end-user, such as buyers in the distribution channels, are similarly motivated, but with the difference that if they can negotiate favourable deals some of the gain can be passed downstream to strengthen their own trading positions. Producers often attempt to reduce the power of channels through exclusive arrangements with distributors and retailers. Sometimes suppliers may market directly to consumers. Component manufacturers seek to influence assemblers by creating preferences for their components with downstream customers. Intermediate customers and customers who are not the end-user, such as buyers in the distribution channels, are similarly motivated, but with the difference that if they can negotiate favourable deals some of the gains can be passed downstream to strengthen their own trading positions.

The bargaining power of suppliers

If suppliers can influence the flow of products and resources to an industry's competing organizations, they can negotiate higher prices, or shift costs to other participants in the industry. Suppliers are able to act independently in relation to an industry's customers if any of the following conditions apply:

1 Suppliers are more concentrated than a particular industry and its customers.

2 Suppliers are not dependent upon a single industry for its revenues. Where a supplier is serving a number of different industries a supplier may extract high returns from each. Alternatively, suppliers may want to protect an industry through agreed and reasonable prices, and assist in other supply chain activities such as quality management or promotion.

3 Suppliers have customers with high switching costs. Suppliers may have favoured supplier status and may be clustered close to large customers.

4 Suppliers have differentiated products and services.

5 Suppliers have products and services for which there are no substitutes.

6 Suppliers have a potential to integrate forward and enter the industry and a customer's market.

The threat of substitute products and services

A substitute creates an equivalent value for a customer as an industry's product, but in a different way. This is not to be confused with substitute rivals, but the products and services that may compete with those of an industry. The threat of substitution can work indirectly or downstream in the industry.

Substitutes are nearly always present, but are difficult to identify if they appear different in form from an industry's products or services. This is particularly so when conditions are fluid and changing radically in other industries and markets, so that it is difficult for an industry's participants to understand what is happening. The threat of substitutes influences an industry's profitability because an industry's prices must remain attractive or an industry's customers may go elsewhere.

The threat of substitutes is high if it is apparent to a customer that an alternative offers an attractive price/performance trade-off to the industry's offer. The customer's switching cost must also be low, not just in terms of costs but also in terms of convenience and assurance. The possibilities work both ways: it may be possible to exploit emerging opportunities in one's own industry to develop substitutes for products in other industries.

Rivalry among existing competitors

Normally the most powerful of the five forces, since how aggressively rivals are actively using the other forces to strengthen positions, increase revenue and save costs determines success. The intensity of rivalry is strong when competitors are roughly of equal power and size and are numerous. In this case it is difficult for any organization to win customers without taking them from rivals. Unless the industry has an industry leader to set the competitive conditions for the industry, the competitive behaviour is likely to be unstable and costly for the industry as a whole.

Slow industry growth can stimulate intense competition for market share. This is especially so when exit barriers are high, because, for example, competitors are locked into technologies and own specialized resources of limited value in other industries. This may lead to a chronic excess capacity and encourage discounting. Organizations may also be present for a variety of reasons that do not give a central role to profitability. Competitors may be part of a larger organization, which has a presence in other industries; these units may be there to search for opportunities for growth or to gain experience of the industry's technology and business. Other competitors may have social as well as profit-seeking objectives,

which influence how they compete; for example, a public service may aim to keep its prices low.

The costs of competition can work to raise prices and reduce the number of customers. Price competition, however, works to win new customers. This may reduce the opportunities for such non-price enhancing factors as product functionality, and if it reduces the share of value created by the industry by passing it on to consumers, it can reduce an industry's profitability and limit investment and industry development. Intermediate customers and customers who are not the end-user, such as buyers in the distribution channels, are similarly motivated, but with the difference that if they can negotiate favourable deals some of the gain can be passed downstream to strengthen their own trading positions.

Price competition can occur especially when the products and services of rivals are very similar and switching costs for customers are low. High fixed costs and low marginal costs lead to pressures for rivals to lower prices below average costs to win customers to help cover fixed costs. Essential investment often requires unavoidable large additions to capacity, which also tempts suppliers to discount prices to grow sales. Other impulses to cut prices involve cases of perishable goods, which must be sold quickly to prevent losses from sales because of poor quality, obsolescence or changing product information.

Non-price factors, such as product and service features, branding and experience, allow market segmentation to take place, when a low price segment can be clearly managed apart from segments with more economically stable and higher prices that reflect the extra value these factors create for customers. In this way, non-price competition is less likely to erode an industry's profitability than price competition, since market segmentation can support above-average profitability.

The overall structure of all forces

The five competitive forces determine how the economic value created by an industry is retained by

> ## Every company should already know what the average profitability of its industry is and how it has been changing over time. The five forces reveal *why* industry profitability is what it is. Only then can a company incorporate industry conditions into strategy.

the organizations operating in the industry, and how much of it is bargained away by customers and suppliers, limited by substitutes, or constrained by potential new entrants. It is necessary for a strategist to keep the overall structure in mind rather than only one of the forces. To quote Porter:

Understanding the forces that shape industry competition is the starting point for developing strategy. Every company should already know what the average profitability of its industry is and how it has been changing over time. The five forces reveal why industry profitability is what it is. Only then can a company incorporate industry conditions into strategy.[28]

An organization's strategy, in Porter's view, can be based on building defences against the competitive forces, or in finding a position where the forces are weakest. This is important to deciding an organization's competitive advantage on which to base a generic strategy (cost leadership, differentiation and focus, see Chapter 6) that can be implemented at a single business level.

PRINCIPLES IN PRACTICE 4.2
Barriers to entry in retail banking

Barriers to entry

New entrants to retail banking must meet domestic regulatory requirements and have in place the appropriate processes concerning access to IT systems, appropriate payment schemes, information and sufficient finance. Strategically, retail banks must attract customers to achieve a viable scale of operations that will recover start-up costs, grow market share and maintain a successful presence in the market. The most important barriers to entry into domestic banking is the low level of customer switching, existing high levels of brand loyalty and a consumer preference for providers with a branch network.[29]

Of course, there are relative factor differences, especially between affluent and the less affluent customer, and for urban and rural areas, and so on. It may be possible for new entrants to enter neglected parts of a market and from there build up over time a base for expansion and trust in a new brand.[30]

One such example is Metro Bank, which is the first bank in the UK to be awarded a full-service banking licence for over 150 years. This bank opened its first branch in 2010. Its customer value proposition is to emphasize good customer service, and its strategy is to offer long opening hours over the whole seven days, and the possibility of opening accounts with debt and credit cards in just 15 minutes. The model is based on the success in the United States of the Commerce Bank, which grew quickly from one to 500 branches, before the bank was sold on to a larger retail bank. The Metro Bank aims to establish 200 branches in the Greater London area over the next 10 years. As part of a bid to shake off the image of queues and stuffy premises, Metro (and similarly Virgin Money) have sought to reposition branches as 'stores' or 'lounges', where coffee and easy chairs are available.

Big store groups

The banks that belong to the big store retailing groups have been relatively unaffected by the global financial crisis. However, the poor image of banking and of some of the long established brands promises enhanced opportunities for growth. Looking back to the Great Depression of the 1930s, the success of the American diversified conglomerate, General Electric's financial services division, was based on the introduction of hire purchase to help financially stricken customers buy its durable products. In the UK there is a long history of retail groups looking to stretch their brands into other areas, including financial services, especially consumer lending.

According to Michael Lafferty, of Lafferty Group the retail banking research house, there is a chance for a new renaissance of big store based consumer lending.[31] For example, Tesco, a large supermarket chain, has pledged to become the 'people's bank'. Although it entered banking in 1997, it has only recently considered offering current accounts and mortgages. In fact, the big stores have not found banking easy. The banking sector requires the requisite infrastructure and IT systems and skills in the management of liquidity and capital. There are also risks to reputation if, for instance, Tesco were to start repossessing its customers' houses. There is, anyway, some suspicion about how large supermarkets contribute to local communities.

On the other hand, consumers may have a deeper relationship with a general grocer, than with a retail bank, which brings a higher general level of trust and can be used to extend a brand across different retail sectors. A general store's core retailing service can be used as a gateway product from which to sell financial services into an existing large customer base. However, there are differences in the fundamental business model.

Robert Jones, a brand specialist at Wolff Olins, comments that no 'retailer will want to go into the banking arena to then behave like a traditional bank. There is no value in doing that. They will want to go into banking to do it in a different way. That may well be a proposition that consumers find very attractive'.[32]

Grocery shopping is placed at the core of the supermarket retail model for financial services. It promotes trust, value, service and convenience. This compares to the bank retail model that places current account or mortgage provision at its centre. The bank model promotes trust, security and integrity. These models are discussed and given as reasons for the likelihood of long-term success for supermarket banking in a report by IBM Business Consulting.[33]

If it is true that the operating costs of supermarket brands may be as little as a quarter of the average for retail banking (op cit.), then the supermarkets may be better placed than other challenger or new entrant banks; as these must achieve a critical mass of customers to cover their costs. At the time of writing, it seems unlikely that Virgin Money, the Metro Bank, or other smaller UK retail banks will be able to offer competitive saving rates and compete effectively.[34] The new competition for the established retail banks is still likely to come from the supermarkets.

Question: Do the five forces apply to the banking industry?

The five competitive forces and the Internet

E-business began to become important the late-1990s. Many observers questioned the traditional ideas in strategic management, especially Porter's exposition of competitive strategy. Porter struck back in 2001 when he argued that the Internet is not a strategy, but only a means for doing business.[35] Sustained competitive advantage is about strategic positioning: the need to deliver a value proposition. He applies the five-force framework to the Internet as follows:

Threat of new business

Barriers to entry are reduced as the Internet requires a smaller sales force, access to channels, and fewer physical and costly assets. The nature of software and Internet applications normally enables easy imitation by rivals, thus allowing entry into the market.

Bargaining power of customers

Powerful channels are eliminated or bargaining power over traditional channels is improved. General bargaining power is shifted to the end user, and switching costs are reduced.

Bargaining power of suppliers

Intervening companies are reduced as the Internet allows direct access from suppliers to end users. There is a shift of power to suppliers as barriers to entry are reduced.

Threat of substitute products or services

The size of the market can be expanded as the overall industry becomes more efficient. New substitute threats are created as the Internet becomes proliferated.

Rivalry among existing competitors

Visible differences between competitors are difficult to see by customers, thus creating more rivalry. The geographical market is increased, thus increasing the number of competitors. The likely differentiable variable is likely to shift to price, rather than company differences.

The survival of the organization, Porter argues, depends on assessing the external environment in respect of the five forces. In the long term, Internet provision will be standardized and it will become difficult for customers to distinguish their difference.

Question: Is the Internet an industry or is it something else?

A competitive strategy will position an organization to leverage its strengths when they will make the most difference in using and defending the effects of the five forces. However, Porter warns that in shaping a strategy, an organization should be careful not to set in motion dynamics that will undermine the attractiveness of the industry in the longer term. The five forces are about how an organization can understand an industry to establish what determines the level of its average profits over the long term. However, for some industries, especially those emerging from new technologies, the shorter term may be more important.

KEY DEBATE 4.2

Are the five forces still relevant for today?

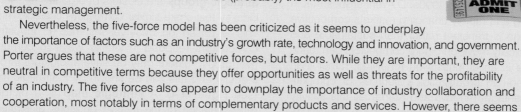

ichael Porter introduced his competitive forces in the *Harvard Business Review* in 1979, and the journal invited him to revise the paper, which was published in 2008.[36] His ideas continue to be (probably) the most influential in strategic management.

Nevertheless, the five-force model has been criticized as it seems to underplay the importance of factors such as an industry's growth rate, technology and innovation, and government. Porter argues that these are not competitive forces, but factors. While they are important, they are neutral in competitive terms because they offer opportunities as well as threats for the profitability of an industry. The five forces also appear to downplay the importance of industry collaboration and cooperation, most notably in terms of complementary products and services. However, there seems to be little reason for not considering this within the existing parameters of the framework.

One issue is the question about how to define an industry. Porter uses the official industrial classifications. It is perhaps not exactly what defines an industry so much as how the competitive forces influence a position within the industry that is crucial.

Yip argues that most of the examples used by Porter, such as Southwest Airlines and IKEA, are already enjoying an established profitable industry position.[37] Porter notes the importance of time for building up a unique competitive position.[38] For some industries with high velocity markets there may be little time to do this (see hypercompetition).

Question: Porter's five forces help an organization to sustain a long-term competitive position within its industry, but how can a new entrant to an industry achieve such a position?

KEY DEBATE 4.3

Should strategy be stable over time, or should it be changing?

onstantly changing strategy is bad for morale if it creates an impression that an organization's senior managers do not know their own minds, so frequent changes in strategy should be avoided. It is also difficult to sustain and make a strategy stronger if changes are always taking place. This suggests taking a constrained or even a conservative view of the external environment.

Some observers, on the other hand, think that organizations should be ever changing, even inconsistent, if they are to be truly creative, innovative, and are to keep their competitors on their toes. The iconoclast, Tom Peters, is well known for slogans such as 'Incrementalism is innovation's worst enemy', and 'Obsolete ourselves or the competition will win'.[39] In a sense constant change is a strategy, or at least a strategic posture. The Virgin group of companies was strongly influenced by Peters. Similarly, Gary Hamel, perhaps inspired a bit too much by the creativity and innovation of the dot.com boom, argued that strategy should be revolution and based on innovation.[40]

Question: Strategic management is about achieving a consistency of purpose; does constancy matter as much?

Hypercompetition

The shorter term is especially so in conditions of **hypercompetition**, described by Richard D'Aveni to explain a dynamic competitive state of constant disequilibrium and change.[41] The concept gained widespread use in strategic management during the time of the rise of the dot.com enterprises trading on the Internet in the late 1990s. D'Aveni argues that in emerging and rapidly changing markets competitive advantage is transient rather than sustainable and rivals typically move on before competitors can react. So there is an emphasis on renewing, rather than protecting, an organization's sources of competitive advantage. Rindova and Kotha call this activity 'morphing', constantly changing shape to suit circumstances.[42] This behaviour calls for an ability to focus short term, a honed ability to read a market and to generate creative innovations continuously.

A related idea is **disruptive innovation**, a concept introduced by Christensen, to signify a revolutionary product that replaces existing ways of competing.[43] There are two basic forms: the first acts to create new competition with new markets and customers; the second acts to generate new value for existing customers who are located in a low value-added part of a market and where the existing competition moves offers up-market rather than defending these low-end segments. The Virgin Group has consistently followed the second course and entered traditional industries, such as insurance and air travel, to offer value based on the excitement of its brand to steal market share from the existing players. At Virgin the strategic question is one of why not?, rather than why? Virgin will enter an industry if it can challenge existing norms, to give customers a better break, be entertaining and 'put a thumb in the eye' of the complacent incumbents.

The rapid technological change in the new economy has led, in the view of Michael Porter,[44] many authors to claim that little or no advantage can be sustained over time. Organizations, it is believed, should not make longer-term strategic choices but be nimble, quick and learn as change happens. Porter sees that while this may be true, the danger is that it leads organizations to compete only on best practice rather than competitive difference. In the end, because rivals do similar things and offer similar products and services, customers choose only on prices, and the resulting price competition will eventually undermine industry profitability.

Strategic groups

Strategic groups are clusters of organizations in an industry that share similar competitive characteristics. This is based on observations that an industry's competitors respond in similar ways to competitive forces.[45] There may be several clusters in one industry and this can be shown by a strategic map (see Figure 4.4). A **strategic map** is a pictorial representation of the relative positions of strategic groups in an industry. (A strategic map should not be confused with a strategy map used with the balanced scorecard, see Chapter 3).

Within a group, rivals offer similar products to the same customers and competition can be intense. A strategic map is used to assess and predict the possible strategic moves of the groups and for the identification of strategic space – that is, areas of strategy not covered by the groups. For example, these may include variables such as price, differentiation of product range, geographic coverage, the degree of vertical integration and use of distribution channels and service. Pairs of such differentiating features can be used to plot the locations of organizations on the strategic map to see how these cluster and form a similar group. Figure 4.4 illustrates five strategic groups, which are shown in the form of varying shaped pie-charts. The shape of the group will vary depending on the competitive characteristics (made up of combinations of the two axes).

In the example, the characteristics are geographical coverage (as a percentage of the whole market) and marketing intensity of the organization (as a percentage of marketing cost to sales revenue). Hence, three zones of strategic space become apparent. Strategic space 3 (represented by the dark blue boxes at the bottom right) concerns an uncompetitive position as marketing costs are high, covering only a small area of the market; the strategic position achieved is therefore of national or regional branders only. Strategic space 1 (represented by the light blue boxes at the top left of the figure), by contrast,

FIGURE 4.4 A strategic map

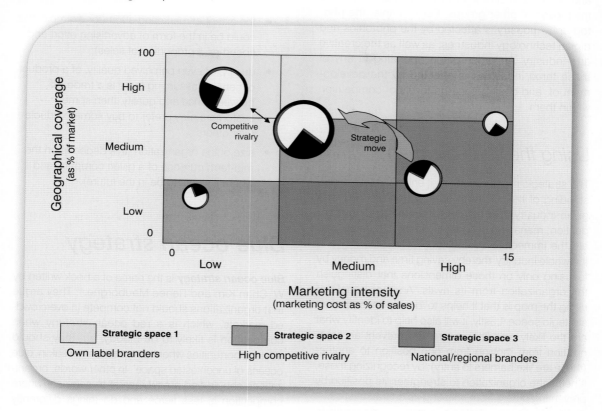

concerns companies with many advantages that enable them to sustain a position that has small marketing costs (in relation to sales) but achieves a high geographical coverage. This is a high-performing competitive position, and the result is that the market will have mainly own-labels. Strategic space 2 (represented by orange boxes) is betwixt the two extremes, and can include characteristics of low marketing cost with low geographical coverage, high marketing cost with high geographical coverage, or an intermediate quantity of both.

It is normally desirable for an organization to move away from strategic space 3 to strategic space 1, as strategic space 2 is highly competitive. This is because the gap between the two strategic groups represents the degree of competitive rivalry (the narrower the gap, the greater the degree of competitive rivalry). Note, however, that it is not always the case that organizations will desire to move in this direction, as it depends on the dimensions of the

axes, and what opportunities are presented within each strategic space. An organization will need to carefully analyze the gains when making each strategic move (a move in the direction that better achieves its longer-term strategy).

In drawing a strategic map, circles are marked around each strategic group, making each proportionate to the size of the group's respective share of the industry's sales revenue. The dual variables should not be highly correlated, and should expose differences between the groups in how they position themselves in the industry. It may be possible to draw several maps, using different axes to give a good overview of how organizations are competing. The shape of an industry is likely to be influenced by the number and size distribution of the groups, and the degree of market interdependence between them.

Individual organizations focus on improving their competitive position within their strategic group. However, these typically have similar market shares and respond in similar ways to external trends and the moves of other groups. For example, the photography industry is affected by the photonics and digital technology industries, as well as the creative arts industry. An organization operating in any of these three industries is affected by the development of, and changes in, the levels of competition within them.

Using the strategic map

The strategic map is useful as it enhances our understanding of the nature of strategic choices within a given industry. It is helpful for understanding competition; managers can identify more accurately who are the immediate competitors rather than those in the whole industry, thereby saving time and money by focusing only on those dimensions that distinguish the organization from its rivals. Another benefit of using the map is that it helps to identify unconquered strategic space. Lastly, it will also help to identify what are the likely mobility barriers that prevent an organization from moving from one position to another (these are like barriers to entry); by recognizing these, it helps the organization to strengthen its position by preventing others from imitating its characteristics.

In identifying strategic groups, organizations may differ in terms of the scope of activities and the resource commitment. The scope of activities may include any of the following:

- the extent of product/service diversity (for example, a computing company may just sell PC software or it could as sell accessories, like Microsoft sells computer mice and keyboards as well as computer software);
- the extent of geographical coverage (for example, Taiwanese laptop producer Asus's market is predominantly Asia, whereas another a Taiwanese laptop producer, Acer's market includes Europe and other continents);
- the range of distribution channels in use (for example, Dell's main distribution channel is through the Internet, whereas Hewlett Packard sells through both the Internet and computer stores).

Resource commitment includes:

- the extent of marketing effort (for example, this could be in the form of advertising effort and spend as a proportion of sales);
- quality, or even perceived quality, of a product or service (assuming there is a trade-off between price and quality, then some customers may prefer to buy some products over others);
- size of the organization (this depends on the mid-term purpose of a given company and where it wants to be in the future).

Blue ocean strategy

Blue ocean strategy is the name of a book written by W. Chan Kim and Renee Mauborgne.[46] They argue that organizations should not compete in overcrowded markets, which is a red ocean strategy when competition is likely to be bloody, but they should seek opportunities where competition is weak in 'blue oceans of uncontested space'. In other words, organizations should find a new market or segment where competition is less fierce and do things differently from its rivals. The idea stands apart from strategic mapping because it involves the creation of new demand rather than trying to win customers with product and service attributes that rivals have already.

Competing in overcrowded industries is no way to sustain high performance. The real opportunity is to create blue oceans of uncontested market space.[47]

New types of business should be created by finding gaps in the red ocean by using a **value curve** (see Figure 4.5) to assess how market rivals compete on relative value-creating attributes, such as price, delivery, quality, functional aspects, service and so on.

The figure shows value curves for existing premium and average airlines. The area where this existing competition seems to offer least value is located towards the lower part of the figure labelled blue ocean: here there is space for a new budget airline based on a new market wanting a low price, less airport congestion, and is not overly concerned with customer service and in-flight service.

FIGURE 4.5 A value curve showing areas of blue and red oceans

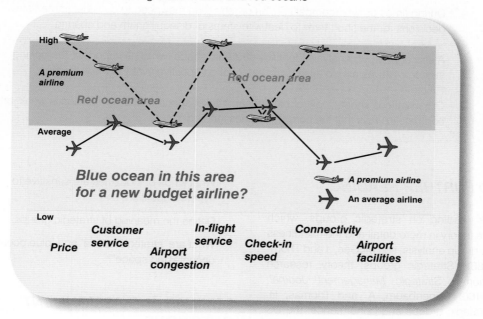

Strategic fit

Strategic fit is the process of matching the opportunities of the external environment with an organization's internal capabilities.[48] The opportunities suggested by PESTEL, the industry life cycle, the five competitive forces, strategic group and blue ocean analyses, must be judged in accordance with an organization's internal environment. How good a fit is between the external and the internal environments of an organization will be an important determinant of the success of the organization's purpose.

SUMMARY OF PRINCIPLES

1   The starting point for effective strategic analysis is to understand the external environment.

2   The factors that relate to the general environment can be summarized in the form of a mnemonic – PESTEL: political, economic, social, technological, environmental, and legal. This is useful as a framework for identifying and following trends.

3   The industry life cycle goes through four distinctive stages: introduction growth, maturity and decline; each stage is subject to different competitive conditions.

4   An industry's attractiveness is determined by the intensity of competition, which is influenced by the threat of new entrants; the bargaining power of customers; the bargaining power of suppliers, and the threat of substitutes.

GUIDED FURTHER READING

For further reading on strategic groups, which explains the theory in more detail and the usefulness of strategic group analysis, see McGee, J and Thomas, H (1986), 'Strategic groups: theory, research and taxonomy', *Strategic Management Journal*, 7(2): 141–160; Fiegenbaum, A. and Thomas, H. (1990), 'Strategic groups and performance: the US insurance industry 1980–84', *Strategic Management Journal*, 11:197–215,

A good exposition of the five competitive forces is given in Porter, M. E. (2008), 'The five competitive forces that shape strategy', *Harvard Business Review*, 86(1):58–77. For a critical view that examines its static nature, see Grundy M. (2006), 'Rethinking and reinventing Michael Porter's five forces model', *Strategic Change*, 15:213–229.

REVIEW QUESTIONS

1   What purpose is achieved by analyzing an organization's external environment?

2   What does a PESTEL analysis do?

3   Why is the global financial crisis a structural break?

4   What is strategic risk management?

5   Why is it helpful to know the stage of an industry's life cycle?

6   Why should organizations consider an industry's attractiveness in terms of its five competitive forces?

7   What kinds of industries are sensitive to hypercompetition?

8   Define the meaning of strategic groups.

9   What are 'strategic space' and 'blue oceans of uncontested space'?

SEMINAR AND ASSIGNMENT QUESTIONS

1   Why is it important for strategic management to see the 'strategic wood, rather than the operational trees'? Discuss this in relation to another idea that a 'whole is greater than the sum of its parts'. Consider the implications of these ideas for how a strategist should look at and evaluate the general external environment.

2   Choose an industry and work out how the intensity of competition is influenced by the five forces. Define and compare the different competitive positions of the main players. Give your opinion on the strengths and weaknesses of the five-force model for your chosen industry. Reach a conclusion and provide a summary of the logic for reaching your conclusion.

3   When economic times are good, popular business books and gurus are apt to say that change is necessary because the environment is dynamic. When economic times are bad, they are still apt to say that change is necessary, but this time it is because change is needed to recover and get ahead of the competition before the economy recovers. Is there any other advice you could offer?

CHAPTER END-NOTES

1 The acronym was originally coined as 'BRIC' in Wilson, D. and Purushothaman, R. (2003), *Dreaming with BRICs: The Path to 2050,* Global Economics Paper, 90, New York: Goldman Sachs. In 2011 the BRIC countries asked South Africa to join to add the leading economy in Africa to their number, and BRIC became BRICS.

2 PESTEL was first developed as PEST by Andrews, K. (1987), *The Concept of Corporate Strategy,* (1st, 3rd edns) Homewood IL: Irwin: and developed by Steiner, G. A. (1979), *Strategic Planning: What Every Manager Must Know,* New York: Free Press.

3 McKinsey (2011), 'What China's five-year plan means for business', *McKinsey Quarterly,* July, www.mckinseyquarterly.com and Hook, L. and Crooks, E. (2011), 'The way the world turns; China's rush into renewables', *Financial Times, 29* November.

4 See contrasting articles: Reed, J. and Schafer, D. (2010), 'Cheap cars to drive growth, says Ghosn', *Financial Times, 20* September, and Schafer, D. (2010), 'Porsche focuses on China front', *Financial Times, 20* September.

5 Zukin, S. (2004), *Point of Purchase: How Shopping Changed American Culture,* London: Routledge. See also Jopson, B. (2011), 'The mobile allure', *Financial Times,* 21 December.

6 Metro International S.A. (2011), *Annual Report 2011,* www.metro.lu/files/2011Annual Report.pdf.

7 Welch, J. (with Welch, S.) (2005), *Winning,* New York: Collins, pp. 165–166.

8 McKinsey (2008), 'How companies respond to competitors: A McKinsey global survey', *McKinsey Quarterly,* www.mckinseyquarterly.com.

9 Teece, D. C. (2007), 'Explicating dynamic capabilities: the nature and microfoundations of (sustainable) enterprise performance', *Strategic Management Journal,* 28:1319–1350.

10 Ohmae, K. (1982), *The Mind of the Strategist,* New York: McGraw-Hill.

11 Hamel, G. (1997), 'Killer strategies that make shareholders rich', *Fortune, 23* June, 70–88, p. 97.

12 Taleb, N. N. (2007), *The Black Swan: The Impact of the Highly Improbable,* New York: Random House. A second edition was published after the global financial crisis in 2010.

13 Rumelt, R. P. (2008), 'Strategy in a structural break', *McKinsey Quarterly,* December, *www. mckinseyquarterly.com.*

14 A scenario is a possible future situation. Scenario planning is a way of analyzing an environment and organizational purpose in strategic planning; it visualizes alternative futures and encourages the design of flexible strategies to meet them. It also can be used to question fundamental assumptions and taken-for-granted preconceptions about purpose, competition, and an organization's environment. It was used by Royal Dutch Shell and helped condition its decision-makers to cope more favourably with the first oil price shock in 1973: see Van der Heijden, K. (1996), *Scenarios: The Art of Strategic Conversation,* Chichester: Wiley & Sons. Well-rehearsed improvization, although it clashes in ordinary times with conventional planning approaches, it may work well in the face of extreme events: see Czarniawska, B. (ed.) (2009), *Organizations in the Face of Risk and Threat,* London: Edward Elgar.

15 Carey, D., Patsalos-Fox, M. and Useem, M. (2009), 'Leadership lessons for hard times', *McKinsey Quarterly*, July, www. mckinseyquarterly.com.

16 Sharman, R. and Smith, D. (2004), 'Enterprise risk management', Chapter 6, in the Professional Accountants in Business Committee (eds), *Enterprise Governance: Getting the Balance Right,* PAIB Committee report, New York; International Federation of Accountants.

17 United States Securities & Exchange Commission (2006), *The Electronic Data Gathering, Analysis and retrieval System,* www.sec.gov/edgar.shtml.

18 See Gadwell, M. (2000), *The Tipping Point: How Little Things Can Make a Big Difference,* New York: Little Brown.

19 Henderson, B. (1976), *The Rule of Three and Four*, Boston Consulting Group, www.bcg.com.

20 Darwin, C. (1859), *On the Origin of Species.*

21 The life cycle concept was presented by Theodore Levitt as a product life cycle: see Levitt, T. (1965), 'Exploit the product life cycle', *Harvard Business Review,* November-December, 81–94.

22 This is known as the sailing ship effect, see Gilfillan, S. C. (1935), *The Sociology of Invention,* Chicago: Follet.

23 Abernathy, W. J. and Utterback, J. M. (1978), 'Patterns of industrial innovation', *Technology Review,* 80 (7):40–47.

24 Porter, M. E. (1979), 'How competitive forces shape strategy', *Harvard Business Review*, March-April, 93–108; the article was up-dated in Porter, M. E. (2008), 'The five competitive forces that shape strategy', *Harvard Business Review,* January, 79–93. There is an appendix about how to conduct an industry analysis in Porter, M. E. (1980), *Competitive Strategy: Techniques for Analyzing Industries and Competitors,* Boston MA: Free Press.

25 Adapted from Porter, M. E. (1979), 'How competitive forces shape strategy', *Harvard Business Review,* March-April, 93–108.

26 Porter, M. E. (2008), 'The five competitive forces that shape strategy', *Harvard Business Review,* January, 79–93.

27 *ibid.* p. 82.

28 *ibid.* p. 88.

29 Office of Fair Trading (2010) *Review of Barriers to Entry, Expansion and Exit in Retail Banking,* report, OFT1282, November.

30 Goff, S. (2011), 'Branch banking stages a revival', *Financial Times*, 8 July.

31 Felsted, A. (2011), 'Trust the stores to get into banking', *Financial Times,* special report on Global Brands, April 28:3.

32 Felsted, A. (2011), *Ibid.* 3.

33 IBM Business Consulting Services (2003), *Supermarket Banking – Fulfilling the Potential*, report, IBM Financial Services Sector, London, www.ibm.com.

34 Moore, E. (2011), 'Virgin takeover offers little hope for rates', *Financial Times,* 18 November.

35 Porter, M. E. (2001), 'Strategy and the Internet', *Harvard Business Review*, March, 63–78.

36 Porter, M. E. (2008), 'How competitive forces shape strategy', *Harvard Business Review*, January, 79–93.

37 Yip, G. S. (2004), 'Using strategy to change your business model', *Business Strategy Review,* 15(2):17–24.

38 Porter, M. E. (1996), 'What is strategy?' *Harvard Business Review,* November-December: 61–78.

39 Peters, T. (1997), *The Circle of Innovation,* London: Hodder & Stoughton, pp. 26, 85.

40 Hamel, G. (1998), 'Strategy innovation and the quest for value', *Sloan Management Review,* Winter, 7–14.

41 D'Aveni, R. (1994), *Hypercompetition: Managing the Dynamics of Strategic Manoeuvring,* NY: Free Press.

42 Rindova, V. P. and Kotha, S. (2001), 'Continuous morphing: competing through dynamic capabilities, form and function', *Academy of Management Journal,* 44 (6):1263–1280.

43 Christensen, C. M. (1997), *The Innovator's Dilemma: When New Technologies Cause Great Firms to Fail,* Boston MA: Harvard Business School Press.

44 Porter, M. E. (1999), 'A conversation with Michael E. Porter: a "significant extension" toward operational improvement and positioning, an interview by Richard M. Hodgetts', *Organizational Dynamics,* 28(1):24–33.

45 The concept dates from a doctoral thesis that indicated performance differences between firms across an industry as well as between industries: Hunt, M. S. (1972), *Competition on the Major Home Appliance Industry,*

1960–1970, Harvard University, and a study: Cool, K. and Schendel, D. (1988), 'Performance differences among strategic group members', *Strategic Management Journal,* 9(3):207–223. A widely quoted definition comes from Porter, '*A strategic group is the group of firms in an industry following the same or a similar strategy along the strategic dimensions*': Porter, M. E. (1980), *Competitive Strategy: Techniques for Analyzing Industries and Competitors,* Boston MA: Free Press, p. 129.

46 Kim, W. C. and Mauborgne, R. (2005), *Blue Ocean Strategy: How to Create Uncontested Market Space and Make the Competition Irrelevant,* Boston MA: Harvard Business School Press.

47 Kim, W. C. and Mauborgne, R. (2004), 'Blue ocean strategy', *Harvard Business Review,* October.

48 Child, J. (1974), 'Managerial and organization factors associated with company performance: part 1', *Journal of Management Studies,* 11: 175–189.

CASE 4.1 How PESTEL shapes L'Oréal

L'Oréal was founded in 1907 when Eugene Schueller, a chemist, developed a new hair colour formula. It is now a multinational with headquarters in Paris and with revenues in 2012 of over $28 billion it is the world's largest cosmetic company. A publicly listed company, a quarter of its equity is owned by the Swiss food company, Nestlé, and another quarter by Liliane Bettencourt, the founder's daughter. The company's advertising slogan, 'because we're worth it' is well-known throughout the world; it has 27 international brands active in 160 countries. This case illustrates how the PESTEL framework is important to its long-term survival. The company's purpose or mission is shown in Exhibit 4.1.

Political: always risky

A major political issue that is growing in importance across the world is health and its associated dietary and self-esteem problems. Beauty has been represented for decades in films and by the media as young women with flawless skins and super-slim bodies, but which in practice does not seem to reflect reality. This may be linked the growing health problems with anorexia and bulimia.

The reality question recently surfaced in the UK when politicians complained to the Advertising Standards Authority. The Authority forced L'Oréal to withdraw advertisements featuring film star Julia Roberts and supermodel Christy Turlington. The complaints alleged that the images used had been digitally manipulated, and were not representative of the effects the products could achieve. Julia Roberts, the face of the Lancôme brand, was promoting a skin foundation called Teint Miracle, a product that claimed to create a natural light that emanates from beautiful skin.[2] L'Oréal did not help its case when it refused to make the original photos available thus preventing a comparison of before and after.

EXHIBIT 4.1 L'Oréal's purpose

OUR MISSION

'BEAUTY FOR ALL'

For more than a century, L'Oréal has devoted itself solely to one business: beauty. It is a business rich in meaning, as it enables all individuals to express their personalities, gain self-confidence and open up to others.

Beauty is a language.

L'Oréal has set itself the mission of offering all women and men worldwide the best of cosmetics innovation in terms of quality, efficacy and safety. It pursues this goal by meeting the infinite diversity of beauty needs and desires all over the world.

Beauty is universal.

Since its creation by a researcher, the group has been pushing back the frontiers of knowledge. Its unique research arm enables it to continually explore new territories and invent the products of the future, while drawing inspiration from beauty rituals the world over.

Beauty is a science.

Providing access to products that enhance well-being, mobilizing its innovative strength to preserve the beauty of the planet and supporting local communities. These are exacting challenges, which are a source of inspiration and creativity for L'Oréal.

Beauty is a commitment.

By drawing on the diversity of its teams, and the richness and the complementarity of its brand portfolio, L'Oréal has made the universalization of beauty its project for the years to come.

L'Oréal, offering beauty for all.[1]

Another issue of growing importance is animal testing. In November 2012 the European Union's Health and Consumer Affairs Commissioner, Tonio Borg, proposed a marketing ban on animal-tested cosmetics. In China the government is taking its first steps to introduce non-animal testing.[3] While governments have generally been reluctant to ban animal testing for health and safety reasons, animal testing for cosmetics is increasingly frowned upon. L'Oréal has maintained that it has not been involved in animal testing since 1989, although some ingredients in their products have been tested on animals for health reasons.

L'Oréal is a French corporate champion and its relationship with the Swiss food company, Nestlé, has been carefully monitored in government circles. The French government is concerned that if L'Oréal should be acquired by Nestlé, then strategic decision-making may drift abroad with adverse consequences for research activities and domestic jobs.[4] However the national interest may serve to limit L'Oréal's expansion as a global company.

Economic: counting on people

The major economic issue for L'Oréal is globalization.

It all started about ten years ago. We were dealing with new populations of consumers in emerging countries, whose household equipment and daily environment were very different from those of our

European customers ... How do you wash your hair in India? How does a Japanese woman apply mascara or lipstick? What are the beauty rituals in South Africa?[5]

The growing global market is more diverse and younger, but in the developed countries, the populations are growing older and may be more conservative, although with more wealth. The global financial crisis has probably had more effect in developed countries, and in these regions it is the more specialized market segments that are increasing in value. Market differences are complex and serving different countries and segments in different ways is likely to prove more expensive than hitherto.

Social: living with the changing times

Particular concerns to a cosmetics company are social aspirations and lifestyle. There is no single model for beauty as the world's populations have their own specific features. Traditionally they have included brands based on national aspirations: for example, Italian elegance, New York street smart, French beauty, and British classicalism. However, young markets across the world exhibit excitement and trendy images. For this reason L'Oréal bought the edgy California makeup brand, Urban Decay. This uses attractive packaging with names like Stray Dog, which uses an ash-brown eye-shadow: 'It is the makeup specialist we needed to fully satisfy young women in search of playful colours and inspiration, at an accessible price point' (Nicolas Hieronimus, L'Oréal Luxe president).[6] The universal standards for beauty may be breaking down or the very opposite could be happening with the rise of celebrity culture in the urban centres of the world.

Technological: making things work

Advances in technology have been used by L'Oréal to expand its range of products and they have become ever more important as discoveries mount in the biological sciences. However technology and beauty may be uneasy bedfellows:

There is undoubtedly a culture in which the pursuit of beauty is deemed to be inherently trivial, in which the use of anti-aging products is perceived as a foolish quest for youthfulness by those old enough to know better. In this case, the association of beauty with cosmetics is sufficient to undermine or trivialize the quality of scientific research undertaken in anti-aging.[7]

The survival of L'Oréal depends upon the underlying technology and science of its products. It has to conduct its own research and development. In a report about skin care the company states it must look ahead and ask:

What advances in skincare are ahead? What is next for the industry? How will developments in science change our skincare habits and what products will we be using in the years ahead?[8]

It is likely that in the not too far distant future, some cosmetic companies will be in new markets where changing and remaking faces will be as common as changing clothes and outfits. This will be a more technological driven activity – today many markets are driven by natural ingredients and natural beauty.

Environmental: that's natural!

When L'Oréal took over The Body Shop in 2006, a retailer of small (often unpackaged) products with natural ingredients, it acquired a green edge that perhaps the company had not had previously. L'Oréal would learn much from The Body Shop's community trading, especially with regard to L'Oréal's sustainability policies:

Our values are present in all aspects of our activities. The most visible examples are of course our strong sustainable development and diversity policies but they are integrated into less visible aspects such as our Purchasing Department's responsible sourcing policy and our high standards regards product quality and safety.[9]

Legal: getting it right

Globalization requires a multinational to be sensitive to the prevailing standards of behaviour in a national economy. This reaches beyond a country's written rules and regulations to codes of practice and business ethics: 'At L'Oréal, we consider that ethics continues where rules end and that we should always ask ourselves not "can we do it" but "should we do it"' (Emmanuel Lulin, Group Director of Ethics).[10] L'Oréal was one of the first companies in France to establish a code of business ethics; this was in 2000 and a director of ethics was appointed in 2007.

Strategy

PESTEL factors shape the reasons behind L'Oréal's mission:

> With the opening up of the emerging markets, L'Oréal's mission is broadening in response to the vast diversity of populations. The whole company is focused on this new horizon: teams enriched by their cultural diversity, a portfolio of international brands present in the different distribution channels, and research that is capable of grasping the world's complexity.

The company is broadening its consumer base and increasing the number of its products and brands. It hopes to be the United Nations of beauty. As the world's markets for cosmetics mature, the company must develop new business and products to compete for a more diverse and demanding customer base. Thus L'Oréal is moving into niche and small category segments that the company has not focused on for a long time.[11]

Discussion questions

1 Given the above PESTEL factors and others not listed, what are the opportunities and threats facing L'Oréal given the emerging trends in the general environment?

2 Are there possible alternatives to L'Oréal's present strategy? The company has a lot of brands; there may be too many and do they have enough universal appeal to be profitable?

3 If, as the old adage has it 'beauty is in the eye of the beholder', is L'Oréal's mission really a meaningful one for developing global markets?

Case end-notes

1 L'Oréal (2012), *'Our Mission'*, Company Overview, loreal.com.

2 Sweney, M. (2011), 'L'Oréal's Julia Roberts and Christy Turlington ad campaigns banned', *The Guardian*, 27 July.

3 CosmeticsDesign-Europe (2012), *Animal Testing*, Breaking News, CosmeticsDesign-Europe.com, November, www.comesticsdesign-europe.com.

4 Betts, P. (2010), 'L'Oréal brushes up well as a potential Nestle target', *Financial Times*, 17 September.

5 L'Oréal (2011), *Sustainable Development Report 2011*, www.loreal.com.

6 Moulds, J. (2012), 'L'Oréal strikes deal to buy Urban Decay', *The Guardian*, 26 November.

7 L'Oréal and Mintel (2012), *Here Comes the Science Bit: A Review by L'Oréal of Skin Science and What's to Come*, L'Oréal Corporate Communications, www.loreal.com.

8 L'Oréal and Mintel (2012), *Here Comes the Science Bit: A Review by L'Oréal of Skin Science and What's to Come*, L'Oréal Corporate Communications, www.loreal.com.

9 L'Oréal (2011), *Sustainable Development Report 2011*, www.loreal.com.

10 Nichol, K. (2010), 'L'Oréal recognised as one of the world's most ethical companies', *Newsletter*, March, CosmeticsDesign-Europe.com, www.comesticsdesign-europe.com.

11 Pitman, S. (2010), 'L'Oréal unveils three-pronged strategy for future growth', *Newsletter*, CosmeticsDesign-Europe.com, www.comesticsdesign-europe.com.

Chapter 5

THE INTERNAL ENVIRONMENT

The internal environment

An organization's **internal environment** consists of the conditions inside an organization, including its strategic resources, abilities and management capabilities.

KEY TERMS

benchmarking

core competences

deutero learning

double loop learning

dynamic capability

exploitative learning

exploratory learning

internal environment

just-in-time management

lean working

PDCA cycle

performance excellence models

resource-based view of strategy

single loop learning

strategic lock-in

strategic resources

SWOT

total quality management

VRIO framework

LEARNING OBJECTIVES

This chapter provides you with an understanding of the following:

1 The internal environment

2 How strategic resources convey competitive advantage

3 The concepts of core competences and dynamic capabilities

4 The meaning of strategic resources in relation to management philosophies and business methodologies:
   - lean working
   - total quality management
   - performance excellence
   - benchmarking

5 Organizational learning

6 The role of SWOT analysis in auditing the external and internal environments

Business vignette Using the nature of who you are for a strategy to manage authentic Chinese food

What you are can give you a competitive advantage if it works to serve up something special that makes your products and services stand out. The choice of which strategy an organization should adopt to achieve its strategic objectives is based heavily on its ability to carry it out and the appropriateness of its internal environment. This also concerns the need to ensure that all the competences of how an organization, or an entity that needs to be successful, configures all of its strengths in a way it can take full advantage.

For example, Ching-He Huang, a Taiwanese-born British celebrity chef, earned fame when she first appeared on television in 2005, and then in 2008 in a BBC cookery series, *Chinese Food Made Easy*. This was accompanied by her first two cookery books, *China Modern* and *Chinese Food Made Easy*, which immediately became best-sellers. Her success may have been due to a number of factors, but what lies in the very heart of her style is the Chinese philosophy of yin and yang (balancing negative and positive forces that affect existence), which she has used in all her accompanying business activities.

She first set up a healthy foodstuff company called Fuge Ltd[1], followed by the release of a healthy drink product called Tzu[2], made from sorghum vinegar. The name links the drink to a Buddhist charity called the Tzu-Chi Foundation, which is headed in the United Kingdom by her father. These activities are premised around the core belief of managing yin and yang.

Huang commented: 'we believe there is this philosophy of yin and yang, a balance of cooling foods and heating foods, to give you a good balance of life force (or chi) energy ... in any dish, you combine this balance for ingredients and cooking methods'.[3]

Celebrity chef, Ching-He Huang, demonstrating Chinese cooking

According to Richard Teece and others, an organization's competitive advantage primarily depends upon its managerial and organizational processes.[4] All organizations are different and this difference can be recognized by management and used to direct the strategy process from the inside-out.

The resource-based view of strategy

The **resource-based view of strategy (RBV)** is a school of strategy that believes competitive advantage is based on strategic resources; those internal resources (or assets) that are unique to a particular organization, and are important to its competitive advantage. **Strategic resources** are combinations or bundles of tangible resources (which are economic and tradable) and intangible ones (such as organizational culture and the way people work, which are idiosyncratic and have little external value). An organization's strategic resources are difficult for competitors to understand and imitate. Strategic resources include the concepts dynamic capabilities and core competences.[5]

The origin of RBV ideas lie in articles by Wernerfelt, Rumelt, and Barney.[6] The influence of economics and the *Strategic Management Journal* have been important, but more generally in economics an evolutionary

view of market forces has prevailed to downplay the role of managerial intentionality and its part in sustaining long-term competitive advantage.[7] The normative implications of evolutionary theory tend to an understanding of general (even naturalistic) behaviours rather than an understanding more useful to the management of the individual firm.[8]

An early economics scholar, Edith Penrose[9], however argued that managers can influence the direction and growth of the firm. She also suggested that 'resources' should be more broadly defined for economic analysis – for example, many essential resources, such as a special quality of water, are free but are valuable to the firm concerned. The RBV in the popular business literature is much more centred on managerial intentionality.[10]

The RBV is sometimes contrasted to Porter's ideas in the sense that he emphasizes industry factors and the RBV is about firm-specific resources. Teece and others point out that the ideas underpinning the competitive forces framework are really about the impediment of competitive forces, and that generic strategy aims to alter a firm's position in the industry in relation to its competitors and suppliers (see Chapter 6). Industry structure plays a central role in Porter and differences between organizations relate primarily to ones of scale. The RBV, on the other hand, understands competitive advantage to be rooted in the development of firm-specific strategic resources and the internal capabilities to manage them.

> Strategic resources are organizational assets, or attributes, which when combined in ways that are uniquely specific to an organization, constitute its competitive advantage. Strategic resources are not economic resources, because they are valuable only to the organization that uses them and they have no external value.

The VRIO framework

Jay Barney offers criteria to identify strategic resources, which he calls the **VRIO framework**.[12] He suggests that above-average profits are likely if an organization's attributes are:

- Valuable – when they enable an organization to implement strategy that improves its effectiveness and efficiency.

- Rare – few, if any, other competing organizations have these valuable attributes.

- Inimitable – attributes may be too difficult to emulate because they have a unique history, their nature is ambiguous, or socially complex.

- Organizable – the organization can exploit the competitive potential the other three.

In the instance of a university, attributes are valuable when they are core to the university's competitive difference. For example, its teaching and research distinguish clearly from other universities. The university may have areas of expertise that other institutions lack; this rareness will attract students for courses in certain subjects. The established reputation, traditions, physical surroundings, and facilities perceived and associated with how and what the university does make it difficult for a rival to attract funding to develop a similar expertise and offer the same quality of courses. Finally, the university should be able to organize these attributes in ways to build and reinforce its competitive difference.

Differences may be enhanced in many different ways, for instance, through the recruitment of people with certain aptitudes and knowledge, patents and

---

KEY DEBATE 5.1

Is competitive advantage found in the industry or the organization?

In an influential paper, Rumelt[13] suggested that competitive advantage is associated with factors at the individual firm level, such as through resources and the specific strategy that is adopted, rather than the structure (and therefore the attractiveness) of the industry. He found that industry factors explained about 9–16 per cent of variations in profit, against around 46 per cent for factors that were specific to individual organizations. Being in the right industry is important but if a specific organization is good at what it does, especially if it is done better and in ways that other rivals cannot easily copy, firm-specific factors matter more.

However, the comparison may vary for different industries, especially for services.[14] Industry structure plays a central role for Porter and a successful strategy primarily relates to how an organization takes this into account in choosing its competitive position.[15] While exponents of the resource-based view claim it is 'arguably the dominant theoretical foundation in strategic management today',[16] there is little empirical evidence to conclusively support the notion that strategic resources generally account for sustained competitive success.

Scholars, such as Priem and Butler,[17] assert that the resource-based view defines strategic resources too inclusively, and it is poor at discriminating between resources that can be practically manipulated, and those which are beyond managerial control. Hoopes and others[18] argue that the perspective assumes what it seeks to explain and defines, rather than hypothesizes. In short, the resource-based view is not very helpful to practitioners.

Jarzabkowski[19] argued that RBV research has resorted 'to positivistic methods that are too coarse to access deep understandings of how firms differ and, indeed, what difference that makes'. The value of deriving generalizable evidence in statistically based studies is doubtful if the nature of strategic resources lies in their uniqueness, but the strategic management literature typically marginalizes the managerial micro-foundations or activities that go on in organizations.[20] There is a tendency for scholars, anyway, to oversimply RBV concepts, and thus squeeze out the quintessential intangibility of practice that makes RBV so insightful for understanding strategic management.

On the other hand, industry analysis also has its difficulties, not least in working out what are an industry's boundaries. If an industry and its competitive influences seem unknowable, it may be better to configure an organization around its core competences to give the organization a competitive uniqueness and a dynamic capability it would otherwise lack in the face of change.

Question: How can competitive advantage found within the organization and in the industry be reconciled?

proprietary technologies, physical assets like buildings and other facilities, location, social and business networks, alliances, and so on. However, the importance of intangible resources, such as corporate image, brands, customer service, is fundamental in establishing how people perceive the difference between organizations and the things they offer. Intangibility is quintessentially a holistically sensed quality. All organizations are to some extent unique bundles of attributes and it is how these are used and managed that determines differences in organizational performance.

The key thing is to integrate resources so the intangibility of the whole creates an image that puts the organization apart from its rivals. Robert Grant uses the example of McDonald's.[21] The organization has outstanding functional capabilities in product development, market research, human resource management, financial control and operations management; however it is how all these are integrated to provide a consistency in its products and services in thousands of its restaurants across the world that really accounts for its success. Barney explains VRIO as a framework for identifying strategic resources. By itself it does not constitute a source of competitive advantage, since the identified resources must be combined and managed as an integrated set.

Distinctive capabilities

John Kay argues that corporate success derives from a competitive advantage that is based on distinctive capabilities, which are derived from an organization's relationships with its suppliers, customers, or employees.[22] The continuity and stability of relationships allows for flexible and cooperative responses to change. There are three types of distinctive capabilities:

- Architecture – these are structures created to coordinate employees, customers and suppliers, to build a mutual commitment in an organization's distribution and supply chains to its unique ways of working.

- Reputation – this is built up through a customer's own experience, the organization's marketing, how the organization seems to compare with its rivals.

- Innovation – usually this can be copied, so what counts is how an organization can support innovation with strategies that are designed to make this difficult; for example through patents or secrecy that make it difficult for a rival to copy.

A key requirement is that an organization's people should have the necessary knowledge and skills to be proficient in delivering the unique value customers want and expect. In other words, an organization must have the necessary core competences.

Core competences

Core competences are the organization-specific abilities people have, which they use in common to work together, to learn and apply knowledge, to be able to manage strategic priorities in ways that will create and sustain competitive advantage. They embody an organization's collective learning, particularly how to coordinate diverse production skills and integrate multiple technologies. Core competences have the following advantages:

- They are hard for rivals to understand how they work, and difficult to emulate: how people

A RBV of strategy at Google

Speaking in 2008, the then chief executive, Eric Schmidt, explained Google as an emerged rather than a planned organization.[23] The founders' (Larry Page and Sergey Brinwork) work grew out of an academic culture of innovation based on the Internet. Google employees are empowered to develop their own ideas and self-organize into projects, some of which occasionally result in an 'amazing achievement'.

Schmidt has said it took him six months of talking to understand how broad Larry and Sergey's vision was ... I remember sitting down with Larry, saying, 'Tell me again what our strategy is', and writing it down.[24]

Senior managers influence the number of projects by prioritizing them as a 'top 100 list', although the actual number tends to be higher. With its increasing size Google's scope has become universal, and an early slogan was 'to organize the World's information and make it universally accessible'. The company's activities have expanded across a range of information and media interests.

Google uses ten principles[25] to guide everybody's actions:

1 Focus on the user and all else will follow.
2 It's best to do one thing really well, really well.
3 Fast is better than slow.
4 Democracy on the web works
5 You don't need to be at your desk to need an answer.
6 You can make money without doing evil.
7 There's always more information out there.
8 The need for information crosses all borders.
9 You can be serious without a suit.
10 Great just isn't good enough.

Every issue is debated according to the principle of the wisdom of the crowd. There is a 'reasonable person' rule: an individual must listen, interact with others, and build partnerships. No one is in charge, but senior managers do shape what people are doing. Google is not looking overtly for opportunities to make a big profit and shareholder value is not the purpose of the business, but it is a consequence of a vision based on end-users:

... to deliver relevant results across all data sources – the Internet, a user's local computer, and the corporate network. In pursuing this goal, we maintain a maniacal focus on the end user experience.[26]

Writing about Google, Kieran Levis worries that while present management has no evil intent, many people find Page's view that 'ultimately you want to have the entire world's knowledge to be connected directly to your mind', and Brin's statement 'the perfect search engine would be like the mind of God', a little chilling and certainly hubristic.[27]

The disclosure in 2010 that research for Street View had included identifying and holding information on individuals' wireless Internet access has fuelled these doubts.

Question: Why is strategic management at Google driven inside-out?

work together and the context of any particular organizational culture is difficult for an outsider to understand.

- They are suitable to influence a range of markets and industries: it may be possible to use an organization's core competences to produce a varied range of products and services.

- They help with an understanding of management's priorities: core competences provide a shared understanding of an organization's purpose, and top-down objectives are likely to be better understood and more easily implemented.

- They are useful for cross-functional working: people from different technical and departmental backgrounds are more likely to understand each other's needs if they share core competences, and it improves team working and project management generally.

- They facilitate common approaches for managing strategically related objectives; core competences are typically associated with a common language of objectives, which are managed in a similar way across the organization.

- They promote a common set of learning-based tools and working principles: a common approach to learning and knowledge is likely to promote similar approaches and methods for solving problems.

- Bottom-up management is facilitated: effective responsibility for decision-making is passed down to the lowest level that is capable of accepting it.

A core competence is not simply an ability to be good or even to excel at something, if this something can also be achieved by a rival. So, for example, it is not a retailer's ability to retail as such, but rather how this is done differently from the competition, such as how the retailer's staff work to enhance the customer's shopping experience so it confers greater value than is available elsewhere. An organization's strategic resources can be characterized as bundles, or patterns of skills, knowledge and supporting resources, which give to the organization its idiosyncratic competencies that are core to its strategic purpose. These develop in part from organizational learning and are typically reinforced and strengthened over time, so that they follow a path or trajectory.

Strategic lock-in

Strategic lock-in is brought about when core competences are sticky and difficult to change quickly.[28] If knowledge and learning become too institutionalized then organizations run the risk of seeing their core competences turn into core rigidities.[29] Prahalad and Hamel argue risk is manageable if core competences are used to develop a foundation of core products that can be used to develop end-products and services in different industries.[30] Core products are areas of organization-specific expertise and resources. Core competences, on the other hand, are the collective learning abilities of employees, which include how to develop and manage the integration of technologies through cross-functional management and collaborative working.

> A core competence is not simply an ability to be good, or even to excel at something, if this something can also be achieved by a rival. ... it is not a retailer's ability to retail as such, but rather how this is done differently from the competition, such as how the retailer's staff work to enhance the customer's shopping experience so it confers greater value than is available elsewhere.

For example, Canon used core competences to develop its technical competencies in optics, a core product, to serve different industries as diverse as cameras, copiers, and semi-conductor equipment. This flexibility is possible because Canon has a core competence, or capability, where people come together and work in common ways. This gives Canon its organization-specific competitive advantage, which is unseen and is difficult for rivals to understand. The important thing with this example is that the competences involved in building up technology and developing products are different from the core competences required to manage those technologies in a unique way.

Many of the examples used from the 1990s came from Japanese organizations like Canon, and the quality-improvement and deployment methods associated with them have become important tools for the development of competencies. They offer a systematic approach that uses a shared set of business methodologies and management philosophies, which gives to everybody in an organization a common language for team working. Approaches such as total quality management allow a deeper understanding of cause-and-effect relationships, so that the organization is able to refine, test and validate its core competences constantly.[31] The ability of an organization to manage its core competencies over time is referred to in strategic management as a dynamic capability.

Dynamic capabilities

Teece, Pisano and Shuen define a **dynamic capability** as an organization's ability to integrate, build, and reconfigure core competencies to meet change.[32] A more general definition defines them as an organization's ability to renew and recreate its strategic capabilities (including core competences) to meet the needs of a changing environment. Teece and others see a dynamic capability as a high level management process and part of (if not synonymously with) strategic management, which acts to influence lower-level dynamic capabilities and competencies. Lower level dynamic capabilities may still be strategic in the sense that they are cross-functional processes that may create market change, or responses to

change in the external environment, such as including product development, alliance and acquisition capabilities, resource allocation and knowledge transfer routines. However, these are lower level capabilities. It is possible to imagine an organization as a hierarchical nest of dynamic capabilities, which are inserted into each other like a set of Russian dolls. Thus a dynamic capability is a systematic and holistic business process.

Its dynamic quality is based on 'a learned and stable pattern of collective activity through which the organization systematically generates and modifies its operating routines in pursuit of improved effectiveness'.[33] In other words, a dynamic capability drives continuous improvement. Teece, Pisano and Shuen give the example of Fujimoto's account of production activities in the Japanese auto industry and identify the Toyota Production System as an example.[34]

Most auto-makers now have similar production systems to the Toyota system, which means it is not necessarily the dynamic capability itself that is Toyota's competitive advantage, but rather how Toyota uses it. Eisenhardt and Martin point out that dynamic capabilities are often similar and point out that the real differences between competing organizations is in the detail of their application.[35] It is true that common features exist so they can be benchmarked and shared as best practice between organizations; however, because organizational context varies so does the effectiveness of a dynamic capability.

Eisenhardt and Martin suggest there is nothing uniquely distinctive in the learning processes involved; these can be easily copied by a rival organization. Nevertheless they give to an organizational an ability to manage resources in particular combinations, which can be used to design a series of short-term competitive positions. Each position can be used to build up a long-term competitive advantage through stages, much in the way that Hamel and Prahalad suggest Japanese organizations run strategic marathons as a series of short-term challenges to achieve a longer-term strategic intent (see Chapter 3).[36]

The debate about the nature of dynamic capabilities continues in the literature and seems to take different forms depending upon the subject discipline concerned. The original idea seems to have emerged during the 1980s and 1990s when the so-called 'new competition' of the Japanese began to eat away at international markets. Many of today's mainstream management approaches and its associated lean production, come from Japanese management.[37]

These constitute strategic resources in the sense that they offer abilities (how people manage work) and capabilities (a process of work that is being managed), which are important ingredients of many organization's dynamic capabilities and competitive strategy. For example, the Toyota Production System includes aspects of most of them. In the sense that they involve management philosophies or approaches to working and managing, as well as business methodologies or tools, they are also important to core competences.[38] They include:

- lean working (production and services);
- just-in-time management;
- total quality management;
- performance excellence models;
- benchmarking.

Lean working

Lean working (or lean production as it is known in manufacturing) is a management system for ensuring any non-value creating activity is removed. Thus this is important to a customer value proposition (Chapter 2) and requires that end-customers should pull the value they want from production and distribution, rather than have products and services pushed forward to them by the needs of the organization. This requires an organization's production or service system to be flexible (or agile) enough to adapt to the changing needs of the market. Lean production emerged in Japanese manufacturing in the 1960s as an operations system approach.[39] Lean ideas have been developed in the West for a wide range of different industries, such as retailing, banking, and hospitals.

The driving principle is to link the management of an organization's core business processes to strategic objectives to continuously improve productivity through attention to quality (customer value), costs, delivery and processes and people (learning and growth). Many assume that lean is an operational tool used only to save waste and costs, but it is much more than this. Lean practitioners sometimes call their core processes, key or critical business areas. This has a lot in common with Rockart's CSFs (Chapter 3) and Porter's value chain (Chapter 6). The word core refers to processes that are vital to the customer value proposition and competitive strategy. As these are critical to strategic management senior managers identify and specify these areas and give them priority for monitoring and reviewing to ensure the organization remains fit for purpose. Peter Hines and others at Cardiff University give an example from the car industry:[40]

1 Strategy formation and deployment: The strategic management of the company, focusing of change, managing critical success factors and ensuring all employees are fully aligned and empowered.

2 Order fulfilment (new cars, used cars, parts): Taking orders, processing the orders, scheduling planning, taking delivery, inspecting, delivery to customer and payment management.

3 Order fulfilment (car servicing & repairing): taking booking, receiving car, serving car, returning to customer and payment management.

4 Winning business: identifying and targeting new customers or business opportunities in order to trigger the order fulfilment process.

5 People life cycle management: the identification of needs, recruitment, motivation, training, development and reward of people together with the management of their eventual retirement.

6 Information technology: the management of electronic support systems.

7 Legal and financial management: the management of the legal function as well as costs, financial and management.

The nature of services is not necessarily as different from manufacturing as is sometimes supposed. Instead of a factory there is an administrative office block and the organization of routines can be as formal as those in a manufacturing plant. The major difference is normally a greater variation in the nature of demand. For example, John Seddon, formerly of Toyota and now advising public services about lean working, explains it this way:

> Service differs from manufacturing. Aside from the obvious lack of physical plant and goods, in services the customer is involved in production; the service agent is involved too. There is, inherently, much more variety of demand. So instead of thinking of the system as one that pulls physical things together to manufacture at the rate of customer demand (the essence of the Toyota system), you have to think of the system as one that brings (largely) intangible expertise together in response to the variety of customer demands. This different purpose leads to different methods, because there are different problems to solve. Solving these problems teaches how to design services from which customers can 'pull' value – in other words, get what they want.[41]

Seddon argues against functionally based organizing, especially the concept of front and back offices, where the easily dealt with enquiries are covered by first contact at the front-end, and more complex and difficult ones are passed on to experts. He argues this approach is based on minimizing costs to the provider and only causes delays and frustrations to the customer. It lowers value because it causes customers to make more enquiries and complaints and locks costs into the system. A system designed around one office, on the other hand, would build up operator expertise and make the service more responsive and able to cope with a variety of enquiries.

Just-in-time management

Just-in-time management is an advanced form of lean working, and involves managing processes so that they respond to the needs of the next customer in line, as and when the customer requires. In other words, a supplier pulls all the components together as and when they are needed in the production process. The approach is powerful in that it makes an organization subject to the voice of the customer. For example, in Japan no car is built until the customer orders what they want. For western markets it is slightly different because buyers tend to make purchases when they see the car at a showroom. However, Toyota only starts to make cars when dealers place specific orders for them. General Motors, on the other hand, is organized around a much larger inventory system, and will often offer discount incentives to prevent its system becoming clogged. This is an important reason why Toyota's product turnaround in the United States average about 30 days, while GM and Ford turnover on average after 80 days or more.

In principle just-in-time removes the need for buffer stocks and reduces costs. It also requires a strict discipline throughout the supply chain to ensure that parts are delivered exactly to specification every time. This requires excellent quality management.

The Toyota Production System

The Toyota Production System is a production system that involves the elimination of *muda*, which is any non-value creating activity. It is based on two key concepts: *jidoka* (translated from Japanese to mean automation with a human touch) and just-in-time (producing only enough necessary for the next stage of the production process).

JIDOKA: highlighting/visualizing the problems

1 Jidoka means that a machine safely stops when the normal processing is completed. It also means that, should a quality or equipment problem arise, the machine detects the problem on its own and stops, preventing defective products from being produced. As a result, only products satisfying the quality standards will be passed on to the next processes on the production line.

2 Since a machine automatically stops when processing is completed or when a problem arises and this is communicated via the *andon* (problem display board), operators can confidently continue performing work at another machine, as well as easily identifying the problem cause and preventing its recurrence. This means that each operator can be in charge of many machines, resulting in higher productivity, while the continuous improvements lead to greater processing capacity.

JUST-IN-TIME: productivity improvement

1 When a vehicle order is received, a production instruction must be issued to the beginning of the vehicle production line as soon as possible.

2 The assembly line must be stocked with small numbers of all types of parts so that any kind of vehicle ordered can be assembled.

3 The assembly line must replace the parts used by retrieving the same number of parts from the parts-producing process (the preceding process).

4 The preceding process must be stocked with small numbers of all types of parts and produce only the numbers of parts that were retrieved by an operator from the next process.[42]

Question: Does the TPS constitute a competitive advantage?

Total quality management (TQM)

Total quality management is an organization-wide philosophy and set of management principles for improving continuously the quality of a product/service to meet customer needs.[43] Quality in this sense is not an absolute product or service attribute. It is possible to have poor quality in a luxury car, as it is to have high quality in an economy car. If a customer's expectation is not being met, then quality is poor. The word 'total', means that the philosophy must apply at every business level and to every process. Quality is only as good as the weakest link in the quality chain (see Figure 5.1). Every part of the production and delivery chain has to be good enough to give the next work process exactly what it wants for it to be able to produce what is exactly needed by the following process, and so on.

FIGURE 5.1 Getting quality right at every stage of the supply chain

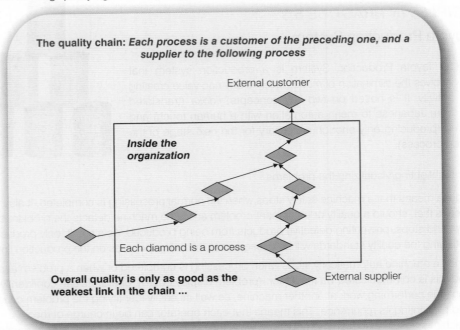

The quality chain: *Each process is a customer of the preceding one, and a supplier to the following process*

External customer

Inside the organization

Each diamond is a process

Overall quality is only as good as the weakest link in the chain ...

External supplier

If everybody has control over their work to the extent that they have a responsibility to meet their immediate customer's requirements, then they are likely to see their work not as a static, stand-alone process, but as a dynamic activity which must change with the needs of the ultimate customer. The guiding principle is that every process is managed according to the **PDCA cycle** (see Figure 5.2), where 'P' is plan (the work), 'D' is do (carry out the work to plan), 'C' is check (to see if progress is satisfactory), and 'A' is act (take corrective action if progress is unsatisfactory). The principle should be used for any process, including the organization's strategic management. It forms the basic mechanism for all types of organizational learning.[44]

The guiding principle is that every process is managed according to the PDCA cycle, where 'P' is plan (the work), 'D' is do (carry out the work to plan), 'C' is check (to see if progress is satisfactory), and 'A' is act (take corrective action if progress is unsatisfactory). The principle should be used for any process, including the organization's strategic management. It forms the basic mechanism for all types of organizational learning.

FIGURE 5.2 The PDCA cycle

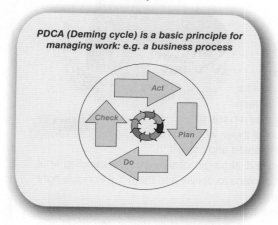

PDCA (Deming cycle) is a basic principle for managing work: e.g. a business process

Another principle of TQM is to solve problems in ways to make sure they do not recur. PDCA should be about finding root causes and ending them, no matter where they originate from in the organization, especially if they are a result of management. This calls for enabling and facilitating styles of senior

management and an organizational culture that is conducive to organization-wide problem solving and project working. Nonaka and Takeuchi argue that effective knowledge management is a mixture of explicit and tacit knowledge (which is felt but hard to articulate).[45]

It is necessary to encourage people to interact and share the tacit skills they have developed, but to make this work, senior managers must establish a common working culture that is fully understood and supported by the organization's managers. The key thing is to enable people through the organization to take responsibility for managing their work. If anything is happening to influence somebody's work adversely, then management must ensure that the issue can be properly problem-solved, no matter where the source of the problem is. Otherwise PDCA stands for 'Please Don't Change Anything'.

A business process is influenced by five areas of quality (see Figure 5.3):

1 the quality of a plan (or design);
2 the conformance of work to plan (the fitness of the process);

FIGURE 5.3 Process management: PCDA and five control areas

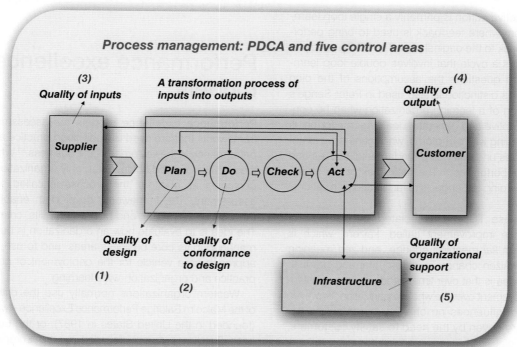

Process management: PDCA and five control areas

3 the quality of inputs (from suppliers);

4 the perception of output (good insight and feedback from the customer is essential);

5 the organizational support.

Corrective action is primarily a single loop learning system where feedback is used to bring performance back to the original plan. The PDCA principle, however, is a cycle that involves double loop learning, which questions the assumptions of the plan itself.[50] This distinction is also used in Peter Senge's description of a learning organization when he contrasts adaptive and generative learning: the former is about dealing with symptoms, while generative learning involves understanding fundamental causes and seeing opportunities.[51] The main task of the strategist, according to Senge, is to facilitate organizational learning.

Japanese TQM is associated with a form of continuous improvement called 'kaizen', which is taken from *kai* meaning change, and *zen* meaning good.[52] Kaizen change is incremental and gradual, but the idea is that over time it adds up to a substantial improvement over the whole organization. However, the main influences on change, as shown in the figure, are driven by the need to satisfy customers, and are classically associated with the need to have

organizational routines under control. Kaizen is also driven by strategic change. This involves senior managers in setting strategically linked objectives, which other levels take account of when forming their plans (see *hoshin kanri*, Chapter 10).

Performance excellence models

Performance excellence models are assessment frameworks that are used to audit good practice and performance in the key areas of the business.[53] When the activity is carried out involving only organizational personnel as auditors, the process is called self-assessment. The frameworks cover both enabling (how things are done), and business results, criteria. The idea is to evaluate how an organization is being managed in its core business areas, and to use the approach as a vehicle for the deployment of good practice and organization-wide learning.

Western organizations normally use the criteria of the Malcolm Baldrige Performance Excellence Award (founded in the United States in 1987), or the European Excellence Award (founded by the European

W. Edwards Deming, who popularized the PDCA Cycle after WWII

are many other awards across the world, including the oldest in Japan, named after the American quality guru, W. Edwards Deming (established in 1951). The criteria for these awards are similar. Organizations apply to be assessed and if successful win the award. The assessment process involves external auditors who award scores for each category of the models (see the example of the European model, Figure 5.4).

The scores for the European Excellence Award are broken down as follows: leadership accounts for a potential 10 per cent of the overall points, people (8 per cent), policy and strategy (8 per cent), partnerships and resources (9 per cent), processes (14 per cent), people results (9 per cent), customer results (20 per cent), society results (6 per cent), and key performance results (15 per cent). The potential overall score is 1000 points, and an organization is rated excellent at over 700.

A version of the PDCA principle is central to how the assessors evaluate practices: that is, they expect processes to be planned, implemented effectively, subject to monitoring and review, and show evidence of effective follow-up, including where it is necessary to make modifications to the original plans. The model distinguishes between enablers and results, reflecting a balance between the drivers and the outputs of performance. The figure shows the direction of influence of the categories from the enablers, which produce the outputs, and innovation and learning, which are fed back to inform the enablers.

Foundation for Quality Management in 1992). The Baldrige framework for strategic planning is summarized in Chapter 1. These were originally established as regional quality awards, but the term 'excellence' is now used to signify their role for benchmarking best practice, rather than just quality management. There

FIGURE 5.4 The European Excellence Model[54]

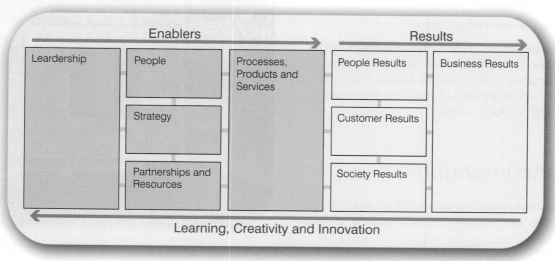

Organizations typically apply for the awards to improve their organizational cohesiveness; for example,

The company I work for was awarded a Recognized for Excellence in Europe award in 2005. We adopted EFQM and pursued the award for strategic reasons (differentiation from competitors in a contract tender). I would suggest that even without the focus being one of improving our end-to-end quality, there was a recognized benefit from the senior managers who were involved ... The perceived benefit in helping breakdown silos was sufficient that all the managers involved requested that we continue to work within the EFQM framework and aim for further awards (Phil Francis, Project Manager, Capita Insurance Services).[55]

These models do not assess the content of an organization's actions, such as whether a purpose statement and a strategy are appropriate, but that certain processes should be in place and it must be proved that they are used. To win high marks for the 'policy and strategy' category, the European Excellence Model requires that an organization needs to show that policy and strategy are:

1 based on the present and future needs, and the expectations of stakeholders;

2 based on information from performance measurement, research, learning and creativity related activities;

3 developed, reviewed, and updated;

4 deployed through a framework of key processes;

5 communicated and implemented.

The criteria used in performance excellent models have been incorporated as an international standard for managing organizations (ISO 2004).[56] Such standards help organizations benchmark themselves for best and desired practice.

Benchmarking

Benchmarking is a comparison of an organization's practices with those of other organizations, in order to identify ideas for improvement and the adoption of useful practices, and sometimes to compare relative standards of performance. There are two main types. The first is competitive benchmarking, where the benchmarks are normally expressed as measured reference goals for aggregate performance, such as the output of a production line. The other is process benchmarking, where teams may visit another organization, often in an unrelated industry, to study analogous business processes.

Process benchmarking was used extensively early on at Xerox to learn from other organizations, and it was linked to the company's business excellence model.[57] For instance, it used a study of the London ambulance service to improve its emergency call-out service for its engineers to visit customers. More recently, however, benchmarking has been scaled down and is used mainly as an internal activity to compare practices across Xerox's business units. Its internalization results from two difficulties: the problem of obtaining access to other organizations, and the cost and time it has involved.

Benchmarking is useful for smaller projects, but as an approach for understanding organization-wide systems, it has problems. Part of the problem is that managers not only do not understand the

other organization as a whole system, they also do not always understand their own in these terms. All generic frameworks are likely to need modification for individual applications and specific contexts. It is not a case of copying practice *per se*, but rather that benchmarking can be a useful catalyst for ideas and change.

From the resource-based view of strategy, the replication of best practice may be illusive, since the managerial practices that are most central to competitive advantage are likely to be specific to an individual organization, and which are irrelevant to another organization's strategic management. Michael Porter agrees but for a different reason; he thinks that capabilities can be copied, and so cannot be sources of lasting competitive advantage, only operational effectiveness:

> The more benchmarking companies do, the more they look alike. If every company offers more or less the same mix of value, customers are forced to choose on price. This inevitably undermines price levels – and devastates profitability. At the same time, competitive convergence leads to duplicate investments and a strong tendency to overcapacity.[58]

On the other hand, former GE chief executive, Jack Welch, thinks this is wrong:

> I've heard it said that best practices aren't a sustainable competitive advantage because they are so easy to copy. That's nonsense. It is true that once a best practice is out there, everybody can imitate it, but companies that win do two things: they imitate and improve ... imitating is hard enough ... But to make your strategy succeed, you need to fix that mindset – and go a lot further ... about finding best practices, adapting them, and continually improving them. When you do that right, it's nothing short of innovation. New product and service ideas, new processes, and opportunities for growth start to pop up everywhere and actually become the norm. Along with getting the right people in place, best practices are all part of implementing the hell out of your big idea and to my mind, it's the most fun. It's fun because companies that make the best practices a priority are thriving, thirsting, learning organizations. They believe that everyone should always be searching for a better way. These kinds of companies are filled with energy and spirit of can-do. Don't tell me that's not a competitive advantage![59]

Indeed, emulation is the basis of me-too competing. For example in Shanghai in China, there is a restaurant called Cheers; the name is taken from a US situation comedy, with a slogan taken from the show, 'It's a place where everyone knows your name'. The business was founded by business students who had taken inspiration from a case study about Starbucks – a company that had started out as a small coffee shop in Seattle and is now expanding in China. One of the founders, Jeff Wei, said: 'We felt that there was no similar business model in the city and that if we could get it right, we'd be quite successful'.[60] Shortly, another Cheers will open, and there are plans to grow by 20–30 per cent in the next two years. Of course, the test will be when Starbucks comes to Shanghai, but by then it is unlikely that Cheers will be worried.

 I've heard it said that best practices aren't a sustainable competitive advantage because they are so easy to copy. That's nonsense. It is true that once a best practice is out there, everybody can imitate it, but companies that win do two things: they imitate and improve ...

KEY DEBATE 5.3

General Motors and the Toyota Production System

An early example of benchmarking involved a General Motors–Toyota joint venture at a car plant in California. For GM this aimed to introduce American managers to the Toyota Production System (TPS). It was largely unsuccessful, and it was only years later before GM was able to refine its own version of lean production.

Knowledge cannot be appropriately valued if it cannot be understood. Knowledge associated with the TPS was particularly difficult to understand because of its systemic and integrated nature, which leads to a second factor ... Within GM there was a belief that the 'secret' to the TPS was observable and transportable, i.e., 'if we could just get the blueprints for stamping'. However, the knowledge was not easily broken down into transportable pieces. The knowledge about TPS and lean manufacturing was deeply embedded in the Toyota context and was tied into an integrated system.

As a manager said, 'You cannot cherry pick elements of lean manufacturing: you must focus on the whole system. Once you learn how the system works you need a good understanding of the philosophy that underpins it'.

The initial learning challenges are summed up in the following statement from a GM manager:

We started with denial that there was anything to learn. Then we said Toyota is different, so it won't work at GM. Eventually we realized there was something to learn. The leaders initially said: implement lean manufacturing, but they did not understand it ... We went to Japan and saw 'kanban' [just-in-time management] and 'andon' [whereby employees are empowered to stop the production line to solve problems] but people did not understand why [these approaches] work. We did not understand that the TPS is an integrated approach and not just a random collection of ideas ... We implemented parts of the system but did not understand that it was the system that made the difference ... We did not understand that the culture and behaviour has to change before the techniques would have any impact.[61]

The TPS is a lean production system. Organizations are still learning about it and it is being applied in service as well as production environments. Lean working needs to be understood carefully by senior managers. There is the issue of dependency between all the parts of a system. These must be learned and understood, for if one part fails then the rest might not do so as well. If the system is strategic, then it must be considered a whole integrated system of principles and methodologies. Many firms compromise, especially where there are production and service variations outside of the control of the organization.

Question: Why did benchmarking not work for GM?

Organizational learning

Central to the resource-based view and the strategic management of core competences is the nature of organizational learning. Argyris and Schon[62] distinguish three different kinds of organizational learning. The first is **single loop learning**. This is when organizational members respond to and correct errors and resolve issues to maintain the present way of working. There is a single feedback loop, which connects to organizational strategies and assumptions so that they can be modified to keep performance within the range set by organizational norms. This is also called a closed system. The second kind of organizational learning is **double loop learning**. This involves a double feedback loop, which connects the detection of errors not only to strategies and assumptions, but to the questioning of the norms that define effective performance. This is an open feedback system since it looks beyond the present ways of doing things. The third is **deutero learning**. This is where an organization learns how to learn, which involves monitoring and reviewing how people learn and use ways to manage things – an essential prerequisite for organizational adaptation.

These three types of learning determine the nature of different forms of review in strategic management. Single feedback is most associated with operations, while double feedback is central to reviews of strategy, while deutero learning is important to audits of how people manage; for instance, using a dynamic capability for developing core competences, or a performance excellence model to appraise management more generally. (Strategic review and control are discussed in Chapter 10).

James March, writing from the resource-based view of strategy, makes a distinction between **exploitative learning**, which occurs within an organization's routine processes and is based on experience and existing knowledge, and **exploratory learning** that occurs as a result of new and unfamiliar information, which is obtained from outside the experiences of existing organizational routines.[63] The former is primarily about market-based opportunities in an organization's external environment, while the latter concerns resource-based opportunities within the internal environment. Exploration covers search, unfamiliar variation, risk taking, play, flexibility, discovery and innovation. Its essence is experimentation with new alternatives when the returns are uncertain, distant and often negative. Exploitation is concerned with refinement, production, efficiency, selection, implementation and execution. Its essence is the refinement and extension of existing competencies, technologies and paradigms when the returns are proximate and predictable. Expressed succinctly, exploration is the pursuit of new knowledge of things that might come to be known, while exploitation is the use and development of things already known.[64] Senior managers must be good learners; March

argues that they must exploit the known while also exploring the unknown.

Sustainable radical innovation is built up collaboratively through periods of incremental change that for longer-term success requires much time and experimentation. This is different from those radical changes brought about by business process re-engineering and other similar top-down led initiatives. These exploit opportunities in the shorter term and typically seek change that comes quickly. The learning process is likely to favour exploratory learning that is externally focused on opportunities and change in industries and markets, rather than exploitative learning that is based on the experience of existing organizational routines, competencies, and trajectories, where an emphasis is placed on continuous improvement and incremental change.[65]

Benner and Tushman[66] suggest that firms will do better to use exploratory learning if their industry environments are unstable, while the use of exploitative learning is preferable for stable conditions. The dynamism of globalization up to 2008 may have favoured explorative rather than exploitative learning. If so, and if the world economy is now back to lower growth and quieter times, global environments may now favour exploitative learning.

Nonaka and Takeuchi,[67] proponents of knowledge management, argue that learning is a spiral process of interaction between explicit knowledge, which can be articulated in formal language, and tacit knowledge, which is hard to articulate. This interaction generates organizational knowledge. It is necessary to encourage people to interact and work together to share the tacit skills they have gained from different experience and career paths. This seems to happen in Japanese organizations, and approaches such as TQM can provide a common language and management tools for handling change, problem solving and reaching agreement in planning and strategy deployment.

Using SWOT analysis for strategic decisions

To be effective, a strategy must be consistent with the need to take account of both the opportunities and

FIGURE 5.5 SWOT analysis in its role for developing a strategy

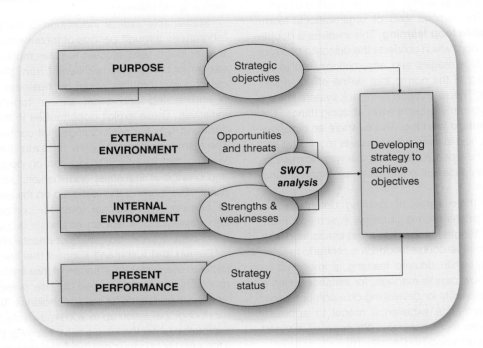

threats of the external situation, and the strengths and weaknesses of the organization's internal situation. This must be worked out in relation to purpose and the strategic objectives (see Figure 5.5).

SWOT is a mnemonic used to analyze an organization's strengths, weaknesses, opportunities, and threats. It is used to match an organization's strengths and weaknesses of its internal environment, with opportunities and threats in the external environments. The origins of SWOT go back to a similar technique that was used by Albert Humphrey, at Stanford University, to see why corporate planning failed in large American companies; although the first use of the actual acronym, SWOT, seems to be by Urick and Orr at a conference in 1964. It can be a quick and ready tool or a detailed and comprehensive organizing framework.

It is important that a SWOT starts with a desired end-state. Otherwise relative terms like 'strength in customer service' are meaningless without a context to explain what it is actually being compared with. A strategic SWOT generally involves the specification of strategic objectives and identifying the external and internal influences that are favourable and unfavourable in achieving these objectives (see Figure 5.6).

A strategic SWOT comprises the following:

- Strengths are attributes of the organization that are helpful to achieving the strategic objectives.

- Weaknesses are attributes that are unhelpful or require attention to make them helpful to achieve the strategic objectives.

- Opportunities are external influences, which are helpful for achieving the strategic objectives.

- Threats are influences that could harm, or prevent, the achievement of strategic objectives.

These are indicated on the right hand side of the figure. The opportunities and threats relate to the strategic objectives of the financial and customer perspectives of the balanced scorecard, where the outside-in influences of the external environment are important. The strengths and weaknesses relate to the strategic objectives of the internal processes and learning and growth perspectives, where the inside-out influences of the internal environment are considered.

FIGURE 5.6 Using SWOT with strategic objectives

SWOT ANALYSIS

Financial performance	Financial objectives and measures	**OPPORTUNITIES THREATS**
Environmental and competitive situation	Customer objectives and measures	*PESTEL factors* *Industry profitability and competitive forces* *Changes in industry groups* *Market life cycle*
Core capabilities	Internal process objectives and measures	**STRENGTHS WEAKNESSES**
Core competences	Learning and growth objectives and measures	*Value creation process management* *Price and quality* *People skills and values* *Location*

BALANCED SCORECARD

The SWOT analysis process is driven by four basic questions:

1 How can each strength be used and developed to advance the strategic objectives?

2 How can each weakness be improved and converted into a strength?

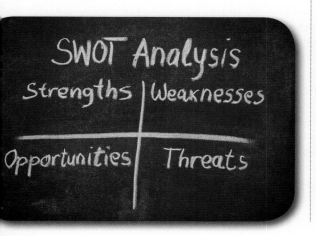

3 How is it possible to exploit and benefit from each opportunity?

4 How can each threat be addressed, and possibly converted into an opportunity?

SWOT is a simple, but a much abused, idea.[68] If it is not to become a simple list of bullet points of equally weighted factors, prioritization is necessary to determine which strengths, for example, matter more than others. In the case of strategic objectives, SWOT analysis should be centred on the critical success factors for achieving the objectives. It is therefore helpful if it is carried out alongside the use of a strategy map. This can be used to identify the primary cause-and-effect relationships and will help the participants to identify and sort out the most important SWOT factors.

In carrying out a SWOT analysis, generally the following principles should be observed:

• Be as realistic as possible.

• Distinguish where the organization is now, and where it wants to be in the future.

- Be as specific as possible to avoid ambiguity and confusion.
- Keep the SWOT short (for example, focused on a small number of CSFs) and comprehensible.
- Question several times to clarify the logic of why a factor is relevant.

The composition and number of participants are important. As a team they should be representative of the core business areas and be able to see the overall and complete picture. The ideal number for an open discussion is eight. Using a balance scorecard approach for SWOT analysis helps to bring a balance of external and internal considerations to the process. Otherwise there is a tendency to favour either exploratory or exploitative sources of information depending upon the focus and location of the SWOT team in the organization.

For example, strategy making in the periphery of an organization may be more externally oriented than the case at the centre, which could be more internally focused. So, for example, decision-making that is closer to markets may involve more exploratory learning activities, such as scanning and scenarios. Decision-making at the centre of an organization may involve more exploitative forms of learning, such as monitoring and forecasting.[68] The aim should be to strike an overall balance.

We have explained SWOT as an approach to help review or choose a strategy. Of course, a SWOT can be used for other purposes, including for strategically related decisions in any part of the organization. The important point remains, however, that the objective of the SWOT must be clear at its start, if it is to be a meaningful activity.

SUMMARY OF PRINCIPLES

1   Once the opportunities and threats of the external environment are understood, it becomes possible to strategically fit internal strengths to purpose.

2   The resource-based view capitalizes on how the internal strategic resources of the organization are managed in a particular way to sustain a competitive advantage.

3   An organization's strategy should take into account its strategic resource strengths and possibilities, in terms of those core competences and dynamic capabilities in which it is particularly effective.

4   A core competence contributes to competitive difference. It is not so much what people do that matters so much as that they should do it in a way that is unique to their organization.

5   A dynamic capability enables an organization to manage its core competences to give a competitive advantage.

6   The central principle of lean production is to manage an organization's core business processes to manage activities continuously to contribute to value.

7   In TQM, quality is defined by the customer, and the guiding principle for managing a business process is the PDCA cycle.

8   To be effective, a strategy should be consistent with the need to take account of both the opportunities and threats of the external situation, and the strengths and weaknesses of the organization's internal situation.

9   Senior managers must be good learners and they should exploit both the known while also exploring the unknown.

10 SWOT analysis must start with a desired object to make it work properly.

GUIDED FURTHER READING

Jay Barney's books and articles are expositions of strategy seen from the resource-based view, see his early paper: Barney, J. (1991), 'Firm resources and sustained competitive advantage', *Journal of Management,* 17:99–120.

Many of the RBV ideas, especially about dynamic capabilities, are still developing. The most comprehensive review of dynamic capabilities is Helfat, C. E., Finkelstein, S., Mitchell, W., Peteraf, M. A. Singh, H., Teece, D. J. and Winter, S. G. (2007), *Dynamic Capabilities: Understanding Strategic Change in Organizations,* Oxford: Blackwell Publishing.

Total quality management takes a wide variety of confusing forms. Cole gives an excellent retrospective commentary, and Witcher explains how 'quality' has been interpreted in different ways: Cole, R. E. (1998), 'Learning from the quality movement: what did and didn't happen and why?' *California Management Review,* 41:43–73; Witcher, B. J. (1995), 'The changing scale of total quality management', *Quality Management Journal,* 2:9–29.

REVIEW QUESTIONS

1   What is a strategic resource?

2   What makes a company competence a 'core competence'?

3   What is the difference between how a dynamic capability is defined by Teece *et al.* and Eisenhardt and Martin?

4   What is the meaning of 'lean' in the context of lean production?

5   Is 'please don't change anything' the correct meaning of the acronym PDCA?

6   What does 'total' mean in the context of total quality management, and who defines the level of 'quality' and why?

7   What is the purpose of benchmarking?

8   In SWOT analysis, how do we know how strong, weak, or what an opportunity or threat, is?

SEMINAR AND ASSIGNMENT QUESTIONS

1   Use a performance excellence model to evaluate an organization known to you personally. Don't forget to use PDCA!

2   Examine Michael Porter's 1996 *Harvard Business Review* paper, about real strategy and operational effectiveness. Discuss evidence and other arguments for and against his point of view. Reach a definite conclusion.

3   Make a list of different organizations and compare their unique features. Come to definite conclusions about how these differences are important to their strategic management. Discuss how they manage this difference.

CHAPTER END-NOTES

1   Fuge (2008), home page, www.fuge.co.uk.

2   Tzu (2008), www.tzu-balanceyourself.com.

3 British Broadcasting Corporation (2008), www.bbc.co.uk/chinesefoodmadeeasy/aboutching, 5 August.

4 Teece, D. C., Pisano, G. and Shuen, A. (1997), 'Dynamic capabilities and strategic Management', *Strategic Management Journal,* 18:509–533.

5 This definition of strategic resources is primarily an economics one. However in taking a managerial perspective it is useful to make a further distinction between strategic resources that are primarily strategic assets, which have to be managed; and strategic management, which is about how people manage strategically by using core competences and dynamic capabilities.

6 Wernerfelt, B. (1984), 'A resource-based view of the firm', *Strategic Management Journal,* 5:171–180; Rumelt, R. P. (1984), 'Towards a strategic theory of the firm', in Lamb, R. B. (ed.), *Competitive Strategic Management,* Englewood Cliffs, NJ: Prentice Hall; Barney, J. B. (1986), 'Strategic factor markets', *Management Science,* 32:1231–1241.

7 Nelson, R. R. and Winter, S. (1982), *An Evolutionary Theory of Economic Change,* Cambridge MA: The Belnapp Press of Harvard University Press.

8 Dosi, G. and Malerba, F. (1996), 'Organizational learning and institutional embeddedness: an introduction to the diverse evolutionary paths of modern corporations', 1–24, in Dosi, G. and Malerba, F. (eds) *Organization and Strategy in the Evolution of the Enterprise,* London: Macmillan Press.

9 Penrose, E. T. (1959), *The Theory of the Growth of the Firm,* Oxford: Basil Blackwell.

10 Popular management writers who have championed a RBV include one of the biggest best sellers, namely Hamel, G. and Prahalad, C. K. (1994), *Competing for the Future*, Boston MA: Harvard Business School Press.

11 Bryson, B. (1995) *Made in America,* London: Minerva, pp. 402–406.

12 The original Barney model was VRIN, where 'N' denotes non-substitutability (that the other three attributes do not have substitutes which rivals can apply), see Barney, J. B. (1991), 'Firm resources and sustained competitive advantage', *Journal of Management,* 17(1): 99–120. The VRIO version is found in Barney, J. B. (1997), *Gaining and Sustaining Competitive Advantage,* Harlow: Addison-Wesley Publishing Company.

13 Rumelt, R. P. (1991), 'How much does industry matter?' *Strategic Management Journal,* 12(3):167–185.

14 McGahan, R. G. and Porter, M. E. (1997), 'How much does industry matter, really?' *Strategic Management Journal,* 18, Summer Special Issue, 15–30.

15 Porter, M. E. (1985), *Competitive Advantage: Creating and Sustaining Superior Performance,* New York: Free Press.

16 Stieglitz, N. and Heine, K. (2007), 'Innovations and the role of complementarities in a strategic theory of the firm', *Strategic Management Journal,* 28:1–15.

17 Priem, R. and Butler, J. E. (2001), 'Is the resource-based view a useful perspective for strategic management research?' *Academy of Management Review,* 26(1):22–40.

18 Hoopes, D. G., Madsen, T. L. and Walker, G. (2003), 'Guest editors' introduction to the special issue: why is there a resource-based view? Toward a theory of competitive heterogeneity', *Strategic Management Journal,* 24:889–902.

19 Jarzabkowski, P. (2005), *Strategy as Practice: An Activity-Based Approach,* London: Sage.

20 Johnson, G., Melin, L. and Whittington, R. (2003), 'Micro strategy and strategizing: towards an activity-based view', Guest Editors' Introduction to a special issue, *Journal of Management Studies,* 40(1):3–22.

21 Grant, R. M. (1991), 'The resource-based theory of competitive advantage: implications for

strategy formulation', *California Management Review,* 33, Spring, 114–135.

22 Kay, J. (1993), *Foundations of Corporate Success,* Oxford: Oxford University Press.

23 Schmidt, E. (2008), video, interviewed by Gary Hamel, at the *Management Laboratory Summit,* Half Moon Bay, California, May.

24 Levis, K. (2009), *Winners & Losers: Creators & Casualties of the Age of the Internet,* London: Atlantic Books, p. 208.

25 Google (2010), Corporate Information, Our Philosophy, /www.google.com/corporate/tenthings.html.

26 Google (2010), *ibid.*

27 Levis (2009), *Winners & Losers: Creators & Casualties of the Age of the Internet,* London: Atlantic Books, p. 208

28 Dierickx, I. and Cool, K. (1989), 'Asset stock accumulation and sustainability of competitive advantage', *Management Science,* 35(12): 1504–1511; Tushman, M. and Anderson, D. (1986), 'Technological discontinuities and organizational environments', *Administrative Science Quarterly,* 31:439–465.

29 Leonard Barton, D. (1992), 'Core capabilities and core rigidities', *Strategic Management Journal,* 13:111–125.

30 Prahalad, C. A. and Hamel, G. (1990), 'The core competence of the corporation', *Harvard Business Review*, May-June, 79–91.

31 Doz, Y. (1996), 'Managing core competency for corporate renewal: towards a managerial theory of core competencies', 155–178, in Dosi, G. and Malerba, F. (Eds) *Organization and Strategy in the Evolution of the Enterprise,* London: Macmillan Press.

32 Teece , D. C., Pisano, G. and Shuen, A. (1997), 'Dynamic capabilities and strategic Management', *Strategic Management Journal, 18:509–533.*

33 Zollo, M. and Winter, S. G. (2002), 'Deliberate learning and the evolution of dynamic Capabilities', *Organizational Science,* 13:339–351, 340.

34 Teece, D. C., Pisano, G. and Shuen, A. (2000), 'Dynamic capabilities and strategic Management', 334–362, in Dosi, G., Nelson, R. R. and Winter, S. G. (eds.) *The Nature and Dynamics of Organizational Capabilities,* Oxford: Oxford University Press.

35 Eisenhardt, K. M. and Martin, J. A. (2000), 'Dynamic capabilities: what are they?' *Strategic Management Journal,* 21(10–11):1105–1121.

36 Hamel, G. and Prahalad, C. K. (1989), 'Strategic intent', *Harvard Business Review*, May-June, 63–76.

37 Kenneth and William Hopper (2009) argue that the origin of the success of the large American corporations is owed to basic cultural attributes, which were transferred to Japan by engineers on loan from AT&T during America's occupation after the world war in the 1940s. These attributes included an aptitude for the exercise of mechanical skills, a moral outlook that subordinated the interests of the individual to the group, and exceptional organizing ability. See Hopper, K. and Hopper, W. (2009), *The Puritan Gift,* London: I. B. Tauris.

38 These philosophies and methodologies are conventionally an important part of strategic operations. In strategic management they become important when they are strategically linked to the organization's purpose and strategic objectives.

39 See Monden, Y. (1998), *Toyota Production System: An Integrated Approach to Just-in-Time,* (3 edn), Norcross, Georgia: Engineering & Management Press (published in Japan, 1983, Institute of Industrial Engineers), and Womack, J. P., Jones, D. T. and Roos, D. (1990), *The Machine That Changed the World*, New York: Rawson Associates.

40 Hines, P., Silvi, R. and Bartolini, M. (2002), *Lean Profit Potential*, Cardiff: Lean Enterprise Research Centre, Cardiff Business School, Cardiff University.

41 Seddon, J. (2008), *Systems Thinking in the Public Sector: The Failure of the Reform Regime and a Manifesto for a Better Way,* London: Triarchy.

42 Toyota (2008), *Production System,* www.toyota.co.jp/en/vision/prodiuction_system/.

43 TQM has been described in very many ways and its history is a story of expanding horizons, see Witcher, B. J. (1995), 'The changing scale of total quality management', *Quality Management Journal*, 2:9–29.

44 Deming, W. E. (1986), *Out of the Crisis: Quality, Productivity and Competitive Position*, Cambridge: Cambridge University Press.

45 Nonaka, N. and Takeuchi, H. (1995), *The Knowledge-Creating Company,* Oxford: Oxford University Press.

46 Porter, M. E. (1996), 'What is strategy?' *Harvard Business Review,* November-December, 61–78.

47 Dean, J. W. Jr., and Bowen, D. E. (1994), 'Management theory and total quality: improving research and practice through theory development', *Academy of Management Review*, 19:392–418.

48 Powell, T. C. (1995), 'Total quality management as competitive advantage: a review and empirical study', *Strategic Management Journal*, 16:15–27.

49 Douglas, T. J. and Judge, Q. (2001), 'Total quality management implementation and competitive advantage: the role of structural control and exploration', *Academy of Management Review,* 44(1):158–169.

50 Argyris, C. and Schon, D. (1981), *Organizational Learning*, Reading, MA: Addison-Wesley.

51 Senge, P. (1990) (2006: revised edition), *The Fifth Discipline: The Art and Practice of the Learning Organization*, New York: Doubleday.

52 Imai, M. (1986), *Kaizen: The Key to Japan's Competitive Success*, New York: McGraw-Hill.

53 Performance excellence models are used in a wide variety of organizations. They formed the basis of the British government's 'Public Sector Excellence Programme' (Cabinet Office, 2003). Although some observers have alleged that the model has been used for controlling civil servants rather than as a framework that helps learning, in Massey, A. and Pyper, R. (2005), *Public Management and Modernisation in Britain,* Basingstoke: Palgrave. More recently the UK civil service has used capability reviews, which are similar but place a greater weight on policy delivery including the role of strategy: see Civil Service (2009), *Capability Review: Refreshing the Model of Capability,* London.

54 EFQM (European Foundation for Quality Management) (2013), *The EFQM Excellence Model,* Brussels: EFQM, www.efqm.org.

55 Francis, P. (2007), email, *Performance Management Forum*, 20 February.

56 See International Standards Office (2009), *ISO 2004: Managing for the Sustained Success of an Organization – A Quality Management Approach,* (3 edn 2009, November, ISO 9004: 2009(E), www.iso.org.

57 Camp, R. C. (1989), *Benchmarking: The Search for Industry Best Practices that lead to Superior Performance*, Milwaukee: ASQC Quality Press.

58 Porter, M. E. (1996), *op cit.,* 82.

59 Welch, J. (with Welch, S.) (2005), *Winning,* New York: Collins.

60 Ryan, F. (2010), 'One restaurant, nine MBAs,' *Financial Times,* 11 October.

61 Inkpen, A. C. (2005), 'Learning through alliances: General Motors and NUMMI', *California Management Review,* 47(4):114–136.

62 Ackoff, R. L. (1971), 'Towards a system of systems concepts', *Management Science,* 17(11):661–671. See Argyris and Schon (1981), *op cit*.

63 March, J. G. (1991), 'Exploration and exploitation in organizational learning', *Organization Science,* 2(1):71–87.

64 Dosi, G. and Malerba, F. (1996), *op cit*.

65 Fiol, C. M. and Lyles, M. A. (1985), 'Organizational learning', *Academy of Management Review,* 10(4):803–813.

66 Benner, M. J. and Tushman, M. (2003), 'Exploitation, exploration, and process management: the productivity dilemma revisited', *Academy of Management Review,* 28(2):238–256.

67 Nonaka, I. and Takeuchi, H. (1995), *The Knowledge Creating Company: How Japanese Companies Create the Dynamics of Innovation.* New York: Oxford University Press.

68 Hill, T. and Westbrook, R. (1997), 'SWOT Analysis: it's time for a product recall', *Long Range Planning,* 30(1):46–52.

69 See Regner, P. (2003), 'Strategy creation in the periphery: inductive versus deductive strategy making', *Journal of Management Studies,* 40 (1):57–82; March, J. G. (1991), 'Exploration and exploitation in organizational learning', *Organization Science,* 2(1):71–87.

CASE 5.1 Nissan's dynamic capability for managing core competences[1]

The Nissan Way

Nissan has a statement of values it calls 'The Nissan Way'. This reflects the importance to the company of its employees working in similar ways to be able to communicate and help each other. This is central to the executive team's ability to manage its competitiveness dynamically as the Nissan businesses and the environment change.

Nissan seeks to develop corporate-wide 'business methodologies and management philosophies'.

These are designed to help cross-functionality and to assist its employees to solve problems easily and quickly, to modify behaviours as necessary, and to identify and take advantage of opportunities as they arise.

Nissan defines 13 cross-functional processes as its core business areas. These are critical for maintaining the overall value-adding capability of the firm. They must be managed effectively across the organization: (1) *hoshin kanri*, (2) fundamental daily management (*nichijo kanri*), (3) production

maintenance, (4) standardization establishment, (5) productivity improvement activity, (6) inspection, (7) production control and logistics, (8) personnel and labour management, (9) cost management, (10) quality control (including just-in-time management, process control), (11) engineering capability, (12) parts localization, and (13) purchasing.

The inclusion of *hoshin kanri* is significant. It is explained in Chapter 10, but note here that it is an organization-wide methodology for the deployment and management of strategically related objectives, and is therefore important to the implementation of strategy. A *hoshin* is a strategic objective with a brief explanatory guideline about its context.

Top executive audits (TEAs)

A top executive audit is an annual examination by executive management of the organization's management of Nissan's core business processes. Its purpose is given such that:

> A top shindan audit is defined as a detailed audit performed to obtain an overview of each activity that is supporting the company's stated strategic goals and objectives. The senior executive of the company always conducts the audit, which is focused on an individual's function and proposed improvement activity.

(The word, *shindan*, translates into English as 'executive'.)

Nissan specifies seven business methodologies and management philosophies; these are: (1) daily control, (2) the determination of *hoshins* (the review of hoshin related work and set up activity), (3) the coordination of hoshin development and deployment for hoshin/business plan and control items, (4) the establishment of control items, (5) analytical and problem solving abilities, (6) check and action taken, and (7) leadership and participation by high-ranking personnel.

They constitute the core competences that everyone is expected to apply. These are used by senior managers to audit the organization's proficiency in managing the 13 business processes. There are other important competences, but these are functionally based rather than cross-functional and value-centred. During the course of the audit the seven competences are called diagnostic items.

The audit's activity examines the application of the seven competences in all of Nissan's units and determines how they are used in the 13 core processes; this is done in the light of Nissan's broader corporate purpose and medium-term plan.

Assessments are made by the executive management auditing team for each of the core business processes on a one-to-five scale of competency. This scale is similar to that used by the Philip Crosby's maturity grid – a scheme that offers five stages in the development of company-wide quality management. At Nissan the idea is expressed simply as: 'stage one, not aware'; 'stage two, aware'; 'stage three, starting'; 'stage four, getting there', and 'stage five, arrived'. This scale is used by the auditor to summarize progress on the condition of the diagnostic items found in the core business processes, and only after reaching stage four on all seven categories would Tokyo consider that an overseas company had implemented the Nissan Way philosophy successfully.

The status of competency for each of the diagnostic items is judged against a benchmarked series of standards that are specified through the engineering department at head office. These provide guides to what competency and practice should look like for each of the five stages. So, for example, taking one of the core business processes, '*hoshin kanri*', and for one of the diagnostic items, 'hoshin determination – its review and set up activity for hoshin content', the five stages that are used to evaluate the progress of a Nissan unit, are specified as follows:

- Step 1:
  – Hoshins are contained in slogans meant for everybody. Measures are not determined even though objectives exist.

- Step 2:
  – Hoshins resulting from precise definition of desired objectives.
  – Not concentrated to the vital subjects in this year.
  – Objectives and measure have been determined.
  – Measures determined without understanding present situation.

- Step: 3
  – Accurate formation of aim arrived at through distillation of the year's important points.

- Annual plan and mid-term plan (3 years) are not matched.
- Understanding is present and is related to objectives, which establish measures.
- No analysis done, but have decided measures through experience.

- Step 4:
  - Stress is made on the formulation of hoshins with solutions given for important problems, based on review.
  - Annual plan and mid-term plan are matched.
  - Set up measures by using QC method for grasping problem.
  - Procedure of hoshin determination has been laid down as rule.

- Step 5:
  - Formulation of the year's hoshins, which bear a relation to middle term plans.
  - Understood present situation, make clear contribution rate of each factor.
  - Revision of hoshins is appropriately being done.

Each business unit is notified about its competence level. So, for example, Nissan South Africa's hoshin kanri competency was judged at a level of 4.5 – a level of 'getting there'. Overall, on all of the seven diagnostic items, the policy management core business process at Nissan South Africa was judged to be 4.7, which in fact made its hoshin kanri one of the better managed of the Nissan group. All the units are given advice about how they should follow up the audit for each of the seven competences. In the Nissan South Africa case, for the 'hoshin kanri determination' competency, the advice for improvement was:

- *To clarify the main activity, to become more priority oriented and to reduce the number of control items.*
- *To clarify responsibility and accountability.*
- *To follow up the last actions at review time.*

Discussion questions

1 How does Nissan use its values statement, The Nissan Way, to manage strategic objectives?

2 What is the difference between Nissan's core business processes and its seven core competences? Why is it important for senior managers to conduct the audit?

3 If the top executive audit is a dynamic capability, how does it work to configure and reconfigure strategic resources?

Case end-notes

1 Witcher, B. J., Chau, V. S. and Harding, P. (2008), 'Dynamic capabilities: top executive audits and hoshin kanri at Nissan South Africa', *International Journal of Operations and Production Management*, 28(6), 540–561.

'ALL MEN CAN SEE THE TACTICS WHEREBY
I CONQUER, BUT WHAT NONE CAN SEE
IS THE STRATEGY OUT OF WHICH GREAT
VICTORY IS EVOLVED.'
SUN-TZU, A MILITARY STRATEGIST
OF THE FOURTH CENTURY, BCE

Strategy

Part 3 introduces three levels of strategy: for an individual business, for multi-businesses of a corporation or group, and at a global or international level.

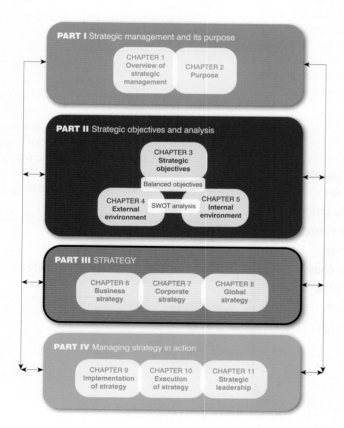

Chapter 6
BUSINESS-LEVEL STRATEGY

Business-level strategy

This chapter considers the organization as a single business operating in a single industry. The business may be operating independently, or it may be a part of a larger multi-business organization, such as a corporation (corporate strategy is discussed in Chapter 7). A **business-level strategy** is an organization's fundamental approach for enabling a single business to sustain a competitive advantage within a given industry.

Business vignette Strategies involve inter-connecting and tailoring activities ...

The main emphasis must always be on our basic range – on the part that is 'typically IKEA'. Our basic range must have its own profile. It must reflect our way of thinking by being as simple and straightforward as we are ourselves. It must be hard-wearing and easy to live with. It must reflect an easier, more natural and unconstrained way of life. It must express form, and be colourful and cheerful, with a youthful accent that appeals to the young at heart of all ages.

The concept of a low price with a meaning makes enormous demands on all our co-workers. That includes product developers, designers, buyers, office and warehouse staff, sales people and all other cost bearers who are in a position to influence our purchase process and all our other costs – in short, every single one of us! Without low costs, we can never accomplish our purpose.

The business strategy for IKEA according to its founder, Invar Kamprad (*The Testament of a Furniture Dealer*).[1]

> **Competitive advantage ... grows fundamentally out of value a firm is able to create for its buyers that exceeds the firm's cost of creating it. Value is what buyers are willing to pay, and superior value stems from offering lower prices than competitors for equivalent benefits or providing unique benefits that more than offset a higher price.**

Competitive advantage and generic strategy

Strategic management aims to provide a strong long-term competitive position that over time will benefit the organization's stakeholders more lastingly than, for example, short-term profitability. Because the external environment is subject to sudden shocks as well as continuous change, it is necessary to ensure that the organization's strategic priorities are consistent and, as far as possible, constant, so that the organization's people are clear about purpose and can adjust to change accordingly; so that customers and other stakeholders will continue to receive value.

Michael Porter writes that competitive strategy for a particular industry should grow out of an understanding of the collective strength of the five competitive forces (Chapter 4), since the ultimate aim of strategy is to cope with and, ideally, influence the forces in the organization's favour.[2] Competitive advantage:

> ... *grows fundamentally out of value a firm is able to create for its buyers that exceeds the firm's cost of creating it. Value is what buyers are willing to pay, and superior value stems from offering lower prices than competitors for equivalent benefits or providing unique benefits that more than offset a higher price.*[3]

Porter argues that there are four general types of competitive strategy based on competitive advan-

tage and competitive scope (see Figure 6.1). He refers to these as types of strategy and calls them **generic strategy**. When an organization targets the whole industry then a strategy is either a cost-leadership generic strategy or industry-wide differentiation generic strategy. When an organization targets a part of an industry, such as a market segment, then the generic strategy is either cost focus, or differentiation focus. The detail of a generic strategy will depend on the organization's needs and a given industry's circumstances. However, Porter maintains that whatever shape the strategy takes, to be effective it must conform to one of the four generic types.

FIGURE 6.1 Four generic strategies[4]

		Competitive advantage	
		Lower cost	Differentiation
	Broad target	*Cost leadership*	*Differentiation*
Competitive scope	Narrow target	*Cost focus*	*Differentiation focus*

Cost-leadership generic strategy

For an organization to have a **cost-leadership generic strategy** it is necessary for it to have lower costs per unit produced than its competitors and any potential rivals can achieve in that industry. The word 'leadership' is important, since this requires the organization to be *the* cost leader, and not just one of several organizations competing on costs. If an organization has a larger share of its industry's markets than its rivals, then it can achieve relatively greater economies of scale and scope. Economies of scale are obtained through cost savings that occur when higher volumes allow unit costs to be reduced. Economies of scope involve cost savings that are available as a result of separate products sharing the same facilities.

The advantages of scale and scope are associated with the experience curve effect, an idea introduced by the founder of the Boston Consulting Group, Bruce Henderson.[5] He argued that when the accumulated production of an organization doubles over time, unit costs when adjusted for inflation have a potential to fall by 20–30 per cent. This is not just the result of scale, but of a combined effect of learning, specialization, investment and scale. To paraphrase: the more that an organization does, the lower the cost of doing it. When cumulative volume doubles, the extra costs, including those in administration, marketing, distribution, and manufacturing, fall by a constant and predictable percentage.

The experience curve idea has encouraged organizations to try to gain a large market share quickly by investing heavily and aggressively down-pricing products and services; the high initial costs can be recovered in the longer term once the organization has become the market leader. Organizations should certainly seek to learn and improve continuously before their competitors do. However, while there is (probably) a discernable effect like an experience curve in many industries, its exact nature is difficult to understand.

The sources of cost advantage are varied, and include such things as proprietary knowledge and technology, preferential access to industry distribution channels and sources of supply, as well as effective cost management. Low-cost leaders often sell a standard or no-frills product and service. They place considerable emphasis on taking advantage of scale, but also are likely to take advantage of any other opportunities to lower costs.

A low-cost leader does not necessarily have to lower its prices below those of its rivals. It may do this to win more customers, and to reap more economies of scale, but if its costs are lower than the industry's average, then to earn above average returns all it has to do is command prices at or near the industry average. However, typically a cost leader can benefit from a market perception that its prices are attractive compared to its rivals. This is reflected in a view from UK's Asda, a supermarket subsidiary of Walmart, in an interview with Judith McKenna, its chief operating officer:

> … *our whole ethos is focused on what we can do on driving our prices down, rather than what everybody else is doing … we are number one for price for the 14th year running and we intend to keep it that way.*[6]

At the time of writing Asda was second in terms of market share, which it was continuing to increase, unlike its rivals in the recession-hit economy. Of course, price competition can be dangerous if it sparks a long price war and discounting eats into profits. Leadership is important. If an organization's market share is only 10 per cent and a rival in the industry has 50 per cent, then it is unlikely to be possible to compete effectively over the short term to increase market share.

Differentiation industry-wide generic strategy

A **differentiation industry-wide generic strategy** offers unique value for an industry's customers in a way that more than offsets the costs of differentiation to enable the organization to earn above average profits for the industry. This may involve a capacity to be able to offer product and service attributes that are offered differently, and are different from those of other participants in the industry, such as special qualities, delivery and reliability features, corporate and brand images, advanced technological, service and support arrangements, and so on.

Of course, the organization concerned will seek to reduce its costs, but only in a way that does not affect the sources of differentiation and the value it creates. The 'industry-wide' position is important, since it involves a comprehensive coverage of the whole or at the very least the major part of the industry and its markets. Unlike cost-leadership, there can be more than one successful industry-wide differentiation competitive position in an industry. This happens when there are significantly different and distinctive customer groups that value product and service attributes in contrasting ways.

An example of differentiation is the case of Canon's success at creating an industry position in relation to Xerox, which had dominated the corporate copier market by following a clear strategy with machines that offered high-speed and high-volume reproduction. The big industrial customers required a direct sales force, and Xerox machines were leased, instead of sold, to the customers. Canon decided to target small- and medium-sized organizations and produced smaller machines for individual use. These were sold through a dealer network rather than leased. Canon decided to differentiate its offer from Xerox by offering quality and price. Unlike Xerox's machines, if Canon's copiers were more reliable and less liable to have service problems, customers would have less of a need to spread their risk by renting a machine rather than buying. The copier industry now had two successful organizations each with a different strategy.

The development of an industry's markets over time tends to favour differentiation, especially if the industry is associated with consumer preferences associated with change and affluence. In general, as consumers become more affluent, they do not necessarily want lower prices, but a more intense consumer experience.[7] Rather than buying a standard smartphone, a consumer might rather buy one that costs twice as much and feels twice as nice. This is why the Apple style and brand of the iPhone continues to prevail in the industry.[8]

Even for a more commodity-type product, variety still seems to provide some spice to life. The Oscar winning film, The Hurt Locker, has a soldier newly returned from the war in Iraq who, when shopping in his local supermarket, is hopelessly confused by the wide variety of dozens of breakfast cereals. They all do a basic job of providing a similar meal but the choice on offer seems a waste in economic resources (especially in the context of the war in Iraq). In fact much of modern industry is driven by differentiation. An industry-wide differentiator has a strong competitive position if it can offer a range of products which offers above average profits for the industry.

Cost focus and differentiation focus generic strategy

A **focus generic strategy** is narrowly based on a particular part of the industry, such as a market segment or niche, where an organization can design its strategy to meet the needs of customers more closely than its competitors. A focuser does not have an overall industry competitive advantage, but it is able to achieve one in its target segment based on a low cost base, or differentiation. Both these strategies depend on the perception that a target segment is different from others in the industry.

The implication of a focus generic strategy is that more broadly targeted competitors cannot deliver a comparable value to the focuser's target customers. The competitors may be under-performing in the sense that in meeting the needs of more general customers they are unable to meet the more specialized needs of the segment, or over-performing in the sense that they are bearing a higher than necessary cost in serving the segment. Both will produce returns in that segment that are likely to compare unfavourably with those of a focused competitor. However, there is normally room for a number of focus strategies within an industry if the focusers choose different target segments.

An example of a cost focus generic strategy is H&M (Hennes & Mauritz). The Swedish company designs cheap but chic clothing for men and women aged 18 to 45, children's apparel and its own brands of cosmetics. It opened its first store for women in 1947 as Hennes (Swedish for 'hers'), and bought the men's clothing store, Mauritz Widforss. Since then it has consistently focused on its segment of the retail market and has grown to more than 1500 stores in about 25 countries.

An example of focused differentiation is McLaren Automotive, a Formula One racing car constructor. The company is capitalizing on its racing success to manufacture road cars and it is an example of an organization that specializes in things in which it does exceptionally well. In 2012, it introduced a sports car called the McLaren MP4-12C. The designation, MP4, refers to a chassis design which McLaren uses for its formula one cars and the '12' refers to a Vehicle Performance Index that it uses to rate key performance criteria for its competitors and its own cars; the 'C' refers to the use of carbon fibre composite for the car's chassis.

The industry segment of the sports car market that McLaren has targeted is the supercar. The price of the McLaren MP4-12C Spider (the soft top variant) is around £200 000. The aim is to sell a thousand cars a year initially expanding to four or five thousand over the next five years. According to Antony Sheriff, McLaren's managing director, the strategy is to compete in a number of international markets, selling to the very rich, but keeping sales to the lowest minimum in each region to sustain its exclusivity.[9] The nearest competitor in the supercar category is the Ferrari 458, and McLaren expects to secure only a fraction of this market. The new car's differentiation from possible rivals is based on exploiting racing technology, particularly its type of carbon fibre composite chassis which is unique to McLaren.

However, it is also based on perfection. In the words of Ron Dennis, executive chairman of McLaren:

It's a mindset thing ... we clean people's feet as they come in [to work at McLaren] by going down different surface finishes, and ... we try to do it with their minds as well, we try to get them into a tranquil mindset, which is consistent with what we want to achieve in our building ... we are focused on trying to be the best, and therefore you've got to have a certain mindset, a certain buy-in to the McLaren DNA.[10]

It seems that when you own a McLaren supercar, you are as close to the real thing as you can get.

Generic strategies are mutually exclusive

The important thing to note about the four generic strategies is that an organization must choose one only and not a combination of them. An organization that chooses a strategy that is part cost and part differentiation is called a **straddler**. In Porter's view an organization must avoid becoming a 'Jack of all trades and master of none': 'Being "all things to all people" is a recipe for strategic mediocrity and below-average performance, because it often means that a firm has no competitive advantage at all'.[12]

Being stuck in the middle is typically a result of an organization's unwillingness to make choices about how to compete. An organization's strategy if it is, as it should be, a fundamentally different approach for sustaining a competitive advantage, calls for managing organizational activities in ways to sustain the strategy. This gives to the organization the power to deliver value that no one else can provide.

PRINCIPLES IN PRACTICE 6.1
Strategy at Whole Foods Market

Founded as a small store in Austin, Texas, Whole Foods Market now claims to be the world's largest retailer of natural and organic foods with more than 270 stores.[11]

Whole Foods Market's strategy is focused on differentiation. Its products are 'unadulterated by artificial additives, sweeteners, colourings and preservatives', and the company aims to give an 'extraordinary customer service'.

Its employees are 'passionate about food'. They are 'well rounded human beings' who are expected to be involved in community service work, neighbourhood events and the work of non-profit organizations. In particular, the company aims to educate its customers and gain their loyalty on the basis of their knowledge about natural and organic foods, health, nutrition and the environment.

Whole Foods Market is still focused only on parts of the North American and the United Kingdom retail food industry. Its focus is based on natural produce and so its costs require the company to

charge premium prices. The extra costs take in those other unusual activities, which are carried out to an extent that is unusual, such as its community service work.

Many supermarket chains offer organic produce and participate to some extent in neighbourhood projects, but Whole Foods Market makes these central to what it does in ways that are impossible for the larger retailers. Unlike its rivals, Whole Foods Market tailors its activities to sustain a perception among its customers that whole foods are desirable for community and whole earth reasons.

Question: Is WFM's differentiation strategy an industry-wide or a focused one?

> Being 'all things to all people' is a recipe for strategic mediocrity and below-average performance, because it often means that a firm has no competitive advantage at all. Being stuck in the middle is typically a result of an organization's unwillingness to make choices about how to compete.

The value chain

A **value chain** is an organizational framework for disaggregating and showing an organization's strategically relevant activities in order to understand the behaviour of costs and the existing and potential sources of differentiation. The performance of a value chain does not depend upon how its parts act independently, but on how they interact together. According to Michael Porter an organization sustains its competitive advantage by performing these strategically important activities more cheaply or better than its competitors.[13]

Value is represented in the value chain as the amount customers are willing to pay for the organization's products and services. Porter stressed the importance of activities rather than functions (such as departments) in adding value. Value is shown in the value chain as a 'margin', which is gross revenue (the aggregated value created for customers) minus costs, or the net margin received by the producer as gross profit (see Figure 6.2). The value creating activities in the chain are depicted as primary and support activities.

Primary activities add value through the transformation of resources into products and services through the following stages:

- inbound logistics – activities bringing in inputs;
- operations – activities turning inputs into outputs;
- outbound logistics – activities getting finished products to customers;

FIGURE 6.2 The value chain[14]

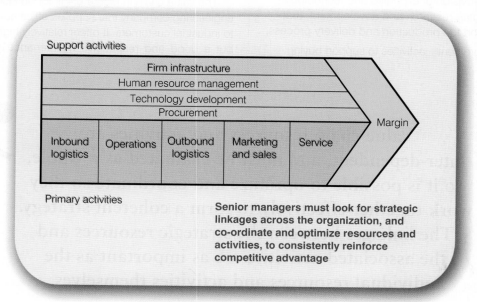

Senior managers must look for strategic linkages across the organization, and co-ordinate and optimize resources and activities, to consistently reinforce competitive advantage

- marketing and sales – activities enabling customers to buy and receive products;
- service – activities maintaining and enhancing value.

Conventionally, these are associated with the line functions of a business. However, a value chain is concerned only with those attributes and activities that are strategically relevant, and the value chain is concerned with how these interact and can be integrated as a whole system, and not in isolation from the perspective of any one functional part of the organization.

Support activities add value by facilitating and assisting the primary activities. Conventionally, support activities are typically staff functions and the responsibility of a dedicated department, although they are normally cross-functional in orientation. Figure 6.2 shows four examples (it is possible to have additional and other support activities, such as quality management):

- Firm infrastructure – activities, such as planning, legal affairs, and finance and accounting, which support the general management of the primary activities.
- Human resource management – activities that support the employment and development of people.
- Technology development – activities such as the provision of expertise and technology, including research and development, that support the production and delivery process.
- Procurement – activities to support buying.

A value chain is used to identify strategic activities and to manage them over time once a strategy is in place. Value chain activities are inter-dependent and therefore must be evaluated as a whole, so it is possible to optimize and coordinate them to work together effectively to sustain a coherent strategy. The linkages between the activities are as important as the individual activities themselves. Managing an activity in one area of the organization is likely to have effects for other areas; for example lowering costs in a department may be sub-optimal if it works to raise costs elsewhere. Coordination is necessary for linking activities to each other; for example it is necessary to coordinate delivery, service and payment activities so that they work consistently in common to enhance reputation and sustain customer value. A distinctive customer relationship management requires both optimization and coordination to control those activities that influence every part of the customer experience, rather than relying, say, on separated specialist functions, such as sales or customer orders.

The value chain illustrated in Figure 6.3 is an example for an insurance company that offers low price policies and aims to achieve economies of scale through taking a large market share. Its internal organization is formal when an emphasis is placed on efficiency. The value chain tasks are to coordinate and optimize costs across these activities to reduce the cost base continuously.

The value chain in Figure 6.4 is for an electronics engineering company that supplies office equipment to industrial customers. It offers relatively high prices but a good and responsive maintenance service.

> Value chain resources and activities are inter-dependent, and must be evaluated as a whole, so it is possible to optimize and coordinate so they work together effectively to form a coherent strategy. The linkages between the strategic resources and the associated activities are as important as the individual resources and activities themselves.

FIGURE 6.3 Cost leadership

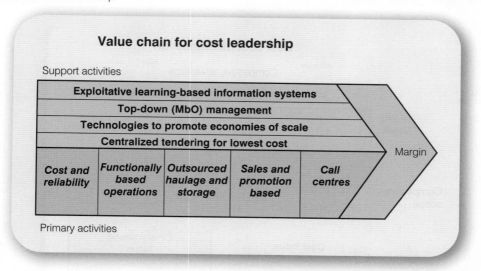

Value chain for cost leadership

FIGURE 6.4 Differentiation

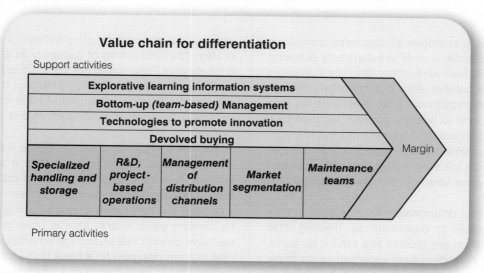

Value chain for differentiation

Its organizational culture is collegiate and informal, and there is a strong tradition of innovation. It takes a relatively large market share, which is based on providing its customer with a customized service. The value chain tasks are to coordinate and optimize the effectiveness of activities that support a customized service.

Generic strategy and the resource-based view

The rise of new Japanese competition during the last quarter of the 20th century seemed to call into question the exclusivity of choosing one

FIGURE 6.5 Hybrid generic strategy

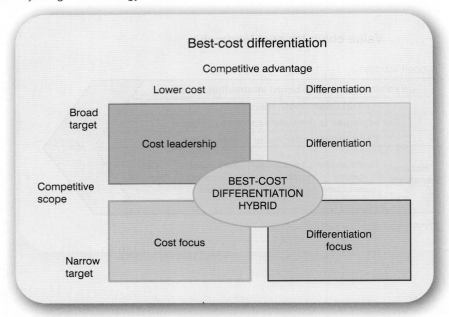

of the generic strategies as Japanese companies offered differentiation while simultaneously achieving lower costs that were better than their Western rivals could achieve. They did this largely through superior organizational capabilities, such as lean production and its associated core competences, such as those relating to business process management and customer focused organizing. The Japanese seemed to be following a **best-cost differentiation generic hybrid strategy**, or **hybrid strategy** (see Figure 6.5).

A best-cost differentiation strategy aims to offer superior value to customers by meeting their expectations on key product and service attributes, while also exceeding their expectations on price. This in effect extends beyond value for money, to a definition of quality that incorporates a perception and expectation of continuous improvement.

Examples of best-cost differentiation hybrid generic strategy are used by Western observers as examples to illustrate the resource-based view of strategy (see Chapter 5). In fact, the resource-based view has been contrasted to Porter's generic strategy. His defence was to explain Japanese strategy as operational effectiveness, not real strategy (the relationship of capability as a means to create what Porter called real competitive strategy is examined in Chapter 5). Regardless of this, it is still possible to use a value chain for the management of a best-cost differentiation hybrid generic strategy.

The value chain illustrated in Figure 6.6 is an example for an auto company. While it aims to minimize its costs through economies of scale, lean production and just-in-time management facilitate a demand pull rather than a supply push approach for creating value. *Hoshin kanri* is used to deploy top-down policies that encourage bottom-up strategies that are designed to achieve both productivity improvements and continuous improvement in customer value. In other words, the value chain tasks are to coordinate and optimize activities that continuously improve value for customers. The value chain for a best-cost differentiation hybrid generic strategy is concerned with strategic resources, including dynamic capabilities and core competences which support primary activities such as those shown in Figure 6.6.

FIGURE 6.6 Best-cost differentiation

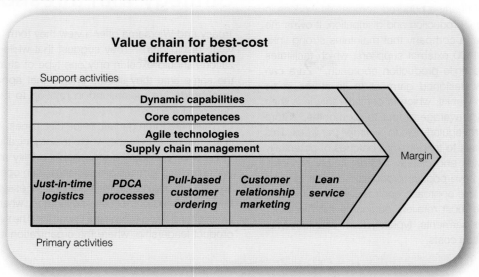

Extending the value chain into the supply chain

The value chain concept can be extended beyond the boundaries of the organization to include those strategic resource related activities positioned in distribution and the **supply chain**. This can be illustrated diagrammatically as a series of linked value chains for the relevant distributors and suppliers. The idea is that suppliers, particularly the first tier suppliers which supply products and services that are crucial to the creation of an industrial customer's creation of value, should manage their activities in ways that are consistent with the strategy of their customer. There may also be synergies between the core competences of an organization and those of its upstream suppliers, and even between its downstream distributors and customers.

The greater the possibilities for managing a sequence of processes both internal and external, then the more difficult it is for rivals to copy you. Companies such as Apple orchestrate the sequences of technologies which drive its product innovation.

This is also true for long established industries: for example, Wolfgang Eder, the chief executive of Voestalpine, Austria's largest steel-maker, feels that the key to success for many manufacturers in high cost countries is to:

> … design complexity into … production processes and have the skills to manage these operations, that give you the power to make products that no one else can make. … You can also provide opportunities for cost reductions which can be a step ahead of what other businesses can do.[15]

However, the extent to which the strategy and value chains of independent suppliers can be influenced to reinforce an organization's own strategy and value chain is often problematic. Even for some exemplar industries, such as cars, in recent years there have been high profile troubles with quality for Toyota[16] and differences in thinking in the strategic tie-up between Volkswagen and Suzuki.[17] For relatively small and specialized suppliers there is also a fear of losing their bargaining power and when they are making products tailored towards one big customer, it is difficult to spread risk by extending the customer base. For example, Samsung does not want its Korean contractors to supply parts to Apple or LG Electronics.[18]

On the other hand, Inditex is a Spanish corporation made up of nearly a hundred companies working in textile design, production and distribution. It owns the retailer Zara, a company that maintains strong links to around 1400 external suppliers, which facilitates an in-house agile production approach.[19] Zara can ship a new designed garment to its stores in as little as two weeks, which is considerably less than the industry's average of four to six months.[20] Store deliveries are regularly two to six times per week. This allows retailers to try out small batches of potentially popular styles and display a wide variety of looks. If batches prove popular production can be ramped up rapidly. This approach contrasts with the industry norm where most retailers outsource the manufacture of their garments, typically from countries with low production costs.

Strategy with thresholds

Treacy and Wiersema offer a view they term 'generic value disciplines'.[21] They suggest that while organizations should excel in only one type of strategy, at the same time they should ensure that appropriate **thresholds** are maintained in relation to the other generic strategies.

There are three generic value disciplines. The first is operational excellence, where the organization aims to excel by providing a reasonable quality at a very low price; this focuses on efficiency, lean operations, and supply chain management. This is essentially a low-cost based competitive advantage, where high-turnover and basic service are important. The second is product leadership, where the organization is strong

---

KEY DEBATE 6.1

Generic and hybrid strategy

Porter[22] argues that organizations should choose only one of the generic business strategies, and avoid using a hybrid and taking a straddler position. There is no broad empirical consensus that the pursuit of a pure generic business strategy does result in a superior performance. Stewart Thornhill and Roderick White in a study of 2351 businesses report a significant positive relationship between the purity of a strategy and performance.[23]

This is unlikely to still the critics. David Teece questions whether a static position can shield an organization from competition. He argues that an industry's structure is determined by the competing organizations themselves and he advocates that organizations should build a dynamic capability to build strategic resources.[24]

Miller and Dess suggest that if one looks beneath the surface of a generic strategy, its methods of implementation and execution are diverse: it is not so much the choice of the generic strategy that is important as is how activities complement and reinforce each other.[25] Campbell-Hunt, on the other hand, finds the opposite: it is the choice of a strategy rather than its detail that really matters.[26]

In practice many organizations seem to have hybrid or dual strategies. Loizos Heracleous and Jochen Wirtz[27] write that Singapore Airlines has dual strategies and achieves both service excellence and cost-efficiency. They argue that dualities are culturally embedded in Eastern thought: for example the concept of yin and yang in Taoist philosophy encapsulates the idea. They maintain dual strategies are embraced more easily by Asian organizations such as Banyan Tree, Haier, Samsung, and Toyota, than by Western companies.[28]

Question: If a hybrid strategy dissipates an organization's energies, is there a danger of becoming a 'Jack of all trades and master of none'?

TABLE 6.1 Generic business models for Internet businesses[29]

- Brokerage (market makers, auctions)
- Advertising (display, classified etc.)
- Infomediary (information intermediaries)
- Merchant (wholesaler/retailer)
- Manufacturer (direct sales/lease)
- Affiliate (click to partner sites)
- Community (open source and content, e.g. web public broadcasting)
- Subscription (both free and fee premium content)
- Utility (pay on-demand/metering)
- Freemium (something offered free in return for your personal details – aim of customer relationship building)
- Add-on (a paid ancillary product/service)
- Bait and hook (free main product, price for its use, refills etc.)
- Franchise (royalties for buying a model)
- Internet bubble (e.g. Twitter, work model out later when popularity is assured)

in brand marketing and innovation, and operates in dynamic markets. The focus here is on development, design, time-to-market, and relatively high margins. The third is customer intimacy, where an organization aims to excel in customer attention and service. The focus is on customer relationship marketing, where service and delivery are reliable and are relatively customized. These last two are primarily differentiation strategy.

Business models

A **business model** is a description of an organization's core business processes that describe the fundamentals for achieving the overall purpose of the organization. It is similar to Peter Drucker's theory of the business.[30] In the most basic sense, a business model is the methods of doing business by which an organization sustains itself – that is, how it generates

revenue. In other words, a business model spells out how an organization makes money.

The term has been frequently employed for organizations actively involved with Internet businesses; in particular, for describing generic business models. A generic business model is not unique to the organization using it, but it is a model used generally within an industry by organizations to create value. As such it is normally an established strategy, and not one for making a fundamental change to how an organization already works, such as a visionary strategy may do. The basic categories of business models used to generate revenue for web businesses are summarized in Table 6.1.

A related management tool is the business model canvas.[31] This is a template for developing a new or documenting an existing business model. It is primarily a chart that describes the parts of an organization that are important to it carrying out its purpose. These parts may include a value proposition, key partners, key activities, key resources, customer relationships, channels, customer segment, cost structure and revenue streams. The canvas is used to identify an organization's key activities and to show how they may **trade-off** against each other. The aim is to help senior managers align activities. It is a mixture of external and internal and the management task is to fit these together in a related way which will be the most effective for the organization.

The extent to which a business model is specific to an individual organization determines its competitiveness. Joan Magretta describes business models for Dell and Walmart. Dell based its competitive

PRINCIPLES IN PRACTICE 6.2

A strategy is creeping up on Twitter

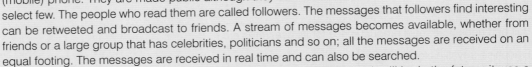

Twitter began as a service in 2006 and by 2013 had achieved 200 million active users. It is used to broadcast short messages of no more than 140 characters. These are called tweets and are typically about what people are currently doing, their moods and thoughts. They are mostly one-liners.

The tweets are posted either from a personal computer or a cell (mobile) phone. They are made public although they can be limited to a select few. The people who read them are called followers. The messages that followers find interesting can be retweeted and broadcast to friends. A stream of messages becomes available, whether from friends or a large group that has celebrities, politicians and so on; all the messages are received on an equal footing. The messages are received in real time and can also be searched.

In its first five years Twitter did not seem to have a picture of what it will be in the future; it was a strategy of 'build it, and it will come'.[32] Like many of the Internet entrepreneurial companies it was oriented towards exploration and discovery. Typically such enterprises make progress through trial and error.[33]

Biz Stone, a co-founder, has said Twitter will never charge a fee for its basic service, although it has considered charging business users for extra functions. Plans were announced in 2010 to offer businesses promoted tweets to appear in selective search results on the Twitter website, in a similar way to Google's Adwords advertising model. Twitter charges advertisers by their engagement with users through clicks, replies, retweets or follow ups, and adverts can generate social media conversations around a brand. Trending topics facilitate instant news about what's going on around the world. The company has plans to bring its promoted tweets to mobile devices. Users' photos also generate royalty-free revenue. Twitter started to earn revenues in 2010, and in the following year it was thought to be earning around £71 million, which could rise to as much as a billion by end-2013.

Many think that if it continues to develop as a mass medium, the service is likely to provide a platform for related products and advertising that existing social networking services like YouTube and Facebook have provided. The Internet barriers to entry are low so new competition is possible. For example, Sina Weibo is a hybrid of Twitter and Facebook, and it dominates microblogging in China with about 300 million users. Twitter has achieved a high usage in other countries such as Japan and Brazil, by engaging in partnerships with Google and Microsoft to design apps to develop localized versions overseas.

See what people are saying about...

Question: In an emerging industry is it better to find a strategy than to decide on one too early?

strategy on a model of working directly with customers bypassing the conventional wholesale and retail channels, to be able get new technology to customers faster. Walmart put large sized retail stores into little 'one-horse towns', which other retailers were ignoring. Both models depend upon effective centralized logistical and IT systems that can respond quickly to requests for product.[34] Magretta observes that business models should consider an organization's critical dimensions and how all the elements of a business should fit together – it should not, in other words, only consider competitive performance.

The concept is not equivalent to a strategy, even though many people use the terms interchangeably. In the strategic management literature Chesbrough and Rosenbloom argue that the function of a business model is to articulate the value proposition, select the appropriate technologies and features, identify target market segments, define the structure of the value chain, and estimate the cost structure and profit potential.[35]

George Yip makes a distinction between strategy and a business model.[36] Strategy, he suggests, should be used when it is necessary to change the underlying business model, since it relates to those dynamic activities that are used to change either a market or a competitive position, while a business model is comprised of elements that make up a static position. He asserts that most of the examples used by Porter and many other strategists describe static business models, in the sense that they are stable and their management reinforces the sustainability of the strategy. This is true as far as it goes, but an overall strategy should be relatively stable over time (Porter suggests decades), or otherwise the strategy will lack the consistency of behaviour and constancy of purpose that is necessary to build and sustain an effective strategy and competitive position in an industry over time.

Complementarities

Work by economists, Peter Milgrom and John Roberts, has been influential in emphasizing the part played by **complementarities** in strategic management. An activity is complementary when doing more of it increases the returns to doing another activity. This is a view of thinking about strategy as a complementary set of activities that reinforce each other as a complex set of inter-relationships. This goes beyond those activities that are captured by a value chain and centres on how management practices may be mutually complementary, and, as for many Japanese organizational innovations, should be adopted as such as an integrated package.[37] While this principally is about organizing, complementarity also applies to markets. For example, Intel, the manufacturer of microprocessors, has encouraged other companies to come up with novel products that open up new consumer markets and which incorporate the Intel chip.[38] In the sense that complementarities work together internally, from the perspective of the resource-based view of strategy, complementarities are managed by dynamic capabilities:

> Internal fit implies not only consistently, but reinforcing complementarities among the organizational elements as well … An important lesson of resource-based theory is the [strategic] resources and capabilities come in bundles … How these bundles form, how they change, and how they are managed by means of various integration and coordination processes … dynamic capabilities brings to the fore.[39]

The advantage behind effective complementarity is organizational synergy – when an organizational whole adds up to more than the sum of its parts. The idea that organizational practices and activities should be mutually reinforcing is basic to the reasons for having an organization in the first place.

According to Michael Porter a strategy involves a collection of activities, not a collection of organizational parts. Activities are 'narrower than traditional functions such as marketing or R&D, they are what generate cost and create value for buyers; they are the basic units of competitive advantage'.[40] A competitive advantage comes from the way activities fit and reinforce each other and typically they cut across functional units.

The tighter activities fit together, the more likely it is that the organization concerned will be able to lock out its competitors by making it difficult not only to emulate, but also to understand the nature of the competitive advantage. An interlocking array of activities makes it difficult for a rival to get any equivalent benefit from imitation unless they can match the whole system successfully.

IKEA, the Swedish home furnishings retailer, targets young furniture buyers who want style but at an affordable cost. The company tailors its activities as a whole set that is different from competitors. In the words of Henry Mintzberg, IKEA is a good example of successful strategy:

An organization that I think has a wonderfully integrated strategy is IKEA. Think about all the intricate interconnections and how that strategy has worked out piece by piece in all kinds of intricate, fascinating ways by people living every aspect of it.[41]

IKEA's value chain is based on serving customers who are satisfied with trading off service for a relatively lower cost. The generic strategy for a typical furniture store company is one that maximizes service and customization, but at a higher cost. However, IKEA does offer extra facilities targeted at young families such as in-store child care and extended hours. Anders Dahlvig, a former chief executive of IKEA, explains the organization's competitive advantage as a totality of many things:

Many competitors could try to copy ... The difficulty is when you try to create the totality of what we have. You might be able to copy our low prices, but you need our volumes and global sourcing presence. You have to be able to copy our Scandinavian design, which is not easy without a Scandinavian heritage. You have to be able to copy our distribution concept with the flat-pack. And you have to be able to copy our interior competence – the way we set out our stores and catalogues.[42]

A strategy guides managers in their activities. But it requires discipline to be true to a strategy. It is not possible to do everything, or meet every need a customer expresses, without eventually blurring the organization's distinct positioning by becoming all things to all customers – a Jack of all trades. A successful strategy is as much about not doing the wrong things that dilute effort and impact, as it is about doing those right things that focus effort and impact. A clear strategy requires understanding by everybody, and having the necessary discipline to carry it out.

Strategies require decisions that involve trade-offs between strategically incompatible activities. A trade-off occurs when doing more of one activity necessitates doing less of others. For example, a budget retailer may seek to emulate an up-market rival by extending its customer services; however, this is likely to increase pressure on costs and if it works, to increase prices may blur the perceived difference customers have of the two retailers:

Managers at lowest levels lack the perspective and the confidence to maintain a strategy. There will be constant pressures to compromise, relax trade-offs and emulate rivals. One of the leader's jobs is to teach others in the organization about strategy – and to say no. Thus strategy requires constant discipline and clear communication. Indeed, one of the most important functions of an explicit, communicated strategy is to guide employees in making choices that arise because of trade-offs in their individual activities and in day-to-day decisions.[43]

> **One of the leader's jobs is to teach others in the organization about strategy – and to say no. Strategy renders choices about what not to do as important as choices about what to do ... Thus strategy requires constant discipline and clear communication. Indeed, one of the most important functions of an explicit, communicated strategy is to guide employees in making choices that arise because of trade-offs in their individual activities and in day-to-day decisions.**

Competitive versus non-competitive strategy

The strategy literature is dominated by competitive strategy and the need for organizations to be distinctive and different in what they do and how they do it. Indeed some scholars define strategy only in these terms. Yet many organizations do not have a direct competitor and they may not wish to compete.

In a sense there is always competition in that there are alternatives in terms of other ways of doing and buying things, and there is always competition for limited resources, income and other funding. No organization sits on an island complete unto itself. Porter argues that competitive strategy is 'real strategy' and only this can give an organization sustainable above average profits.[44]

However, strategic management is about managing those critical success factors for which a strategy is needed to focus the organization where it can make the most contribution with the resources available.[45] The determination of a strategy begins with purpose. Whether an organization is in a competitive environment or not, it will still require a strategy as a framework to help managers identify and sustain those activities that sustains purpose and creates value of the organization's customers (and sometimes other stakeholders).

Question: In principle for strategic management there is no difference between competitive strategy and non-competitive strategy: do you agree?

Summary note to chapter

This chapter has been about strategy at a single business level. This may apply to a single business, or to a business division, such as a company that is part of a larger corporation. Porter's generic strategies in particular apply to a single industry or market, where a specific approach is required to position the organization against its rivals. Business strategy can be used for a large corporation as a whole, but in this case, the organization is typically operating in a single (typically international) industry. The next chapter considers the multi-business organization.

SUMMARY OF PRINCIPLES

I   There are two sources of competitive advantage: lower costs and differentiation.

2   Generic strategy is based on sources of competitive advantage and scope.

3   Organizations must choose and sustain only one of the four generic strategies: cost leadership, differentiation, cost focus, and differentiation focus.

4   With generic strategy it is possible to vary strategy providing the activities that sustain strategy keeps within the four groups.

5   The value chain is used to coordinate and optimize organizational activities so that they reinforce the chosen strategy.

6   Both an organization's business model and its strategy should be managed together as an integrated part of the strategic management process.

7   Strategy involves making trade-offs and is as much about what not to do, as it is about what to do.

GUIDED FURTHER READING

The theory of generic strategy is best covered in Michael Porter's original and seminal books, see Porter, M. E. (1980), *Competitive Strategy*, and Porter, M. E. (1985), *Competitive Advantage,* both New York, Free Press.

A business model is sometimes described as a unique dynamic capability, in particular, Makadok examples as the yield management system of American Airlines, Walmart's docking system, Dell's logistics system, and Nike's marketing capacity, see Makadok, R. (2001), 'Towards a synthesis of resource-based and dynamic capability views of rent creation' *Strategic Management Journal,* 22(5):387–402.

REVIEW QUESTIONS

1   What are the sources of competitive advantage?

2   What is meant by leadership in a cost leadership generic strategy?

3   Why are generic strategies mutually exclusive?

4   What is a hybrid strategy?

5   Why were the Japanese successful?

6   Why should a value chain differ for different generic strategies?

7   What are complementarities?

SEMINAR AND ASSIGNMENT QUESTIONS

1   Compare four organizations that use a cost-leadership, differentiation, cost focus and differentiation focus, generic strategies. Consider in each case how each organization holds its competitive position in its industry in relation to its main competitor.

2   Sketch out value chains for the organizations you used in (1) above.

3   Sketch out the linkages between the important activities at your college, or university, that sustain your institution's overall strategy.

CHAPTER END-NOTES

1   Kamprad, I. (2007), *The Testament of a Furniture Dealer: A Little IKEA Dictionary,* Inter IKEA Systems B. V.

2   Porter, M. E. (1985), 'Competitive strategy: the core concepts', Chapter 1 in *Competitive Advantage: Creating and Sustaining Superior Performance,* New York: Free Press.

3   Porter, M. E. (1985), 'Competitive strategy: the core concepts', see p. 3 In *Competitive Advantage: Creating and Sustaining Superior Performance,* New York: Free Press.

4 Adapted from Porter, M. E. (1985), *Competitive strategy: the core concepts*, see p. 12 In *Competitive Advantage: Creating and Sustaining Superior Performance,* New York: Free Press.

5 Henderson, B. D. (1974), 'The experience curve reviewed, II. History', *Perspectives,* The Boston Consulting Group, and 'The experience curve reviewed, III: Why does it work?' *Perspectives,* The Boston Consulting Group, www.bcg.com.

6 De Vita, E. (2012), 'Judith McKenna', *Management Today,* April, p. 30.

7 For an entertaining elaboration of this view see Davis, E. (2011), *Made in Britain: How the Nation Earns its Living,* London: Little, Brown.

8 In 2012 Samsung overtook Apple for world sales of smart phones. Even so, Apple continues to struggle to meet the demand for its most recent model and for the time being its competitive position as an industry-wide differentiator appears secure.

9 Bloomberg (2012), video interview, 21 October, www.bloomberg.com.

10 Davis, E. (2011), Made in Britain: *How the Nation Earns its Living*, London: Little, Brown. pp. 118–119.

11 Whole Foods Market (2008), *Welcome to Whole Foods Market*, www.wholefoodsmarket.com.

12 Porter, M. E. (1985), 'Competitive strategy: the core concepts', see p. 12 In *Competitive Advantage: Creating and Sustaining Superior Performance*, New York: Free Press.

13 Porter developed the concept from the McKinsey & Company's business systems model of the firm as a series of functions, which must then be analyzed to understand how each is performed relative to those of rivals. This addressed broad functions rather than activities; it did not distinguish among types of activities nor show how they may be related. See Porter, M. E. (1985), 'Competitive strategy: the core concepts', see p. 36 In *Competitive Advantage: Creating and Sustaining Superior Performance,* New York: Free Press.

14 Adapted from Porter, M. E. (1985), 'Competitive strategy: the core concepts', see Figure 2.2 In *Competitive Advantage: Creating and Sustaining Superior Performance,* New York: Free Press.

15 Marsh, P. (2011), 'Closed encounters with suppliers', *Financial Times,* 7 July, p. 14.

16 See Kang, M. (2010). 'Risks of global production systems: lessons from Toyota's mass recalls', *SERI Quarterly,* July, 65–71; Reed, J. (2012), 'Toyota learnt of door fault four years ago', *Financial Times,* 12 October, p. 23.

17 Soble, J. (2011), 'Suzuki demands divorce from VW', *Financial Times,* 13 September.

18 Mundy, S. and Jung-a, S. (2012), 'Samsung's might creates unease in S Korea', *Financial Times,* 15 November, p. 21.

19 A distinction is sometimes made between 'lean' and 'agile', which means the firm and the supply chain can respond rapidly to unpredictable changes in demand, unlike lean, which may have no surplus capacity. Lean is then more appropriate to high volume, low variety and predictable environments, while agility is necessary when the demand for variety is wide and the environment unpredictable.

20 Reeves, M., Love, C. and Tillmanns, P. (2012), 'Your strategy needs a strategy', *Harvard Business Review*, September. See also Inditex (2012), *Global Growth Opportunities,* www.inditex.com/en/downloads/pres-grupo-12.pdf.

21 Treacy, M. and Wiersema, F. (1995), *The Discipline of Market Leaders: Choose Your Customers, Narrow Your Focus, Dominate Your Market,* Reading, MA: Addison-Wesley.

22 Porter, M. E. (1985), *Competitive Advantage: Creating and Sustaining Superior Performance,* New York: Free Press.

23 Thornhill, S. and White, R. E. (2007), 'Strategic purity: a multi-industry evaluation of pure vs. hybrid business strategies', *Strategic Management Journal,* 28:553–561.

24 Teece, D. C. (2007), 'Explicating dynamic capabilities: the nature and microfoundations of

(sustainable) enterprise performance', *Strategic Management Journal,* 28:1319–1350.

25 Miller, A. and Dess, G. (1993), 'Assessing Porter's 1980 model in terms of its generalisability, accuracy and simplicity', *Journal of Management Studies,* 30(4):553–585.

26 Campbell-Hunt, C. (2000), 'What have we learned about generic competitive strategy? A meta-analysis', *Strategic Management Journal,* 21:127–154.

27 Heracleous, L. and Wirtz, J. (2010), 'Singapore Airlines Balancing Act', *Harvard Business Review,* July-August, 145–149.

28 Porter argues that Japanese firms do not have real strategy, but operational effectiveness: see Porter, M. E. (1996), 'What is strategy', *Harvard Business Review,* November-December, 61–78.

29 For more detail on the first nine listed models, see Rappa, M. (2010), 'Business models on the web', *Managing the Digital Enterprise,* http://digitalenterprise.org.

30 Peter Drucker's earlier theory takes into account the basic assumptions for managing a business: see Drucker, P. F. (1997), *Managing in a Time of Great Change,* Oxford: Butterworth-Heinemann.

31 The canvas has its origins in Osterwalder, A. (2004), *The Business Model Ontology – A Proposition in a Design Science Approach,* doctoral thesis, University of Lausanne.

32 Waters, R. (2009), 'Sweet to tweet', *Financial Times,* 27 February, 10.

33 Levis, K. (2009), *Winners & Losers: Creators & Casualties of the Age of the Internet,* London: Atlantic Books.

34 Magretta, J. (2002), 'Why business models matter', *Harvard Business Review,* May, 86–92. Both the Dell and Walmart models are a form of customer-pull based on a kind of JIT management. An essential component for effective JIT is lean working; this requires the identification of the core processes that contribute to adding value for the customer; this is similar to the business model canvas approach.

35 See Chesbrough, H. and Rosenbloom, R. S. (2002), 'The role of the business model in capturing value from innovation: evidence from Xerox Corporation's technology', *Industrial and Corporate Change,* 11(3):529–555.

36 Yip, G. S. (2004), 'Using strategy to change your business model', *Business Strategy Review,* 15(2):17–24.

37 Milgrom, P. and Roberts, J. (1995), 'Complementarities and fit: strategy and organizational change in manufacturing', *Journal of Accounting and Economics*, 19(2/3): 179–208. Milgrom and Roberts illustrate how practices combine and reinforce each other in Japanese practices: see Milgrom, P. and Roberts, J. (1994), 'Complementarities and Systems: Understanding Japanese Economic Organization, *Estudios Economicos,* 9(1):3–42.

38 Gawer, A. and Henderson, R. (2007), 'Platform owner entry and innovation in complementary markets: evidence from Intel', *Journal of Economics & Management Strategy,* 16 (1):1–34.

39 Helfat, C. E., Finkelstein, S., Mitchell, W., Peteraf, M. A., Singh, H., Teece, D. J. and Winter, S. G. (2007), *Dynamic Capabilities: Understanding Strategic Change in Organizations,* Oxford: Blackwell Publishing.

40 Porter, M. E. (2004), *Competitive Advantage,* (export edit.) London: Free Press, p. xv.

41 de Holan, P. M. (2004), 'Management as life's essence: 30 years of the Nature of Managerial Work', an interview with Henry Mintzberg, *Strategic Organization,* 2(2):205–212, p. 208.

42 Brown-Humes, C. (2003), 'An empire built on a flat-pack', an interview with A. Dahlvig, A., *Financial Times,* 24 November, 12.

43 Porter, M. E., Takeuchi, H. and Sakakibara, M. (2000), *Can Japan Compete?* London: Macmillan, p. 77.

44 Porter, M. E. (1996), op cit.

45 Rumelt, R. (2012), *Good Strategy, Bad Strategy* (paperback edition), London: Profile Books.

CASE 6.1 Ryanair's strategy

Ryanair is an Irish-owned and European based short-haul airline. Growth of the company has been spectacular. It was founded by Tony Ryan in 1985 and by 2008 it was carrying around 40 million passengers, which by 2013 had grown to about 85 million. During its early years Ryanair was unable to turn rapidly rising passenger numbers into profits, and the company's founder, Tony Ryan, brought in his personal assistant, Michael O'Leary, an accountant, to investigate the airline's problems. It took O'Leary about two years to work out where the money was going, and at one point, he was pessimistic enough to suggest to Ryan that the company should be sold.

Two things stand out about O'Leary's strategic management: first, a cost-based strategy that is used as a discipline to focus everybody (including customers) on Ryanair's competitive advantage, and second, a set of business activities that sustains the strategy.

Michael O'Leary, CEO of Ryanair, posing in front of a budget passenger aircraft

We have the lowest cost base of any airline in Europe. Business is simple. You buy it for this, you sell it for that, and the bit in the middle is ultimately your profit or loss. We have low-cost aircraft, low-cost airport deals, we don't provide frills, we pay travel agents less, our people are well paid but work hard and we deal in efficiencies ... nobody else has our discipline.[1]

Strategy is about focus and discipline; O'Leary notes it is not about saving paper clips but about instilling discipline: 'It's the decision that one guy down in operations can make on one Friday evening on leasing in an aircraft that can cost you £10 000 or £20 000 at a stroke. It's those decisions that we have to clarify and clear up in people's minds'.[2]

If Ryanair could have lower costs than anyone else, it could also have lower prices. And if prices were low enough, it could fill seats on almost any route ... [which] led Mr O'Leary to three further conclusions. The first was to increase capacity relentlessly, even during downturns in a notoriously cyclical industry. The second was that there are all manner of ways of wringing money from the business other than selling tickets. Passengers were not only captive customers for food and drink but, from Ryanair. com, they could be sold car hire, insurance, hotel bookings and airport transfers. The third was that those marginal, out-of-the-way airports would pay Ryanair to bring them passengers.[3]

If these three conclusions are considered strategic themes it is possible to illustrate how these link the key activities that sustain Ryanair's strategy by using Porter's mapping activity system (in Exhibit 6.1). The three themes are represented by the emboldened circles, and the other circles are the supporting activities. Ryanair seeks to increase its profits not only by saving costs, but also by raising ancillary revenue, achieving favourable conditions at airports, and maximizing the number of passengers. The supporting activities are listed below.

EXHIBIT 6.1 Ryanair's activity mapping system

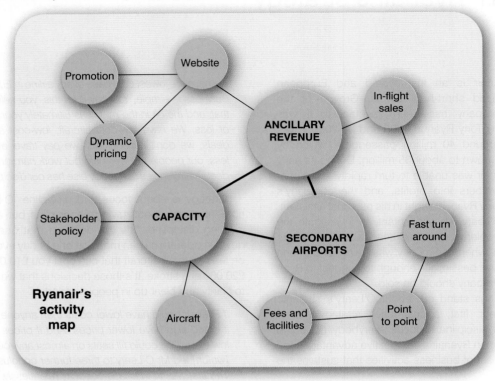

Ryanair's activity map

Dynamic pricing

Fares vary according to purchase dates. Around 70 per cent of passengers get low fares for early booking, but late bookings are expensive. A dynamic pricing system allows Ryanair to price up to its rivals when they raise their prices, and also offer relatively low prices when it is necessary to gain market share. This process is facilitated by the absence of travel agents and the ability of Ryanair through its website to react immediately to prevailing market conditions. There are no special programmes such as a frequent flyer programme and penalties for 'no show' passengers. However, there is no airline policy of over-booking and so there is no risk to the passenger of missing the flight.

Promotion

This is low cost promotion, with the same simple message of cheap fares. Its advertising is often controversial, involving attention-grabbing issues. The emphasis is on promotions that advertize special deals, discounts via the web, and email advertizements. Ryanair has an uncompromising corporate image – cheap, but no concessions. Ryanair has a history of bad publicity, such as booking problems, charging for wheelchairs, and uncompensated damage to baggage. Many of these incidents are trivial cost concerns, but they reinforce the company's image that Ryanair is cheap, and offers no concessions. The company's aggression also makes it seem a formidable competitor and negotiator. O'Leary likes to project himself as the underdog scrapping for a fair chance to take on the big guys. That sense of smallness, of being an entrepreneurial company in a world of state-owned or recently privatized behemoths, is critical to the company's culture.

Website

No travel agents are used to sell tickets and there are no Ryanair retail ticket outlets. Passengers have to book their flights through the company's website. This saves on the costs of using travel agents and gives Ryanair an immediate flexibility to adjust prices as needed. In September 2007, the airline ended its online booking fee (although there is a significant credit card charge), and introduced extra charges for passengers choosing to use the check-in facilities at the airport (travellers with limited mobility, or who are visually impaired, families with infants, and groups of more than nine, must check-in). Passengers are encouraged to check flights and print boarding passes from the website. The website is also used to raise ancillary revenue, such as hotel accommodation, car hire, and insurance.

In-flight sales

Ryanair does not offer in-flight free services such as free sweets, newspapers, food and beverages. This, and the sale of on-board items, such as insurance, adds to revenue. Passengers have to pay for in-flight services and this reduces the quantity of items and helps to simplify cleaning and speed up turnaround.

Point-to-point

Ryanair is a basic, point-to-point service and no arrangements can be made for passengers to connect to other destinations and airlines. For each additional leg of a journey passengers must collect their bags, clear customs, and check in again. For Ryanair the absence of interlining simplifies check-ins and avoids any need for interlining alliances with other airlines.

Fees and facilities

Landing fees and the costs associated with large airports are lower at secondary airports. There may also be opportunities for negotiated concessions. Ryanair believes that if it operates its routes from the cheapest airports, then passengers will follow. While the airports are typically located away from major urban destinations they offer to customers ease of access, fewer delays to flights and relatively low costs from congestion. To Ryanair this creates

opportunities for deals with bus and hire-car firms, and hotels.

Fast turnaround

Check-in is kept simple and there are no seat allocations. The relative lack of congestion and delay at secondary airports, and their smaller size, which enables passengers to walk directly on to their planes, helps to speed up Ryanair's aircraft turnaround time. This is typically under 25 minutes and compares very favourably with about one hour for the major airlines using large airports. O'Leary is very clear about the advantage: 'We can fly six aircraft a day where Aer Lingus or British Airways could fly four … Where they get six in the air, we fly eight. So we're 20–25% more efficient from the very start. It's so simple a four-year-old could work it out.'[4]

Aircraft

Ryanair uses one class of plane: it has over 300 Boeing 737-800s, which accommodate only the ordinary traveller (there is no business class) and which increases the number of seats per aircraft permitting a higher load factor. The single type of plane means that staff training time and maintenance costs are simplified. It is also believed that Ryanair has effectively timed and negotiated its purchases to achieve favourable discounts from Boeing.

Stakeholder policy

Ryanair has amassed large cash reserves, which it argues are necessary to pursue capacity and organic growth. The company has pursued a no-dividend policy; its shareholders have, however, benefited from the rise in the capital value of Ryanair shares, which is based on the company's growth record and promise of future revenues. There are similar incentives for Ryanair's staff, who are shareholders, and whose promotion prospects also depend upon the profitable growth of the company.

O'Leary took many of his ideas from Southwest Airlines.[5] However, there are some differences, notably Ryanair's greater use of secondary airports.

Ryanair did not adopt the Southwest model all at once. Changes were introduced slowly and opportunistically, and today's low-cost model took time to evolve and continues to change; at the time of writing, 2013, prices have been increasing significantly, although in general they still remain below those of rivals.

Some ideas were tried, but failed: for example, in-flight entertainment was announced at the end of 2004, but it was soon abandoned when it was found passengers would not pay over short flights. The Ryanair offer is not a low quality one in the sense that its service represents low customer value, but rather it offers a clear low budget and no-frills alternative to a higher price and a full flight service of a traditional carrier.

Discussion questions

1 What kind of generic strategy is O'Leary following and what would his company's value chain look like?

2 What is Ryanair doing right to make strategy distinctive from rivals like easyJet and the other budget airlines?

3 Ryanair has made four attempts to acquire Aer Lingus, an Irish competitor which also provides long-haul services, especially to the United States. O'Leary has said he would not be able to strategically manage Aer Lingus in the same way as Ryanair. What then would his strategy be for managing the two airlines?

Case end-notes

1 Ruddock, A. (2007), *Michael O'Leary: A Life in Full Flight,* Dublin: Penguin, p. 223.

2 Ruddock, A. (2007), *Michael O'Leary: A Life in Full Flight,* Dublin: Penguin, p. 75.

3 *Economist* (2007), 'Snarling all the way to the bank, review of Ruddock, A. (2007), *Michael O'Leary: A Life in Full Flight,*' 23 August.

4 Ruddock, A. (2007), *Michael O'Leary: A Life in Full Flight*, Dublin: Penguin, p. 223.

5 A mapping activity system for Southwest Airlines is given in Porter, M. E. (1996), 'What is strategy', *Harvard Business Review,* November-December, 61–78.

Chapter 7

CORPORATE-LEVEL STRATEGY

Corporate-level strategy

This chapter considers the nature of **corporate-level strategy**: that is, a corporate centre's or corporate parent's strategy for strategically managing a multi-business organization.

Business vignette
Corporations grow given the opportunities facing them, but also because of the choices corporate management gives itself ...

n the late 1980s, Microsoft had a corporate commitment to the computer software industry. There was, however, strategic uncertainty about how best to compete in that space. And so the company pursued a number of different trajectories simultaneously. MS-DOS was their bread-and-butter product for both personal and corporate computing customers. Yet Microsoft was collaborating with IBM on the OS/2 graphical interface operating system, even as it was developing its own graphical Windows systems, while exploring a version of Unix targeted at commercial markets. And on the applications front, the company was writing Excel and Word for the Apple OS.

This was not diversification designed to create a portfolio with uncorrelated fortunes and cash flows. Rather, it was a carefully constructed set of hedges, some of which could prove enormously useful to each other. Some of these strategic options, like OS/2, never ripened and were abandoned. Others, in particular the Windows OS and its complementarity with Word, Excel, and other applications, became the foundation of decades of profitability and industry dominance.

Today, Microsoft continues to build and manage a portfolio of strategic options. The Windows OS platform and Office applications suite are the company's current bread and butter, but strategic uncertainties abound. What will the next platform, or platforms, for personal computing be? Mobile

Bill Gates, co-founder and former CEO of Microsoft

devices? Game players? What about content, search, or online services? From the perspective of the corporate office, Microsoft's investments in Windows mobile, X-box, MSNBC, and MSN can be seen as strategic options that create the ability, but not the obligation, to morph the OS division in a number of very different ways, depending on how the industry evolves over the next five to seven years, arguably the long term in this industry. The result is an ability to mitigate strategic risk in ways that the divisions, and shareholders, cannot replicate.

It would appear that ... managers responsible for each of these product groupings – Windows Mobile, Xbox and MSN, for example – quite likely view the ventures they guide not as options but commitment. That is, each manager must choose how best to make the operation as successful as possible in the medium term – say, three to five years.[1]

Multi-business organizations are of a sufficient size to operate in more than one industry and several markets. A corporate centre is typically the organization's headquarters, which may manage corporate growth strategy, mergers and alliances, strategic portfolio analysis, and influence the activities of businesses in ways much like how a parent might try to influence the behaviour of children. Figure 7.1 shows a strategy hierarchy where corporate strategy is conducted centrally, and corporate businesses have their own business-level strategy which will differ according to the industry each business is in. Each business will have its own levels of departmental strategy. The corporate centre may provide value chain support activities depending upon the degree of the relatedness of the businesses.

Corporate synergy and corporate development

A concern for any organization but especially for an organization made up of multi-businesses is how to manage strategically so that the different organizational

FIGURE 7.1 Corporate business management

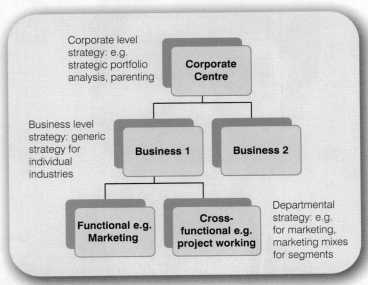

> Igor Ansoff explained corporate synergy as the
> '2+2 = 5 effect' ... the firm seeks a product-market
> posture with a combined performance that is
> greater than the sum of its parts.

parts work together effectively to achieve strategic purpose. Igor Ansoff explained this as **corporate synergy**, a '2+2 = 5 effect ... [when] the firm seeks a product-market posture with a combined performance that is greater than the sum of its parts'.[2] Many multi-business companies have businesses that could exist independently. However as Goold *et al.* (1994) put it: in a corporation, 'businesses perform better in aggregate under a parent's ownership than they would if they were independent entities, and that the parent creates a sufficient value to more than offset its cost'.[3]

Synergy is achieved by the centre's emphasis on the whole organization, while respecting the organizational parts. For a diversified organization a balance must be achieved between integration and differentiation. Some corporations encourage internal competition, while others seek cooperative approaches to integrate intra-business activities to share common technology, and core competences, for example, may be managed across the corporation as com-

mon ways of working to instil a desired corporate culture. Much depends upon how corporations grow and how they are managed as multi-business units.

Figure 7.2 outlines two broad approaches for corporate development. The first is growth strategy, based on organic growth, and inorganic growth by mergers and acquisitions (M&As); while the second is concerned with multi-business strategy involving either strategic portfolio analysis, or parenting. This chapter considers each of these in turn.

The product expansion grid

The advantage of organic over inorganic growth is that it is less risky. For instance this view is given by Tidjane Thiam, chief executive of Prudential Insurance:

> *My primary focus is on organic growth ... We know that 80 per cent of acquisitions fail and that is a very well known statistic, it's a risky business. And for us we are so busy just capturing the growth potential we have that M&A will only come in the picture if it generates profits that are over and above the very high returns we get from organic growth. We are a bit unique in that respect and if you look at us we have not done a lot of M&A and it's for that reason because we just ... you know, you look at the US and we made more profit in the first half than in the whole previous year, and that's just organic. It's an organic consolidation and we are gaining market share without having to buy or integrate anybody.*[4]

Ansoff explains there are four main directions to take in developing an organization's markets and products, which he illustrates as a product-market

FIGURE 7.2 Two broad types of strategy for corporate development

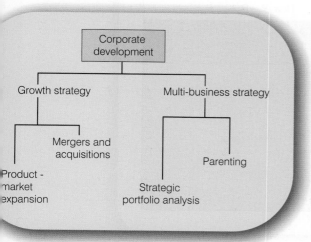

expansion grid, sometimes called the growth vector matrix (Figure 7.3). Depending upon whether products and markets are new or not, four growth strategies are possible. The four distinctive positions are formed through different combinations of current and new products (represented by P) and markets (represented by μ): market penetration, market development, product development, and diversification. The size of each of the four quartiles that make up Figure 7.3 symbolizes both the potential gain opportunities for that given option as well as the potential risk associated with it, the smallest being market penetration and the largest being diversification.

Market penetration

This involves using the existing product range to increase an organization's share of its existing markets. This is the least risky strategy of the four options. An organization, for example, should be able to understand its existing customers and be able to use existing activities to encourage them to buy more. Prospective customers, who may be currently buying a competing offer, or additional prospects that can be added through geographical extensions, for example, may also be encouraged.

Market development

This strategy introduces an organization's existing products and services into new markets. The move into new areas usually requires good research and marketing strategy to provide an initial entry, target segments, and effective organizational learning about the new market. There are likely to be potential differences between existing and new markets.

Product development

This strategy introduces new products and services into existing markets. Ideas for new products typically come from understanding the needs and behaviour of existing customers. The risk of new product failure can be minimized if innovation is piloted or developed with familiar customers.

Diversification

This strategy involves introducing new products and services into new markets. This is the riskiest option if the organization has to take time to develop new resources to understand its products and

FIGURE 7.3 The product-market growth grid[5]

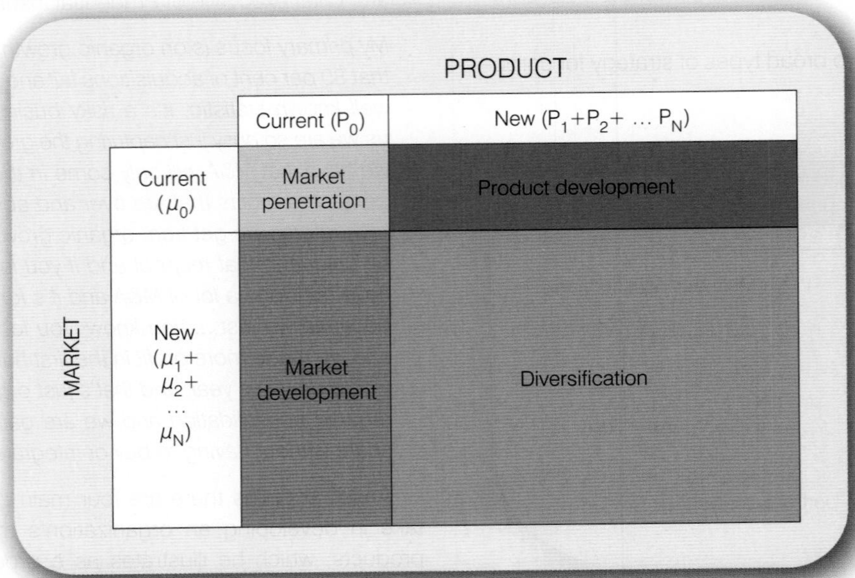

market. For large organizations that can command the backing of investors, mergers and acquisitions offer an opportunity by which to enter new markets and industries.

The American conglomerate, 3M, has built its reputation and grown through using innovation to develop new products and markets. It has four overall strategies; each of these corresponds to an Ansoff quartile (see Figure 7.4). 3M aims to continue expanding sales of its existing core products and markets. It will continue to expand its existing products into new world markets. It is also taking advantage of the opportunities offered by its research and development to develop new products. Finally, it will continue to diversify through acquisitions.

Prospectors, analyzers, defenders, and reactors

In their influential 1978 book, *Organization Strategy, Structure, and Process,* Raymond E. Miles and Charles C. Snow, argue that strategy is not based on industry and market opportunities alone, but is also influenced by how organizations decide to address three fundamental problems.[7] The first is the entrepreneurial issue of how to choose a general and target market; the second concerns an engineering issue of how to decide the most appropriate means to make and offer products and services, and the third is about the administrative issue of how to organize and manage the work. They suggest there are four distinct types of organizations: prospectors, analyzers, defenders and reactors.

Prospector organizations put an emphasis on new opportunities and choosing the right products and services, so that the organization's growth comes through the development of new markets. These organizations use a variety of technologies and are characterized by flexibility: co-ordination and facilitation are important, and the nature of planning is broad and sensitive to external changes. Prospectors are likely to be first-movers: for example, Amazon.com was the first major online bookstore. It established an early lead over later entrants, which it has continued to hold. The traditional booksellers could have been much more powerful rivals if they had become online book sellers earlier. The Amazon success has provided a foundation for moves into other markets.

FIGURE 7.4 Corporate strategy at 3M[6]

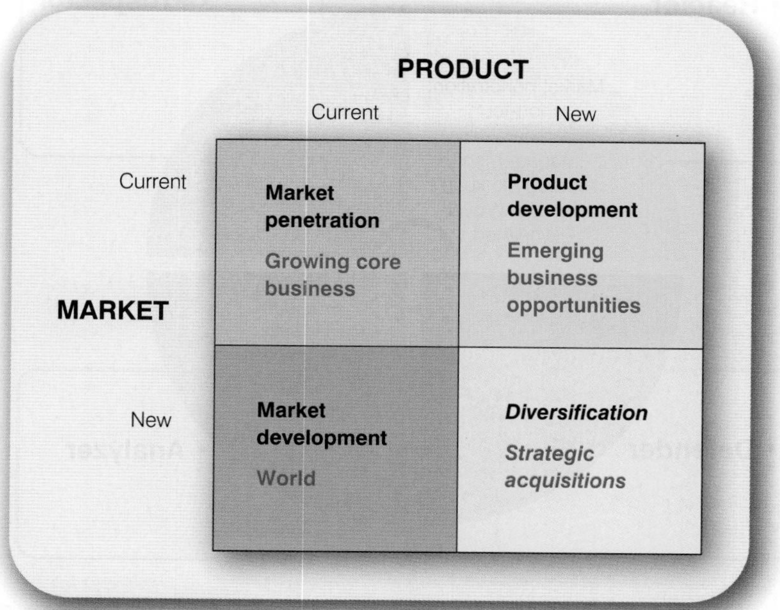

Defender organizations target a narrow market and concentrate mainly on the engineering issue of how to produce products and services to deliver value. They seek improvement in what they do, concentrating on core technologies, where control is relatively centralized and sensitive to internal conditions; such organizations are more functionally based with finance and production dominant. In China, state-owned organizations have tended to adopt defender strategies.[8]

Analyzer organizations are a combination of these two strategies. They avoid excessive risks, but hope to do well in the delivery of new products and service. These are represented by the larger companies, which cover a variety of markets and industries. In China these may be organizations that are foreign owned.[9] **Reactor organizations** respond to change in ways that are inconsistent and inappropriate; typically the reason is a mismatch in the management of the three issues. They often have little control over their external environment.

Miles and Snow argue that an organization's strategy, structure and processes, should be consistent,

although different strategies can be used by a single organization for different projects. In fact they suggest that no single strategy is best, but what determines the ultimate success of an organization is the fact of establishing and sustaining a systematic strategy that takes into account the organization's environment, technology and structure. In other words, pick a strategy and stick to it. The Miles and Snow model remains an attractive scheme for scholars who are interested in typologies or the study and interpretation of types. On the whole, research tends to confirm the general idea and the terms, prospector, analyzer, defender and reactors, have common usage in the strategy literature.

They can be used to associate an organization's propensity to adopt Ansoff type strategies. In Figure 7.5 a prospector strategy is associated with diversification, an analyzer with market development, a defender with product development, and a reactor with market penetration. The arrows denote a potential cycle of strategy movement – when an organization diversifies it moves next to an analyzer position, followed

FIGURE 7.5 Types of organizations and their strategic approach to change

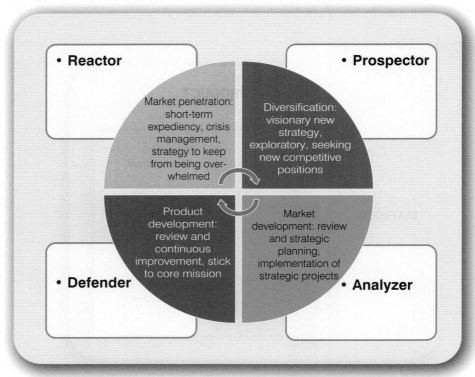

by defender and then rector positions. This change of approach will happen subtly and probably will not be noticed by the organization concerned until an exogenous change in an industry makes the organization's position obvious. Then it becomes necessary to adopt a new prospector approach to find and implement a more radical strategy to retake the initiative in the industry; this typically is a turnaround strategy and has been employed effectively by large companies such as IBM.[14]

Mergers and acquisitions

Inorganic organizational growth is brought about by adding extra size by mergers and acquisitions (**M&As**).

A **merger** is the agreement of two organizations to integrate their operations as a combined organization under a common ownership. A merger of equals is unusual, since one of the organizations is usually more dominant, and its management is likely to be favoured after merger negotiations and reorganization. An **acquisition** is when one organization buys a controlling interest in another, with the aim of creating a larger entity, or with a view to restructuring the acquired organization to re-sell at a profit. A **takeover** is made when the target organization has not sought the acquisition and if it is unwanted, it is called a hostile takeover. A friendly takeover occurs when the target's board of directors indorses the terms of the bid and recommends it as a desirable offer for the shareholders. Surveys carried out by McKinsey[15] suggest M&As are a necessity for growth, and the most common rationale cited for deals is to acquire new products, intellectual property, and capabilities. Other reasons include a need to incubate new businesses, to enter new geographies, or to acquire scale.

The direction of integration: vertical and horizontal

Vertical integration is the growth of an organization by expanding its operations downstream or forwards along the distribution chain towards the ultimate customer, or upstream or backwards along the supply chain towards the primary sources of supply. Backward vertical integration enables an organization to control some of the resources that are used as inputs in the production of its products and services. For example, Suzlon Energy, an Indian wind energy company, which started manufacturing wind turbines with just 20 people, has now grown substantially to around 13 000 people; it has started to develop manufacturing capabilities for all its critical components, which, in the words of Mr Tani, the company's founder, brings into play economies of scale, quality control, and assurance of supply.[16]

Forward vertical integration enables an organization to control the distribution centres and retailers where its products are sold. Alliance UniChem, a pharmaceutical wholesaler, acquired in 2006 the Boots Group, a United Kingdom owned pharmaceutical retailer, to form Alliance Boots. This forward move up the supply chain enables Alliance to position itself as an industry leader with expertise in distributing brands in pharmacy-led health and beauty retailing, as well as in wholesaling.

The exact forms of horizontal and vertical integration vary. An organization's control of an industry's participants in a supply chain varies, not so much according to how much of a supplier it owns, as the influence it exerts through its purchasing power. This is often a preferred strategy if the organization wants to spread its risk over several suppliers.

Horizontal integration occurs when an organization grows by taking over or merging with competitors, or organizations that offer complementary products and services, perhaps by moving into a business outside the industry. For example, in the United Kingdom, Sir Philip Green founded a new clothing retailing company, Arcadia Group, in 1997

out of the old Burton Group. Green revitalized the group by growing it horizontally to take a larger share of the clothing retail business on the high street. This has been done organically by developing existing brands, such as Dorothy Perkins and Evans, and introducing new ones, Topman and Topshop, but the group has also acquired Miss Selfridge, Wallis, and Outfit.

Over time industries become more concentrated as horizontal integration driven M&A activity narrows down the number of rivals. However, Clayton Christensen[17] of Harvard, suggests that while industries tend to be vertically integrated in the early stages of their industry's life cycle, they disintegrate into specialized segments once technology becomes more mature. Mediatek, a Taiwanese company and now the largest supplier of mobile phone chips to China, offered a design that made it possible for Chinese phone makers to get into the business by making *shanzai* or bandit phones.[18]

Effectiveness of M&As

In general, M&A activity is a fast way for an organization to increase its market power. This may be achieved through horizontal and vertical integration, especially if growth brings new knowledge, technologies, competencies and resources. It can take the acquiring organization into new markets and industries. M&As are classically associated with new and expanding industries and markets.

> M&A activity is a fast way for an organization to increase its market power. This may be achieved through horizontal and vertical integration, especially if growth brings new knowledge, technologies, competencies and resources. It can take the acquiring organization into new markets and industries. M&As are classically associated with new and expanding industries and markets.

Vodafone, the mobile phone company, used M&A as a central focus in its dash for growth during the deregulation of national telecommunication services and at a time when the expansion of the industry was spurred on by emerging new technologies. The acquisitions included taking over Airtouch in the United States for £42.7 billion, and Mannesmann in Germany for £101 billion. However, Vodafone spent relatively little cash on its global expansion, less than £15 billion; the rest was raised through shares issues. The company in 2002 was never 'deals for the sake of deals', but the strategy had aimed to capture the mobile phone sector as it was going through rapid consumer growth. It coincided with a strong general rise in shares, which gave Vodafone 'an acquisition currency'. More recently, Vodafone's chief executive, Arun Sarin, has said, he 'inherited a company that was created out of a lot of M&A. There was no operating principle to the company.' Now this period is over, he says, 'Today this feels like a good, well-run company'.[19] Does this mean that Vodafone was lucky?

Some companies in other sectors of telecommunications were not: notable failures included WorldCom and Marconi, which through a combination of bad timing, and perhaps some ill-thought out ambition, disappointed their shareholders and fell into bankruptcy.

In another, more mature industry, the Vidal Sassoon range of hair and beauty products was acquired by Procter and Gamble in 1985 as part of its purchase of Richardson-Vicks. Sales peaked ten years later and afterwards, when Vidal Sassoon had left the company, the brand declined and lost its premium position. Sassoon launched a lawsuit against Procter and Gamble for 'systematic neglect, mismanagement, sabotage and the destruction of brand'.[20] He alleged that his life's work was being destroyed by the corporation, which had starved his products of advertising, relegated them to bargain bins and planned to remove them entirely in the US and Europe.

Acquisition integration

Success requires a clear strategy before an acquisition is completed. To achieve synergy the integration process needs to be prompt and decisive once the financial transaction is over. Without a planned integration a company achieves little but financial diversification. A basic understanding of the acquired company is needed on the part of senior management and this is difficult. Some of the most successful mergers have been between companies with a previous history of partnerships such as through joint ventures or alliances.

A McKinsey study that followed the progress of 160 deals consummated in 1995 and 1996, found that only 12 per cent managed to accelerate sales growth in the three years after a merger.[21]

t can probably never be proved, but many people seem to think that most M&As fail. It is hard to know what that means since most of the large corporations have grown as much through M&A as through organic growth when growth is generated internally.

There have been many high profile costly acquisitions. UK companies such as the Royal Bank of Scotland's acquisition of part of ABN just before the global financial crisis, BP's integration of Amoco and Arco was flawed, and the price paid for Mannesmann by Vodafone was expensive, all seem to be lessons that favour caution. However, with the possible exception of RBS, these companies would not be the size they are today without M&A activity. Problems often seem to occur 'when there exists a temptation for seasoned dealmakers to do the Big One – egged on by investors who have reaped the rewards of previous deals'.[22]

Porter found in a study of corporations between 1950 and 1986 that a majority of them had divested more acquisitions than they had integrated.[23] This may simply reflect an active use of strategic portfolio analysis. The notion that acquisitions are forever is problematic. Many acquisitions involve re-structuring and the reselling of some or parts of the acquired organization which is profitable for shareholders.[24]

When a very large organization merges with another, it is difficult to tell what 'success means'. Is not the size of the majority of today's large corporations due to M&A? The Hewlett-Packard/Compaq merger was undoubtedly painful for its first few years. Today, with HP's process management and Compaq's PCs (and perhaps problems at Dell), things seem better. The truth may be that it takes years, rather than months, to achieve a high level of organizational synergy, especially in terms in organizational culture.[25]

Question: Is growing your organization a personal thing for some chief executives?

The McKinsey study noted that mergers typically create uncertainty. The top salespeople became recruitment targets for rivals, post-merger redundancies damage morale, and consumers are sensitive to signs that product or service quality is slipping. While cost cutting and rationalization boost profits and earnings for a short time, long-term progress is impossible if management is damaged or stagnates.

A McKinsey study that followed the progress of 160 deals consummated in 1995 and 1996, found that only 12 per cent managed to accelerate sales growth in the three years after a merger. The reasons were that mergers typically create uncertainty.

FIGURE 7.6 Acquisition integration approaches[26]

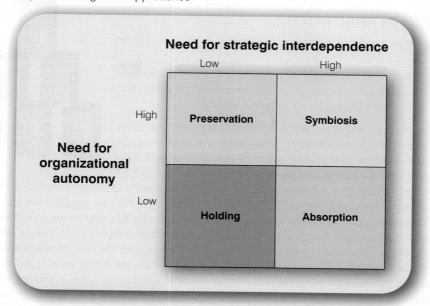

Philippe Haspeslagh and David Jemison offer a matrix for classifying integration approaches (see Figure 7.6). This is based on the need for strategic interdependence after the merger, and the need for the acquired organization to have autonomy. Strategic interdependence is conditioned by the need to create extra value from the acquisition. There are four main sources: (1) sharing resources at the operating level, (2) transfer of functional skills by moving people or sharing knowledge, (3) transfer of management to improve control and insight, (4) combined benefits created by leveraging resources, borrowing capacity, added purchasing power, and greater market power.

Managers should not damage the value of the acquired organization and a judgement is necessary about the degree of required organizational autonomy. This can be determined by asking three questions: (1) Is autonomy essential to preserve the strategic capability that was bought? (2) If so, how much autonomy should be allowed? (3) In which areas specifically is autonomy important?

Depending on whether strategic interdependence, and organizational autonomy, are low or high, the preferred acquisition approaches are:

- Absorption: the acquisition should be fully integrated into the organization.

- Preservation: the focus should be to keep the source of the acquired benefits intact.

- Symbiosis: integration should be gradual, while the existing boundary is maintained, it should be permeable.

- Holding: no intention to integrate, advantages come from financial transfers, risk sharing, and general management capability only.

In recent years some important mergers have come to grief. Two of the most prominent were the break-up of the American-German car company, DaimlerChrysler, and the troubles and changes in senior management at the American-French telecoms equipment group, Alcatel-Lucent.[28]

Jack Welch, an M&A master, emphasizes the importance of 'cultural fit', where the organizational culture of the acquisition should be compatible with that of the acquiring company (see organizational

culture, Chapter 1). It is relatively easy, he writes, to evaluate strategic fit (and possibly also strategic interdependence) since most managers have the tools to assess whether two companies complement each other in geography, products, customers, or technologies. But cultural fit is difficult because companies have unique and often very different ways of doing business.

I passed over deals on the west coast in the '90s because of my concerns about cultural fit … The booming technology companies in California had

their cultures – filled with chest thumping, bravado, and sky-high compensation. By contrast our operations in places like Cincinnati and Milwaukee were made up of hard working, down-to-earth engineers, most of whom were graduates of state universities in the Midwest. These engineers were every bit as good as the west coast talent, and they were paid less well but not outrageously. Frankly, I didn't want to pollute the healthy culture we had. Every deal affects the acquiring company's culture in some way, and you have to think about

what is going in. The acquired company's culture can blend nicely with yours. That's the best case. Sometimes, a few of the acquired company's bad behaviours creep in and pollute what you've built. That's bad enough, but in the worst case, the acquired company's culture can fight yours all the way and delay the deal's value indefinitely.[29]

Related and unrelated diversification

Diversification is when an organization is active in different types of business area. The degree of difference varies. So, for example, Citigroup is a large American company that offers many different products and services in distinct business areas, but these are related in the sense they are the financial services industry. This is an example of **related diversification** and it typically offers up a strong potential for corporate synergy through corporate parenting (see below). **Unrelated diversification** offers contrasting products and services in different markets and industries, which have little or no relation to each other. Ansoff argued that unrelated diversification has risks associated with the unfamiliar (see diversification in relation to the product-market growth grid, above). However, selling multiple products and services to different markets in different industries potentially provides security by spreading the risk of market

failure in any one industry. The most extreme form of unrelated diversification is the conglomerate.

The middle of the 20th century saw a strong growth in conglomerates when companies such as Litton Industries in the United States, and Hanson Industries in the United Kingdom, developed as corporate groups of autonomous operating companies, which seemed to offer little or no synergies. Many of these conglomerates added value for their financial stakeholders by imposing radical rationalization and aggressive management on the acquisitions; in its extreme form, this kind of M&A activity is known as asset stripping, when an acquired organization is broken up and its parts sold off.

In recent times, some important conglomerates have emerged in developing countries, where industrial groups had been encouraged by government policies that both limited foreign competition and encouraged indigenous economic development.

In India, for example, many of these are long-established family firms, such as the 140-year-old Tata group, which developed a range of diversified infrastructural-based businesses in India, and has now become an important global corporation. Many of the world's largest corporations are American and the greater proportion of these is comprised of diversified organizations.

To determine the relative strategic importance to a corporation of its diversified businesses a portfolio analysis approach is used.

A portfolio is the collection of businesses that make up a corporation, which can be figuratively represented in a way to show the relative strength/weakness of each business in relation to its attractiveness to the corporation. The aim is to decide which businesses should receive more or less investment, develop growth strategies that involve expanding and adding new businesses, and which businesses ought to be maintained, or divested.

KEY DEBATE 7.3

Is related better than unrelated diversification?

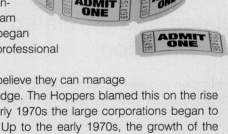

I n their book about the growth of large American corporations, from the end of the 19th century to the global financial crisis of this century, brothers Kenneth and William Hopper argue that the move into unrelated businesses began when the senior managers of the corporations became professional managers.[30]

Managers became expert and mobile in the sense they believe they can manage any sort of business, without the necessary domain knowledge. The Hoppers blamed this on the rise of the business schools in the 1950s in America. In the early 1970s the large corporations began to diversify and strategic portfolio analysis became popular. Up to the early 1970s, the growth of the large corporations had been driven by internally financed investment; after that time, external borrowing became important and a greater emphasis was placed on the shorter-term performance of the corporate businesses.

The generally favoured response given to the work of Goold et al.[31] about parenting and the rise of Japanese competition, with organizations built around related diversification, saw a swing away from unrelated diversification.

Andrew Pettigrew and others suggest that European organizations have been narrowing their 'spheres of activity', toward a dominant business and a set of related businesses.[32] Even so, conglomerates, such as General Electric, and the Virgin Group, continue to do well.

Question: Is it possible for a large company to grow without diversification?

Strategic portfolio analysis

Strategic portfolio analysis is used at a corporate level by executives and central management to appraise the performance of a portfolio of the corporate businesses. It is used primarily as a corporate framework to manage a group of corporate businesses as a single set of distinct investments. It is not meant to be a vehicle for analyzing the internal management of the businesses, although it can be used to identify problem businesses, which may then lead to corporate interventions. The two best known portfolio approaches are the Boston Consulting Group **growth–share matrix** (sometimes called the 'Boston Box'), and the **General Electric–McKinsey matrix** (sometimes known as the 'GE–McKinsey Screen').

The growth–share matrix

The growth–share matrix was introduced in 1970 by the Boston Consulting Group to group businesses by overall market growth and market share (see Figure 7.7). The principle is to rank and review the performance of its businesses in an analogous way to a portfolio of investments. A balance of businesses is maintained where each is in a different stage of competitive power and growth. The individual businesses will then each have different investment needs and these are balanced by the centre in the interests of the corporation as a whole. The matrix is similar to the industry life cycle,[33] which can be used in a similar way to fund the investment needs of the new and growing businesses (the businesses of the future), by transferring money from today's successful businesses (today's breadwinners).

The matrix is comprised of high and low relative positions of growth and market share. Market growth rate is ranged between 0 and 25 per cent, and relative market share (to competitors) is ranged between $0.2 \times$ (20%) and $2 \times$ (200%) on a logarithmic scale against the product or service's largest competitor (normally a rival). The size of the circles inside each quartile represents the extent to which a wise organization should invest in its products/services. The figure indicates a balanced portfolio of investments – that being, only a few small investments that are of low market share and growth, some medium sized investments that are of high growth but still have low market share, and greater investment in those of high growth and low/high market share. These distinctive quartiles can then be represented diagrammatically (in the bottom half of Figure 7.7) through the use of the well-known business metaphors, 'cash cows', 'stars', 'question-marks' and 'dogs'.

The stars and cash cows are businesses in industry leadership positions in expanding, and

FIGURE 7.7 The Boston Consulting Group's growth-share matrix[34]

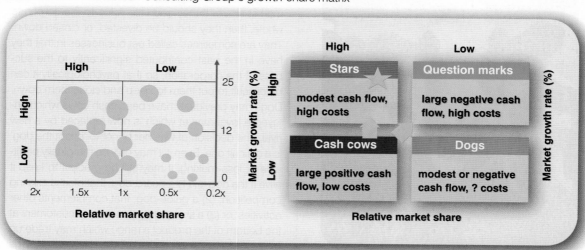

mature markets respectively. Question-marks and dogs are in weak competitive positions in uncertain, and declining, markets respectively. Cash cows provide investment funds for stars and question-mark businesses. Dogs should be divested.

Cash cows

These have a high market share in a slow growing, typically a mature, industry. They are likely to generate cash in excess of the amount needed to invest to maintain the health of the business. The excess cash can be milked off to provide investment funds for stars and question marks. Of course, the managements of cash cows may not be happy to have investment funds transferred from their business to another, especially if a local management is prevented from diversifying into new business itself. From the perspective of the corporate whole, however, the principle is that these generally slow growing, but cash rich, businesses should provide the investment necessary for the milk cows of the future.

Stars

These have a high market share and are in expanding markets. The expectation is that stars will become the cash cows of tomorrow. For the present, however, they

are likely to require more funds than they can generate if their high growth rates are to translate into sustainable leadership positions. The principle is to grow star businesses as fast as possible by removing any resource constraints; for example, growing businesses typically need to add capacity ahead of demand.

Question marks

These have a low market share, but are in fast growing markets. A question mark business is sometimes called a problem child because typically it does not generate much cash and its future is uncertain. While a question mark has the potential to become a star, it is likely they will require a lot of cash, especially when a market begins to turn upwards. This is typically the commercialization stage of innovation, when the cost of R&D and market development becomes much more expensive. Corporations are typically involved in a number of promising, but unproven, businesses, where the corporate centre is essentially watching developments. At this stage, these may be relatively inexpensive, but the principle is to be prepared to move resources into expanding businesses, but at the same time, noting that caution is necessary as well.

Dogs

These have a low market share and are located in low-growth markets. While these may break even, they may not generate enough cash to maintain their present market share. If they add little value to the corporate whole, then they should be divested, or closed down. They are sometimes called pet businesses in that they have in the past contributed significantly to the success of the corporation, so that psychologically it can be difficult to put them to sleep and close them down. Dogs may previously have been cash cows which enjoyed a loyal market which is now replaced by a new rival. The decision of whether or not to 'shoot the dog' is a difficult one. Even if it may only be marginally profitable or loss-making, it may still be prudent to keep it alive if the dog is: (1) a guard-dog, that blocks existing competition; (2) a guide-dog, that complements other activities; or (3) a sheep dog, that creates customers at the bottom of the product's range which may trade up to one of its better products later on. However, if dogs

not investing in new and alternative investments are not necessarily a consideration. The emphasis is on the internal competition for funds. However, the approach is not meant to be deterministic, and is only a framework to help guide decisions and as such it is useful for periodic reviews. The approach has been used for a long time, but its form is generally modified to suit a particular organization; a well-known example is the GE–McKinsey nine-cell matrix.

are products that had originally built up a business, managers can be sentimental and reluctant to let pet businesses die. The principle is that these businesses should be terminated as soon as conditions allow.

The General Electric–McKinsey nine-cell matrix

The strengths of the growth–share matrix

The advantage of a growth–share matrix is that it is a straightforward approach for identifying the most attractive corporate businesses into which to put cash. It helps senior managers to compare the businesses on their competitiveness. Of course, cash flow is influenced by more than simply market share and industry growth and many external considerations are ignored that could have a significant impact upon decisions. Return-on-investment and the opportunity costs of

The GE–McKinsey nine-cell matrix was developed in the 1970s by consultants McKinsey and Company for General Electric. It is sometimes called the GE–McKinsey attractiveness screen. The McKinsey framework was based on the growth–share matrix, but to include more detail: it uses a nine-cell matrix; instead of market share and market growth, it uses industry attractiveness and competitive strength (see Figure 7.8). The nine cells are grouped into three zones, and investment decisions are offered for each zone: Zone 1, investment for further growth; Zone 2, selective investment because of weakness; and Zone 3, short-term gains only or pull out.

FIGURE 7.8 The GE–McKinsey matrix[35]

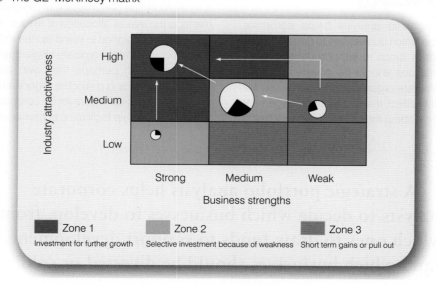

The factors that typically determine the market attractiveness of a business include variables such as market size, growth and profitability, pricing trends, the intensity of competition, the overall risk of return to the industry, entry barriers, the opportunity to differentiate products and services, variability in demand, the segmentation and distribution structure, and, lastly, the stage of technology development.

The factors that typically influence the competitive strength of a business include the strategic assets and competencies, relative brand strength, size and growth of market share, customer loyalty, relative cost structure and profit margins compared with competitors, distribution strength, capacity, ability to innovate and develop technology, quality, access to financial and other investment resources, and management strength.

The sizes of circles plotted on the matrix represent market size; the sizes of the circle segments represent the market share of the business. The arrows represent the expected direction and movement of a business in the future. The order of the stages of analysis follows through:

1 Specify the drivers of each dimension.
2 Weight each driver to prioritize their relative importance.
3 Score each business on each driver.
4 Multiply weights by scores for each business.
5 View the resulting graph and interpret what it means.
6 Perform a sensitivity analysis (adjust weights and scores accordingly).

A strategic portfolio analysis helps corporate analysts to decide which businesses to develop, from which ones to draw funds to support development, and which businesses should be divested or sold. However, if a corporate organization's businesses are unrelated and diversified, the corporate management may know very little about the nature of the work being carried out. In this case corporations are really only collections of autonomous operating companies with no apparent corporate synergies, except financial transfers. From the level of a corporate perspective, it is the overall performance of a business that matters. The advantage to corporate strategic management is to reduce the risk of business cycles by investing in a diversified portfolio of businesses. Also, a spread of different businesses offers opportunities to cover a wide range of possibilities for growth in areas that could become the profitable industries of the future. (General Electric simplified the approach when Jack Welch began his term as chief executive, although he kept to its principles: see Case 7.1.)

Strategic business unit (SBU)

When conglomerate organizations are structured into divisions that have a strong degree of strategic independence from the corporate centre, they are called **strategic business units** (SBUs). Each SBU has a general manager who is assisted by a staff that includes the functional heads working in the division; these are middle managers in the sense they report to senior executives at the corporate headquarters or centre. However, corporate executives are not directly involved with running the strategic management of the divisional businesses; instead, their role is to evaluate the performance of the divisions and to manage the overall allocation of resources.

SBUs are designed to stand alone within the corporate structure, and are typically single business-based enterprises, with perhaps their own business-level generic strategy, and distinctive organizational cultures and competencies. However, a corporate structure with SBUs can help facilitate a corporate-level portfolio

 A strategic portfolio analysis helps corporate analysts to decide which businesses to develop, from which ones to draw funds to support development, and which businesses should be divested or sold.

approach, in that individual SBUs can be added or divested without any significant knock-on effects on the other SBUs in the portfolio. The investment and divestment of SBUs have helped some diversified corporations transform themselves from one type of industry to another.

For example, since the 18th century Whitbread had been a successful brewing company in the United Kingdom with its own estate of public houses. In 2001, it sold its alcoholic beverage based businesses; the Whitbread beer brand is now managed by another company called InBev. Its present businesses include Premier Inn and Costa Coffee, as well as several more restaurant businesses, like Brewers Fayre and Beefeater. The brewing business was at best a cash cow that had started to bark. Whitbread saw the industry as unattractive. Since 2001 it has followed an active portfolio approach which saw the arrivals and departures of such businesses as David Lloyd Leisure, a chain of fitness clubs; the Marriott Hotel group, Pizza Hut, and Britvic, its soft-drink business. Over this short time Whitbread moved from a brewing, to leisure, and now a hospitality industry. It has worked a very successful corporate transformation, which continues through Whitbread's active management of its portfolio of separately managed businesses.

Downscoping and strategic restructuring

Downscoping is a divesture, demerger, spin-off, or some other means of eliminating businesses, which are unrelated or are not core to an organization's corporate strategy.[36] The aim is to refocus an organization on those activities that are central, which

is a principle described by Tom Peters and Robert Waterman as 'sticking to the knitting': organizations should concentrate on those activities that add directly to value and sustain competitive advantage.[37] It is suggested that about 40 per cent of spin-off companies from large corporations in Europe are taken over within two years, and that spin-offs may perform better than when part of a larger corporate whole.[38]

Another, more general, term for this is **strategic restructuring**, when an organization substantially changes the composition of its portfolio of businesses, or breaks the corporation up into different companies. The benefit to shareholder value can increase dramatically if the divested businesses are attractive to investors as a whole. For example, AT&T's market value was $75 billion in 1996, when it was restructured to create three independently listed companies, AT&T, Lucent Technologies, and NCR, with a combined market capitalization of $159 billion only a year later.[39]

Restructuring typically occurs as a result of a crisis, when the organization may be experiencing such a loss of resources that its viability becomes doubtful. A topical example is how some financial institutions have had to restructure their businesses away from investment banking and financial derivatives, to more traditional forms, such as private lending and clearing bank activity. Then a head office will plan a corporate turnaround, when an extraordinary (typically an internal organization-wide) effort is put underway to enable the organization to resume routine working and viability.

Diversification and core competences

The great advantage of a diversified corporation is that it spreads risk if businesses are located in different industries and markets. However, since the 1980s there has been a shift in strategic thinking away from unrelated diversification towards related diversification.[40] Prahalad and Hamel[41] argued risk is manageable if core competences are used to develop core products that can provide a foundation for products in unrelated markets. Core products are not final products, but are areas of firm-specific (and thus unique) expertise and resources that can be configured to produce a range of final products and services for different and unconnected markets.

Prahalad and Hamel define core competencies as the abilities of employees to learn how to develop and manage the integration of technologies, through their expertise in cross-functional management and collaborative working.

Canon used these competences to develop its technical competences in optics, which Prahalad and Hamel call a core product, to serve different markets as diverse as cameras, copiers, and semi-conductor equipment. This flexibility is possible because Canon's people can work effectively together in common ways. Canon's competitive advantage is an internal capability not easily seen or understood by its rivals. It is not the core products and core competences that by themselves provide the strategic capability, but it is also the company's ability, or its dynamic capability, to develop and sustain their core competence that is competitively important.[42] (See dynamic capabilities in Chapter 5.) Prahalad and Hamel likened the company to a tree, see Figure 7.9, so that its competencies

FIGURE 7.9 The diversified corporate as a tree

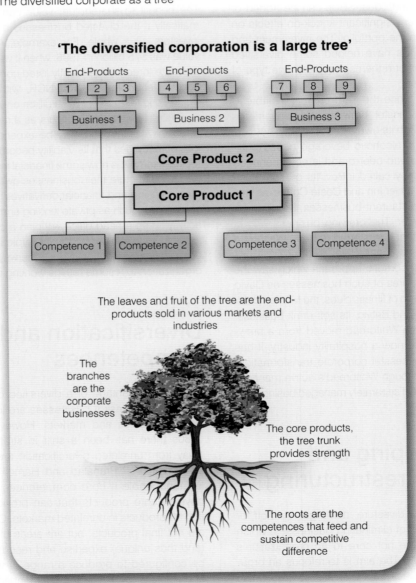

and abilities are like the company's roots, the core products the trunk of the tree, the corporate businesses in their different industries and markets are the tree's separate branches and the leaves and fruit the end-products.

Corporate parenting and related diversification

The idea of core products and competencies offers a resource-based view variation on strategic portfolio analysis and a more necessary involvement of the corporate centre in the strategy of its corporate businesses. Since the centre must understand and develop the corporation's core products it is necessary for the diversified businesses to be related. McKinsey, for example, have argued that the right portfolio strategy is to be a 'natural owner' of the corporate businesses so that the centre is able to build the synergies of the organization through operational synergies, distinctive skills, and specific strengths, such as superior access to capital and talent in emerging markets.[43]

Michael Goold, Andrew Campbell, and Marcus Alexander, contrast unrelated to related diversification strategies, and introduce the concept of **corporate parenting**.[44] They explain how a corporate centre acts like a parent to the corporate businesses by nurturing and growing them synergistically as dependent entities. Parenting aims to create a unique fit between the corporation's capabilities and the critical success factors for each of the individual businesses, so that the value

added by the corporate headquarters to the value of the individual businesses can be maximized. In other words, the corporate centre should create more value for the corporate stakeholders from the businesses it looks after than the value would otherwise be if these same businesses were functioning independently. Otherwise it pays the corporation to sell these businesses as going concerns.

Bad parenting is making bad decisions in allocating resources and setting direction. This is made worse if the centre and the corporate structure work to hinder at the business level, relations with markets, the development of emerging technologies, and flexible responses to the moves of competitors. This is serious if the centre causes delays in making decisions so that it does not respond effectively to emerging opportunities and threats. In order to counter such possibilities some corporations organize their strategy around the needs of divisions, so that the direction of strategy formation is bottom-up rather than top-down. For example, Ed Arditte, senior vice president of strategy and investor relations at Tyco International, feels that for large 'diversified companies, like Tyco, strategy is typically driven by the businesses, with appropriate input and guidance from the corporate centre. That has proved to be a better approach for us than approaching it from the centre outwards'.[45]

> **For large diversified companies, like Tyco, strategy is typically driven by the businesses, with appropriate input and guidance from the corporate centre. That has proved to be a better approach for Tyco than approaching it from the centre outwards.**

Parenting styles

Goold and Campbell offer a typology of three generic parenting styles: financial control, strategic planning, and strategic control.[46] Financial control involves the portfolio approach. This is less about parenting and more about the centre achieving a better investment performance. SBUs manage their strategy within tight financial targets set by the centre. Strategic planning emphasizes linkages, where the centre coordinates and reviews strategy. The centre continues to set tight financial, but also, strategic targets. There is some attempt to create links between the different businesses to create competitive advantage. Strategic control is based on the management of the core business. The centre drives strategy around the development of important synergies and competences and there are strong coordinating actions and linkages between the businesses.

Franchising

Franchising is a contractual relationship between a parent organization (the franchiser) and its partners (franchisees) that specifies the control, sharing, and use, of the franchiser's strategic resources. Some very large corporations have used franchising to expand their overseas markets, where a franchiser's knowledge of local conditions is uncertain and the franchise model offers less risk. Some of the best known names include McDonald's and Starbucks, but also Spain's Zara, Sweden's H&M and the United Kingdom's Mothercare.

The primary role of a franchiser is to develop these resources and capabilities and transfer them to the franchisees to compete effectively at a local level. Franchisees on their part should feed back to the franchiser knowledge about their competitiveness and how to become more effective. In other words, the franchiser works closely with franchisees to develop the whole business and strengthen the franchise's brand. The franchiser charges for the right to make use of its brand name, products, operating systems, marketing etc. The franchisee gains knowledge and skills quickly, and is able to

exploit the reputation, systems (etc.) of the larger group. For the franchiser it is a fairly economical way to grow without raising capital and the extra risk this entails. Franchisers typically own around 15 per cent of the outlets, and the others are owned by the franchisees.

The franchise model is based on a strong centrally controlled form of performance management, in terms of setting boundaries for franchisees and how local employees work and serve customers. This generally aims to impose centrally determined values to support the brand, the use of the associated logo, the necessarily core competence, or the common ways of working that people must be able to perform to provide the same standard of product and service, wherever it is made available.

Franchising is also an effective way for a senior management of a large multinational to retain control over the implementation and execution of its business model without too much structure. However, there may be an adverse trade-off in favour of centralized control, and creativity and innovation at a local level. Toni Mascolo, owner of Toni and Guy, a chain of roughly 250 hairdressing saloons in the United Kingdom, has no doubts. He says it encourages the franchisees to do things for themselves. The important things are the Toni and Guy brand, and the fact that it must be supported by hairdressing academies to teach the latest hair designs.

The easyGroup business model

The speed and easy flexibility of the Internet allows customers of the easyGroup of companies to take advantage of dynamic pricing, when prices are adjusted to match demand, with the best deals offered to advance bookers and off-peak users. easyGroup has a number of different businesses in entertainment, leisure and travel, but all of them have the following features[47]:

A clear value proposition:
The 'easy' concept brings cheap and efficient services to the mass public.

Standard resources:
Only one type of aircraft, the Boeing 737, while the easyCar car fleet has just two or three car models.

A common, pervasive technology, the Internet:
Most customers book online; creating strong brand awareness.

Simple outputs:
Offer no-frills and stripped-down services.

A common type of customer:
Most easyGroup customers are young, urban and 'hip' (or think of themselves that way), with more time than money.

Question: Is the 'easy' concept a related or an unrelated diversified corporate strategy?

SUMMARY OF PRINCIPLES

1   Synergy is achieved when the centre can effectively transfer corporate resources in ways that add value for the group as a whole.

2   Corporate-level strategy concerns the strategic management of an organization's businesses at the corporate centre.

3   An organization grows in four main ways: through market penetration, product development, market development, or diversification.

4   M&A activity is a fast way to grow an organization, but success depends upon an effective integration strategy.

5   There are broadly two kinds of diversification: related and unrelated.

6   Strategic portfolio analysis is used to manage diversified businesses, especially SBUs, to allocate investment between them.

7   A corporate centre is a parent to its businesses when it is able to add value to the businesses that is greater than the centre's cost.

GUIDED FURTHER READING

For a book about mergers and acquisitions see: Gaughan, P. (2010), *Mergers, Acquisitions and Corporate Restructurings'* 5 edn, London: Wiley. About strategic alliances, see: Child, J., Faulkner, D. and Tallman, S. B. (2005), *Cooperative Strategy: Managing Alliances, Networks and Joint Ventures,* 2 edn, Oxford University Press.

For more detailed and up-to-date materials about their approaches to strategic portfolio analysis see the websites of the Boston Consulting Group (www.bcg.com), and McKinsey (www.mckinsey. com); they offer related articles and updates on their matrices.

The ideas of corporate parenting are examined closely by Goold, Campbell and Alexander. In particular, see their parenting fit matrix, which is proposed as a means for assessing the critical success factors of an individual corporate business and for comparing these with a centre's own value creation insights: Goold, M., Campbell, A. and Alexander, M. (1994), *Corporate-Level Strategy: Creating Value in the Multibusiness Company*, New York: John Wiley & Sons.

For a review of the role of the centre in multi-business firms, Constantinos Markides has written an excellent article for the *Handbook of Strategy and Management*, see: Markides, C. (2002), 'Corporate strategy: the role of the centre', in Pettigrew, A., Thomas, H. and Whittington, R. (2002), *Handbook of Strategy and Management,* London: Sage Publications.

REVIEW QUESTIONS

1   What are the two types of corporate strategy for corporate development?

2   What is synergy?

3   What is corporate-level strategy and how is it different from business-level strategy?

4   Name with descriptions, the four parts of the Ansoff matrix.

5   What is the difference between a merger and an acquisition?

6   What is the difference between diversification and integration?

7   What is the importance of integration to a successful merger?

8   What is related and unrelated diversification?

9   What is a strategic business unit and how does it facilitate M&A?

10   What is parenting and how does it add value to corporate businesses?

SEMINAR AND ASSIGNMENT QUESTIONS

1   Strategic fit and cultural fit are different things. Discuss their implications for strategic management.

2   Conduct a strategic portfolio analysis to group different businesses that are part of a single corporation. Recommend a strategy to help the corporate centre manage these. Discuss the reasons for the strategy and suggest any major disadvantages and how the corporate centre should allow for these.

3   How should companies plan and undertake M&A activity? Review journal and newspaper commentary over the last year. Contrast and critically discuss the reasons for M&A over the last year, and assess the likely effects on the strategic management of the organizations involved.

CHAPTER END-NOTES

1   Raynor, M. E. (2007), 'Solving the strategy paradox: how to reach for the fruit without going out on a limb', *Strategy & Leadership,* 35(4): 4–10, p. 7.

2   Ansoff, H. I. (1965), *Corporate Strategy: An Analytic Approach to Business Policy for Growth and Expansion*, London: Pelican edition (published 1968), p. 2.

3   Goold, M., Campbell, A. and Alexander, M. (1994), *Corporate-Level Strategy: Creating Value in the Multibusiness Company*, New York: John Wiley & Sons, pp. 7–8.

4   Davies, P. J. (2009), 'Transcript: interview with Tidjane Thiam', *Financial Times,* online article, 10 September, www.ft.com.

5   Adapted from Ansoff, H. I. (1957), 'Strategies for diversification', *Harvard Business Review,* September-October.

6   3M (2007), *Annual Report: Leading Through Innovation*, Forward by George W. Bockley, Chairman of 3M, www.multimedia.3m.com.

7   Miles, R. E. and Snow, C. C. (1978), *Organizational Strategy, Structure and Process,* London: McGraw-Hill.

8   Peng, N. M., Tan, J. and Tong, T. W. (2004), 'Ownership types and strategic groups in emerging economies', *Journal of Management Studies,* 41:1105–1129.

9   Peng, N. M., Tan, J. and Tong, T. W. (2004), 'Ownership types and strategic groups in emerging economies', *Journal of Management Studies,* 41:1105–1129.

10 Penrose, E. T. (1959), *The Theory of the Growth of the Firm,* Oxford: Basil Blackwell.

11 Foster, R. and Kaplan, S. (2001), *Creative Destruction: Why Companies that are Built to Last Underperform the Market – and How to Successfully Transform Them,* New York: Doubleday.

12 Miller, D. (1991), *The Icarus Paradox,* London: Harper Business Books.

13 Frankl, P. and Rubik, F. (2000), *Life Cycle Assessment in Industry and Business: Adoption Patterns, Applications and Implications,* Berlin and Heidelberg: Springer-Verlag.

14 A subtle and gradual change in a strategic position is called strategic drift. The story of IBM illustrates this type of cycle and the company has been very successful (so far) as a turnaround-prospector organization, see Maney, K., Hamm, S. and O'Brien, J. M. (2012), *Making the World Work Better: The Ideas That Shaped a Century and a Company*, London: IBM Press/Pearson.

15 McKinsey (2011), 'Organizing for M&A: McKinsey global survey results', *McKinsey Quarterly,* December. www.mckinseyquarterly.com.

16 Suzlon Energy (2009), *Our Company, History.* www.suzlon.com.

17 Christensen, C. M. (1997), *The Innovator's Dilemma: When New Technologies Cause Great Firms to Fail,* Boston MA: Harvard Business School Press.

18 Kwong, R. (2010), 'King of the bandit phones has the last laugh', interview with Tsai Ming-kai, *Financial Times,* 18 October, p. 16.

19 Burt, T. (2002), 'The winners are concentrating on cash-generation, cost controls and subscriber margins', *Financial Times*, 23 November; Parker, R. and Edgecliffe-Johnson, A. (2007), 'Vodafone survivor sets a course for convergence', *Financial Times,* 17 November, p. 16.

20 *The Times* (2012), 'Vidal Sassoon, the upwardly mobile East End boy who turned hairdressing into an art', 10 May.

21 Cited in London, S. (2002), 'Secrets of a successful partnership', *Financial Times,* 6 February, p. 12.

22 Hill, A. (2011),'Chance encounters of the M&A kind', *Financial Times,* 8 November, p. 12.

23 Porter, M. E. (1987), 'From competitive advantage to corporate strategy', *Harvard Business Review*, 65(3):43–59.

24 Baghai, M., Smit, S. and Viguerle, S. P. (2008), 'M&A strategies in a down market', *McKinsey Quarterly,* August, www.mckinseyquarterly.com.

25 Gerstner, L. V. Jr. (2002), *Who Says Elephants Can't Dance?* New York: Harper-Business.

26 Adapted from Haspeslagh, P. C. and Jemison, D. B. (1991), *Managing Acquisitions: Creating Value through Corporate Renewal*, New York: Free Press.

27 Burgelman, R. A. and McKinney, W. (2006), 'Managing the strategic dynamics of acquisition integration: lessons from HP and Compaq', *California Management Review,* 48 (3):6–27.

28 Hall, B. (2008), 'Russo and Tchuruk are paying the price for failure', *Financial Times,* 30 July, p. 20.

29 Welch, J. (with Welch, S.) (2005), *Winning,* New York: Collins, p. 226.

30 Hopper, K. and Hopper, W. (2009). *The Puritan Gift, Reclaiming the American Dream Amidst Global Financial Chaos,* London: I. B. Taursis.

31 Goold, M., Campbell, A. and Alexander, M. (1994), *Corporate-Level Strategy: Creating Value in the Multibusiness Company*, New York: John Wiley & Sons.

32 Pettigrew, A. M., Massini, S. and Numagami, T. (2000), 'Innovative forms of organising in Europe and Japan', *European Management Journal,* 18(3):259–273.

33 Another portfolio analysis method, the Arthur D. Little (ADL) matrix, directly uses industry life cycle stages to assess the strength of a business's competitive position for each stage. The approach requires the determination of an industry's current life cycle, which is always difficult.

34 Adapted from Henderson, B. D. (1984), *The Logic of Business Strategy,* New York: Ballinger Publishing.

35 Adapted from Coyne, K. (2008), *Enduring Ideas: The GE–McKinsey Nine-Box Matrix*, McKinsey & Company, September. www.mckinsey.com.

36 Hoskisson, R. E, and Hitt, M. A. (1994), *Downscoping: How to Tame the Diversified Firm,* Oxford: Oxford University Press.

37 Peters, T. J. and Waterman, R. H. (1982), *In Search of Excellence*, London: Harper and Row.

38 Sanderson, R. and Parker, A. (2010), 'Spin-offs show demergers are staging comeback', *Financial Times,* 30 March, p. 17.

39 Klepper, S. J. and Subramaniam, S. (2008), 'Breaking up is good to do', *McKinsey Quarterly,* December, www.mckinsequaterly.com.

40 Strategic portfolio analysis continues to be used widely and conglomerates continue to do well, but the frameworks have been subject to much criticism in the academic literature: for a review of this criticism see Untiedt, R., Nippa, M. and Pidan, U. (2011), 'Corporate portfolio analysis tools revisited: assessing causes that may explain their scholarly distain', *International Journal of Management Reviews,* 14(3), 263–279.

41 Prahalad, C. A. and Hamel, G. (1990), 'The core competence of the corporation', *Harvard Business Review*, May-June, 79–91.

42 It has been argued elsewhere that it is how Canon uses its capabilities dynamically that really accounts for its competitive advantage over time: see Stalk, G., Evans, P. and Shulman, L. E. (1992), 'Competing on capabilities: the new rules of corporate strategy', *Harvard Business Review,* May-June, 57–69.

43 McKinsey (2008), 'Is your company the natural owner of its business?' *McKinsey Quarterly Chart Focus Newsletter,* July, 18. www.mckinseyquarterly.com.

44 Goold, M., Campbell A. and Alexander, M. (1994), *Corporate-Level Strategy: Creating Value in the Multibusiness Company,* New York: John Wiley & Sons.

45 Dye, R. (2008), 'How chief strategy officers think about their role: a roundtable', *The McKinsey Quarterly,* May, www.mckinseyquarterly.com.

46 Goold, M. and Campbell, A. (1991), *Strategies and Style: The Role of the Centre in Managing Diversified Corporations,* London: Blackwell.

47 Delbridge, R., Gratton, L. and Johnson, G. (2006), *The Exceptional Manager,* Oxford: Oxford University Press.

Corporate strategy at General Electric

The American-based conglomerate General Electric (GE) is one of the world's largest multinationals, employing just over 300 000 people in 160 countries.[1] The company's origins lie with Thomas Edison, who established his Electric Light Company in 1876, and a merger with the Thomson-Houston Electric Company created the General Electric Company in 1892. In 2012 the company recorded £95 billion revenue. It calls itself a diversified technology, media and financial services company. It is an important company to strategic management, because no organization has contributed more to thinking about corporate-level strategy.

Changes in GE's corporate-level strategy

The history of GE shows how the strategic management of a large corporation develops in ways that

reflect changes in corporate agenda and the management style of a chief executive. In a review of strategic planning at GE since the 1940s, Ocasio and Joseph observe that each chief executive had changed the design of the strategic planning system to meet their own priorities and to reflect their own experience, management style and background, as well to take account of the changing market and institutional environments.[2]

During the 1960s and early 1970s Fred Borsch moved the group from a form of strategic management that was based on financial performance to one that took into account industry attractiveness and competitive strength, and established a large central corporate planning department. His successor, Reginald Jones, was more financially oriented and had a more detached management style; this was facilitated by building up a more elaborate system of SBUs, which reported to central planning.[3]

In the early 1980s GE was hit by recession and a new chief executive, Jack Welch, downsized the corporation and drastically reduced the corporate planning office. He restructured the corporate divisions and ended the strategic independence of the SBUs to make them more accountable to the centre. Welch followed an extensive M&A programme to reposition the group's strategy away from one based on commoditization to a value-added strategy.[4]

Jeffrey Immelt, the current chief executive, is largely following the Welch strategy, although there seems to be more emphasis on organic (internally generated) growth rather than on M&As. The corporation is now divided into four main businesses: technology infrastructure (made up of units in aviation, enterprise solutions, healthcare, transportation), energy infrastructure (energy, oil and gas, water and process technology), GE Capital (aviation financial services, commercial finance, energy financial services, GE Money, Treasury), and NBC Universal (cable, film, internal, network, sports and Olympics).

GE's strategy

Our strategy was ... directional. GE was going to move away from businesses that were being commoditized towards businesses that manufactured high value technology products or sold services instead of things. As part of that move, we were going to massively upgrade our human resources – our people – with relentless focus on training and development. We chose that strategy after getting hammered by the Japanese in the 1970s. They had rapidly commoditized businesses where we had reasonable margins, like TV sets and room air conditioners ... Our quality, cost, and service – the weapons of a commodity business – weren't good enough in the face of their innovation and declining prices ... That's why we divested businesses like TV sets, small appliances, air conditioners, and a coal company, Utah International. It is also why we invested so heavily in GE Capital, bought RCA, which included NBC; and poured resources into developing high technology products in our power, medical, aircraft engine, and locomotive businesses.

Now, in such changing times, how and why did GE stick with one strategy over twenty years? The answer is that strategies, if they're headed in the right direction and are broad enough, don't really need to change all that often, especially if they are supplemented with fresh initiatives. To that end we launched four programmes to bolster our strategy – globalization, service add-ons, Six Sigma, and e-business. More than anything, though, our strategy lasted because it was based on two powerful underlying principles: commoditization is evil and people are everything. Virtually every resource allocation decision was based on those beliefs ...

My advice, then, is when you think strategy, think about de-commoditizing. Try desperately to make products and services distinctive and customers stick to you like glue. Think about innovation, technology, internal processes, service add-ons – whatever works to be unique. Doing that right means you can make a few mistakes and still succeed. That's enough theory![5]

Welch had been impressed by the returns to financial services at GE Capital. This was founded in the 1920s to offer hire purchase to help customers buy

GE products. However, its involvement in real estate and commercial loans meant that when the global financial crisis came along in 2008, GE shares fell 70 per cent and lost its triple-A rating, which it had carefully safeguarded since 1965.

Corporate mission

According to Welch, the corporate mission was sometimes mistaken by outsiders as GE's strategy:

From 1981 through 1995, we said we were going to be 'the most competitive enterprise in the world'. By being No. 1 or No. 2 in every market – fixing, selling, or closing every under-performing business that couldn't get there. There could be no doubt about what this mission meant or entailed. It was specific and descriptive, with nothing abstract going on. And it was aspirational, too, in its global ambition.[6]

This mission was used in combination with a new framework for classifying GE businesses that replaced the GE–McKinsey nine-cell matrix. He grouped GE's businesses into three, designated technology, services and core, and another group which didn't fit into these; the groups are shown on the left-hand side of Exhibit 7.1. The 'Invest and grow' businesses were number one or two in their markets, while select growth and defend were designated as important to GE's longer-term future. The harvest businesses provided cash for the first two groups, and 'Exit and divest' ones were to be sold.

Strategy at divisional level

At a divisional level, managements were advised to do strategy in three steps. 'Over my career, this approach worked incredibly well across varied businesses and industries, in upturns and downturns, and in competitive situations from Mexico to Japan.'[7]

The steps were (1) come up with the big idea (Welch calls it the 'aha') for the business, which must be a smart, realistic, and a relatively fast way to gain sustainable competitive advantage; (2) put the right people in the right jobs to drive it forward; and (3) relentlessly seek out the best practices to progress your strategy (continuous improvement).

EXHIBIT 7.1 GE's business grouped in terms of four priorities[8]

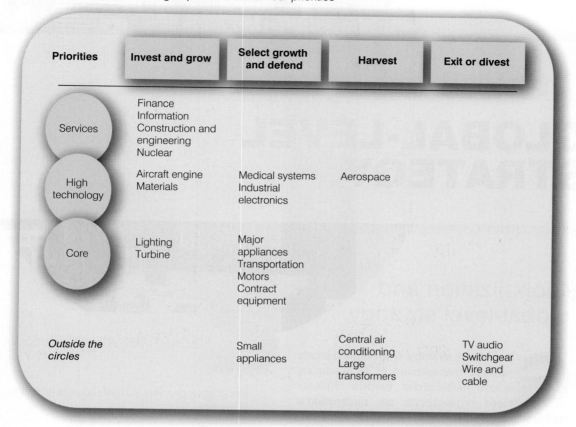

Priorities	Invest and grow	Select growth and defend	Harvest	Exit or divest
Services	Finance Information Construction and engineering Nuclear			
High technology	Aircraft engine Materials	Medical systems Industrial electronics	Aerospace	
Core	Lighting Turbine	Major appliances Transportation Motors Contract equipment		
Outside the circles		Small appliances	Central air conditioning Large transformers	TV audio Switchgear Wire and cable

Discussion questions

1   Using web resources and the latest opinions about GE, critically evaluate and decide if GE's reputation as one of the world's most admired corporations is still deserved. In particular, take into account if the move away from a commodity to a value-added business has helped it during the economic downturn caused by the financial crisis.

2   Jack Welch believed that strategy should be kept simple. This seems difficult given GE's size and complexity. Critically examine the grounds generally for thinking along these lines in the strategic management literature.

3   Evaluate the job of a chief executive at GE. How does it involve synergy and can a single person, such as Jeffrey Immelt, ever be said to strategically manage an organization like GE?

Case end-notes

1   General Electric (2008), www.ge.com.

2   Ocasio, W. and Joseph, J. (2008), 'Rise and fall – or transformation? The evolution of strategic planning at the General Electric Company', 1940–2006, *Long Range Planning*, 41:248–272.

3   Pascale, R. T. (1991), *Managing on the Edge*, New York: Simon & Schuster.

4   Welch, J. (with Welch, S.) (2005), *Winning*, New York: Collins.

5   Welch (2005), *Winning*, New York: Collins, pp. 170–171.

6   Welch (2005), *Winning, New York:* Collins, p. 15.

7   Welch (2005), *Winning, New York:* Collins, p. 167.

8   Adapted from Rothschild, W. E. (2007), *The Secret of GE's Success*, London: McGraw-Hill, Exhibit 12.1.

Chapter 8

GLOBAL-LEVEL STRATEGY

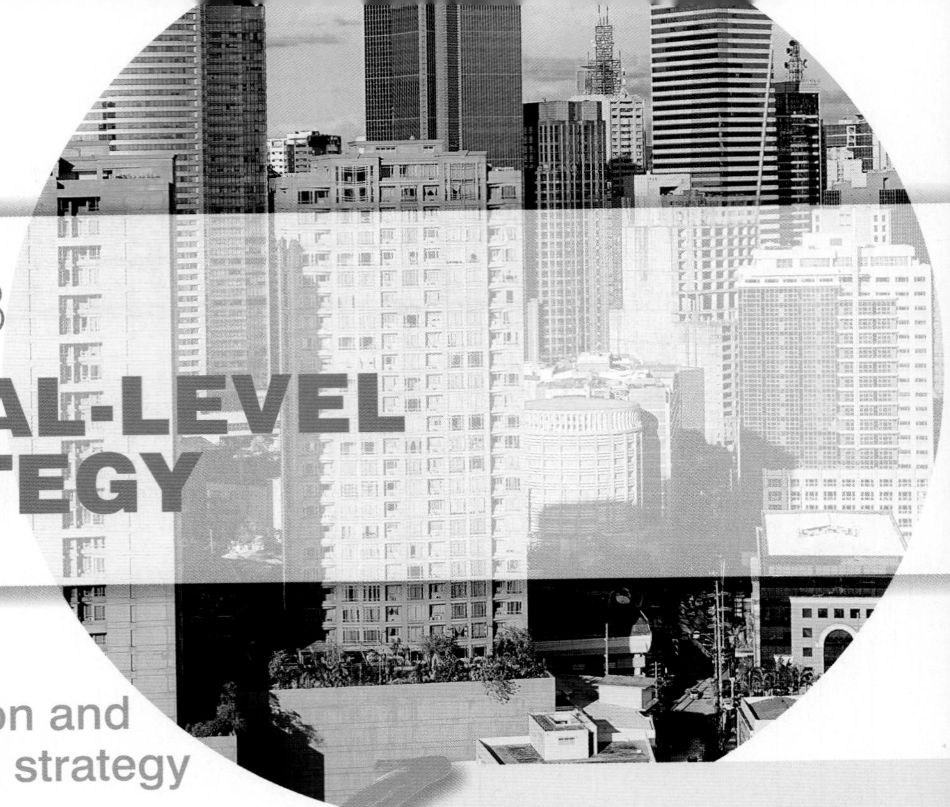

Globalization and global-level strategy

Global-level strategy is an organization's strategic management of its operations across multi-national borders. Typically these organizations are **multinational corporations (MNCs)**.

KEY TERMS

brand
commoditization
co-opetition
coordinated market economy
diamond model
global strategy
global-level strategy
globalization
glocalization
international strategy
leveraged buyouts
liberal market economy
micro multinational
multi-domestic strategy
multinational corporations (MNCs)
state capitalism
strategic alliances and partnerships
technology-based strategic platform
transnational strategy
varieties of capitalism

LEARNING OBJECTIVES

This chapter provides you with an understanding of the following:

1 Globalization
2 The competitive advantage of nations
3 The four strategic approaches for global-level business:
- global strategy
- multi-domestic strategy
- international strategy
- transnational strategy

4 Micro-multinationals
5 Strategies for local companies
6 The influence of national cultures
7 Varieties of capitalism
8 Strategic alliances and partnerships
9 Co-opetition and strategic platforms
10 Private equity

Business vignette The world is flat

One of the most influential business writers on globalization is Thomas Friedman. He writes in his bestselling book, *The World is Flat,* how he thought of its title.

Friedman describes a visit to the Indian company, Infosys Technology, and its chief executive, Nandan Nilekani. He recounts that at one end of the company's conference centre was a massive wall-size screen. This had been constructed from 40 digital screens and was probably the largest flat-screen TV in Asia. Infosys used it to hold virtual meetings with people, who Nilekani described as the key players in the company's global supply chain to discuss any project at any time. So, for example, American designers could be on the screen talking with their Indian software writers, and their Asian manufacturers, all at once.

According to Nilekani, 'We could be sitting here, somebody from New York, London, Boston, San Francisco, all live. And maybe the implementation is in Singapore, so the Singapore person could also be here ... That's globalization'.

Above the screen there were eight clocks and these summed up the Infosys workday: 24/7/365. The clocks were labelled US West, US East, GMT, India, Singapore, Hong Kong, Japan, and Australia.

Nilekani summed up the implications, 'Tom, the playing field is being levelled ...'

In Friedman's words:

He meant that countries like India are now able to compete for global knowledge work as never before ... I kept chewing on that phrase: 'The playing field is being levelled'. What Nandan is saying, I thought, is that the playing field is being flattened. Flattened? Flattened? My God, he's telling me that the world is flat![1]

as Friedman

Sometimes referred to as multinational enterprises or transnational corporations, these are enterprises that are active in more than one country and the very largest can have a strong influence on local economies. Overall they exert a driving role in globalization. **Globalization** is a phenomenon of changing commonalties and differences associated with a world-wide perception that the world is becoming smaller, more alike, and more inter-connected.[2] This chapter covers the background of globalization before discussing the four types of international strategy. It then considers strategic alliances and partnerships, and the rise of leveraged buy-outs.

Globalization

Globalization is a growing world phenomenon of connections, associations, differences and commonalities, which influence national markets and international industries. It is an idea that human activity, in particular commercial activity, is converging and becoming more inter-connected all over the world. Some observers have called the present period a post-industrial or post-modern age: a shrinking world that is growing basically more alike (or flat!), but at the same time is becoming more global and stylistically divergent. This perception is heightened by the growth of world communications media and a pervasive feeling that the world ecology is not as safe as we used to think. If we can call this 'globalization', then it is the most important change phenomenon of our time, and is inextricably tied up with the great international debates concerning climate change and the economic management of our planet.

Technological developments, such as satellite broadcasting, computers, email and the Internet, and parallel developments in liberalizing trade and movements in international capital, have helped drive globalization. The concentration of investment activity through international banks and other financial institutions, in large companies, and in accompanying insistence on the part of international investors that commercial organizations should grow in size, and adopt global practices, have been important influences.

For example, in a review of the pulp and paper industry, Lilja and Moen conclude:

> *During the 1990s leading firms have become Europe-wide or even global as a result of their production systems ... The concentration process has transformed pulp and paper mills into multinational companies ... Investment banks have had a major role. They have acted as architects, messengers and bankers between firms ... As a result, leading firms have learnt to construct strategy projects that appeal to transnational investors and financial analysts.*[3]

The pressure to internationalize approaches to organizational management has been important in

 Global-level strategy is an organization's strategic management of its operations across multi-national borders. Globalization is a growing world phenomenon of connections, associations, differences and commonalities, which influence national markets and international industries.

As the world economy converges countries are likely to become richer and consumer tastes are likely to change. This is likely to be disruptive for how it will question traditional ways of being and thinking. There are many who are concerned with the associated implications and consequences for socio-economic issues, such as an unequal distribution of income and the ecological effects on the health of the planet.

In particular, hostility over aspects of American foreign policy, and questions about the businesses ethics of some conglomerates, have spilled over to influence how people see globalization. This has focused particularly on the power of brands, such as Nike, Shell, Walmart, Microsoft and McDonald's (see Klein's *No Logo*[4]).

Researching the thoughts of young South America for Levi, Amaranta Wright, is worried that 'Perhaps one day there will be no authentic thoughts and feelings left, only branded ones, formulated to inspire needs before needs exist'.[5]

A contributory factor may be a lack of scruples at boardroom level. American big business, say Kenneth and William Hopper, has forgotten the original reasons for making profits, which is to serve society.[6]

The tenants of current global business ideology, such as shareholder value, free trade, intellectual property rights, and profit repatriation, are not universally accepted. The importance of the Internet and the threat of censorship and manipulative ideologies, are becoming major concerns.

The global financial crisis is probably the first big test for the principles of international integration: the deregulation and liberalization of trade. Things could go into reverse. However, it is likely that international forums will become more important, and groups such as G-20 will be more active: this is a group of around 20 nations, which represent both the advanced and most important emergent economies; it was created in 1999 to promote international financial stability.

Question: Rather than coming closer together, will the world become more adversarial?

nearly all areas of administration, including those in government, religion, charity, sport – just about every human activity that requires organizing and management has been influenced by the idea that the world is somehow increasingly becoming joined-up. However, success in international markets may begin with a strong base at home.

Competitive advantage of nations

The importance of a strong home base as a foundation for global expansion was made the subject of research by Michael Porter, which was sponsored by the government of the United States in the late 1980s.[7] He investigated 20 industrial sectors in 12 countries. It was found that many internationally leading industries were clustered in geographical regions. For example, the most successful global parts of the film industry, as well as the IT industry, are centred in California. Porter's research pointed out the importance of developing and nurturing a geographical concentration of suppliers, specialized resources, and the importance of getting a balance between an industry's home-based activities and those dispersed abroad. Porter argues that an organization's competitive advantage in part depends upon local advantages that cluster as a regionally localized industry. Porter illustrated the influences of the competitive strength of a nation as a diamond (see Figure 8.1).

FIGURE 8.1 Porter's diamond of competitive advantage of nations[8]

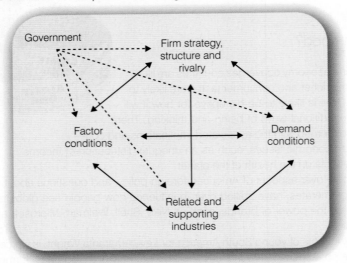

Firm strategy, structure and rivalry

The intensity of domestic competition works to compel organizations to work for improved productivity and innovation. This follows on from Porter's ideas about industry competitiveness (see Chapter 4). An important factor is a country's capital market. When relatively short-term returns to investment are expected, such as in the United States, then industries with short investment cycles are encouraged, such as in computers and films. In countries where the investment cycle is longer, such as in Japan, then investment favours more radical technology, such as Toyota's hybrid car, which the company started to develop in the 1990s.

Demand conditions

The presence of demanding and sophisticated customers will spur on greater efforts and competitiveness. Domestic industries are encouraged by open competition, since this raises expectations about the standard of service and products a market wants, and this spurs local organizations to innovate and improve. The large important leather and footwear industries in eastern England succumbed quickly in the late 20th century, when markets were opened up to competition from Italy and other countries; largely because they were unable to innovate after years of protected markets.

Related and supporting industries

This source of competitive advantage is concerned with the need for a sufficient density of related and supporting organizations, especially the proximity of distributors, suppliers, and other organizations, that facilitate an industry's activities. For example, the number, and close proximity, of clothing wholesalers and fashion houses in Milan have provided an important springboard for the Italian textile industry.

Factor conditions

These are the available specialized factors of production, which include skilled labour, capital and infrastructure. They do not include general-use factors, such as unskilled labour and raw materials, which are generally available and do not contribute to a nation's competitive advantage, such as general education because specialized training is more important for generating innovation that leads to a sustainable competitive advantage. The Dutch horticultural industry is a world leader in produce that includes tomatoes and dahlias, but it has no natural resources that are particularly suited to these plants. The origins of Dutch horticulture lie in the 17th century when the Netherlands was internationally famous for tulips. Since that time the country has been able to build up its specialist marketing and other resources across the world.

Robert Kaplan and David Norton observe that strategies for creating value have shifted from managing tangible assets to knowledge-based strategies; these favour an organization's strategic resources that include its intangible assets, and a focus on product and service differentiation.[9] They give examples of close customer relationships, innovative products and services, high quality and responsive operating processes, skills and knowledge of the workforce, supporting IT infrastructure which link an organization to its suppliers and, finally, an organizational climate that encourages innovation, problem-solving and continuous improvement.

So the importance of clustering is especially felt in the knowledge-based industries where people prefer to work near other similar working people. This preference means that a compact geographical concentration of similar organizations can foster an environment of both cooperation and competition, which are conducive to creativity and the development of new ideas. The competition acts as a driver, while cooperation provides insights that can be exploited. While physical items are made in scattered factories, knowledge is concentrated in networks of skilled people.

The role of government

The purpose of government, according to Porter, is to provide and facilitate economic conditions that act as a catalyst and encourage enterprise. Local rivalry can be stimulated by policy that limits direct cooperation and enforces anti-trust regulations. In the diamond, 'government' is shown as a periphery influence. This reflects Porter's view that the role of government is neutral: in other words, government can be good or bad.

However, there is no denying that policy interventions often work well to build infrastructure, develop specialist resources, and can boost investment to encourage innovation. According to Kenneth Galbraith, the mighty public investment in the American defence industry has been a primary driver of the country's dominance in key technologies, such as computing and aircraft.[10] Peter Drucker compared the success of Japan to the failure of the United Kingdom to support innovative industries that would have maintained the country's technological leadership.[11] The profound importance of the interdependence of business and society for the creation of long-term value was noted long ago in Adam Smith's *The Wealth of Nations*.

The usefulness of the diamond model

The **diamond model** is not meant to be a practical strategic management tool to help specific organizations compete more effectively. Porter designed it to help understand why a nation is successful in some industries and not in others. However, this can help strategists understand how their organizations can use the resources and networks in their home base to build a firmer foundation for success in global markets.

Regional clusters, of course, do not necessarily last. In the United States under the pressures of global competition there has been a discernible move of car manufacturing away from Detroit. This has been in part because of relatively high production

costs and location of Japanese subsidiaries on green field sites in the less expensive parts of the United States.

Porter's ideas are an extension of the old idea of the comparative advantage of nations. Some economists have argued that regions rather than countries are important; Rugman and D'Cruz propose a double diamond that covers more than one country, to explain the success of large multinationals from small nations.[12] Others, argue the model runs counter to the idea of globalization itself, for example, as Dunning argues, organizations may gain innovation from factor conditions in a foreign location.[13] Since Porter introduced his diamond, globalization has made it seem that a favourable domestic base may not be as important as it once was.

Supply-side reasons for moving operations overseas

In terms of assembly and raw material costs in manufacturing, and because of favourable exchange rates, emerging economies may themselves offer a comparative advantage for large international companies, especially the large multinationals. Many of them have moved component production to low wage Asian countries. This is in part a result of **commoditization**: the transfer of unsophisticated production and service units from advanced economies to developing countries where the cost of labour is low, and reflects a general move on the part of multinational companies to slim down operations and use contractors, while they focus on managing supplier relationships in core areas that add more value such as product development, marketing and services.

Nokia, the Finnish mobile phone manufacturer, caught by surprise by the rapid success of high-priced smartphones, especially the Apple's iPhone, moved in 2012 to cut jobs at its European and American factories to shift production to Asia. Niklas Savander, executive vice-president for markets, said: 'Shifting device assembly to Asia is targeted at improving our time to market. By working more closely with our suppliers, we believe we will be able to introduce innovations into the market more quickly and ultimately be more competitive'.[14]

The automotive multinationals have probably gone furthest in organizing and managing international supply chains. To an extent this reflects a desire on the part of the car makers to align and harmonize objectives downstream in their industry value chains (see Chapter 6).

A similar trend has been happening to services where notably banks and insurance companies have taken advantage of improved information technology to standardize their business processes on a global scale. An example is the use of offshoring for call centres. Offshoring involves a transfer of a company's activities and jobs from its domestic base to other regions overseas. These new locations offer opportunities for green-field development with cheaper resources, in particular, relatively low labour costs. Offshore activities may be organized within the existing organization, or they could be out-sourced to other independently owned organizations.

Aviva is the world's fifth largest insurance group, serving around 50 million customers. By 2008 the company had moved 6000 jobs offshore to India and most of these involved call centre based processes such as the routing of customer service requests to different parts of Aviva across the world. It requires a capacity for real-time matching of customer profiles with agent skill profiles on a global basis. Aviva worked with an Indian business process outsourcing firm (a BPO) called 24/Customer. Aviva has to have visibility as to the type of customer, loads, and the quality of agents and their skills in their various locations.

However, perhaps globalizing internal processes can be overdone. Following UK customer complaints about its call centres, Aviva has brought most of its call centre jobs in-house; they remain based in India. The company claims it was always part of its outsourcing policy to do this, and that using BPO partnerships had offered an economical and low risk way of building an initial global capability. Aviva's old BPO partners now continue as independent companies, which are looking to build services with other clients (they continue to perform some Aviva outsourcing). The Aviva call centre activities remain in India. What Aviva has done is to bring into the company those processes that are core to its global strategy; these are now more closely managed in-house, to maintain the quality of service

FIGURE 8.2 Four types of strategy for international markets

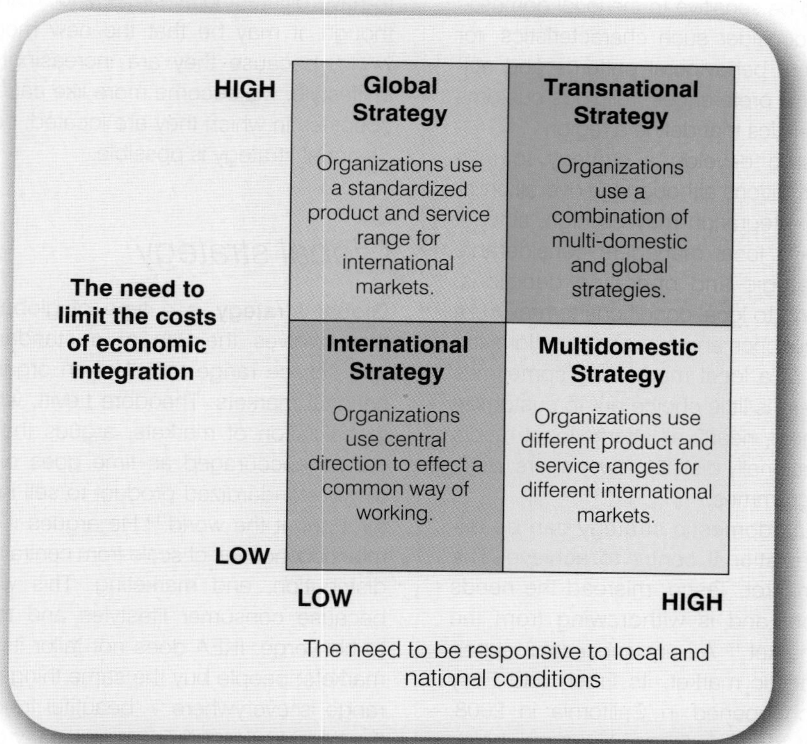

necessary to sustain those service-based core competences that underpin its competitive advantage.

Some large American multinationals seem to be bringing back manufacturing. General Electric is investing $1 billion in appliances to move most of its appliance manufacturing back to the United States from China and Mexico. Apple is also to resume manufacturing in the United States. Such moves represent only a small proportion of the manufacturing sent overseas, but factors such as materials costs and time-to-market, as well as quality problems, have made the home country look more attractive for some western multinationals.[15]

Demand-side global-level strategy

There are also demand-supply side advantages for going global. The promise of the sheer size and growth of markets in the emergent economies with large populations, offer many large multinationals the scope for expansion in sales that in their domestic markets would be impossible. There are four types of strategy approaches for global-level business, according to the pressures on an international company to keep its costs of economic integration low, and the strength of the need to be responsive to local and national conditions (see Figure 8.2): multi-domestic, global, international and transnational strategy.[16]

Multi-domestic strategy

Multi-domestic strategy is a type of global-level strategy that involves using different products and services to suit different markets in different countries. This approach is based on knowledge that markets in different countries or regional parts of the world are distinctly different from, and independent of, each other. A simple transfer of an existing strategy that has been effective in a domestic market, or another foreign market, may not necessarily work for a new country. The strategy should be sensitive to the local domestic environment, and consider such characteristics, for example, as different behavioural patterns and attitudes, including food preferences, religious customs and other characteristics that define a region.

The solution is to develop a strategy to take account of local conditions although the overall organizational costs of integration may be high, since it is necessary to give local managers considerable autonomy for strategic and operating decisions. The need to respond to local conditions to maximize revenue takes precedence and compensates for extra costs. The needs of a local market are sometimes so specific that there is little choice but to customize strategy; for example, nearly all international media companies offer nationally distinct newspapers, radio and television programmes.

However, a multi-domestic strategy can be difficult for an organizational centre to achieve. The UK-based supermarket, Tesco, misread the needs of the US shopper and is withdrawing from the American retail market.[17] A very successful supermarket in its domestic market, its Fresh and Easy retail stores, which opened in California in 2008, were very different to its traditional business, being designed to suit local conditions to meet a low price demand for fresh food. However, the company misread the needs of the local shopper who likes to pick up and touch their fruit and vegetables, which was difficult with the Fresh and Easy pre-packaged products.

Expansion into foreign markets can involve the acquisition of companies that are familiar with local conditions. This can also be risky if local knowledge and experience are turned against a parent organization, perhaps because there is a clash of organizational cultures, or the parent is thought to be too slow to support local decisions. The intervention in key issues at a local level could also be misinterpreted as uninformed interference by local management.

Consultants, McKinsey & Company[18] argue that for emerging economies, such as the BRICS, it is not enough to develop a country-level strategy, but it is necessary to go deeper. Companies should target city clusters (McKinsey have identified 22 of them in China). In these areas, competitive intensity is typically higher than in the country at large; typically the emerging middle class is concentrated in them. However, there are opportunities in both city clusters, and in the areas outside them; the important thing is to have different local strategy for both. Paradoxically though, it may be that the new megacities of the world, because they are increasingly metropolitan in lifestyle, will become more like each other that the countries in which they are located, so that a variant of global strategy is possible.

Global strategy

Global strategy is a type of global-level strategy that involves the use of a standardized product and service range for all of an organization's international markets. Theodore Levitt, writing about the globalization of markets, argues that organizations will be encouraged as time goes on to develop a single standardized product to sell in the same way throughout the world.[19] He argues it will bring enormous economies of scale from centralized production, distribution, and marketing. This will be possible because consumer lifestyles and tastes are likely to converge. IKEA does not tailor its stores to local markets: people buy the same things, and the same range is everywhere – 'beautiful functional items at the lowest prices'.[20] There are many other examples, usually associated with global brands.

A **brand** is a name or label that incorporates a visual design or image, which differentiates a product, service, or an organization, from others. Various positive attributes are associated with the brand through communication media and advertising to add a value that goes beyond the intrinsic functional value of the product or service bought. When branding is effective it offers attractive price premiums to the producer, and creates strong loyalty to the brand from the customer.

Brands are important to global strategy as they signify a standardized offer and a consistent promise of benefits regardless of where purchases are made. Global brands reach across the world. Some brands that were originally domestic in conception, have in the wake of changes in new communications media, developed into a new dimension. A spectacular example is the globalization of sport. The English Premier Soccer league is located in England but it is no longer a domestic competition. The competition has developed into an international showcase for clubs that are often foreign-owned, with foreign football managers and star players from all over the world. The competition is (probably) the best in the world, but English players no longer necessarily play a very important part. The television presenter, Evan Davis, observes that economists call this 'Wimbledonization', after the role Wimbledon plays in 'hosting the best tennis tournament' (at least on grass) but, as he says, the home nation does not 'expect to play a very prominent part in the tennis'![21]

New international brands are also emerging, particularly from China, and these could threaten long-established brands. One of the most famed is Li-Ning, founded in 1990, and named after its chairman who was an Olympic gymnast. It is a new sports brand that originally was modelled in the image of Adidas and Nike, but which has developed its own identity. For instance, once with a slogan, 'Anything is Possible', which resembled the 'Impossible is Nothing'

KEY DEBATE 8.2

Global or regional strategy?

The approaches used by large multinational to manufacture products and serve markets may be less global and local, and more regional in orientation, when groups of countries rather than the world as a whole are considered. In the view of David Simchi-Levi, a professor in supply chain management at the Massachusetts Institute of Technology: 'Many ... companies are starting to move from a global manufacturing strategy to a more regional strategy. That's a completely different strategy from what we saw companies using ten to fifteen years ago'.[22] An important reason is that cultures are distinctly different between regions. It may also be the case that varieties of capitalism differ for regions, so that a region's institutions may work in ways that are unique to that region.[23]

Pankaj Ghemawat, writing in the *Harvard Business Review,*[24] cites Jeffrey Immelt, chief executive of GE, saying regional teams are the key to GE's globalization initiatives, and that he had moved to graft a network of regional headquarters onto GE's otherwise lean product-division structure. John Menzer, president and chief executive of Wal-Mart International, was reported telling employees that global leverage is about playing 3D chess – at global, regional and local levels. Ghemawat claims that many see the emergence of regional blocs as an impediment to the process of globalization, when it is really an enabler of increasing cross-border integration.

Kenichi Ohmae in 1985 suggested the world is divided into three regional areas that he called the triad: namely the American, European and Asian regions.[25] Rugman and Verbeke argue that 'in virtually every case ... companies have developed a regional triad-based strategy. They first do well in their home markets and then expand out in their home triad markets.'[26] Alan Rugman questions the grounds for so-called global strategy and thinks the real drivers of globalization are the network managers of large multinationals. Their business strategies are regional and responsive to local customers.[27]

The formalization of regional trading areas, ranging from economic and political unions such as the European Union, to looser free trade agreements like the Association of Southeast Nations, place a special prominence on institutional harmonization and regulation.

The original manifesto for globalization was written in the *Harvard Business Review* by Ted Levitt,[28] and others, notably George Yip, have argued that 'companies now assume that they should globalize unless they can find very good reasons not to'.[29] Schlie and Yip have argued that regional strategy is a step towards a global strategy.[30]

Question: Is regional strategy a first step for achieving a global strategy, or is it distinctly different?

of Adidas, the company now has a new one, 'Make the Change': 'The message seems to be you don't need an expensive Western brand to get the values you aspire to. At first you copy, then you invent your own.'[31]

However, local brands are likely to suffer when faced with competition from multinationals. Seven out of China's top eight beverage companies have been merged with Coca Cola or Pepsicola. Foreign firms now account for an estimated 90 per cent share of the carbonated drinks market. Aiming to take advantage of foreign technology and management experience through joint ventures to develop their own brands, some Chinese companies have lost out as the dominant foreign brand eventually replaces local ones.[32]

International strategy

International strategy is a type of global-level strategy that uses central direction to achieve a common way of working across all of an organization's subsidiaries. This is a resource-based view of international strategy that makes use of an organization's core competences and dynamic capabilities. The focus is managing from the multinational's centre, when corporate businesses are aligned around a common corporate culture (or shared values[33]) and ways of working. This reflects the Prahalad and Hamel idea that a related diversified organization depends upon the corporation's core products rather than its end-products and services (see Chapter 7). What counts are the organization's abilities to exploit innovation appropriate to its different markets.

A survey of *Fortune*'s 'world's most admired companies' suggested that such companies are more focused on managing from the centre than on local initiatives. For example, they are focused on enterprise-wide objectives and these are better managed from the centre. These companies are more likely to develop new practices centrally and diffuse them to subsidiaries than other companies. They also have centralized pay policies and keep incentives consistent from country to country. Foreign experience is a prerequisite for senior management. These companies also claim they have succeeded in building a one corporate culture across all their divisions.[34]

Procter & Gamble has changed its global strategy to shift more of its resources to low-income markets in overseas' markets. The company is using new approaches in its consumer research, which involve time spent in the homes of low income consumers and the development of new forms of communication. At first glance this looks like an organization that focuses on low value added products. However, Procter & Gamble are using core competences to manage their core products of advanced technology and marketing to design low-income products in ways that local competitors find difficult to emulate. For example, it is producing a disposable nappy for no more than the price of a fresh egg (or ten cents).

Transnational strategy

Transnational strategy is a type of global-level strategy used to exploit markets in different countries by using a mixture of multi-domestic and global strategies. The interplay of local and global interactions is sometimes called **glocalization** – a portmanteau of globalization and localization. Transnational strategy recognizes that the global market is not just a single homogenous one, but that it is comprised of many locally different ones. The local markets are globally accessible but they have different cultural conditions that require a more regionally customized one. A multinational organization must balance the interests of the greater organization with the needs of local management and its need to make local strategic decisions.

According to Akio Morita, chairman of Sony Corporation, it is possible for a company to be both global and local:

For companies operating worldwide, true localization is the first step towards becoming a global enterprise. Managers of such global enterprises must consider how to closely knit together or integrate each of their localized operations so that they function as a single corporate entity. What is essential to this end is a universally common management philosophy and technology on how to develop and market products. I introduced a slogan – 'global localization' – to let Sony People know the importance of these concepts. It is another Sony word, like Walkman, and who knows, the phrase may one day appear in a Webster's dictionary either under the word, global or local. I believe that I share the same idea with Mr. Gozueta [chairman of Coca-Cola], who in the past advocated the concept, 'Think globally and act locally'.[35]

Coca-Cola was a single brand company for nearly a century, but it now has over 200 products and many of these are local brands (there are 47 in China). Coca-Cola gives some degree of autonomy to local marketing; however, the centre's overall strategy has been to give more prominence to Coca-Cola's global drive to expand its range of beverages beyond fizzy drinks. This has led to buying Russia's second largest juice maker, Multon, in 2005.[36] The overall concept is now 'think globally, act locally'. According to its chief executive, Douglas Daft, Coca-Cola had made the mistake of centralizing its 'decision-making and standardized its practices. We were operating as a big slow, insulated, sometimes even insensitive global company and we were doing it in a new era when nimbleness, speed, transparency and local sensitivity had become absolutely essential to success'.[37]

A transnational strategy is a way for reaching underdeveloped markets. Unilever has for a long time favoured a more decentralized approach and given its local managers more autonomy to make decisions. It works well for food because products can be adapted to meet local tastes. It is less effective in household and personal care, where the same products, such as nappies, toilet rolls, razors, can be more easily marketed and sold globally. Even so, Hindustan Unilever successfully sold a local brand, Wheel, a detergent to low income consumers in India. C.K. Prahalad advocates a strategy aimed at the bottom of the economic pyramid, which requires a low-price, low-margin, and high volume approach.[38] This assumes that a large turnover can be achieved quickly for a new product.

One form of transnational strategy is based on flexible manufacturing, which uses common production platforms that facilitate the use of the same type of modular components world-wide.[39] The best examples belong to the car industry. During the 1980s and 1990s General Motors (GM) and Ford both sought to develop a world car. They aimed to gain economies of scale by selling the same car everywhere, rather than developing vehicles separately for each region. In the end, finding out that roads are different across the world and demand different things from cars, they abandoned this ideal in favour of platforms (or architectures) designed to produce a common group of basic models; these are used but are varied at the local levels of assembly and marketing units to suit local national conditions. Car companies centralize their R&D, while dispersing manufacturing to relatively low-cost assembly units and suppliers.

Micro multinationals and born global organizations

A **micro multinational** is a small to midsize manufacturer that maintains a hub in a domestic economy, while its industrial customers are spread out, and who are typically carrying out production in low-wage regions of the world. A micro multinational is typically located in a niche sector of an industry where novel technologies are used that are esoteric yet vital to a larger industry. Competitors are usually few in number.

Wendy Chilton runs R.A. Chilton, a small company that invented and produces a specialized coating used for air-bearing spindles. These are small cylindrical devices used in machines that bore tiny holes in printed circuit boards, which are used for products such as mobile phones. R.A. Chilton's technology adds a sticky layer of copper that does not come loose even when a component is rotating at the speed of sound. Tens of thousands of electronic companies, many of them in China, rely on Chilton's coatings. Of course, small companies must be forever on their toes. According to Wendy Chilton, 'there's a chance that the Chinese will work out how to do this. But as long as we continually improve what we do, we feel we can keep one step ahead'.[40]

Before the advent of the Internet, organizations had to be large to gain a global reach, but this is no longer the situation. From start-up, entrepreneurs and the self-employed can access international markets at little initial cost. Such enterprises are sometimes referred to as born global organizations.[41] While many of these have chequered histories, some of the most successful have become very big indeed and are the household names we know so well, such as Amazon and eBay.

Wu Fangfang founded the Shanghai Qianrui Garment Company in 2005 with a girls' clothing brand, called Miss de Mode.[42] She designed, manufactured and promoted her brand through retail stores. In 2008 she employed 30 people, but the global financial crisis of the year saw retailers reneging on contracts to expand sales.

She decided to move from a bricks-and-mortar to an online business. She used the Taobao Mall, a business-to-consumer online market place, owned by Alibaba, the Chinese e-commerce group, which has a free online payment system and instant messaging. Prices were brought down to about half those in the shops, and the company has introduced new clothes lines.

The company now has a new factory and employs 200 garment workers with orders around £1 million. Having her own factory means that the company 'can respond to the market and needs very quickly. Less than 6 per cent of our stock remains unsold'. The business now employs a design team of 60 people and the fulfilment and e-commerce centre has another 120. The company has obtained venture capital from the US and aims to list as a public company in either Hong Kong or in the US, in 2014.

In 2008 when financial problems threatened to overwhelm her company, 'I didn't panic ... I used the situation to coolly evaluate my business model and decided that over the long term, I will be fine because children's clothes and e-commerce were both growing sectors in China.'

Question: Is the Internet the future for business in an emergent economy?

Strategies for local companies in emerging markets

Niraj Dawar and Tony Frost suggest a strategic framework for local companies to assess their competitive strength in an emerging market.[43] This is based on two parameters: the strength of globalization pressures in an industry, and the degree to which a company's assets are transferable internationally (see Figure 8.3).

If globalization pressures are weak, and the local company assets are not transferable, then the company should defend its own position. Dawar and Frost use the example of Shanghai Jahwa, a Chinese cosmetics group. The company has developed low cost mass-market brands that are positioned around beliefs about traditional ingredients. If globalization pressures are weak but the company's assets can be transferred, then the company may be able to extend

FIGURE 8.3 Positioning for emerging market companies[44]

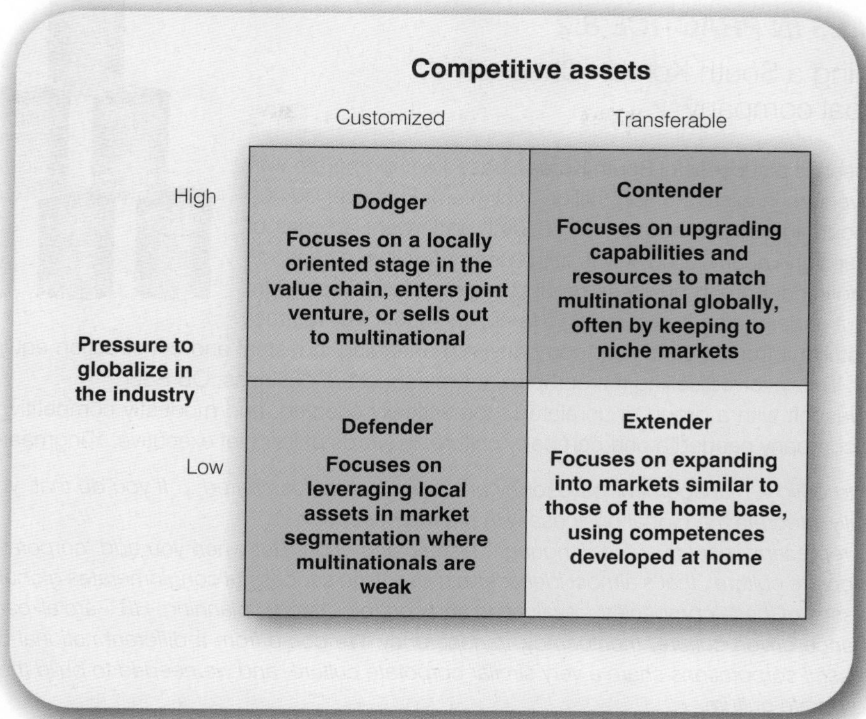

Competitive assets

	Customized	Transferable
High	**Dodger** — Focuses on a locally oriented stage in the value chain, enters joint venture, or sells out to multinational	**Contender** — Focuses on upgrading capabilities and resources to match multinational globally, often by keeping to niche markets
Low	**Defender** — Focuses on leveraging local assets in market segmentation where multinationals are weak	**Extender** — Focuses on expanding into markets similar to those of the home base, using competences developed at home

Pressure to globalize in the industry (vertical axis, High to Low)

its business to some other markets. Jollibee Foods is a family-owned chain of fast food restaurants based in the Philippines. After meeting fierce competition from McDonalds the company opened restaurants in Hong Kong, the Middle East, and California, to offer its traditional meals to expatriate populations.

If globalization pressures are strong and a company's assets are suitable only for home, then it will need to depend on its ability to dodge the multinationals by restructuring to serve those parts of the value chain where its local assets are still valuable. Skoda, the Czech Republic's car company, entered into a joint venture with Volkswagen; the alternative would have been to sell out entirely. If globalization is strong, and a company's assets are transferable, then it may be able to compete globally with the multinationals. Acer of Taiwan, and Samsung of Korea, have become very successful in international markets.

Local companies typically start with a cost advantage over the multinationals and this can be used to give them a foothold in some markets. Embraer, founded by the Brazilian government in 1969, has become the fourth largest manufacturer of business jets and commercial airplanes by sales, behind Boeing, Airbus, and Canada's Bombardier. Brazil's low labour costs have been important. In 2002 they came to $26 000 per employee which was very low compared to its nearest rival, Bombardier's $63 000; Embracer has centred its operations on final assembly, which is the most labour-intensive part of the production process, and has outsourced other operating activities to its suppliers.[45] It has taken a long time, but Embracer has successfully competed against the world's established plane makers using the advantages of lower labour costs that Brazil has offered. There is some evidence that local businesses based in low income markets, do better when they leverage their activities on the strengths of the existing market environment, than if they were to focus on overcoming weaknesses.[46]

Similarly, China's relatively cheap and large workforces are a great advantage to its industries, especially those companies doing final assembly for Western and Japanese companies. The Hon Hai Precision, known by its trade name as Foxconn, has

Transforming a South Korean Chaebol into a global company

Doosan is a successful South Korean based conglomerate with revenues in excess of £15 billion, which employs over 30 000 people in 30 countries. In the 1990s it underwent a series of crises and nearly failed; it was at that time a family-run *chaebol*, which is a traditional Korean business group comprised of independent companies but under the control of a single family. In 1996 it was restructured to transform it from a consumer company into a leading industrial and construction equipment manufacturer. This involved selling the company's profitable core business, OB Beer.[47]

Doosan was left with a group of unrelated, domestically oriented, and modestly competitive businesses. The company needed a one-company culture. In words of its chief executive, Yongmaan Park:

> You have to build a management philosophy and value set that is shared ... If you do that, you can successfully integrate the global business with the mother business.
>
> Culture represents country, race, language, history, and such. But when you add 'corporate' and make 'corporate culture', that's almost identical in most of the successful conglomerates globally. The key processes of these companies – evaluation and control, strategic planning, HR – are all based on a performance-driven culture, meritocracy, transparency. We come from a different national culture, but successful corporations share a very similar corporate culture, and we needed to build the same kind of corporate culture.
>
> We want to become a global company that happens to come from Korea. Nestlé is a good example. Most people even in the business community, don't see the colour and taste of Switzerland in Nestlé. It's simply a multinational company that happened to originate in Switzerland. I want to build Doosan to such a global company.[48]

Question: Do large multinational companies constitute a distinct variety of capitalism?

headquarters in Taiwan, but most of its one million employees are based in mainland China. It is the world's largest contract electronics manufacturer, doing work for Apple, Dell, Hewlett-Packard and Sony. Already located in some other parts of the world, including Europe, it has recently embarked on a major expansion in Brazil. It has often entered new geographical areas by taking over and making more efficient factories once owned by its customers. However, Foxconn is notorious for its autocratic management style, which has led to clashes with its employees in several countries including China itself. While the company claims it is sensitive to local cultures, Terry Gou, Foxconn's chairman, is reported to have said, 'a harsh environment is a good thing'.[49]

National cultures

The importance to multinationals of one-company organizational cultures was noted above in the context of international strategy. There is evidence that organizations active in different countries can build a one-company culture, and for Japanese companies business methodologies and management philosophies do transfer between countries.[50] This is important to organizations which, like Toyota, take a resource-based view of competitive advantage.

If national cultures create insurmountable barriers to the transfer of organizational core competences and capabilities, then a competitive advantage built on strategic resources will be at risk.

Toyota's executive vice president, *Mitsuo Kinoshitsa,* admits that adapting to individual communities can be challenging:

> *In India the cultural differences are nothing like those in the United States. Indians are often quite sensitive to criticism, resisting Toyota's culture of constant improvement through problem identification, and deadlines are often not viewed with high importance ... The French and the Japanese have vast cultural differences ... Japanese are known to work long hours, but in France, a 35-hour work-week prevails for most professionals.*[51]

Most importantly for strategic management, of course, the national culture of senior management is a factor that is likely to influence management style. Carlos Ghosn, chief executive of Renault-Nissan, thinks that 'One of the great challenges that Renault has faced in its globalization is the fact that a part of its management still sees itself as exclusively French. It goes without saying that French culture is very important in the culture of the company, and again we mustn't lose sight of that fact. But we can't stop there'.[52]

In India the cultural differences are nothing like those in the United States. Indians are often quite sensitive to criticism, resisting Toyota's culture of constant improvement through problem identification, and deadlines are often not viewed with high importance ... The French and the Japanese have vast cultural differences ... Japanese are known to work long hours, but in France, a 35-hour work-week prevails for most professionals.

Many of the theories about how to manage come from the United States. However, Hofstede finds there are no universal management styles because of differences in national cultures.[53] He identifies five dimensions of national culture that influence how organizations are managed:

1 Power distance – which is the degree of inequality a national culture considers normal. Hofstede found this to be greatest for Latin and Asian, African and Arab countries. It is low for northern European countries. The United States was found to be in the middle.

2 Individualism versus collectivism – the extent a culture thinks it is appropriate for people to look after themselves and be cared for. The more economically developed countries have the greatest individualism.

3 Masculinity versus femininity – the acceptable balance between dominance, assertiveness, acquisition, on the one hand, and regard for people, feelings, quality of life, on the other. The Nordic countries have the lowest difference, while masculinity is very high in Japan.

4 Uncertainty avoidance – the degree of preference for structured versus unstructured situations. This is high for Latin American countries, southern and eastern Europe, including German speaking countries and Japan. They are lowers for Anglo-American, Nordic and Chinese culture countries.

5 Long-term versus short-term orientation – saving/persistence to reach a future, versus present, tradition and other social obligations. Long-term orientations are found in China and Japan, and are low in Anglo-American countries, Islamic countries, Africa and Latin America.

Such cultural dimensions are associated with differences in the nature of social and economic institutions between countries. This is likely to have strong influences on how large organizations, especially multinationals, organize and manage their strategic management across borders. Since the 2008 global financial crisis much has been written about a crisis of capitalism, in particular about which are the most appropriate forms or varieties of capitalism for global-level strategy.

Varieties of capitalism

The economists Peter Hall and David Soskice argue there are systematic differences for corporate strategy across nations; they make a distinction between two kinds of market economy, which they call **varieties of capitalism**.[54] These are based on five questions about how organizations are to coordinate resources: (1) How to coordinate bargaining over wages and working conditions with the representatives of labour and other employers; (2) How to secure a workforce with suitable skills, and how workers must decide in which skills to invest; (3) How to access finance and reconcile the needs of investors about the returns on their investments; (4) How to relate to other enterprises, especially customers and suppliers to secure a stable demand for products and services, and secure access to appropriate inputs and technology; (5) How to develop the requisite competencies and abilities to cooperate with others, to advance the purpose of the firm.

The important point they make is that the nature of national capitalism depends upon the strategic interactions and complementarities between institutions and firms in any one economy. These provide the prevailing mode of coordination of resources that firms will use for their strategic management.

Hall and Soskice identify two contrasting modes of market economy. The first is a **liberal market economy** where the five spheres are coordinated through competitive market arrangements and hierarchies (following Williamson[55]), and the second, is a **coordinated market economy** where the spheres are coordinated around collaborative institutional relations, which act to reduce uncertainty on stakeholder longer-term purpose. These represent two opposite characterizations and Hall and Soskice suggest there will be variations within these extremes.

In a liberal market economy the near-term needs of a firm's financial stakeholders are primary. These are typically equity shareholders, when it is a priority for executives is to maintain a level of dividend and a high share price that will protect the firm from a hostile takeover. A government policy emphasis is placed on the encouragement of free competition, and regulation may work to discourage inter-firm collaboration and those alliances that seem counter to free markets.

The Renault-Nissan Alliance

I n 1999 Renault and Nissan entered an alliance, which is a strategic partnership not a M&A. It has since served as a model for other alliances, notably General Motors and PSA Peugeot Citroën, PSA Peugeot Citroën and Mitsubishi, and Volkswagen and Suzuki (although this later failed amid accusations of non-collaboration). The alliance has broadened to include partnerships with Germany's Daimler, China's Dongfeng Motor, and Russia's AvtoVAZ.

Renault originally took a 36.8 per cent stake (now 44 per cent) in Nissan, and Nissan in turn now has 15 per cent in Renault. Renault's motive was to reduce its dependence on Europe, and Nissan offered access to the North American and Asian markets. It would also give access to Nissan's management philosophies and business methodologies. The Nissan Group in Japan was primarily a property company, which had incurred substantial debts, which limited the car company's ability to invest. Renault invested $5.4 billion and this saved Nissan's investment grade status. The agreement is subject to three principles: Nissan will retain its name; its chief executive is appointed by the Nissan board, and Nissan would take the principal responsibility for implementing a revival plan (which proved very successful).

ALLIANCE VISION – DESTINATION[56]

The Renault-Nissan Alliance is a unique group of two global companies linked by cross shareholding.
They are united for performance through a coherent strategy, common goals and principles, results driven synergies, shared best practice.
They respect and reinforce their respective identities and brands.
The Alliance is based on trust and mutual respect. Its organization is transparent.

It ensures: clear decision-making for speed, accountability and a high levels of performance, maximum efficiency by combining the strengths of both companies and developing synergies through common organizations, cross-company teams, shared platforms and components.

The Alliance attracts and retains the best talents, provides good working conditions and challenging opportunities: it grows people to have a global and entrepreneurial mindset. The Alliance generates attractive returns for the shareholders of each company and implements the best established standards of corporate governance.

Objectives

The alliance develops and implements a strategy of profitable growth and sets itself the following three objectives:

1 to be recognized by customers as being among the best three automotive groups in the quality and value of its products and selling in each regional and market segment;

2 to be among the best three automotive groups in key technologies, each partner being a leader in specific domains of excellence; and

3 to consistently generate a total operating profit among the top three automotive groups in the world, by maintaining a high operating profit margin and pursuing growth.

Question: Besides access to international markets and Nissan's management capabilities, what other advantages (and disadvantages) are there for Renault?

In a coordinated market economy, stakeholders include institutions such as business and employer associations, strong trade unions, and professional networks that involve cross-sharing of support and ideas. The regulatory systems in these economies work to facilitate a free movement of information and industry collaboration. A firm's attractiveness as a collaborator may be dependent on its reputation as a consensual decision-taker, and its history as a developer of specific firm and industry skills, and other strategic resources.

Of the large OECD nations Hall and Soskice identify six that are liberal market economies: namely the USA, UK, Australia, Canada, New Zealand and Ireland. Ten are identified as coordinated market economies: Germany, Japan, Switzerland, the Netherlands, Belgium, Sweden, Norway, Denmark, Finland and Austria. Another six economies are in 'more ambiguous positions' and these include France, Italy, Spain, Portugal, Greece and Turkey. Hall and Soskice point out how, for example, the economies of the United States and the United Kingdom are characterized by a free market ethos, while the German economy is characterized by close cooperative relations between firms, banks, owners and employees. Similarly, in Japan, its economy functions as a closely coordinated partnership of professional societies, commercial, sometimes family, banking and industrial groups, and government agencies.

Richard Whittington has written that for a period between 1960 and 1990, it was the coordinated market economies that were the most successful. This was an era of large-scale mass-production of cars, consumer electronics, and chemicals, when economies were largely stable and strategic planning was important. The core strategic concerns of this period were continuous improvement in quality, cost, delivery, and employee development. This changed around 1990, and until the onset of the global financial crisis in 2008, it was the liberal market economy countries that became more successful: 'It looks like the fast-moving, flexible and sometimes ruthless strategizing of the Anglo-Saxon [the liberal market] economies is better suited to the emergent economic conditions of the 21st century than the careful instrumentalism of Germany and Japan.'[57]

Until the events of 2008, some strategists had argued that varieties were converging, and that multinational firms were increasingly developing their own form of capitalism.[58] Certainly national differences in the nature of strategic leadership and the role of executives in strategic management may have played their parts (see Chapter 11) in bringing about the crisis.

State capitalism is a form of a commercial and profit-making activity undertaken by the state. It can include a state where the means of production are privately owned but controlled by strong government influences, especially large-scale businesses, which may be favoured as strategically important enterprises (for example, to ensure an availability of resources for use in time of war). A highly coordinated market economy may be viewed as a form of state capitalism if the state takes a leading role in its management.[59]

The success of China after the economic problems of the late 1990s has caused some observers to see its form of state capitalism as a challenge to free market economies. China is reported to provide aggressive financial support to its companies to invest overseas and sign deals in sectors such as energy and raw materials, to build new multinationals while securing supplies of strategic commodities; there is also increased pressure for foreign multinational to transfer knowledge of important technologies in return for access to the Chinese market.[60]

Strategic alliances and partnerships

Strategic alliances and partnerships are formal and informal associations and collaborations between independent organizations. A formal alliance involves a legally binding collaboration between two organizations to work to a specified purpose and which may involve a major project and shared resources. It can involve forming an independent organization such as a joint venture. This involves establishing a legally separate company, in which the partners take agreed equity stakes. Agreements are made about a common purpose, standards, and contractual arrangements, covering such matters as licensing, franchises, distribution rights, and manufacturing agreements. Organizations can also enter informal alliances, including with customers who have major accounts, key distributors, preferred suppliers, major institutional shareholders, and other stakeholders.

The reasons for alliances and partnership are varied and numerous. Often it is to share knowledge about new technologies. Sony and South Korea's Samsung in 2007 announced a $2 billion joint venture to mass-produce the next generation liquid crystal screens for flat-screen televisions. Sony has a leading share in cathode-ray tube televisions, but its share is falling as flat-screens take more of the market. Both companies will benefit in that Sony will gain from Samsung's technical knowledge and Samsung will be able to exploit Sony's market power.

Alliances also help organizations to find out about another company's management approaches, or about unfamiliar markets. They can help to reduce the cost of capital and spread risk, and sometimes they are a more acceptable form of market entry to regulators. However, they are not without challenges. In a Chinese study of joint ventures, the main difficulties that foreign organizations have had with their Chinese partners, have been cultural differences and communication problems.[61] In 1996 the Chinese Hangzhou Wahaha group entered into a joint venture with Groupe Danone SA of France (the French company had a controlling interest of 51 per cent). The Chinese partner has since developed into the country's largest domestic beverage company. However, in 2012 Danone accused its partner of using the Wahaha brand name to develop businesses (some of them as independent businesses) without its consent since the trademark rights of Wahaha had been transferred to the joint venture.[62] This has fuelled worries in China that foreign multinationals are taking over local brands.

A consortium partnership involves companies that come together to bid for a mutual rival. In 2008 Heineken and Carlsberg, two independent brewers, made a joint take-over of Scottish & Newcastle. Heineken aims to become number one or two in the beer markets in the countries it operates in, but prior to the bid only had 1 per cent of the British market; as a result of the acquisition it is now the largest brewer there. Carlsberg has taken over those parts of Scottish & Newcastle that are important in Eastern Europe and Russia. The Heineken and Carlsberg bid was designed to facilitate a break-up of the British company that would satisfy the Economic Union's competition laws. The companies would not have been able to bid independently. After the bid they were to dismember Scottish & Newcastle in ways that reduced the threat to competition.

The rapid changes in communications technologies, especially the Internet, have given rise to new thinking about alliances. Two important developments are co-opetition and technology-based strategic platforms.

Co-opetition (competition and collaboration)

Co-opetition is a word collapsed from cooperation and competition. It takes its inspiration from e-business. Ray Noorda, the founder of Novell, may have been the first to use the term, and it has now been widely taken up in the IT industry. It means a form of business activity that involves competing organizations that also cooperate with each other. For example, organizations that belong to strategic groups may work together to create barriers to new or outside competition. Adam Brandenburger and Barry Nalebuff in their book, *Co-Opetition*, use examples from the e-economy and ideas from game theory to show how collaboration between rivals can work in the interests of all.[63]

Organizations should consider their industry to take into account how its network of customers, suppliers, and competitors can be used to enhance the value of products and services. This involves identifying potential and actual complementors: those organizations that through their own products enhance the value of an organization's products and services. For example, a rival's software products may complement an organization's hardware products, and vice versa. The e-economy offers a change in strategy thinking from a 'brick and mortar' approach, based on tangible resources, to one more intangibly centred on interacting with inter-organizational networks.[64] Organizations have to determine how possible relationships may be complementary and how they can be used to sustain their competitive advantage.

Technology-based strategic platforms

A **technology-based strategic platform** is a standardized technical system, over which an organization may have property rights, but it can be used by other organizations (and sometimes rivals as in co-opetition) as a platform to develop their own products and services.[65] Microsoft's strategic success is based upon its desktop operating system, which has provided a platform for software groups to develop their own products to use with the Microsoft system. Bill Gates, the former Microsoft chief executive, has been consistent in ensuring that changes to MS-DOS, or Windows, have not meant that customers have had to abandon their existing programs and accessories. This has added complexity and cost to the development process and may have made Windows less reliable. 'Bill Gates' insistence on the strategic imperative has infuriated some of his most talented programmers ... It just keeps plugging on. That is not very glamorous – and it often results in bloated code and feature-laden programs. But it is an extremely effective competitive weapon in an industry where products never get past the 'promising' stage'.[66]

There is a strong functional interdependence among components of a technology-based system –

The front screen of Minitel, the French precursor to the World Wide Web

what David Teece calls a multi-sided market phenomenon.[67] For instance, electronic game consoles need games, and organizations have to work together to co-specialize, and a platform provider must take such activity into account for its strategic decision-making.

It may be difficult to implement platforms without forming alliances with other organizations to coordinate and respond to market changes. The French Minitel videotext system was coordinated by the French government as a telecommunications platform and involved a broad alliance of hardware manufacturers, software designers, and information providers. This facilitated the joint development of organizational competencies that allowed Minitel to offer new products through its on-line access. A similar videotext service failed in the United Kingdom largely because it failed to develop a strategic platform that could be used profitability by its information providers.[68]

KEY DEBATE 8.3

Do national cultures matter?

Referring to the Nissan-Renault alliance, Magee gives an example of how the Japanese and French national cultures influence communications:

The communication methods and habits within the cultures are so different that even when the same language is used, different understandings can result. For instance, Japanese businessmen often say 'yes' repeatedly when being told something. It is a sign that they understand the dialogue and are absorbing it, not that they approve of what is being said. Imagine the potential for confusion.

French: We think we need to close a plant.

Japanese: Yes.

French: Jobs will be lost.

Japanese: Yes.

French: We have no choice. It must be done.

Japanese: Yes.

The conversation ends. The French are moving on, making plans to close a plant. The Japanese are only ready to begin considering it, having said 'yes' simply as conversational confirmation that they understand what was being said.

Confusion never occurred at this magnitude, but cultural communication differences made for some interesting moments during high-level meetings and discussions.[69]

Question: The ideal of a 'global manager' seems a way off. Is it possible that a new class of global manager can emerge with globalization?

Private equity firms

Private equity firms are associated with **leveraged buyouts**, when they buy a publicly quoted company and make it private, so that the acquired company's stock is no longer traded publicly. Private equity firms raise large amounts of debt to finance their purchases, and off-set the costs by re-selling parts or the whole of the acquired companies, and sometimes building them up by adding other companies (called 'bolt-ons') to sell on to other companies. Traditionally, many of the private equity firms provide venture capital to new enterprises, but they have become increasingly involved with buying companies rather than taking shares in them.

Permira is Europe's largest private equity group: it owns several well-known brands, including Birds Eye, the AA (Automobile Association), and the retailer New Look. The world's biggest buy-out occurred in 2008, when Blackstone, founded in 1986, spent £19.8 billion to acquire Equity Office Properties, the largest commercial property group in the United States. Buyouts, however, often involve consortia of investors rather than just a single firm or buyer.

Private equity firms have been criticized for their lack of public accountability, especially in terms of investor names and executive salaries, and also for the very large levels of borrowings they sometimes use to finance deals, which afterwards can burden purchased firms with large debt (which is of some concern to fans of Manchester United, as a subject of a buyout). There are also accusations of asset-stripping and short-term financial, rather than longer-term strategic, management. Others see their role as usefully ruthless, and better able to reinvigorate sluggish companies, that otherwise publicly listed companies might have changed very little. Silverfleet, a United Kingdom private equity firm, bought the Dutch-based TMF, a provider of outsourced administrative services in 2004. It built up the business by making more than 50 bolt-ons, and then sold the business on making a six-fold return on its investment in 2008.[70]

Another form of private equity is the sovereign wealth fund; this is an investment fund held by a national government, which is used to invest in international companies. The history of these funds stretch back to at least the early 1950s, but they have more recently attracted attention for their participation in private equity buyouts. The largest fund seems to belong to Abu Dhabi ($635bn); others include Norway, Singapore, Kuwait, China, and Russia. Some of these owe their existence to dollar surpluses accrued from oil. At the present time sovereign funds account for a low proportion of the world's financial assets, but they are expected to become a significant feature of globalization, prompting disquiet about the possibility that a hostile country take control of companies that are strategically important.

Until the global financial crisis in 2008, private equity had been increasing very quickly. Private equity funding was about 4 per cent of the global M&A market in 2000 and rose to over 20 per cent in 2007. The importance of private equity is likely to remain, but to what extent it will recover is at the moment open to question.

SUMMARY OF PRINCIPLES

1   Global-level strategy must be considered against the main drivers of globalization, but it is important to recognize that global changes are still uncertain, so that organizations should be adaptable.

2   A company's competitive advantage in part depends upon local advantages that cluster as a regionally localized industry.

3   There are four broad strategic approaches for global-level business: multi-domestic, global, international, and transnational (glocalization) strategies.

4 The positioning for emerging market companies depend on the pressure to globalize in the industry and their competitive assets.

5 National cultures play a large influence in the choice of international strategy.

6 Strategic alliances and partnerships enable organizations to learn about technologies, ways of managing, and new markets.

7 Strategic platforms provide a basis for adapted or complementary products and services.

GUIDED FURTHER READING

An essential read for those interested in globalization is Thomas Friedman's *The World is Flat*. It is probably the most influential popular business book of a large and growing library about globalization, see Friedman, T. (2005), *The World is Flat: A Brief History of the Globalized World in the 21st Century,* London: Allen Lane.

For an in-depth treatment of the management of global-level strategy, see Bartlett, C. and Beamish, P. (2013), *Transnational Management: Text, Cases and Readings in Cross-Border Management,* (7 edn) London: McGraw-Hill. Also see: Segal-Horn, S. and Faulkner, D. (2010), *Understanding Global Strategy,* Andover: Cengage Learning.

One of the best books about international business in China is Tian, X. (2007), *Managing International Business in China,* Cambridge: Cambridge University Press. For a review of how the home economies of multinational firms might influence strategic management, see Witcher, B. J. and Chau, V. S. (2012), 'Strategic management and varieties of capitalism', *British Journal of Management,* 23 (March), S58–73.

REVIEW QUESTIONS

1 What is the difference between the following: global-level, global strategy and globalization?

2 Is the dominance of Western economies coming to an end?

3 What are the four drivers of the competitive advantage of nations?

4 What are the four strategic approaches to international strategy?

5 How can local companies compete in emerging economies?

6 Do national cultures influence strategic management?

7 What is a strategic platform and what are its complementors?

8 What are the advantages and disadvantages of alliances?

SEMINAR AND ASSIGNMENT QUESTIONS

1 Put together two lists that compare how national cultures may encourage and discourage any of the four types of global-level strategy.

2 Can international organizations be managed as a single company? Consider if a one-company culture is effective.

3 Are countries like China and India more likely to use the Anglo-Saxon rather than the German/Japanese models for strategic management? Compare the two models and use contrasting examples from America, the United Kingdom, Germany, and Japan.

CHAPTER END-NOTES

1 Friedman, T. (2005), *The World is Flat: A Brief History of the Globalized World in the 21st Century,* London: Allen Lane.

2 One influential definition of economic globalization is: 'the increasing integration of economies around the world, particularly

through the movement of goods, services, and capital across borders. The term sometimes also refers to the movement of people (labour) and knowledge (technology) across international borders. There are also broader cultural, political, and environmental dimensions of globalization'. See 'International Monetary Fund (2008), Globalization: a brief overview', *Issues Brief,* issue 02/08, Washington DC, IMF, p. 2.

3 Lilja, K. and Moen, E. (2003), 'Coordinating transnational competition: changing patterns in the European pulp and paper industry', in Djelic, M-L. and Quack, S. (eds) *Globalization and Institutions: Redefining the Rules of the Economic Game,* Cheltenham: Edward Elgar, pp. 187–160.

4 Klein, N. (2001), *No Logo,* London: Flamingo.

5 Wright, A. (2005, *Ripped and Torn: Levi's, Latin America and the Blue Jean Dream,* London: Ebury Press.

6 Hopper, K. and Hopper, W. (2009), *The Puritan Gift, Reclaiming the American Dream Amidst Global Financial Chaos,* London: I.B. Tauris,

7 Porter, M. E. (1990), *The Competitive Advantage of Nations,* New York: Free Press.

8 Adapted from Porter, M. E. (1990), *The Competitive Advantage of Nations,* New York: Free Press.

9 Kaplan, R. S. and Norton, D. P. (2001), 'Transforming the balanced scorecard from performance measurement to strategic management: part 1', *Accounting Horizons,* 15(1):87–104.

10 Galbraith, J. K. (1975), *Economics and the Public Purpose,* London: Pelican.

11 Drucker, P. F. (1969), *The Age of Discontinuity,* London: Pan Piper.

12 See Rugman, A. M. and D'Cruz, J. (1991), *Fast Forward: Improving Canada's International Competitiveness,* Toronto: Kodak Canada.

13 Dunning, J. H. (1993), 'Internationalizing Porter's diamond', *Management International Review,* 33(2):7–15.

14 Thomas, D. (2012), 'Nokia to slash 4,000 jobs in shift to Asia', *Financial Times,* September, p. 20.

15 It could also signal a move to longer-term thinking rather than an emphasis on maximizing shorter-term shareholder value, see: Denning, S. (2012), 'Why Apple and GE are bringing back manufacturing', *Forbes,* 12 July, www.forbes.com.

16 Bartlett, C. and Ghoshal, S. (1989), *Managing Across Borders: The Transnational Solution*, London: Business Books; Bartlett, C. and Beamish, P. (2010), *Transnational Management: Text, Cases, and Readings in Cross-Border Management,* (6 edn) London: McGraw-Hill.

17 Felsted, A. (2012), 'American dream that died for Tesco', *Financial Times,* 6 December, p. 25.

18 Atsmon, Y., Kertesz, A. and Vittal, I. (2011), 'Is your emerging-market strategy local enough?' *McKinsey Quarterly,* April, www.mckinseyquarterly.com.

19 Levitt, T. (1983), 'The globalization of markets', *Harvard Business Review*, July-August, pp. 92–102.

20 George, N. (2001), 'One furniture store fits all', *Financial Times*, 8 February.

21 Davis, E. (2011), *Made in Britain: How the Nation Earns its Living*, London: Little, Brown, p. 219.

22 Mishkin, S. and Pearson, S. (2013), 'Foxconn faces culture clash as its global reach grows', *Financial Times,* 4 January, p. 15.

23 Witcher, B. J. and Chau, V. S. (2012), 'Varieties of capitalism and strategic management: managing performance in multinational after the global financial crisis', *British Journal of Management,* 23(March), S58–S73.

24 Ghemawat, P. (2005), 'Regional strategies for global leadership', *Harvard Business Review,* December.

25 Ohmae, K. (1985), *Triad Power: The Coming Shape of Global Competition,* New York: The Free Press.

26 Rugman, A. M. and Verbeke, A. (2004), 'A perspective on regional and global strategies of multinational enterprises', *Journal of International Business Studies,* 35(1):3–18.

27 Rugman, A. M. (2005), *The Regional Multinationals: MNEs and 'Global' Strategic Management,* Cambridge: Cambridge University; Rugmand, A. and Hodgetts, R. (2001), 'The end of global strategy', *European Management Review,* 19(4):333–343.

28 Levitt, T. (1983), 'The globalization of markets' *Harvard Business Review,* July-August, pp. 92–102.

29 Yip, G. S. (2002), 'Global strategy in the twenty-first century', in Mazzucato, M. (ed.) (2002), *Strategy for Business, a Reader'*, London: Sage Publications, 358–368. See also: Yip, G. S. (1992), *Total Global Strategy: Managing for Worldwide Competitive Advantage,* Englewood Cliffs: Prentice Hall, and Yip, G. S. (2003), *Total Global Strategy II: Updated for the Internet and Service Era,* Upper Saddle River NJ: Prentice Hall.

30 Schlie, E. and Yip, G. S. (2000), 'Regional follows global: strategy mixes in the world automotive industry', *European Management Journal,* 18:343–205.

31 Davis, E. (2011), *Made in Britain: How the Nation Earns its Living,* London: Little, Brown.

32 Xinhua (2012),'Experts warning: beware mergers that clip local brands', *China Daily,* November.

33 Nohria and Ghoshal explain two alternative approaches: differentiated fit and shared values. The former is when the structure of relations between a headquarters and its subsidiaries is organized to fit the local contexts of the subsidiaries, and the latter is the degree of shared values determining relations between headquarters and the subsidiaries: see Nohria, N. and Ghoshal, S. (1994), 'Differential fit and shared values: alternatives for managing headquarters-subsidiary relations', *Strategic Management Journal,* 15(6):491–502.

34 HayGroup (2006), 'Going global, in The World's Most Admired Companies', The World's Most Admired Companies supplement, *Fortune,* 6 March, pp. 4–5.

35 Senn, J. A. (1995), 'Interview with Akio Morita, Chairman of Sony Corporation', *Global Management Challenges,* Computer Information Systems Department, Georgia State University, cis.gsu.edu/jsenn/morita.pdf.

36 Kwong, R. and Mitchell, T. (2008), 'Coke to squeeze more from China', *Financial Times,* 4 September, p. 20.

37 Tomkins, R. (2003), As hostility towards America grows, will the world lose its appetite for Coca-Cola, McDonald's and Nike? *Financial Times,* 27 March, p. 19.

38 Prahalad, C. K. (2010), *The Fortune at the Bottom of the Pyramid: Eradicating Poverty Through Profits*, London: FT Press. For a perspective that argues high prices are also necessary, see Simanis, E. (2012), 'Reality check at the bottom of the pyramid', *Harvard Business Review,* June, pp. 120–125.

39 Reed, J. (2010), 'A drive to Lego land', Analysis, *Financial Times*, 1 December, p. 15.

40 Marsh, P. (2012), 'Nimble, niche and networked', analysis, *Financial Times,* 13 June, p. 11.

41 See Knight, G. A. and Cavusgil, S. T. (2004), 'Innovation, organizational capabilities, and the Born-Global firm', *Journal of International Business Studies,* 35(2):124–141. The rise of the micro-multinational has encouraged many to see it as a lever to generate jobs in a so-called 'project economy', see Mettier, A. and Williams, A. D. (2011), 'The rise of the micro-multinational: How freelancers and technology-savvy start-ups are driving growth, jobs and innovation', *Lisbon Council Policy Brief,* V(3), Brussels: The Lisbon Council.

42 Hanbury-Tenison, M. (2011), 'Web offers a comfortable fit', *Financial Times,* 24 November, p. 19.

43 Dawar, N. and Frost, T. (1999), 'Competing with Giants: survival strategies for local companies in emerging markets', *Harvard Business Review,* March-April, pp. 119–129.

44 Adapted from Dawar, N. and Frost, T. (1999), 'Competing with Giants: survival strategies for local companies in emerging markets', *Harvard Business Review,* March-April, p. 122.

45 Ghemwat, P. (2003), 'The forgotten strategy', *Harvard Business Review,* November, pp. 76–84.

See also Kandell, J. (2011), 'Is Brazil's Embraer ready to take on Boeing', *Institutional Investor,* 25 July, http://www.institutionalinvestor.com/Article/2869137/Search/Is-Brazils-Embraer-Ready-To-Take-On-Boeing.html.

46 London, T. and Hart, S. L. (2004), 'Reinventing strategies for emergent markets: beyond the transnational model', *Journal of International Business Studies,* 35(5):350–370.

47 Chang, S. J. and Hong, J. (2000), 'Economic performance of group affiliated companies in Korea: Intragroup resource sharing and internal business transactions', *Academy of Management Journal,* 37(2):429–448.

48 Barton, D. and Deutsch, C. G. (2008), 'Transforming a South Korean chaebol: an interview with Doosan's Yongmaan Park', *The McKinsey Quarterly,* September. www.mckinseyquarterly.com.

49 Mishkin, S. and Pearson, S. (2013), 'Foxconn faces culture clash as its global reach grows', *Financial Times,* 4 January, p. 15.

50 Hong, J. F. L., Easterby-Smith, M. and Snell, R. S. (2006), 'Transferring organizational learning systems to Japanese subsidiaries in China', *Journal of Management Studies,* 43(5):1027–1058.

51 Magee, D. (2007) *How Toyota Became #1, Leadership Lessons from the World's Greatest Car Company*, London: Portfolio, Penguin Group, p.170.

52 Ghosn, C. and Reis, P. (2003) *Shift: Inside Nissan's Historic Revival,* London: Currency, Doubleday, p. 166.

53 Hofstede, G. (1980), *Culture's Consequences: International Differences in Work-related Values,* London: Sage Publications. See also Hofstede, G. and Hofstede, G. J. (2005), *Cultures and Organizations: Software of the Mind,* (2 edn) New York: McGraw-Hill.

54 Hall, P. A. and Soskice, D. (2001). 'An Introduction to Varieties of Capitalism', in Hall and Soskice (eds). *Varieties of Capitalism: The Institutional Foundations of Comparative Advantage,* Oxford, Oxford University Press,

1–68, pp. 6–7. Alfred Chandler had earlier conceptualized capitalism in the US as competitive managerial capitalism (where in terms of governance, executives have no connection with the founders and their families and have little equity in the firms); in the UK as personal capitalism (founders and their families continue to be influential shareholders and senior executives, although they have recruited managerial hierarchies), and in Germany as co-operative managerial capitalism (with closer a involvement of other stakeholders, notably the banks, in executive decisions): see Chandler Jr., A. D. (1990), *Scale and Scope: The Dynamics of Industrial Capitalism,* London: Belknap Press.

55 Williamson, O. (1985), *The Economic Institutions of Capitalism: Firms, Markets, Relational Contracting*, New York, Free Press.

56 Nissan (2004), *Alliance Vision – Destination,* Nissan Motor Company. www.nissan-global.com.

57 Whittington, R. (2001), *What is Strategy – and Does it Matter?* (2 edn), London: Cengage Learning, p. 5.

58 Albert, M. (1991), *Capitalisme contre Capitalisme,* Paris: Editions de Seuril. For a review of the subject and how it is associated with different views of strategy, see Witcher, B. J. and Chau, V. S. (2012), 'Varieties of capitalism and strategic management: managing performance in multinational after the global financial crisis', *British Journal of Management,* 23 (March), S58–S73.

59 For a review across the world and particularly China, see *The Economist* (2012), 'State Capitalism', special report, January.

60 Dyer, G. (2010), 'State capitalism: China's "market-Leninism" has yet to face biggest test', *Financial Times,* 13 September.

61 CEIBS (2012), '*CEIBS 2012 Survey: Challenges and Success Factors for Foreign Companies in China',* China Europe International Business School.

62 Zhenghua, W. (2012), 'Family feud between Danone and Wahaha', *China Daily,* November.

63 Brandenburger, A. M. and Nalebuff, B. (1996), *Co-opetition: A Revolution Mindset that Combines Competition and Cooperation – The Game Theory Strategy that's Changing the Game of Business,* New York: Doubleday.

64 Gnyawali, D. R. and Madhavan, R. (2001), 'Cooperative networks and competitive dynamics: a structural embeddedness perspective', *Academy of Management Review,* 26(3):431–445.

65 Evans, D. S., Hagiu, A. and Schmalensee, R. (2006), *Invisible Engines: How Software Platforms Drive Innovation and Transform Industries,* Cambridge MA: MIT Press.

66 Martin, P. (2001), 'Let's hear it for Microsoft', *Financial Times,* 16 October, p. 23.

67 Teece, D. C. (2007), 'Explicating dynamic capabilities: the nature and microfoundations of (sustainable) enterprise performance', *Strategic Management Journal,* 28:1319–1350.

68 Witcher, B. J. (1982), 'Telepropinquity: Implications for Business Trading Systems', in Didsbury, H. F. (ed.) *Communications and the Future,* Washington DC: World Future Society, 296–304.

69 Magee, D. (2003), *Turnaround: How Carlos Ghosn Rescued Nissan,* New York: HarperCollins, p. 135.

70 Arnold, M. (2008), 'How the credit crunch threw a spanner in works for bolt-ons', *Financial Times,* 22 August, p. 21.

Global strategic management at Tata Steel

Background to the Tata group of companies

The Tata group of companies is a large multinational conglomerate that in 2011 employed around 400 000 people and had revenues approaching £54 billion. The group consists of nearly 100 companies and is India's largest private sector group. Its businesses range across seven industrial sectors: information systems and communications, engineering, materials, energy, consumer products, and chemicals. Tata was founded in the mid-19th century, and since that time its declared purpose has been to explore and develop business opportunities, and to assist in the development of India.

When the Indian economy was liberalized in the 1990s Tata rethought its strategic management. A view emerged that the group was too loosely connected to manage itself for globalization.[1] The group moved to reduce its exposure to the Indian economy, by internationalizing its activities, which saw the acquisition of established overseas' companies with global brands, and the adoption of global business methodologies and management philosophies. These changes have required the Tata Group to restructure its traditional shape.

At the group's core is a holding company, Tata Sons, which is owned by three philanthropic charitable trusts and the Tata family; the chairman acts as the chief executive for the Tata Group. Tata Sons owns the Tata name and trademark, and has minority stakes in the other companies. The Tata companies cross-hold stakes in each other, which gives considerable freedom to the individual companies (they also operate as autonomous legal entities, with their own independent boards of directors, and executives).

The number of Tata companies, mostly small and based in India, has been reduced from around 300 to 90 (28 are publicly listed). These changes are intended to make the group more cohesive and competitive. The group has followed an ambitious global acquisition strategy. Between 1991 and 2005, 29 acquisitions were made, and between 2006 and 2010, there have been another 36. Some of the largest were Tata Tea's takeover of the iconic UK brand Tetley, for £290 million in 2000; in 2007, Tata Steel bought Corus, Europe's second largest steelmaker, for £7.8 billion, and just a year later, Tata Motors paid Ford £1.5 billion for Jaguar Land Rover.

The group's strategic objectives are that each company should (1) deliver returns greater than the cost of capital; (2) be in the top three of its industry, and (3) achieve high growth in global markets. According to R.K. Krishna Kumar, a director of Tata Sons, global branding is a natural evolutionary course for the group: 'The Japanese started this way, so did the Koreans, and there's really no reason to ask whether the trajectory is the right one – it's a strategic necessity for companies and countries as they evolve'.[2] The advantages of brands are twofold: they add additional value to products, and by controlling the brand, the corporate group is able to increase its influence on management of the individual companies.

During the mid-1990s Tata Sons introduced a Brand Equity and Business Promotion Agreement, which requires the group's companies to pay a percentage of their annual revenues for using the Tata name and brand. The companies must also apply the group's code of conduct, which documents Tata's general principles and ethics and its Tata Business Excellence Model (TBEM). The model is based on the Baldrige Excellence Framework and it is used to, 'deliver strategic direction and drive business improvement. It has elements that enable companies following its directives to capture the best of global business processes and practices.'[3]

The group's strategic management remains primarily collaborative and emergent rather than controlling and prescriptive. However, it may prove difficult to maintain the distinctiveness of the Tata Brand if the companies are free to pursue their own strategy. For example, in different regions of the world the group seems to be following different approaches: in developing economies Tata companies seem to be diversifying into unrelated businesses, while the opposite is true for more developed economies (conglomerates may have advantages in a developing context, but not in an industrial one).[4]

Vision 2007 at Tata Steel

The originally named Tata Iron and Steel Company was established in 1907, and is now the world's third largest steel company, with an annual crude steel output of around 28 million tonnes. It employs around 83 000 people across 24 countries. In 2002 the company introduced a five-year strategic plan called Vision 2007. This is represented as a pillared house (see Exhibit 8.1), with Tata Steel's purpose placed at its top, supported by values, strategic goals, and strategy.

The purpose of Vision 2007 was twofold: to make Tata Steel's economic value added positive, and to improve the quality of life for employees and the communities the company serves. The company had become perhaps the lowest cost supplier of steel in the world, but the economic value added was problematic.

Ratan Tata, the Tata group's chief executive in July 2001, said: 'We recognized that, regrettably, the steel industry does not cover the cost of capital … If you have to invest … as we did in the modernization of the plant, and if it doesn't give us a return that is equal to the cost of capital, then we have destroyed shareholder value … we have to do much more in steel to make it an investor-attractive area of business'.[5]

Six strategic goals were listed: (1) to move from a commodity-based business to brands; (2) to achieve positive economic value added in core businesses; (3) to continue as the lowest cost producer of steel; (4) to achieve value creating partnerships with customers and suppliers; (5) to have enthused and happy employees; and (6) to achieve sustainable growth.

To achieve these, the following strategies were identified: (1) manage knowledge; (2) outsource those business areas that do effect the company's sources of competitive advantage; (3) encourage innovation and a culture of calculated risks; (4) excel at TBEM; (5) unleash people's potential and create leaders who will build the future; (6) invest in attractive new business that will complement steel; (7) ensure safety and environmental sustainability; and (8) divest chronically under-performing non-core businesses, while merge and acquire those that add synergy and accelerated growth and that can be organized as profit centres.

Several initiatives were introduced, which included new brands, such as Tata Steelium (cold rolled steel), Tata Shaktee (galvanized corrugated sheets), Tata Pipes, and so on, and which were organized as profit centres. Other initiatives included changes to improve the integration of the supply chain. In 2007 the Anglo-Dutch company, Corus, was acquired for £6.7 billion to improve Tata's access to EU markets and expand operations at the high-value end of steel products. In 2005 the company acquired Singapore's NatSteel and Thailand's Millennium Steel, to strengthen its industry position in higher value finished products in the growing Asian markets).[6]

The strategic management process

The TBEM is managed as an annual process; this includes checking and assessing the core values of the Tata group, including business methodologies and management philosophies, such as customer driven processes, a long-range view of the future and a systems perspective. A key part is the strategic planning process: how the company develops strategy, including its strategic objectives, action plans and related human resource plans, and how plans are deployed and performance-tracked (the process is shown in Exhibit 8.2).

Seven strategic tasks are involved, which from right to left in Exhibit 8.2 are purpose statements (vision, mission, values), through to performance and progress review. The exhibit shows beneath these the processes involved in carrying out these tasks, moving through time from left to right. Strategy is developed through a consideration of purpose, an analysis of the environment and opportunities, objectives and targets, and the determination of the key strategic initiatives and functional excellence plans (thus strategy is developed with operational effectiveness).

Balanced scorecards are used to derive the key strategic imperatives from the strategic objectives, which are linked to the needs of key stakeholders. The voice of the customer and the importance of critical success factors are shown carried forward across the departments, and the management of performance and its review. Rewards and recognition refer

EXHIBIT 8.1 Vision, 2002–2007[7]

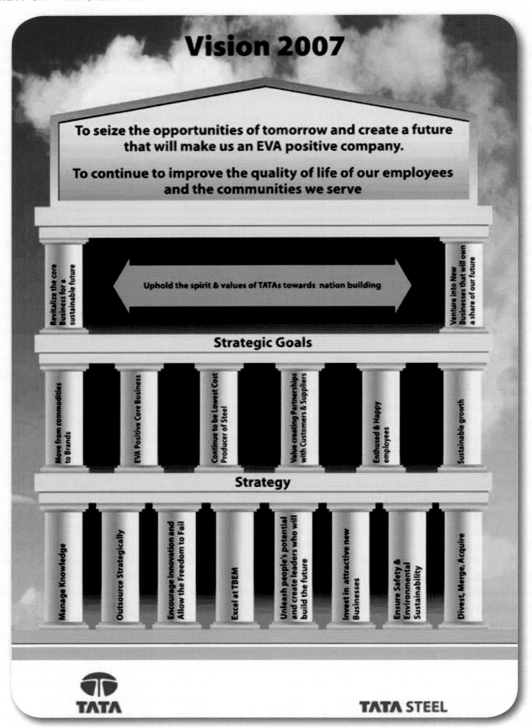

EXHIBIT 8.2 The strategic management process[8]

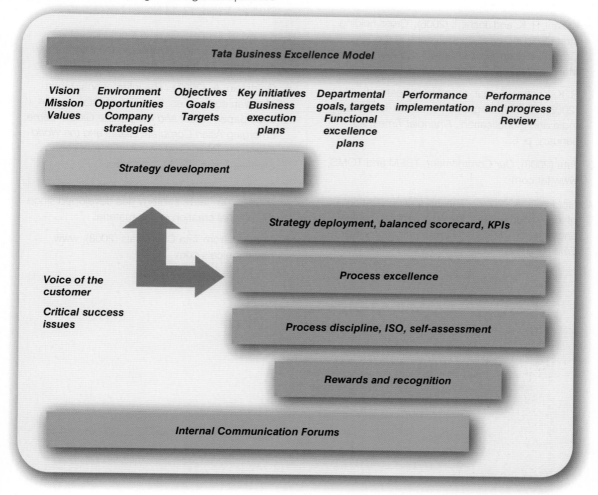

to the alignment of human resource plans, and the internal communication forums are used to provide company-wide feedback for strategy development and deployment.

The TBEM provides a framework for the group to understand how strategy is being applied and how it works at an operational level. Executives from other Tata companies participate in the annual audit activity and play a part in assessing the extent to which Tata Steel conforms to the criteria laid down in the group's Brand Equity and Promotion Agreement. The feedback is used to promote best practice in the wider group through its regional forums.

Discussion questions

1 What is the role played by the group's Tata Business Excellence Model and the Tata brand?

2 Work out how Tata Steel conforms to this book's strategic management model: POSIES. What are the strengths and weaknesses of the group's strategic management in relation to Tata Steel?

3 How does Tata's strategic management of a multinational compare to that of western multinationals?

Case end-notes

1 Kakani, R. K. and Joshi, T. (2006), 'Cross holding strategy to increase control: case of the Tata Group', *Working Paper* 06–03, School of Management, XLRI, Jamshedpur.

2 R. K. Krishna Kumar, reported in Leahy, J. (2008), 'The burning ambition of the Tata group, India and globalisation', *Financial Times,* 25 January, p. 5.

3 Tata (2008), *Our Commitment*, TBEM and TQMS, www.tat.com.

4 Goldstein, A. (2007), 'The internationalization of Indian companies: the case of Tata', conference paper, *Thrust and Parry in the Global Game: Emerging Asian Corporate Giants and the World Economy,* Tokyo Club Foundation for Global Studies, Tokyo, 13–14 November.

5 Kanavi, S. (2001), 'Given the right incentives, India can be a steel supplier to the world', *Business India,* 23 July.

6 Goldstein, A. (2007), 'The internationalization of Indian companies: the case of Tata', conference paper, *Thrust and Parry in the Global Game: Emerging Asian Corporate Giants and the World Economy,* Tokyo Club Foundation for Global Studies, Tokyo, 13–14 November.

7 Tata Steel (2002), *Vision 2007*, Annual Report 2002–2003. Tata's strategy has developed since the original creation of this material.

8 Adapted from Tata Chemicals (2008), www.tatachemicals.com.

'LIFE IS WHAT HAPPENS TO YOU, WHILE YOU ARE MAKING OTHER PLANS.'

JOHN LENNON.

'IT HELPS IF PLANS ARE MANAGED SO THAT THERE MAY BE FEWER NASTY SURPRISES.'

BARRY WITCHER AND VINH CHAU.

Managing strategy in action

This part introduces three important areas of strategy in action. These include how organizations implement strategy by organizing, and how they manage strategic and control strategy at a daily management level. In the end, the success of strategic management depends upon the people who lead their organizations.

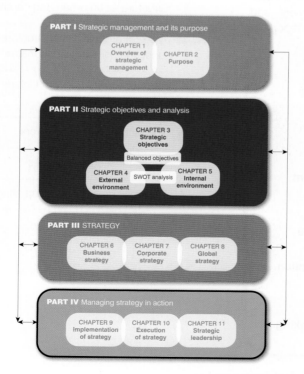

Chapter 9

IMPLEMENTATION: ORGANIZING STRATEGY

Organizational structure

S tructure is the organization of effort into a coherent and working entity. Its characterizing feature is a hierarchy to determine an order of responsibilities; only very small organizations can do without it. **Structure** can be categorized in terms of width and the degree to which decisions are centralized or not, and height, according to the number of levels of management, and a hierarchy formalizing the direction of reporting.

KEY TERMS

business process

business process re-engineering (BPR)

cross-functional

downsizing

functional management

joined-up management

loosely coupled systems

M-form organization

matrix structure

McKinsey 7S framework

medium-term plans

middle management

networks

strategic architecture

strategy implementation

structure

systems

systems thinking

LEARNING OBJECTIVES

This chapter provides you with an understanding of the following:

1 Structure as an organizing capability

2 Types of organizational structure – functional, divisional and matrix

3 Forms of organizing that include networks and internal markets

4 The McKinsey 7S framework

5 Cross-functional structures

6 Business process re-engineering

Business vignette Getting structure right at the oil companies

BP and its larger ExxonMobil rival differ in the degree of how they organize strategically. After a series of operating disasters, most notably in the Gulf of Mexico, BP has been introducing a fundamental change to the way it is structured to counter views among investors that the company has a systemic operating problem. The BP revamp is expected to take five to ten years. The company was organized to be the most efficient cost-cutter in the industry. This may have influenced safety and maintenance has probably contributed to skill shortages within the company. The acquisition of Arco and Amoco complicated this. BP improved Amoco's safety record, but BP admits it failed to integrate fully different safety systems. Its plants still use a range of procedures that are entrenched by local custom and practice.

It seems a gap may have emerged between the corporate centre, which tries to establish clear business principles, and local management, which is focused on day-to-day operational performance. BP's organizational structure is made up of many business units which are profit centres. These contrast the old school style of ExxonMobil, which uses a more centralized structure.

ExxonMobil is the only major oil company with a structure that allows it to face the challenge of taking on huge, technologically challenging projects. Exxon's success resulted from the bitter experience of the Exxon Valdez tanker oil spill in Alaska in 1989. The company overhauled its approach to safety and centralized its businesses, adding checks and balances, and created an internal communications system that improved everything from financial prudence, to physical caution and technological innovation. Based on the approach taken by Dow Chemical, the company structure is now the same around the world. Therefore, employees do not have to relearn Exxon's policies and procedures every time they move. It also allows problems to be communicated throughout the company so that others can help, or at least learn from them.

Mark Albers, president of ExxonMobil Development Company, who oversees all of Exxon's new production and development projects, says the centralized

structure is key to its success. From concept to production, all of Exxon's big projects are managed from Houston.

In terms of the management and service that we provide to each of our affiliates, it's all done in one location, which means we can provide the same world-class service to an affiliate in Angola as in Sakhàlin, as in Qatar. And people are literally just down the hall from people who worked on a similar issue on a project somewhere else down the globe, so the information transfer and the best practice transfer is immediate.

He points out that the projects Exxon operates are within 3 per cent of the unit costs expected at the time of funding, and the company finishes its projects about 5 per cent more quickly than it forecasts.[1]

 Structure is the organization of effort into a coherent and working entity. Its characterizing feature is a hierarchy to determine an order of responsibilities; only very small organizations can do without it.

A difference is sometimes made between local structure (the organization within functional and distributed units) and strategic structures (the organization of the total structure). Broadly, the overall structure of organizations can be grouped into four main types. In Figure 9.1 these are represented by functional, product, regional and matrix forms. The lines between the boxes show the main reporting paths between of the different parts. These also reflect corporate parenting styles, as already discussed in Chapter 7.

Functional structure is based on **functional management**. This involves the division of work into

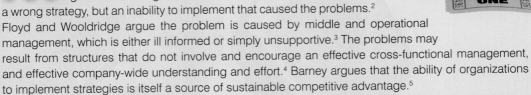

KEY DEBATE 9.1

Is it implementation or strategy that matters?

Many observers argue that the reasons for ineffective strategic management concern poor implementation. Charan and Colvin argue that for 70 per cent of organizations that get into trouble, it was not because of a wrong strategy, but an inability to implement that caused the problems.[2] Floyd and Wooldridge argue the problem is caused by middle and operational management, which is either ill informed or simply unsupportive.[3] The problems may result from structures that do not involve and encourage an effective cross-functional management, and effective company-wide understanding and effort.[4] Barney argues that the ability of organizations to implement strategies is itself a source of sustainable competitive advantage.[5]

Others, such as the processual, or learning school of strategy (see Chapter 1), argue that the distinction between strategy and implementation is a false one anyway.[6] Mintzberg thinks there is a disconnect between grand strategy and operations: this is due to the fact that senior managers do not understand their organizations.[7]

Question: What are the principal tasks of good strategy implementation?

FIGURE 9.1 Four basic types of organizational structure

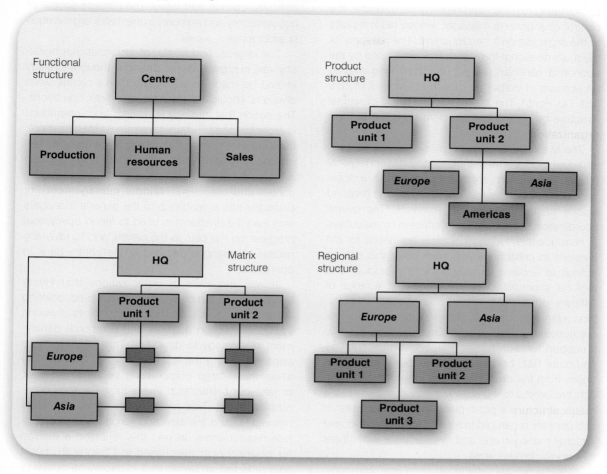

specialist activities. Typically these are organized into departments that specialize in purchasing, manufacturing, marketing, finance and so on. This specialization is characteristic of the division of labour, when work is split into parts so that individuals are more able to carry it out effectively. To work as a complete system the separate parts must be coordinated effectively by a centre, so that the structure must be hierarchical where the centre is positioned at the top of the organization and controls the overall design of the inputs-into-outputs transformation process.

As some organizations grow in size, becoming multi-product and multi-market enterprises, they group their activities into divisions, based on products and geographical regions. These divisions are

organized into functional activities with their own coordinating centre, and are typically under the control of a general manager, whose team reports to the organization's headquarters. The reasons for the multi-divisional form were first articulated by the economic historian, Alfred Chandler, who offered an account of corporate growth at General Motors and Du Pont.[8] The term used for multi-divisional structure by organizational scientists is the **M-form organization**.

The M-form enables each division to specialize in particular products (or brands), or on a distinct regional market. The divisions are thus focused and are closer to customers, so that they can pick up, and respond quickly to, the needs of the markets. The overall coordination of the divisions is effected by executives at headquarters. However, if there are needs for the divisions to collaborate with each other, this can be difficult to achieve formally within the product and regional structural form. If, for example, a range of different products is required for distinct markets, then inter-divisional and inter-departmental projects are necessary. Project teams may be organized by a support function based at headquarters, such as corporate R&D or marketing, with their membership drawn from the divisions. Where inter-divisional projects are central to the organization's core business a **matrix structure** is put in place. In this, project teams and units are organized to report jointly to product and regional management, and to coordinate with others for ongoing project work.

ABB, a global electrical products company, made the product line geographical matrix approach popular in the 1990s, when it organized its hundreds of local business units around the world. In the new structure, each local business unit reported to both a country executive and worldwide line-of-business executive. This allowed the corporation to achieve the benefits of centralized coordination, functional expertise, and economies of scale for product groups while maintaining local divisional autonomy and entrepreneurship for marketing and sales activities. Matrix organizations have proved difficult to manage because of their inherent tension between the interests of the senior executives responsible for managing either a row or a column of the matrix. A manager at the intersection struggles to coordinate between the preferences of his 'row'

and 'column' managers, leading to new sources of difficulty, conflict and delay. The ultimate source of accountability and authority in the matrix organization is ambiguous.

The degree, and levels, of organizational hierarchy vary in organizations. Chandler thought strategy should be made at an organization's centre, while divisions should be involved only with operations. The notion that strategy is distinct from operations is a central one for classical strategic management: the idea that strategic planning is primarily a central and long-term function, while its implementation is carried out through shorter-term management control and operations. **Middle management** (for Chandler this is made up of the general managers who lead the divisions) is used to report operational progress on the plan to the centre, and to relay any necessary changes decided at the centre back to operations.

It was this view of organizations that Henry Mintzberg and James Brian Quinn attacked, pointing out that the idea a centre can control its divisions through detached analysis and a rational deployment of strategy is doubtful.[9] This became more apparent during the last years of the 20th century when many large corporations began to de-layer, or take out hierarchical levels to make their organization flatter. This reduced the ranks of middle managers, and the size and functions at a corporate headquarters. In part this reflected a fashion for downscoping (discussed in Chapter 8), but it also reflected an awareness of Japanese business process and customer-based organizing: for example, total quality management and lean production (Chapter 5).

Problems of functional organization

Functional working has many disadvantages from a strategic management point of view. Strategic priorities are likely to become fragmented, as critical business processes are chopped into disjointed pieces and scattered across several specialized departments. This can result in many hand-offs between activities, which lengthen completion time; and efforts to deal with delays increase the costs of coordination and overheads. There is a risk that essential details fall through the cracks. Breaking objectives down into specialized pieces is also to lose sight of the strategic imperative for an activity, so that employees go through the motions, and do not follow through to make sure the work is being done.

Process organization

A **business process** is a sequence of tasks necessary to deliver a business objective. In the organization science literature, 'processes' are classically understood as (normally) informal cross-functional activities, which flow horizontally across the vertical and hierarchical structure of the organization. The distinction is that a hierarchical structure provides a stable working framework, while processes are essentially the organizing activity within that framework. The new thing about this lies in the relationship of organization to organizing. In Japanese organizations, business processes are organized more directly around the pull of customer requirements, whereas in many Western organizations, the requirements of the customer are less instant, and pushed through the organization through top-down planning and design. The practical difference for organizing is that in a Japanese context the processes decide, bottom-up, what they need from the specialists.

Reporting on the findings of a major international study of organizational forms in Europe and Japan, Andrew Pettigrew with others write that there is 'now an understandable tendency to drop the noun of organization and to use the more dynamic verb of organizing to try and capture the realities of continuous innovation ... Organizing and strategizing are now recognized as truly complementary activities even to the point where the form of organizing, may be synonymous with the strategy of the firm'.[11]

> **There is now an understandable tendency to drop the noun of organization and to use the more dynamic verb of organizing to try and capture the realities of continuous innovation … Organizing and strategizing are now recognized as truly complementary activities even to the point where the form of organizing, may be synonymous with the strategy of the firm.**

Cross-functional structure

In fact, the process orientation of large Japanese organizations is still based within a functional structure, but the difference is that business processes are strategically managed to take account of top-down priorities. Japan has a strong top-to-bottom structure in its organizations that are likely to impede horizontal relations. The solution has been to use cross-functional committees to provide support for how key strategic **cross-functional** objectives are managed in the functional areas of the business. Ishikawa has compared this activity to making cloth, when the horizontal woof (sometimes called weft) of a textile is crossed to bind together the vertical warp into a strongly held together textile (see Figure 9.2).[12]

FIGURE 9.2 Cross-functional woof to weave functional warp

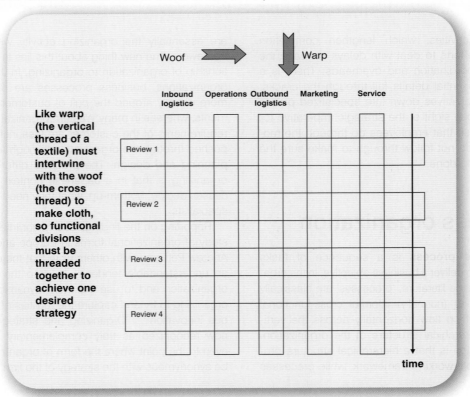

The functional areas of a business are suggested at the top of the figure, and the work of the committees through review is indicated on the left-hand side of the figure.

The cross-functional committees are organized centrally and involve senior management. These work to review periodically the organization-wide progress of a limited number of strategically derived objectives. The objectives are characterized in a similar way to the perspectives of the balanced scorecard (Chapter 3), as quality, cost, delivery, and education – where 'quality' means those objectives that are linked directly to customer-oriented requirements; 'cost' to financial needs; 'delivery' to the strategic needs of the core business processes, and 'education' to the growth and learning needs of the workforce.

At the time when the Japanese were first introducing cross-functional structures, Western corporations were moving away from management by top-down committee towards the devolved and divisional forms of corporate control.[13] In fact, Western corporations never really used the woof–warp structure of review for strategic objectives. Instead, they use matrix organization, where strategically relevant project work is based around specially established multi-skilled teams.

In fact, the Japanese used matrix organization as well, but the work of the project teams is strategically linked to a review of progress carried out within the existing cross-functional structure. In this context, Kondo suggests Japanese organizations do not have as many centralized functions, such as quality planning, coordination, and auditing, as their Western counterparts, but that instead these activities are carried out by line personnel, who have the necessary education and training for managing strategically linked objectives.[14] He pointed out that Japanese central departments are typically small and perform only a limited array of activities, including objective deployment, review and consulting services.

Downsizing

Some observers believe that increasing environmental dynamism and uncertainty from globalization, for example, requires greater organizational flexibility and therefore smaller and new forms of organizing. This is particularly so for industries where hypercompetition is present. **Downsizing** is a reduction in the size of a corporate entity. It reflects a wider revolution in thinking about organizations: a move from the bureaucratic pyramid to what the Yale sociologist, Richard Sennett, termed 'the flexible organization of the new capitalism':

> Cutting-edge firms and flexible organizations need people who can learn new skills rather than cling to old competencies. The dynamic organization emphasizes the ability to process and interpret changing bodies of information and practice ... In work terms a person's human 'potential' consists in how capable he or she is in moving from problem to problem, subject to subject.[15]

This resulted in smaller corporate headquarters for many organizations, and a reduced role for staff at the corporate office. However, downsizing has attracted much adverse commentary, since in several instances its scale was huge. For example, BT cut its workforce from 232 000 in 1990, to 148 000 in 1995; the consequences for employee relations were such that, according to BT surveys, one-fifth of its workforce thought that managers could not be relied upon.[16]

Downsizing is associated with **business process re-engineering (BPR)**, which was originally defined as the use of information technology to radically redesign business processes[17], but it quickly came to mean any breakthrough change in business processes that involves redesigning a set of activities to make them customer rather than functionally responsive. It involves establishing a senior management project team to question how the corporation should be structured if it were to be re-organized from scratch. Its focus is on creating an entirely new organization, so that it can eliminate overheads that are incurred because of excessive specialization. While it produces new forms of flexible organization, because it typically delayers the organization to make it flatter, it also diminishes the role and influence of middle management, which can adversely take away a main support for organizing, and diminishes collective corporate memory.

Downsizing is associated with outsourcing. This concern activities which do not contribute directly to value, and can be performed more effectively by external organizations. For example, Procter & Gamble has outsourced human resources, accounting, and information technology; these are activities that had employed 8000 people in areas that had been considered back office operations.[18] Outsourcing can be risky if things go wrong at the supplier over which the customer organization has no control. British Airways outsourced its in-flight prepared meals to Gate Gourmet, but in 2005 the caterer became involved in an industrial dispute that delayed BA flights and generated a lot of bad publicity.

Networks

Corporate memory is less important if organizations are in areas of dynamic change. Here there is a movement away from traditional hierarchies to modular and network organizations, which offer a new type of learning capability and corporate knowledge. **Networks** comprise informal groups of individuals, who are typically based in distinct and different parts of, and are sometimes external to, the organization. However, they can be organized from the corporate centre.

This happens at Xerox, where specialists manage from the centre cross-functional networks of experts located, sometimes individually, in the different business units acting as consultants in areas like IT, quality and human resources. The networks are informal and involve forums across the organization where ideas are exchanged about best practice, matters of mutual interest are discussed, and intra-organizational learning is facilitated. These networks are also used to manage the Xerox Management Model (see performance excellence, Chapter 5) and the deployment of strategic objectives (see Case 10).

Nearly all organizations have some form of informal networks that are quasi-social in character, and which often cut across formal structure. Compared to hierarchical structure, which is indicative of authority, lines of command and reporting, informal networks are typically about the communication of information and support. In some countries they take on special qualities that are influenced by national cultural practices (for example, see China's *guanxi*, Chapter 2).

Systems and systems thinking

Systems are typically formal and documented codes, policies and procedures, which organizations prescribe as normal or best ways of working. Such systems are important to hierarchical structure to clarify responsibilities and reporting procedures. However, **systems thinking** is different. Broadly it likens organizations to organisms, especially the idea that problems can only be understood by looking at the whole context, rather than by examining the constituent parts. Organizations have sub-systems just as organisms do. Many have boundaries that span each other and many will have interconnected components that work together. A systems way of thinking implies that people will see the whole, whereas in a functionally top-down organization there is always a danger of sub-optimization. This is where one part will act in its own interest, and against the interest of the customer and the whole. A systems approach emphasizes the use of integrative conceptual frameworks to guide strategic decisions, which can provide a consistent and holistic view of an organization's activities. The best known is the McKinsey Consulting Group's 7S framework.

PRINCIPLES IN PRACTICE 9.2

Success depends on being organized to achieve it

Jimmy Greaves, footballer, holds the record for the most goals scored for England. In his autobiography he puts England's success in the 1966 World Cup down to a new approach used by the England manager.

England's historic success was seen to be the result of players being 'professional' and 'doing a professional job'. Alf [the team manager] had had a game plan and he picked the players to suit that game plan. What he didn't do was create a game plan to suit the styles of the players at his disposal. Each player had a job to do within the game plan. They did it and England won the World Cup. Though players enjoyed a degree of freedom with this game plan, there was no place for a player who might want to stamp his own idiosyncratic style on the course of a game. No place for a maverick with a penchant for playing to the crowd. Players had to be professional and do the job they were being paid to do. The modernization of English football had picked up momentum since the late fifties. Even before 1966 coaches were having a bigger say in how the game should be played and teams were better organized … [it was] the death knell for players who were given to fully expressing themselves in the course of a game. Being 'professional' seeped into the subconscious of the game and any player who took it upon himself to play-act in the course of a match, or play to the gallery, was deemed to be unprofessional.[19]

The England World Cup team, 1966

Question: Is the new capitalism still appropriate for organizations since 2008?

McKinsey's 7S framework

The **McKinsey 7S framework** was first published by Waterman with others in 1980, and made popular by Tom Peters and Robert Waterman a couple of years later in their very successful book, *In Search of Excellence*.[20] These authors were McKinsey management consultants, who at the time were strongly influenced by the success of Japanese organizations that take a more organization-wide and integrative view of change management. The McKinsey consultants argue that in looking at an organization as a whole, seven variables are important, but the essential thing about them is that they are inter-linked, so that 'it's difficult, perhaps impossible to make significant progress in one area without making progress in the others as well … it isn't obvious which of the seven factors will be the driving force in changing a

FIGURE 9.3 Organizing for interconnectivity[21]

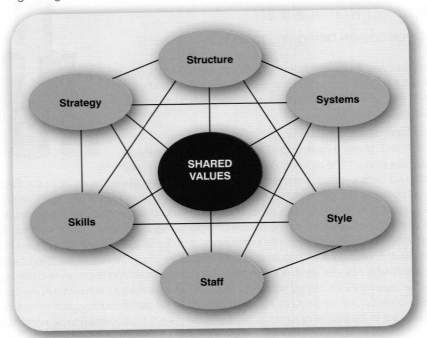

particular organization at a particular point in time'.[22] The seven variables are shown in Figure 9.3 and the lines between them signify their interconnectivity.

- Strategy: those actions an organization plans in response to, or anticipation of, changes in the external environment, its customers and competitors.
- Structure: the organization that divides tasks and provides for their coordination.
- Systems: the processes, procedures, formal and informal, that 'make an organization go'.
- Style: the perception a senior management team creates of itself in the organization.
- Staff: the socialization of managers in terms of what the business is about.
- Skills: the characterization of the organization in terms of what it does best, its dominating attributes or capabilities.
- Shared values (or superordinate goals): the guiding beliefs, or fundamental ideas, around which an organization is built.

Changes in strategy and structure by themselves can be implemented quickly. However, to be effective the other elements must be strategically managed, especially the central place of shared values, a concept that is virtually the same as core values (see Chapter 2). Changes in these other elements can take years to achieve, so that the real pace of change is ultimately a function of all seven variables.

Hard and soft strategic management

Pascale and Athos, who were also McKinsey consultants, used the 7S framework to explore the nature of Japanese management.[23] They found that while there is little difference between Japanese and Western organizations in terms of the management of strategy, structure, and systems, the Japanese give prominence to the other variables. Pascale and Athos call strategy–structure–systems hard-ball variables, and the others, soft-ball. Peters and Waterman used a similar idea they called loose–tight properties, to characterize best practice. These books stress that competitive advantage is based as much on soft-ball as it is on the hard-ball variables. The new competition of the Japanese resulted from a combination of the soft-ball variables of the 7S framework: the Japanese national 'culture gives them ambiguity, uncertainty, and imperfection, and interdependence as the most approved mode of relationship'.[24]

Using mostly Japanese examples, Ghoshal and Bartlett went further and argued for a soft-based approach to running organizations, based on purpose, process, and people.[25] These three things should replace strategy, structure, and systems. This is a flat view of organizational management that favours a minimum number of organizational levels; where a strategic direction is reliant on the creative abilities of people to sense and respond to opportunities. Thus, 'purpose' is the direction of the organization; 'process' involves self-directing teams, where people plan, do, check, and improve their own work, and 'people' are the facilitation of commitment and involvement to make self-management possible.

Strategic architecture

A related term, architecture, is popular in the general management literature where it is used to refer to such things as networks and infrastructural elements, including a mix of formal and informal management systems, frameworks, organizational structure, and culture. Architecture can be understood as those coordinating features that link up activities and influence behaviour, which are 'hard-wired' into an organization in the same way that a building's design will condition how people work. A modern example relates to information architecture, where the design of a database in terms of its applications will determine how people work together.

Hamel and Prahalad give **strategic architecture** a central role: 'a company needs a point of view about the future (industry foresight) and must construct a blueprint for getting there (strategic architecture)'.[26] This 'blueprint' is a framework for core

competence building and must ensure that existing core competencies do not fragment across corporate business units. Although they do explicitly make the link, the role of a strategic architecture is to enable an organization's dynamic capability: the corporate-wide capability to reconfigure and sustain core competencies, or strategic assets (see Chapter 5).

Joined-up management

Joined-up management is 'a strategy which seeks to bring together not only government departments and agencies, but also a range of private and voluntary bodies, working across organizational boundaries'.[27] It aims to address complex social problems, such as social exclusion and poverty, in a comprehensive and integrated way. While such problems have a long history, especially in relation to problems of coordination in government, the term 'joined-up government' came into common use in public sector management in the late 1990s as a criticism of functional departmentalization. However, public sector strategic management has tended to move away from this to favour the possibility that competitive influences can 'incentivize public services' to improve services.

Internal markets

Internal markets are created as quasi-markets to simulate market behaviour inside a single organization or an organizational group, such as a large corporation. The purpose is typically to achieve efficiencies, say, based on competing cost centres or through formal contracts. This approach has been favoured by governments in the United Kingdom for parts of the public sector, notably the National Health Service, where service providers must negotiate contracts with internal suppliers and some types of customers. The aim is to create a more cost-conscious orientation, but this may have been at the expense of a patient-caring organizational culture. More generally, collaborative efforts that encourage learning and technology transfer may be jeopardized if incentives and rewards work to encourage individualism rather than collective behaviours.

Flexible organizations and general strategic resources

The shift from a bureaucratic to a more fragmentary new form of fast-moving agile organization, argues Yale sociologist, Richard Sennett, works to reduce institutional loyalty, trust among workers, and weakened institutional knowledge.[28] He contrasts the bureaucratic pyramid to the 'new flexible organization': explaining its culture, he describes how cutting-edge firms want employees who are able to learn new general skills rather than cling to old competencies.

Employees are understood as a human resource that is capable of moving from problem to problem, subject to subject. This is a general rather than a firm-specific resource. According to the resource-based view, organization (and to some extent industry) resources, such as core competences, underpin competitive advantage. It is organization-specific experience that is valued.

In a liberal market economy the generality of strategic resources make them easier to switch between organizations than in a coordinated market economy which may have more specific and sticky strategic resources. Organizations are easier to assemble and to break up. A concentration of strategic decision-making in a few hands at the top of an organization allows leaders to implement decisions very quickly and any consequential reorganization is relatively straightforward to implement.[29]

As Sennett observes one vice of the old bureaucratic pyramid was its rigidity, its offices fixed, its people knowing exactly what was expected of them. However, it had the virtue of an accumulation of domain knowledge about how to make the system work, and in time experience and trust accumulates: 'the bureaucrat learns how to oil bureaucratic wheels'.[30] The flexible firm is now an influential model for government, but this organizing form may be inappropriate for those public institutions that seek to delivery security and well-being to citizens.

Question: Do resource-based view organizations lack a dynamic capability for managing change?

Loosely coupled strategic management

Karl Weick introduced a more fluid view of strategic organizing when he argued that it is how organizational elements come together frequently and loosely that determines how an organization works as an entity. Using ideas originally associated with biology, Weick argues that frequently in organizations several different means lead to the same outcomes, so that it can be said that means are loosely coupled to an end, in the sense that there are alternative pathways.[31] Rationality and indeterminacy are both accepted, which contrasts with classical views of administrative science, for example, of Simon and his view that complex systems should

be decomposed into stable subassemblies.[32] According to Weick, loose coupling involves impermanence, dissolvability, and tacitness; they are all the 'glue' that holds organizations together. Weick used a metaphor to start his essay about **loosely coupled systems**:

Imagine that you're either the referee, coach, player or spectator at an unconventional soccer match: the field for the game is round; there are several goals scattered haphazardly around the circular field; people can enter and leave the game when they want to; they can throw balls in whenever they want; they can say, 'that's my goal!' if they want to; the entire game takes place on a sloped field; and the game is played as if it makes sense. If you now substitute principals for referees, teachers for coaches, students for players, parents for spectators and schooling for soccer, you have found an equally unconventional depiction of school organizations. The beauty of this depiction is that it captures a different set of realities within educational organizations than are caught when these same organizations are viewed through the tenets of bureaucratic theory.[33]

In many ways strategic management looks more like Weick's unconventional soccer match than it does the old idea that an organization is like car; you assemble the pieces, put in the oil and off it goes.

Strategic planning – revisited

One could be forgiven, especially if one works in them, for thinking that organizations are a mess. Or, in some cases, they run themselves. Where does this leave strategic planning? How is it possible to be deliberate? The days of classical strategic planning, when long-range strategy, structure, and systems, were worked out at an organization's centre by planners for others to implement are now long gone. In the oil industry, for instance, Robert Grant concludes that strategic plans have become shorter term, more goals focused, and less specific with regard to actions and resource allocations, which are worked out informally at local levels. The role of strategic planning systems within strategic management has also changed. It has become less about strategic decision-making and more a mechanism for coordination and managing performance.[34]

Strategy implementation puts in place an organization's strategy. It is carried out through an organization's structure and control systems, and the outcomes are modified during its execution during daily management. 'Implementation' and 'execution' are often used interchangeably. However, an organization's structures and systems must be in place

KEY DEBATE 9.3

The importance of competition to structure

There is an implicit assumption in much of the writing about strategy that the intensity of competition works to sharpen organizations and their managements up through providing incentives for strong leadership and change. This belief can lead to problems when an organization's structure is designed to incentivize competitive behaviour. The logic for organizations (and hierarchies) is that (a market's) competitive behaviour is unfavourable to many purposes: see the original work of Arrow, and Williamson.[35]

The link between competition and good management is uncertain. When a financial perspective dominates a strategic portfolio approach; competition between SBUs within a corporate group may encourage short-termism (see Chapter 7).

The resource-based view argues that hierarchies are created spaces for organizing activity in a non-market like fashion. The things that make an organization competitively unique are core competencies and dynamic capabilities; it is how structure facilitates organizing these that really counts: 'The very essence of capabilities/competencies is that they cannot be readily assembled through markets', writes David Teece.[36]

Initiatives to introduce market influences to achieve hybrid structures have worked against the very organizational complementarity that sustains a hierarchical structure, and have proved dysfunctional enough to spiral hierarchies toward fundamental transformation.[37]

Question: There is a paucity of evidence about how structure promotes competition; can you think of any that motives employees effectively?

prior to execution, or the alignment of strategy with operational activity is unlikely. Strategic planning is today primarily an implementation activity for many large and complex organizations, and works through **medium-term plans**.

The objectives of a strategic balanced scorecard can be written into a medium-term plan under a strategic theme or challenge. The plan provides the signposts or yardsticks for an organization's near future, which will serve as a basis for setting the annual priorities to execute at the functional levels of the organization. These plans start at the senior level and are designed in the form of objectives set for three successive years. Because they relate to the longer-term balanced scorecard objectives, they are normally grouped in a similar manner to the four perspectives of the scorecard. Hamel and Prahalad explain similar plans as challenges, or stages, which will move the organization forward to achieve its longer-term strategic intent (see Chapter 3). Medium-term objectives are developed from the senior level medium-term plan at other units and levels of the organization. The specification and development of objectives is not meant to be prescriptive of the enablers. The modern view of strategic planning is similar to the programmatic view of planning favoured by Mintzberg (see Chapter 1) and his related concept of an umbrella strategy, when a loose and directional form of longer-term strategy is used to guide more detailed short-term action planning.[38] The medium term plan is essentially a guiding framework for the detail which is worked out during annual planning in more detail at a daily management level. This is the subject of the next chapter.

SUMMARY OF PRINCIPLES

1 Structure is necessary for hierarchy. There are four principal types: functional structure, product structure, regional structure and matrix structure.

2 Flat organization is associated with devolved decision-making and has become associated with new forms of flexible organizing, such as downsizing and business process reengineering.

3 Cross-functional structure has the benefits of integrating the strengths of the horizontal (functional areas) and vertical (review areas) of an organization.

4 The McKinsey 7S framework is a systems view of organizations, when the key areas of an organization must be considered as a whole.

5 Strategy, structure and systems are 'hard-ball', while skills, staff, style and shared values are 'soft-ball'.

6 Joined-up management concerns the bringing together of governmental and private bodies across a range of organizational boundaries, mainly to address complex social problems.

7 A number of different means can lead to the same end; the recognition and management of this is called 'loosely coupled management'.

GUIDED FURTHER READING

For a classic text on structures and systems, see Daft, R. (2009), *Understanding the Theory and Design of Organizations,* Andover: Cengage Learning. Karl Weick, who is always interesting, has extended his ideas to situations where there is little or no existing reference frameworks for understanding an organization, see Weick, K. (1995), *Sensemaking in Organizations*, Thousand Oaks CA: Sage.

The use of metaphors for understanding and managing organizations has been covered in several areas of organizational studies. Gareth Morgan uses images, such as plants, as sense-making tools to categorize organizations, and to understand the essence of different organizational forms, see Morgan, G. (2006), *Images of Organization,* (updated edn), London: Sage.

Henry Mintzberg has proposed a new way for understanding organizational structure, called configurations, see Mintzberg, H. and Waters, J. A. (1985), 'Of strategies, deliberate and emergent', *Strategic Management Journal*, 6:257–272, and Mintzberg, H., Lampel, J., Quinn, J. B. and Ghoshal, S. (2002) (eds), *The Strategy Process,* (4 edn), London: Prentice Hall.

REVIEW QUESTIONS

1 What is meant by an organization structure, and why is this important?

2 List the four main types of organizational structure.

3 What is a business process and how do process organizations facilitate this?

4 What is the defining characteristic of Japanese organizational structures?

5 Why has business process re-engineering (BPR) got a bad name?

6 What is the difference between 'hard-ball' and 'soft-ball' variables?

7 What is 'loosely coupled' strategic management about?

8 How has strategic planning changed?

SEMINAR AND ASSIGNMENT QUESTIONS

1 What things need to be taken into account for developing an effective organizational structure that is appropriate to an organization's overall strategy?

2 Use a 7S framework to examine two contrasting organizations. Consider for each case how taking a system's view is likely to improve their strategic management. Are there any disadvantages to the 7S framework?

3 When is structure a strategy?

CHAPTER END-NOTES

1 Hoyos. C. (2006), 'BP battles to clear its Augean stables', *Financial Times,* 20 September, p. 23.

2 Charan, R. and Colvin, G. (1999), 'Why CEOs fail', *Fortune Magazine,* 21 June.

3 Floyd, S. W. and Wooldridge, B. (1996), *The Strategic Middle Manager,* London: Jossey-Bass.

4 Kano, N. (1993), 'A perspective on quality activities in American firms', *California Management Review*, 35:12–31.

5 Barney, J. B. (2001), 'Is the resource-based 'view' a useful perspective for strategic management research? Yes', *Academy of Management Review,* 26(1):41–56.

6 Mintzberg, H., Lampel, J., Quinn, J. B. and Ghoshal, S. (2003) (eds), *The Strategy Process* (4 edn), London: Prentice Hall.

7 de Holan, P. M. (2004), 'Management as life's essence: 30 years of the Nature of Managerial Work, an Interview with Henry Mintzberg', *Strategic Organization,* 2(2):205–212.

8 Chandler Jr., A. D. (1962), *Strategy and Structure: Chapters in the History of the Industrial Enterprise*, Cambridge MA: MIT Press.

9 Mintzberg, H. (1994), *The Rise and Fall of Strategic Planning,* London: Prentice-Hall; Quinn, J. B. (1980), *Strategies for Change – Logical Incrementalism*, Homewood IL: Irwin.

10 Adapted from Drucker, P. F. (1955), *The Practice of Management,* London: Heinemann-Butterworth.

11 Pettigrew, A. M., Massini, S. and Numagami, T. (2000), 'Innovative forms of organising in Europe and Japan', *European Management Journal,* 18(3):259–273, p. 6.

12 Ishikawa, K. (1969), 'Company-wide quality control activities in Japan', *Proceedings of the 1st International Conference on Quality Control,* Tokyo: JUSE.

13 Jantsch, E. (ed.) (1967), *Technological Forecasting in Perspective,* Paris: OECD.

14 Kondo, Y. (1988), Quality in Japan, in Juran, J. M. and Gryna, M. (eds) *Juran's Quality Control Handbook* (4 edn), London: McGraw-Hill, 35F1–35F30.

15 Sennett, R. (2006), *The Culture of the New Capitalism,* London: Yale University Press, p. 115.

16 Micklethwait, J. and Wooldridge, A. (1997), *The Witch Doctors: What the Management gurus are Saying, Why it Matters and How to Make Sense of It,* London: Mandarin.

17 Hammer, M. (1990), 'Re-engineering work: don't automate, obliterate', *Harvard Business Review,* July-August.

18 Saigol, L. (2002), P&G begins global review of back office, *Financial Times,* 26 February, p. 30.

19 Adapted from Greaves, J. (2004), *Greavsie, The Autobiography,* London: Time-Warner, pp. 280–281.

20 Waterman, R. H., Peters, T. and Phillips, J. R. (1980), '*Structure* is not organization', *Business Horizons,* June, pp. 14–26; Peters, T. J. and Waterman, R. H. (1982), *In Search of Excellence,* London: Harper and Row.

21 Adapted from Peters, T. and Waterman, R. H. (1982), *In Search of Excellence,* London: Harper and Row., p 10.

22 Waterman, R. H., Peters, T. and Phillips, J. R. (1980), '*Structure* is not organization', *Business Horizons,* June, pp. 18–19.

23 Pascale, R. T. and Athos, A. G. (1982), *The Art of Japanese Management,* London: Penguin.

24 Pascale, and Athos, A. G. (1982), *The Art of Japanese Management,* London: Penguin, p. 204.

25 Ghoshal, S. and Bartlett, C. A. (1997), *The Individualised Corporation: Great Companies are Defined by Purpose, Process, and People,* London: William Heinemann.

26 Hamel, G. and Prahalad, C. K. (1994), *Competing for the Future,* Boston MA: Harvard Business School Press, p. 280.

27 Bogdanor, V. (2005), 'Introduction', in Bogdanor V. (ed.) (2005), *Joined-Up Government,* Oxford: Oxford University Press, pp. 1–2.

28 Sennett, R. (2006), *The Culture of the New Capitalism,* London: Yale University Press.

29 For an account of change among European airlines: see Lehrer, M. (2001), 'Macro-Varieties of Capitalism and Micro-Varieties of Strategic Management in European Airlines', in Hall, P. A. and Soskice, D. (eds). *Varieties of Capitalism: The Institutional Foundations of Comparative Advantage,* Oxford, Oxford University Press, pp. 361–386.

30 Sennett, R. (2006) *The Culture of the New Capitalism,* London: Yale University Press, p. 69.

31 Weick, K. E. (1979), *The Social Psychology of Organizing* (2 edn), Reading MA: Addison-Wesley.

32 Simon, H. A. (1947), *Administrative Behaviour: A Study of Decision-Making Processes in Administrative Organizations,* New York: Free Press.

33 Weick, K. E. (1979), *The Social Psychology of Organizing* (2 edn), Reading MA: Addison-Wesley, p. 1.

34 Grant, K. E. R. M. (2003), 'Strategic planning in a turbulent environment: evidence from the oil majors', *Strategic Management Journal,* 24:491–517.

35 Arrow, W. (1974), *The Limits of Organizations,* London: W. W. Norton; Williamson, O. E. (1975), *Markets and Hierarchies: Analysis and Antitrust Implications,* New York: Free Press.

36 Teece, D. C., Pisano, G. and Shuen, A. (1997), 'Dynamic capabilities and strategic Management', *Strategic Management Journal,* 18:509–533, p. 517.

37 Zenger, T. R. (2002), 'Crafting internal hybrids: complementarities, common change initiatives, and the team-based organization', *International Journal of the Economics of Business,* 9(1):79–95.

38 Mintzberg, H. (1994), *The Rise and Fall of Strategic Planning,* London: Prentice-Hall.

CASE 9.1 Cross-functional structure at Toyota

Toyota is organized around the way it manages its strategy. It is commonly believed that the company's competitive advantage is based on the Toyota Production System, its lean production approach. In fact, all the global car makers use their own version of Toyota's production system. Corporate management in Japan say (privately) its competitive advantage is based on the company's cross-functional structure, of which its lean production is only one part.

Cross-functional committees

Cross-functional structure began at Toyota in 1961, when it was designed to ensure that company-wide quality control worked at departmental level.[1] Quality assurance and cost management were regarded as purpose activities (core to the reasons for the organization), while others, including engineering (product planning and product design), production (manufacturing preparation and manufacturing),

Eiji Toyoda, former President of Toyota Motor Co.

and commercial (sales and purchasing), were called means activities (enablers). This is similar to Porter's distinction between support and primary activities in the value chain.

Each area of activity has its formal reviews that are separate from departmental ones although they have a shared membership, but both types report to the corporate executive. The flow of the relationship is that cross-functional reviews take corporate strategic decisions, which the departments implement, acting in effect as line management to the cross-functional committees. Once the cross-functional policy is known, a department establishes its plans and holds meetings with its sections. The exact shape and membership of the cross-functional meetings vary according to the urgency and reach of a cross-functional concern at any one time. The cross-functional reviews constitute a formal and permanent structural arrangement, and involve bi-monthly and monthly meetings on quality and cost (although a significant agenda is also required). The immediate purpose of these meetings is to take remedial action on plans and reviews. A more substantial evaluation of progress is done in the middle, and at the end, of the planning year, and this involves the participation of top level, functional, and departmental, managers; the purpose is to provide feedback on the functional policies.

In the following exhibit, Toyota's strategic management starts with Toyota's overall purpose, a vision statement and its values expressed as a set of guiding principles. These are used as reference frameworks to develop Toyota's basic policies and guidelines (Exhibit 9.1), which are used as a basis for the mid-term plan. This is managed using cross-functional structure as described above. A key element is Toyota's *hoshin kanri* (policy management), an approach to policy execution discussed in more detail in Chapter 10. Senior managers translate the mid-term plan into action guidelines and goals (called *hoshins*) for each division of Toyota.

Toyota's Guiding Principles

- Honour the language and spirit of the law of every nation and undertake open and fair corporate activities to be a good corporate citizen around the world.

EXHIBIT 9.1 Toyota's organizing pyramid[2]

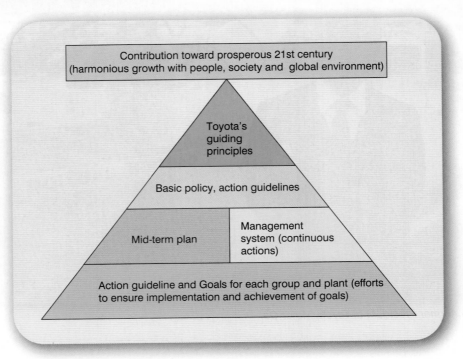

Contribution toward prosperous 21st century
(harmonious growth with people, society and global environment)

Toyota's guiding principles

Basic policy, action guidelines

Mid-term plan

Management system (continuous actions)

Action guideline and Goals for each group and plant (efforts to ensure implementation and achievement of goals)

- Respect the culture and customs of every nation and contribute to economic and social development through corporate activities in local communities.

- Dedicate ourselves to providing clean and safe products and to enhancing the quality of life everywhere through our activities.

- Create and develop advanced technologies and provide outstanding products and services that fulfil the needs of customers worldwide.

- Foster a corporate culture that enhances individual creativity and teamwork value, while honouring mutual trust and respect between labour and management.

- Pursue growth in harmony with the global community through innovative management.

- Work with business partners in research and creation to achieve stable, long-term growth and mutual benefits, while keeping ourselves open to new partnerships.

Example of a basic policy: environmental policy[3]

An overarching concern is environmental policy. However, few firms actually manage the execution of environmental policy through the deployment of related objectives and means as closely as Toyota. This involves the formulation by senior management of three basic policies to last five years; each policy is linked to a number of action guidelines, which are managed continuously, or 'promoted' – the Japanese term, by senior management committees chaired by the President.

Each action guideline is in turn translated into several 'action items' put together as a 'mid-term' (five-year) plan. Generally, in Japanese companies, an 'item' is understood as an item of control, so that in this instance, the items are used to control the implementation of the three policies.

The mid-term plan gives each item its own 'action policy', with its specific goals and implementation items, and which are continuously reviewed by senior management for current status against expected achievement. For example, one of the three basic policies is written thus:

Recognize that the manufacture of automobiles is deeply related to the earth's environment. Combine the strength of all groups with the Company and cooperate with suppliers and distributors worldwide to develop technologies that are gentle on the earth and serve to promote environmental measures.

This policy has seven action guidelines. One of these, for example, is: 'Always be concerned about the environment. Promote programmes to protect the environment: (i) develop low-pollution vehicles; and (ii) develop low-pollution production processes'.

Each action guideline has its own action items, or a statement, which is used as a guide for finding the means to achieve the policy. So, for example, the action guideline to achieve '(i) Develop low-pollution vehicles', has five action items:

- *Reduce exhaust emissions*
- *Reduce noise pollution*
- *Increase fuel efficiency*
- *Develop clean-energy vehicles*
- *Use alternative refrigerants.*

In the 2001/2005 mid-term plan, the 7 action guidelines had in aggregate 23 action items, and each action item had its own 'action policy' and 'specific goals and implementation items'. For example, for the action item, 'reduce exhaust emissions', the mid-term plan had the following:

Action Policy

Promote appropriate emissions reduction responses considering specific urban needs in each country and region:

- Promote technological development challenging zero emissions

- Respond to regulations in developed countries prior to their enactment

- Expand emission control measures immediately in developing countries

The specific goals and implementation items are translated at divisional or business unit level into local mid-term plans. The ones shown immediately below are an example, in this case, for business units and plants in Japan. Local units will translate the mid-term plan into annual priorities or objectives, typically grouped under QCDE targets, for everybody to align and integrate into daily management.

Specific Goals & Implementation items (Japan only):

Further reduction in emissions in gasoline vehicles.

- *Systematically introduce low emission vehicles which emit a quarter of the emissions permitted under Japan's 2000 regulation, starting with Prius.*

Development and introduction of clean diesel vehicles:

- *Introduce vehicles that accommodate the new Japanese diesel long-term regulation prior to its enactment.*
- *Development of ultra-clean diesel vehicles.*

This approach to the deployment of its environmental policies working through a mid-term plan is used by Toyota for its other policies. The unusual aspect is the continuous use of top level management committees to review and drive the action policies against expectations, once the mid-term plan is in place. This continuous review activity is cross-functional and takes priority over the company's departments and functional areas. It is at the heart of Toyota's management system referred to in Exhibit 9.1.

The world's first hybrid car

One of the great successes of Toyota's environmental policies has been its hybrid car. This was launched in Japan in 1997, and was offered for sale in the United States two years later. The former Toyota chairman, Eiji Toyoda, believed Toyota needed to put its time and money into creating a unique product for the next generation of customers, shareholders, and employees. Toyota engineers had been working to develop a hybrid engine technology, a system that reduces gasoline usage by integrating electric power.

After several years in development, the project resulted in the revolutionary Prius Sedan. Using Toyota's own hybrid technology, dubbed the Hybrid Synergy Drive, and patented the design, the Prius was the world's first bona fide twenty-first century vehicle intended for sale on a mass, commercial level. Its development was one of the most difficult challenges in the history of global product design, engineering and manufacturing. Total costs, including the development of the hybrid technology, exceeded $1 billion. Difficulties arose all along the way, but the project received strong encouragement and direction from the highest corporate levels.

...

'There will be great significance in launching the car early', said former Toyota president Hiroshi Okuda, who took charge of the company in the midst of the Prius project, 'this car may change the course of Toyota's future and even that of the auto industry'.[4]

Some observers of the industry had felt that developing a new model for a mass market was an expensive mistake. There was no demand for a small car, a hybrid-engine car, especially as growing world prosperity seemed to favour larger cars. However, the gamble paid off and the company now puts hybrid engines into a range of popular models, and Toyota is now widely considered the leader in alternative transportation, at a time when global warming and rising oil prices are major world concerns.

Discussion questions

1   How does Toyota use organizational structure to implement its strategy?

2   Consider the strengths and weaknesses of a large multi-national corporation of a Toyota pyramid (see Exhibit 9.1).

3   Is Toyota a truly visionary organization, and what constitutes its competitive advantage?

Case end-notes

1   Koura, K. (1990), 'Survey and research in Japan concerning policy management', *ASQC Quality Congress Transactions*, San Francisco, 348–353; Kurogane, K. (1993) (ed.), *Cross-Functional Management: Principles and Practical Applications,* Tokyo: Asian Productivity

Organization; Monden, Y. (1998), *Toyota Production System: An Integrated Approach to Just-in-Time,* (3 edn), Norcross, Georgia: Engineering & Management Press. (Published in Japan, 1983, Institute of Industrial Engineers.)

2 Toyota (1999), 'Ensuring the achievement of the second action plan (FY2000) and taking actions for the 21st century', *Toyota Environment Management,* company document.

3 Information taken from Toyota (1999), 'Ensuring the achievement of the second action plan (FY2000) and taking actions for the 21st century', *Toyota Environment Management,* company document.

4 Magee, D. (2007), *How Toyota Became # 1, Leadership Lessons from the World's Greatest Car Company,* London: Portfolio, Penguin Group.

Chapter 10

EXECUTION: STRATEGIC PERFORMANCE MANAGEMENT

The execution of strategy

The **execution** of strategy is the management of delivery of strategic objectives in daily management and operations. It follows implementation, which is about putting the structures and systems of an organization in place, and the formulation of medium-term strategic plans or programmes.

KEY TERMS

capability review

catchball

CompStat

FAIR

hoshin kanri

management by objectives (MbO)

nemawashi

periodic strategic reviews

policy delivery units

review wheel

strategic control

strategic levers

strategic performance systems

strategic performance management

strategic reviews

LEARNING OBJECTIVES

This chapter provides you with an understanding of the following:

1 Strategic review and the review wheel

2 Strategic performance management

3 The FAIR stages of strategy execution

4 Examples of strategic performance management approaches:
   - *hoshin kanri*
   - CompStat/CitiStat
   - delivery units
   - strategic levers of control

Business vignette Tracking down the detail that adds up to the general shape of change

Whatever the organization, having a strategy does not guarantee it will be managed by others. This applies to Prime Ministers and to business executives alike.

In the words of former UK Prime Minister Blair:

My impatience with the scale and ambition of our reform was now carved in granite. I was going to do it, come hell or high water. I needed to be able to solve the tricky problem questions of policy detail that added up to the general shape of change, and I need to track whether and how the change was being introduced ...

... in domestic policy, changing public service systems inevitably meant getting into the details of delivery and performance management in a radically more granular way. Increasingly, prime ministers are like CEOs or chairman of major companies. They have to set a policy direction; they have to see it is followed; they have to get data on whether it is; they have to measure outcomes.[1]

Dan Simpson, vice-president, head of Strategy and Planning at Clorox, observes:

Execution problems are often symptoms of trouble upstream in the strategy – development process – the strategy process has failed to realistically assess current reality, to honestly understand organizational capabilities, to align key players with those who do real work, or, at the end of the day, to create a compelling, externally driven vision of success.[2]

Making strategy work is the most difficult part of strategic management.

The organization must ensure that its strategic priorities are included and carried out by everyone on a daily basis. This is not purely an operations matter, since it concerns the question of how an organization manages its routines so that they are sensitive to the overall needs of the strategy of the organization.

Strategic review

Kaplan and Norton note that **strategic reviews** play 'a critical role in the executive team strategic-learning process'.[3] Reviews should bring leadership together to focus on improvement, pulling time away from maintenance and putting leadership time into improvement and learning that will build a firm's future. However, Kaplan and Norton warn of a danger that strategic review can be too narrow. They use an example at Kenyon Stores, where strategy meetings were too much about operational issues, where its 'goal was to monitor performance relative to plan and to initiate short-term actions that would bring the organization back into compliance with plan ... Missing was a process to learn whether organizational strategy was working and being implemented effectively'.[4]

Taking, say, a diagnostic approach to consider strategic objectives is in fact fine, but these meetings must consider how progress on one objective is likely to have an impact on others, including longer-term ones. Linking relationships must be understood. In this, organizations should be clear about the difference between operational and strategic review meetings. The whole system of multi-level review should itself be reviewed and understood by senior management.

A review wheel for strategic management

It is necessary to distinguish between (1) longer-term purpose, objectives and strategy; (2) shorter-term implementation and execution; and (3) the overall strategic control of (1) and (2) (see the POSIES model in Figure 10.1). The shaded box in the figure, top left, signifies the longer-term components of strategic management. The shaded box, top right, signifies the shorter-term components. There are several forms of review indicated in this figure. Basic to good management is a need to monitor and review work in progress and this is indicated here by the PDCA cycle: this is the principle that all businesses processes should be managed to Plan, the Doing part should involve monitoring work as it progresses, and the Check component involves a review of progress, with any necessary follow-up Action.

The figure illustrates several levels of review. In the **review wheel**, the first levels of review take place at a daily and operational level, and these are by nature single-looped and exploitive learning processes (see Chapter 5) that are primarily concerned with managing routines and operational issues. The next level involves periodic strategic reviews of the progress of strategically linked priorities. These are primarily double-looped and explorative learning processes. The last level on the wheel is an annual audit of the management of the important businesses processes, including how long-term strategy has been managed as shorter-term priorities. This is primarily a triple-looped learning process, which takes into account long-term strategy and changes in the external environment and the ability of the organization as a whole to strategically manage these.

How these reviews are managed forms a basis for **strategic control**: the monitoring and review of the organization's strategic management of purpose,

FIGURE 10.1 POSIES model of strategic management

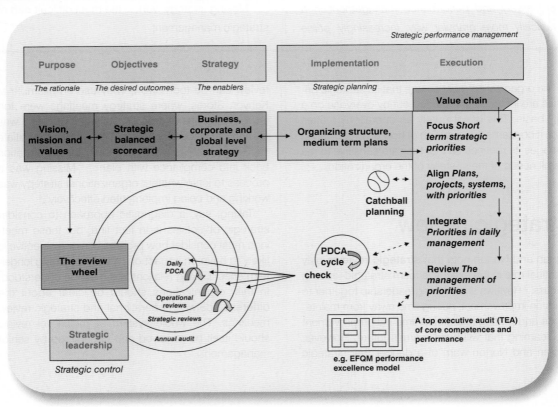

objectives and strategy, and if necessary, to adapt and manage follow-up action. The strategic control of the long-term components of strategic management should be a shaping, reflective and testing activity, but strategy's execution as a shorter-term management of strategic priorities is about strategy in action.

Strategic performance management

Organizations, in addition to organizational structures for implementing strategies, need to install an organizing framework for realizing them.[5] In general, senior managers deal with implementation that is effective immediately after decision-making by putting in place organizational structures and systems, but implementation that is executed through an organizational-wide effort requires a strategically managed system to link daily management to strategy: these are called **strategic performance systems**.

If a strategic objective and its strategy crafted at a senior level are to work at an operational level, then they must be linked in effectively with all the different things the organization is doing already. Without making and managing these connections an all-involving effort to achieve the organization's overall priorities is unlikely to happen. This requires more than a calendar of dates and deadlines; it requires the proactive involvement of senior managers in **strategic performance management**. This helps them to better understand their organization so that they are able to manage strategy execution.

This does not assume a top-down strategy formulation, followed by a strategy implementation, approach as in classical strategic planning. Senior managers in organizations are more likely today to set the overall direction and the organization's strategically-related priorities, which the rest of the organization uses to develop bottom-up action plans for the year. It is within these parameters that local managers have to work out the other organizational activities, such as determining budgets, functional priorities and strategies, as well as departmental control and incentive systems.

Good strategic performance management mobilizes an organization-wide effort to achieve four main things: focus, alignment, integration, and review (**FAIR**; see the right-hand side of Figure 10.1, and Figure 10.2). Managing implementation involves focusing the organization on the needs of the medium-term plan by crafting objectives that the rest of the organization uses to align action plans. When the plans are managed in daily management the objectives are progressed, and towards the end of the planning cycle performance is reviewed, and the lessons are used to inform the re-crafting of the objectives for the next turn of the planning cycle.

FIGURE 10.2 The FAIR framework for managing implementation

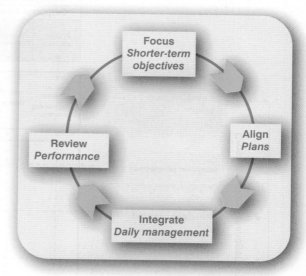

> **Good strategic performance management mobilizes an organization-wide effort to achieve four main things: focus, alignment, integration, and review (FAIR).**

Focus

The primary participants in the focus phase of the cycle are senior managers (see Figure 10.3). The senior management team (top left of the figure) typically comprises departmental and functional heads. The first consideration in crafting the annual objectives is to sort out the needs of the departments (the relationship of a department to the organization's value chain is shown at the top of the figure). This is done within the framework of longer-term purpose (vision, mission, and values), strategic objectives (the balanced scorecard), and overall strategy, and is centred on the organization's need to progress the medium-term plan over the coming year. This involves establishing the opportunities and threats facing the departments, as well working out the strengths and weaknesses, in relation to achieving the objectives of the plan.

The second consideration is to identify the critical needs of the medium-term plan in terms of cross-functional objectives. These are explored from the four perspectives of the balanced scorecard (see left of the figure). The two are brought together to determine the cross-functional objectives that are both critical for the organization and practical in terms of the ability of the functional areas to help deliver them (this is shown stylistically in the figure at the points where the lines cross in the matrix). Some organizations craft two groups of objectives: a small number of breakthrough (or innovatory) objectives, and a larger number of annual improvement targets.

FIGURE 10.3 The determination of shorter-term objectives

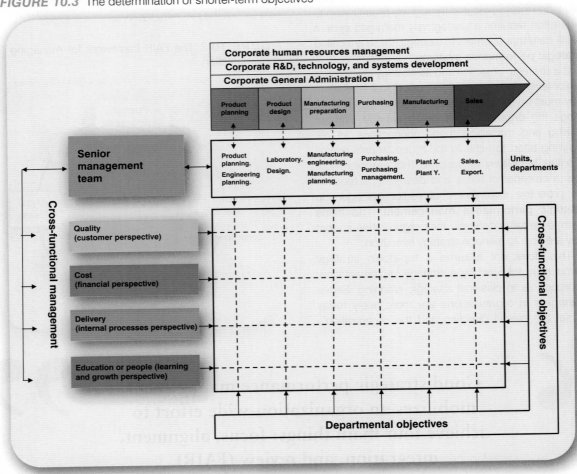

Breakthrough objectives are crafted to encourage exploratory organizational learning and they typically require the organization to rethink its organizational routines. Improvement targets are incremental targets (or key performance indicators) that primarily encourage exploitative organizational learning and normally do not involve any rethinking of existing routines.[6] The organizing principle for establishing a short-term strategic focus is to keep the number of objectives, especially the breakthrough ones, small enough to be manageable, and their relevance vital so people will easily understand why they must be achieved.

Alignment

The breakthrough objectives and improvement targets are taken by the individuals who make up the senior management team when they return to their functional areas. Annual planning at these levels is primarily centred on local priorities, but the objectives and targets take priority in working out everything else. This involves crafting draft action plans and passing them between teams to reach agreements with everybody involved about how the objectives and targets can be achieved (see Figure 10.4).

The objectives and teams are provisionally incorporated into team plans for the coming year. The implications for third parties, and especially for the other team plans, are sounded out. This is an iterative process of throwing ideas and possibilities backward and forward like a game of **catchball**.[7] It is likely that teams will have to change their targets and their proposed means (the strategies to achieve a target), perhaps several times.

Some breakthrough objectives are difficult and may therefore need a long planning or development period to sort out their implications. Typically these objectives need to be developed to clarify the full relevance for a department, or a number of departments in different functional areas. The means of achieving a breakthrough objective may take months to investigate and then this sort of problem-solving activity is usually made into an on-going project.

Department heads need to oversee the planning period to ensure that consensus is established, but primarily to review the overall implications of the agreements reached among teams to check that workload and resources, especially the responsibilities and the timing of the critical events, are all recorded

FIGURE 10.4 Agreeing team plans

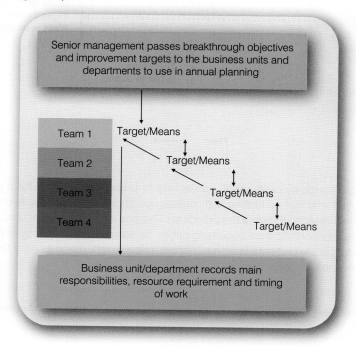

so that everyone is aware of them. This record is checked and reviewed periodically through the year to make sure operations are functioning normally, and that the objectives are on course (these reviews are departmental, not strategic, reviews; see below). Departmental heads also have to ensure their management systems, such as budgets and staff appraisals, are harmonious and consistent with the objectives and the associated working. In particular, it is important to be sure that individuals are not over-loaded and can receive the support they may need for development.

PRINCIPLES IN PRACTICE 10.1

Preparing the ground for implementation

The Japanese take more time and involve more people in the agreement of proposals and plans, so that the implementation of these is quicker and more likely to succeed.[8] This is especially as the people who must carry out the decisions, because they have been involved in making the decisions, understand what is required and what the possible problems will be.

Peter Drucker pointed out that while the Japanese are slower to make decisions than Western organizations they are quicker to implement them …

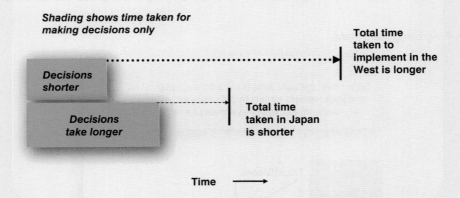

Decisions are conditioned by *nemawashi* – an activity to prepare the ground for a proposal. This involves doing a lot of informal consulting with colleagues (including superiors and subordinates) before there is a formal meeting to agree the proposal.[9] This has the advantage of uncovering unforeseen issues and prevents conflicts from becoming public. Its essence is not directly about agreement as such, but it is about people understanding each others' roles, which makes it easier for everybody to rely on and communicate with each other.

Question: *Nemawashi* may prevent public argument, but could it limit creativity?

KEY DEBATE 10.1

Ford versus Toyota

Themselves the delivery of effective strategy depends to a great extent on how organizations are organized. The car producer, Ford, developed a system of mass production during the first part of the 20th century that extended the ideas of scientific management[10] and which influenced assembly-line operations across the world, which became known as Fordism.[11] The system uses mass production which involves the manufacture of standardized products in huge volumes, using specialized machinery and unskilled labour. Henry Ford took the idea of the division of labour to its extreme, dividing tasks to a bare minimum of components; the boost this gave to productivity allowed Ford to pay double the wages paid to employees by competitors.

In the rebuilding of the Japanese economy after the Second World War, the domestic car market was small with many competitors; the mass production model of Ford was difficult to apply. Productivity required a different system for working, which would enable assembly lines to switch flexibly between small runs and different model of car. Toyota developed a production system based originally on the post-war ideas of Deming and total quality management.[12] Other related philosophies and methodologies reinforced and sustained the system, including just-in-time management. These new ways of working involved degrees of manager-employee collaboration that brought into the organization a new concept, the knowledge worker, very different in conception to the unskilled car worker.

Since the 1980s and 1990s, the effectiveness of the Toyota Production Systems has influenced car companies across the world, including Ford Motor Company, and all of them have adopted similar approaches.[13]

However, the idea that people should work together and agree mutually reinforcing objectives is open to question if it leads to narrow organizational agendas and limits the discussion and exploration of alternatives.[14] Michael Porter and others are critical of Japanese management, arguing that consensual processes have important adverse consequences for strategic positioning.

First, the need to obtain so many approvals almost guarantees that bold or distinctive strategies will not be pursued. The chances of making choices and trade-offs that favour one unit or division over another are minimal. Second, once so many have signed off on a decision, it is very difficult to exit unsuccessful product lines or businesses.[15]

Garrahan and Stewart (1992), in a study of Nissan, assert that lean working has not meant a real change from Fordism, in that the command and control of line employees is now more pressured because the ideas of quality and flexibility has meant a new kind of surveillance through team-working where workers must not only perform but they also have the added responsibility for deciding how to do the work.

This has been recognized to some extent by Toyota: '... when excess workers are eliminated, the JIT system actually forces the remaining workers to work much harder and creates severe work strain.

Therefore, human alienation can result from productivity improvements'. Toyota uses a 'respect-for-humanity' system as part of its JIT management, which includes measuring workloads, idea creation and worker proposals: 'Being involved in improving the work environment is the biggest source of a better quality of life for workers.'[16]

Deming argued senior management should drive out fear, to encourage workers to solve problems and not hide them or seek to blame people; he believed that performance was primarily a result of underlying system factors, which are beyond an individual's control. He argued that individual recognition and appraisals should be abolished because employees should take a team-based approach.[17] Few organizations have followed this advice.

Question: Is there any real difference between Fordism and Toyota's system, and is the way in which employees are managed really important for strategy?

Integration

As soon as plans are completed teams begin to manage their processes with the newly agreed objectives and targets integrated into their routines in daily management. The sources of change associated with continuous improvement in process management were noted in Chapter 5 in relation to total quality management (TQM). This approach for managing work is typically based on the PDCA cycle. However, the real driver of change on the operational processes comes not from doing work better, but from working to objectives and targets that are derived from strategy and the medium-term plan. In other words, the operational processes are as much influenced by strategic considerations as they are by the immediate need to satisfy the present customers: for example, an annual objective may be crafted by senior managers to encourage the organization to build into operations a particular unique advantage to combat the activities of an important competitor.

The organizing principle for the management of objectives is that work should be done along the lines of something like PDCA, where the specification of the work being performed is used to monitor the progress of the work, and that if things are not going to plan, then it is possible to intervene to problem-solve the reasons and put things right. If this requires changes in the objectives and the means to achieve them, then the implications have to be understood and acted upon for anyone else working in the organization. This is the management *of* objectives, and not *by* objectives. Objectives should be managed by people to facilitate their work, and should never be used within a context that is cut off from other objectives and means. In the management of objectives it is the transparency and relevancy of objectives to each other, or the propinquity of objectives, that conditions how people work together strategically.

This is a very different approach from **management by objectives (MbO)**, which is an approach that is still used widely in organizations. MbO is an

> In the management of objectives it is the transparency and relevancy of objectives to each other, or the propinquity of objectives, which condition how people work together strategically.

approach that deploys (or cascades) objectives down through the levels of an organization, by subdividing them, so that a superior's objectives become the sub-objectives of subordinates, who in turn, pass parts of the sub-objective to their own subordinates, and so on.

Originally it was the clarification of objectives, and the self-management aspects of MbO, that were emphasized; the approach was thought to be a way for harmonizing an individual's goals with strategic objectives.[18] However, it has been used by managers to command and control their subordinates to perform to numerical goals, and to hold them to account for their work. In this way authority is imposed in a hierarchical way through top-down objectives, which have little to do with the implementation of strategic objectives.[19] For these reasons MbO is now largely discredited.

Review

There are two kinds of strategic review at a daily management level: the first is a series of **periodic strategic reviews**, held every two or three months to oversee the progress on the annual objectives, and the second, an annually held capability review. These are different in character from operational and departmental reviews, which are primarily used by functional management to oversee and address immediate issues. Strategic review is normally a formal activity that is likely to involve the presentation by a unit's managers to senior managers from outside the part of the organization that is being reviewed. They are held to check progress on the annual strategic objectives; to provide necessary assistance and advice and, if necessary, to commit resources for follow-up action early enough to be sure that the organization's medium-term plan will ultimately be achieved.

For example, Hewlett-Packard's organization-wide planning and review system is based on the following belief: 'The ultimate measure of the success of the planning process is whether the organization achieves its objectives and has the maturity (and early warning mechanisms in place) to take corrective action should progress towards these objectives start to be a concern'.[20]

The ultimate measure of the success of the planning process is whether the organization achieves its objectives and has the maturity (and early warning mechanisms in place) to take corrective action should progress towards these objectives start to be a concern.

Periodic strategic reviews aim to consider only the strategic objectives from the perspective of in-progress issues. A **capability review** is a senior level annual audit of the organization's management capabilities. It considers how the organization's core areas or processes are being managed and has the object of developing good practice (it is sometimes linked to organizational benchmarking; see Chapter 5). The process is usually informed by evidence from the periodic strategic reviews, and from employee and customers, but the focus of attention is on the enablers of performance and good management practice.

The audit takes place towards the end of the planning year and senior managers (and in some organizations, the chairman of the board and non-executives) participate as auditors. This is important, as it is the senior level's check on how the organizational is doing its work to achieve the organization's purpose. In other words, it is an important vehicle for keeping top management informed about how the organization manages the core areas of the business. The involvement of senior managers is important since this keeps them in touch with the operational realities of the business.

An organization typically uses a performance excellence framework to review the organization's management of its core areas. In some organizations, however, the capability review is used as a dynamic capability to develop the organization's core competences. Nissan uses a top executive audit to do this, and one of the core competences is how its units manage strategic objectives in daily management (see Case 5.1). Nissan uses its audit in combination with *hoshin kanri*.

Hoshin kanri

Hoshin kanri is an organization-wide methodology for the deployment and management of senior level policies and the development of the means to achieve them in everyday working.[21] Hoshin kanri is not synonymous with strategic planning, which is the larger system for implementing long-term objectives and overall strategy. It refers instead to the deployment and management of shorter term, usually annual, policy priorities designed to make daily management responsive to the current needs of strategy. Hoshin kanri is used under a number of names in Western firms, such as hoshin planning at Bank of America and Hewlett-Packard; Objectives, Goals, Initiatives, Measures at Proctor and Gamble, and Strategy into Action at Unilever. It has been used widely in the health sector; for example at the Royal Bolton Hospital in the UK (where it is called policy deployment) and at ThedaCare in the USA.[22]

The approach was developed in Japanese manufacturing as long ago as the early 1960s, when it was used as an organization-wide approach for the deployment of cross-functional policies. A *hoshin* is a brief statement about a desired organization-wide policy designed to achieve a specific strategic objective. The original kanji characters for 'ho' are suggestive of 'method' while 'shin' suggests a reflected light from a compass needle to show the way to go forward. The basic principle is that everybody should make some contribution in their routine working to a hoshin, so that the organization as a whole will be moved forward to an extent that otherwise would not be achieved through normal working. For this reason hoshins are sometimes called breakthrough objectives.

Hoshin kanri is conventionally applied within a lean working and a PDCA-TQM conditioned organizational environment. The hoshins are used to bring an external influence to bear on kaizen, or continuous improvement. Because they are linked to strategy, hoshins have priority over other operational objectives, and are the main drivers for change in lean

production, and they provide a frame of reference for organization-wide decisions, including, for example, the much emulated Toyota bottom-up decision-making.

While the details of application vary according to context and organization, hoshin kanri has a common set of working principles. The first is not to overload the vital few hoshins. The number should be as few as possible – perhaps no more than four or five. They are designed to be easily understood by everyone and should relate to a pressing need to achieve a breakthrough: this could, for instance, be the need to achieve a catch-up in performance on the organization's business plan, or to react quickly to a sudden and unforeseen change in the external environment. There is a tendency at the top of an organization to want to achieve too much, which is likely to produce too many hoshins, which causes complexity and measures mushroom out of control.

A second principle is that hoshin plans and projects have to be agreed with everybody who is likely

PRINCIPLES IN PRACTICE 10.2

Bottom-up decision-making in hoshin kanri at Toyota

A practitioner explains how decisions were made at Toyota:

In my experience, agreeing objectives for new programmes was accomplished by employees, engineers and staff, bringing proposals to their supervisors for approval. This is how all new initiatives got started. Through it all, the superiors avoided ever telling anyone exactly what to do. As my first manager and mentor at Toyota told me, 'Never tell your staff what to do. Whenever you do that, you take the responsibility away from them'. So, the Toyota managers, the good ones anyway, would rarely tell their people what to do; they would lay out a problem, ask for analysis or a proposal, but always stop short of saying: 'Do this'. The employee, upon getting the problem to work on (actually, finding the problem to work on was usually his job too), would develop solution options to take to the manager. The manager's first answer was, invariably, 'No'. The employee would return to his desk and rework his proposal – three times, five times, ten times if necessary. The manager was the judge and jury while the employee was the attorney with whom rested the burden of proof to justify his proposal by presenting and analyzing all the viable options. It took me a good three years to figure out how this worked.

This was the famous Japanese 'bottom-up decision making' in action. My initial reaction was a level of disillusionment, declaring bottom-up decision making a huge lie. Wasn't 'bottom-up' supposed to be some kind of enlightened form of democratic self-management whereby people essentially do what they want? It took a while for me to see that this wasn't a lie so much as it was objective management, but it was powerful nonetheless: no one was telling anyone else what to do. What a beautiful answer to the control–flexibility dilemma that dogs all large organizations: the company gets basic adherence to the desired corporate objectives, and the workers are free to explore best possible real solutions to problems that they themselves know best.

... Policy management [hoshin kanri] is often confused with policy deployment, a relatively simple prioritization process in which the desires and objectives of senior management (the company) are deployed throughout the organization (the employees). That is a good first step. But policy management Toyota-style was a much more dynamic process, with lower levels of the organization taking part in formulating policy as well as carrying it out.[23]

Question: What is the difference between the deployment and the management of hoshins?

to be affected by them, or who will be expected to contribute. In Western firms this is the activity described as catchball (above), but in Japan this type of decision-forming appears almost as a natural process called *nemawashi*. This is a term borrowed from horticulture, to describe the process in which a plant is made ready for a move to a new part of the garden. Japanese organizations take long periods to prepare the ground for making major decisions. A key feature of hoshin kanri is that policies and their related objectives are always discussed in the context of their possible means. If objectives are deployed without reference to their means, then the development of hoshins begins to resemble command and control through management by objectives.

Another principle is that problem-solving must be based on current data to take account of reality and current weaknesses, and use a Paretian approach to ensure that effort is spent on the most important issues, where the return is greatest, and the sum of available resources will be able to make the most impact. This involves taking into account a full consideration of relevant cross-functional influences, wherever they may occur, and if necessary, across organizational boundaries. This should not lead to too much emphasis on special task teams. Hoshin projects should deploy through the ordinary organizations, and team members should come from all ranks. This requires a facilitating form of organizational management to work effectively.

The fourth principle is that senior managers must oversee the strategic reviews of progress of the hoshins at an operational level. Also, towards the end of the organization's annual cycle, executives and other senior managers conduct an audit of organization-wide capabilities, the business methodologies and management philosophies (core competencies), which are necessary to manage the hoshins, especially in those key areas where the organization must be fit for purpose. This requires a senior level to understand microscopic as well as macroscopic data. This is not easy for Western organizations which will often see this as a form of micro-management. Hoshin kanri requires the top-most level not only to take full responsibility for the audit, but also to demonstrate this by participating to some extent as auditors, and to gather insights into routine working and talk to other levels.[24]

Hoshin kanri is perhaps the most comprehensive of delivery systems in present use. However, there are two others that are proving influential in public administration. These are the use of a delivery unit used in central government in the United Kingdom, and a city-based system, originally used for New York, called CompStat.

CompStat/CitiStat

When Rudolf Giuliani became mayor of New York in 1993, the city was one of the most lawless in America. By the time he left office in 2004, the city had changed to become one of the world's safest. He used an approach called **CompStat**, which is short for computer statistics or comparative statistics.[25] CompStat is said to have begun with broken window theory, derived from a Police Foundation sponsored study of foot patrols in Newark.[26] Broken windows is the contention that a seemingly minor matter like broken windows in abandoned buildings leads directly to a more serious deterioration of neighbourhoods.

Giuliani argues leaders should sweat the small stuff, because the seemingly less serious things are part of the bigger picture; by solving these, leaders may be able to get on top of the big issues, such as serious crime. William Bratton, who became Giuliani's police commissioner, first used the idea as head of transit police in New York, when he cracked down on fare evasion; it was 'the biggest broken window in the transit system'.[27] It had not seemed worthwhile before, since the cost in police time was high and the cost of a fare is small, but it was discovered that many of the people arrested were causing other problems once inside the subway system. As commissioner, Bratton used 'civil law to enforce existing regulations against harassment, assault, menacing, disorderly conduct, and damaging property ... prevented the [serious] crime before it happened.[28]

According to Giuliani, CompStat works like this:

The police officer in the street makes a report and enters it into his precinct's On-Line Complaint System. The report is transmitted to the CompStat mainframe and entered in two places: (1) on a map that shows geographical concentrations of criminal activity and sorts them by hour of day, type of crime, and day of week; and (2) on a weekly summary of crime complaints that displays trends over a variety of periods, such as week-to-date, month-to-date, and year-to-date, and compares the current year's total with the prior year's and shows the percentage change. The data can only result in a meaningful response if it's accurate. We implemented an auditing system ... It would flag statistically unrealistic performance, allowing us to dig deeper into its accuracy. There were even commanders removed for tinkering with the numbers.[29]

CompStat is more than a computer-based information system. What makes it work strategically is a review meeting that is normally held weekly (twice when it started) with senior managers, police precinct commanders and other operational heads, to discuss progress on the city's strategies. The idea is to discern emerging and established crime and quality of life trends, as well as deviations and anomalies, and to make comparisons between the different precincts and commands to promote debate and learning. It uses presentations by operational heads and their staffs to discuss patterns in terms of the evidence of what is going on, to help the owners of objectives to understand the whole picture. It serves to help senior managers to understand operations, to evaluate the skills and effectiveness of middle management, and to assist in allocating resources for continuous improvement. Because high-ranking decision-makers are present they can commit resources quickly to clear obstacles, and avoid delays that are common in highly structured bureaucratic organizations.

Every precinct commander can expect to be called at random to make a presentation about once a month. According to Giuliani the approach aims to foster a team approach to problem solving, and the use of presentations and objectives acts as a motivational and competitive tool for encouraging accountability. He also makes it plain that managers must work wholeheartedly with the system. It is possible for poor performers to try to hide unfavourable statistics, or to manipulate the recording of statistics to hide the true situation, but as Giuliani writes above, periodic audits are supposed to pick this up.

Critics have pointed out that CompStat may not be the sole reason for lower crime. National crime had already started to decline before Giuliani took office and in other major cities crime had fallen over the same period due to an improvement of the economy. Similarly in Australia a variant had produced large falls in crime, but crime rates were already declining.[30] There were also other factors peculiar to New York, such as the recruitment of extra police.[31] Even so, rates of crime fell faster in New York than elsewhere, and there is evidence that broken windows policing is linked to declines in violent crime.[32]

New York extended the idea to other city agencies. Some other American cities now have their own versions: in Los Angeles where it has been overseen by Bratton, in Philadelphia where it has been used in education, and in Baltimore where it is called CitiStat.[33] Robert Behn, of Harvard's Kennedy School of Government, argues these applications have been effective, but he summarizes some possible dangers.[34] The review meeting can seem to have no clear purpose, and specific responsibilities may be unclear. The meetings are in some places held infrequently or randomly, without any individual authorized to organize and run the meetings. Administrative support is often lacking, especially a dedicated analytic staff. There is no one who manages follow-up. Behn also suggests that agencies seem to find it difficult to strike a lack of balance between a brutal and bland style of leadership. Leadership style seems to be of particular importance for CompStat.

Both NYPD's CompStat and Baltimore's CitiStat are known for being tough and uncompromising with poor performers ... Yet in an overreaction to ... some jurisdictions and agencies have consciously tried to make their meetings as harmonious as possible. As a result, their meetings have become mostly show-and-tell.[35]

A good leader should want to understand more about what is going wrong than about what is going right. CompStat/CitiStat may seem an approach that anyone should expect of a strategic review. Namely, there should be a series of regular and periodic meetings held with senior managers. This should involve current data to examine and explore what is actually going on and the possible follow-ups with middle managers and their staffs. The trick is how to enhance not only the abilities of the agencies and units to enable them to learn from experience and

Broken windows theory for the underground

New York mayor, Giuliani's first police commissioner, William Bratton, had been influenced by broken windows theory.[36] This holds that a seemingly minor matter like broken windows in abandoned buildings lead directly to a more serious deterioration of neighbourhoods. Giuliani argues that the idea is relevant not only to crime but business more generally: leaders should 'sweat the small stuff', because the seemingly less serious things are part of the bigger picture.[37]

Bratton used quality of life issues to help clean up more serious crime. These were small misdemeanours and petty crime, but when they are left unattended, because they seem unimportant, they begin to create a poor environment that begins to encourage more, and often more serious, crime, so that a vicious circle of decline sets in.

Bratton in his previous job as head of transit police in New York had cracked down on fare evasion. It had not seemed worthwhile since the cost in police time was high and the cost of a fare was small. However, many of the people arrested were causing other problems once they got inside the subway system. When he became Giuliani's police commissioner, he used civil law to enforce existing regulations.

Time and time again, when cops interrupt someone drinking on the street or a gang of kids drinking on the corner, pat them down, and find a gun or a knife, they have prevented what would have happened two or three hours later when that same person, drunk, pulled out that gun or knife. We prevented the crime before it happened. New York City police would be about prevention … .[38]

William Bratton, former Police Commissioner for New York City, 1995

Question: Are leaders likely to want to be known for the small stuff since it is often associated with micromanagement?

from each other, but also to help the senior level understand the organization. CompStat is different in this to many other approaches in that it brings a senior team into the same physical place as middle management to review operations in the context of the bigger picture. This is very rare and very difficult to achieve as a routine for most organizations. Usually everybody is just too busy to be in the same place at the same time.

Prime Minister's Delivery Unit

Policy delivery units typically enable an organization's executive level to track the progress of its strategic objectives or targets. In the UK, Michael Barber[39] set up a Prime Minister's Delivery Unit (PMDU) at the beginning of Tony Blair's second term of government. The government had failed to achieve the majority of its targets during its first term. The PMDU employed less than 50 people and reported to the prime minister. Its job was to track the delivery of a small number of key targets. These were originally 15 in number and the responsibility for achieving them lay with individual government departments, namely health, education, the home office, and transport.

> It would focus like a laser on an issue, draw up a plan to resolve it working with the department concerned, and then performance-manage it to solution. It would get first-class data which it would use for stocktakes that I took personally with the minister, their key staff and mine, every month or so. The unit would present a progress report and any necessary action would be authorized ... often it became clear that the challenge was systemic, requiring wholesale change to the way a public service worked, rather than a centrally or bureaucratic driven edict.[40]

The PMDU's concern was not policy (the Blair government had a Strategy Unit to explore and develop strategies), nor was it concerned to tell government departments how they should operate (a Policy Unit assisted departments in planning). The PMDU's contribution to the work of departments was to organize regular reviews of the targets and write delivery reports. It set interim goals for delivery, working with the department concerned to provide delivery maps and plans, the identification of delivery chains, trajectories to show the progress on targets over time, audits of performance, and the compilation of league tables to show the relative performances of the departments.

For the first time the prime minister's executive was receiving real-time data and following it up so that obstacles could be removed and policies adjusted if necessary. Most of all, those charged with delivering in the departments knew they were being monitored, and the consummate skill of Barber was to make performance measurement be a partnership. Published reports from existing government inspection and review took months and sometimes years to deliver, but the unit aimed to close its investigation of any issue within a month. The process would involve working out the delivery chain, a broad view about how policies are implemented, which maps out the participants in a chain of cause-and-effect.

> For any given target, a joint review team of five or six people from the relevant department and the Delivery Unit ... [would] pull together all the data they could assemble on the issue and generate some hypotheses and answer the key questions: Were we on track to deliver the target? If so, what were the risks? If not, what could be done to fix the problem?
>
> ... [they] would then go and see for themselves the reality on the ground. Often they would visit a place where progress was good and ask why, and a place where it was poor and ask the same question. They would ask everyone they met the same questions: is the target understood? What are the successes? What are the barriers? What action is needed to strengthen delivery? Finally they would invite interviewees to identify their top three messages for the Prime Minster – an invitation few could resist. This way the team could test and refine their hypotheses. In effect they checked every link in the delivery chain to see how it could be strengthened.[41]

This is an approach consistent with joined-up government which crosses organizational boundaries. It addresses complex social problems, such as social exclusion and poverty, in a comprehensive integrated way, and in as much as it includes a range of

KEY DEBATE 10.2

Do targets work?

B y [Prime Minster] Blair's second term, the target culture was near maniacal. The Audit Commission league tables scored [local government] councils by how many 'library items were issued per head of the population'. They recorded how many 'nights of respite care were supplied per 1,000 of the adult population'. They recorded what percentage of statements on special needs children were prepared per six months. Lest anyone query the answers, private auditors from [accountants] KPMG were hired to audit the audit. Quangos recruited internal and external auditors to mark the Treasury's public auditors. Turnbull, then head of the civil service, was a defender of targets, deriding old guard public administrators as 'knightly professionals left to their own devices'. He felt that doctors, teachers, police chiefs and housing officers have for too long been content with a comfort zone level of service. Targets, said Turnbull, had made public servants 'focus their efforts, requiring them to work more closely with others in the delivery chain'. Yet even he admitted that targets had sometimes proved too top-down, demeaning professional standards, encouraging gaming, undermining trust, distorting priorities.'[42]

Looking back on his time as Prime Minister, Blair remembers there:

... was a lot of exaggerated nonsense about targets and so on in the public sector. ... as I used to say to ministers and civil servants ... cut [targets] down to the essentials, unwind any conflicts, grant a sensible discretion on how they should be met – but don't think for an instant that in any other walk of life you would spend these sums of money without demanding a measurable output.[43]

Steven Kelman writes of value infusion, where targets are used to connect with agency purpose.[44] In practice, however, they often create goal displacement, when people orient themselves too narrowly to attaining a target rather than its underlying goal.[45]

Quality guru, Deming, wrote: 'Goals are necessary for you and me, but numerical goals set for other people, without a road map to reach the goal, have effects opposite to the effects sought'.[46] Often targets encourage gaming and a waste of resources.[47]

The setting by superiors of targets without an understanding of how implementers are to carry it out, without guidelines or a trajectory, is likely to prove ineffective. Quite often targets are achieved but not in the way that those who set the targets intended. If managers do not understand the practicalities of implementation, then they are also unlikely to be able to tell if what has been achieved is really up to their expectations.

John Seddon makes a distinction between targets and measures. He writes that where targets are essentially arbitrary and express a top-down aspiration, a measure is used more usefully locally to help check progress on work. 'At the heart of a system approach is a change to measures. The choice of measures is governed by the purpose of the service from the customer's point of view.'[48]

Question: Should targets in the public sector be put into the 'too-difficult' box?

stakeholders, it serves to build greater legitimacy for policy. Barber summarized what the most important things about the PMDU were. This includes a consistent focus on the key priorities in domestic policy; the provision of an emphasis on the 'how of getting things done' rather than the 'what to do'; it also brought a real and powerful belief in the importance of data and evidence.[49] The idea has been copied in other countries.[50]

Levers of strategic control

Robert Simons has offered a framework to describe how senior managers use four ways for gathering information about how strategy is working and to discover opportunities for new strategic themes and opportunities. He points out that control systems must accommodate not just intended strategies, but also strategies that emerge from local experimentation and independent employee initiatives. He maintains that such systems should do four things: 'to signal the domain in which subordinates should search for opportunities, to communicate plans and goals, to monitor the achievement of plans and goals, and to keep informed and inform others of emerging developments'.[51]

Each of these four information-based activities is a control system for sustaining or influencing patterns of behaviour in the organization. In the sense that senior managers can use these to lever the organization into a desired strategic position, they can be called the organization's four **strategic levers**: beliefs systems, boundary systems, diagnostic control systems, and interactive control systems (Figure 10.5).

FIGURE 10.5 The four levers of strategic control[52]

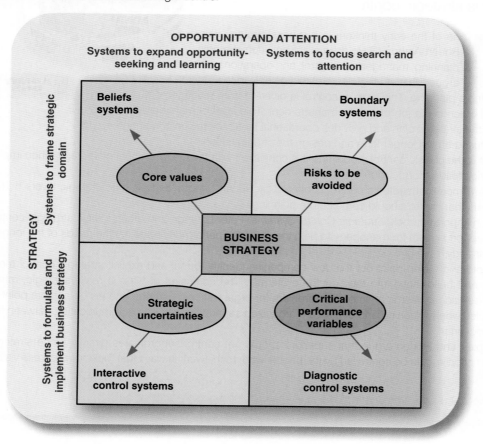

Principally, *beliefs systems* are there to inspire and direct the search for new opportunities; *boundary systems* set the limits to this opportunity-seeking behaviour; *diagnostic systems* motivate and monitor current behaviour towards the achievement of the specified goal; and *interactive control systems* stimulate the organization by provoking newer ideas that emerge. The two levers on the left hand side of the four quadrants are considered by Simons to be the yang (representing warmth, positivism and light, as positive forces) control levers, while the two on the right hand side, are the yin elements (of cold and darkness, which are the negative forces). The yang and yin tensions come from Taoist I-Ching philosophy, and the key thing about them is that they must be in balance.

The two levers, beliefs systems and boundary systems, relate to the framing of strategy and must be in balance with the other two levers, diagnostic control systems and interactive control systems, which relate to the formulation and implementation of strategy. A successful balance will result in the achievement of the organization's strategic goals.

KEY DEBATE 10.3

What is strategic control?

One of the early thinkers in business strategy was Robert Anthony.[53] He drew a line between strategic planning, management control, and operations, and argued that strategic control relates only to the control of strategic planning. This form of control is different from management control which is the job of middle management. This level of management implements the strategic plan and provides operational feedback to senior managers who are focused on the longer-term and design the strategic plan.

This is the classic control model and it is consistent with the design school of strategy, when implementation follows formulation.

A new model of strategic control is offered by Robert Simons and his four strategic levers.[54] This suggests that control should come before planning.

In an important book, *Strategic Control Systems,* Peter Lorange and others define strategic control as a support system for managers, to help them assess performance against the needs of the longer-term strategy.[55]

Goold and Quinn point out that few companies identify formal and explicit strategic control measures, and build these into their control systems.[56] The confusion of what is really strategic, rather than operational, seems an important problem for organizations. Lorange and his co-authors point to examples where planning and control are organized separately, with little communication between the two functions.

Kaplan and Norton argue that superiors should not control subordinates directly, since strategy-linked action should be controlled by the people who do the work in ways that make its progress visible to all.[57]

Question: Does the word 'control' mean the same thing as 'management'?

Lever 1: Beliefs systems

Beliefs systems are an explicit set of organizational definitions that senior managers communicate formally, and reinforce systematically, to provide the basic values and direction for the organization. They inspire and help direct staff in the search for new opportunities. The notion of beliefs systems considers the values that are rooted deeply within an organization which underlie the purpose of its existence. This control system is imperative although Simons had originally omitted this from discussion in his earlier work.[58] His change of mind probably reflects contemporary discussion that places a stress on leadership and the importance to it of vision and values. These may be explicitly written into the original articles of the organization or implicit in the nature of the work it does.

Where the organizational purpose is explicit, a beliefs system is indicated by its purpose statements that are used to document basic values and the direction for the organization. Where purpose is implicit and not so clear, the beliefs system must inspire and guide the organization's search and discovery of that purpose; for example, the beliefs system can be used to motivate individuals to find new ways for creating value for the organization. The formal articulation of beliefs systems in purpose statements becomes more important with growth. Whereas in smaller organizations personnel are intuitively clear about the purpose of the organization, this weakens as complexity increases, and there is a need to document beliefs formally. However, beliefs systems are typically too brief and vague to guide implementation on their own and need the second lever of control, boundary systems.

Lever 2: Boundary systems

Boundary systems cover those sets of rules and sanctions that restrict search, and which help clarify those areas of risk that the organization ought to avoid. In other words, they set limits on opportunity-seeking behaviour. As individuals are opportunity seekers who create value for the company by overcoming obstacles, they must process new information and

situations presented before them. In other words, metaphorically, they are the breaks of a car, and the faster the car the more effective the breaks need to be. However, as it is impossible for senior management to understand all likely contingencies and problems, boundary systems must be robust enough to be flexible for a range of possible opportunities. One way is not to tell individuals what exactly to do, but instead to tell them what not to do. Boundary systems, therefore, set the limits of organizational opportunism and activity.

When new situations arise, untested organizational responses may be used to deal with them. Various organizational factors may affect this, such as specific and stringent codes of conduct. These factors are equivalent to dominant stakeholders overlooking the operations of the company. They affect the enforceability of issues. These may include codes of conduct promulgated by a regulator, as well as political and public opinion. Nonetheless, where these codes or factors have strong similarities with the core values of the company, these operate beneficially. The role of senior management is to state and cascade the core values and visions of the organization, analyze business risks and delimit competition so that the work of subordinates can be eased.

Levers 2 and 3 operating together provide the strategic domain of the organization, but in order to sustain resources and organizational strengths, managers must concentrate on positioning the organization

Lever 3: Diagnostic control systems

Diagnostic control systems are formal systems that are designed to monitor the progress of objectives in the implementation of strategic and related plans. They provide a diagnostic check on how strategy is working. They also motivate, monitor, and reward the achievement of specified goals. Diagnostic control systems are designed to serve predictable goal achievement. They are feedback systems which are core to management control. Managers obtain feedback from their subordinates to align the organization's activities with the organizational goals.

There are three principles for managing diagnostic control systems: first, is the ability to measure the outputs of a process; second, to have predetermined standards against which actual results can be compared; and third, to be able to correct deviations from these standards. These ensure that managers can control outputs through a careful selection of inputs, and can deal with critical performance variables that represent important dimensions of a given strategy. Critical performance variables take many forms; these are not just financial, but may also include customer satisfaction and quality.

Diagnostic control systems can be devolved to local management. Unlike boundary systems, the freedom is left to the individuals to accomplish the desired ends, as superiors will have already agreed the process specification, and the process team can intervene to take corrective action if performance starts to drift from the original specification. Senior managers will only become involved by exception.

Lever 4: Interactive control systems

Interactive control systems comprise formal information systems that managers use to involve themselves regularly and personally in the decision activities of subordinates. Many kinds of interactive control are used, but the important element is the personal participation of senior managers in monthly reviews of progress and action plans that involve other levels in face-to-face meetings. These enable senior managers to try out and introduce new possibilities for change. This activity helps form the agendas for wider debate and includes information gathering from outside routine channels.

This control system brings the organization in line with the changing external environment, since effective managers scan for disruptive changes that signal the need to change organizational structures, capabilities and product technologies. For interactive control systems to function properly, organization-wide involvement is required. When external opportunities and threats are identified, it is important that people across the organization provide input about how organizational capabilities can be changed and brought into play to meet them.

Essentially, there are four distinctive characteristics which form the backbones to interactive control systems: (1) information must be generated by the system and addressed by senior management; (2) operating managers, and other levels of the organization, must review the system frequently; (3) the data generated, must be discussed face-to-face in meetings at all levels; and (4) the system must be the catalyst for all the action plans of the organization.

Interactive control systems must take into consideration various factors. In technology dependent companies, senior managers must focus on responding to customer needs, as technological advances are so rapid. In companies with complex value chains, accounting-based measures provide opportunities and threats to the company, but where this is simple, they need only focus on input and output measures. In regulated public utilities, Simons notes specifically, companies must pay attention to public sentiment, political pressures, and emerging regulations and legislation.

The strategic levers are ways that a senior management can manage the strategic performance of an organization. Of course, how senior management use each of the strategic levers, and more generally their propensity to use strategic performance management at all, will ultimately depend upon styles of strategic leadership and management (see Chapter 11).

SUMMARY OF PRINCIPLES

1 Good strategic performance management mobilizes an organization-wide effort to achieve four things that are vital to the effective management of strategy implementation: focus, alignment, integration and review (FAIR).

2 The objectives translated from the needs of the medium-term are of two sorts: a very few vital breakthrough objectives, and more numerous improvement targets. The former may require exploratory thinking and re-working of routines. The latter involve only incremental changes.

3 These objectives drive improvement in daily management. Breakthrough objectives bring an external influence to bear on the management of the internal processes.

4 The management of objectives is more effective than management by objectives.

5 There are two kinds of strategic review at the daily management level: periodic strategic review and an annual capability review.

6 Delivery systems are important to the strategic management of the public sector and these function through the discipline of review and follow-up.

GUIDED FURTHER READING

For a very good comprehensive text about execution and the management of delivery, see Kaplan, R. S. and Norton, D. P. (2008), *The Execution Premium; Linking Strategy to Operations for Competitive Advantage*, Boston MA: Harvard Business Press. For an in-depth account of the delivery of strategic priorities in government, see Barber, M. (2008). *Instruction to Deliver: Fighting to Transform Britain's Public Services*, (revised paperback edn), London: Methuen.

A wider interpretation of strategic performance management has been given by de Waal's book. This includes the definition of mission, objectives and strategy and their measurement through KPIs: de Waal, A. (2007), *Strategic Performance Management: A Managerial and Behavioural Approach*, London: Palgrave.

The seminal text about Japanese hoshin kanri is an edited book by Akao and other Japanese writers, see Akao, Y. (ed.) (1991), *Hoshin Kanri:*

Policy Deployment for Successful TQM, Cambridge MA: Productivity Press. It is technical and may be too difficult for non-specialists; an easy introduction is Witcher, B. J. (2003), 'Policy management of strategy (hoshin kanri)', *Strategic Change*, 12, March-April, 83–94.

REVIEW QUESTIONS

1 What is FAIR?

2 Why must objectives be kept to the lowest number possible?

3 What is the difference between breakthrough and improvement objectives?

4 What is the difference between the management of objectives, and management by objectives?

5 How does TQM make objective management easier?

6   What is the difference between a performance excellence framework and a top executive audit approach?

7   Is CompStat too authoritarian?

8   What are the four levers of control?

SEMINAR AND ASSIGNMENT QUESTIONS

1   Evaluate how a balanced scorecard's strategic objectives can be translated into annual strategically relevant objectives/means. What kind of scorecard can be used in daily management to help FAIR?

2   Put together a team to draw up agendas for a periodic strategic review, capability review, and a strategy review. Make a list of guidelines for managing a review meeting.

3   The use of delivery and review systems to drive progress on social objectives is controversial. One of the problems is that a strategic priority implies ignoring other things that one expects from a universal service. Are 'objectives' really necessary for effective performance management in the public sector and what is the role of 'management'?

CHAPTER END-NOTES

1   Blair, T. (2010), *Tony Blair, A Journey,* London: Hutchinson.

2   Dye, R. (2008), 'How chief strategy officers think about their role: a roundtable', *The McKinsey Quarterly,* May, www.mckinseyquaterly.com.

3   Kaplan, R. S. and Norton, D. P. (1996), *The Balanced Scorecard: Translating Strategy into Action*, Boston MA: Harvard Business School Press, p. 262.

4   Kaplan, R. S. and Norton, D. P. (1996), *The Balanced Scorecard: Translating Strategy into Action,* Boston MA: Harvard Business School Press, p. 264.

5   Using survey data, Kaplan and Norton argue that organizations with a formal execution process, more than half the organizations sampled, outperform organizations without one: see Kaplan, R. S. and Norton, D. P. (2008), *The Execution Premium: Linking Strategy to Operations for Competitive Advantage,* Boston MA: Harvard Business Press, p. 4.

6   March, J. G. (1991), 'Exploration and exploitation in organizational learning', *Organization Science,* 2(1):71–87.

7   Catchball is term used in Western forms of hoshin kanri, see Watson, G. H. (1991), 'Understanding hoshin kanri', in Akao, Y. (ed.) (1991), *Hoshin Kanri: Policy Deployment for Successful TQM,* Cambridge MA: Productivity Press, xxi–xxiv. Its Japanese version is *nemawashi*.

8   Monden, Y. (1998) *Toyota Poduction System: An Integrated Approach to Just-in-Time,* (3 edn), Norcross, Georgia: Engineering and Management Press.

9   Drucker, P. F. (1971) 'What we can learn from Japanese management', *Harvard Business Review*, March-April: 11–23.

10 Taylor, F. (1911), *The Principles of Scientific Management*, New York: Harper & Row.

11 De Grazia, V. (2005), *Irresistible Empire: America's Advance through Twentieth Century Europe,* Boston: Belknap Press. The origin of the term is associated with Antonio Gramsci, a political philosopher, in 'Americanism and Fordism' in (1934), *Prison Notebooks*.

12 Deming, W. E. (1986), *Out of the Crisis: Quality, Productivity and Competitive Position*, Cambridge: Cambridge University Press.

13 Womack, J. P., Jones, D. T. and Roos, D. (1990), *The Machine That Changed the World*, New York: Rawson Associates.

14 Janis, I. L. (1982), *Groupthink: Psychological Studies of Political Decisions and Fiascos,* (revised edn of *Victims of Groupthink,* 1970) Boston MA: Houghton Mifflin.

15 Porter, M. E., Takeuchi, H. and Sakakibara, M. (2000), *Can Japan Compete?* London: Macmillan, p. 163.

16 Monden, Y. (1998), *Toyota Production System: An Integrated Approach to Just-in-Time,* (3 edn), Norcross: Georgia: Engineering and Management Press, pp. 369 and 374.

17 Deming, W. E. (1986), *Out of the Crisis: Quality, Productivity and Competitive Position, Cambridge:* Cambridge University Press.

18 Drucker, P. F. (1955), *The Practice of Management*, London: Heinemann Butterworth. (1954, American edn), New York: Harper Row; Humble, J. W. (ed.) (1970) *Management by Objectives in Action*, New York: McGraw-Hill. There are indications that MbO may work differently (and more collaboratively) in different national cultures, see Hofstede, G. (1980), 'Motivation, leadership and organization: do American theories apply abroad?' *Organizational Dynamics*, Summer, 42–63.

19 Hewlett-Packard (undated), Planning and Review Process, internal document.

20 Witcher, B. J. and Butterworth, R. (2000), 'Hoshin kanri at Hewlett Packard', *Journal of General Management,* 25(4):70–85.

21 Witcher, B. J. and Butterworth, R. (2001), 'Hoshin kanri: policy management in Japanese-owned UK subsidiaries', *Journal of Management Studies*, 38(5):651–674.

22 Royal Bolton (2009), Annual Plan 2009/10, Bolton: Royal Bolton Hospital NHS Foundation Trust; ThedaCare (2011), 'Strategy deployment', Healthcare Value Reports, ThedaCare Center for Healthcare Value, April, www.createhealthcare value.com.

23 Shook, J. Y. (1998), 'Bringing the Toyota Production System to the United States: a personal perspective', in Liker, J. K. (ed.) *Becoming Lean: Inside Stories of US Manufacturers,* Portland OR: Productivity Press, 40–69, pp. 58–59.

24 Witcher, B. J., Chau, V. S. and Harding, P. (2008), 'Dynamic capabilities: top executive audits and hoshin kanri at Nissan South Africa', *International Journal of Operations and Production Management,* 28(6):540–561.

25 Giuliani, R. W. with Kurson, K. (2002), *Leadership,* London: Little, Brown.

26 Wilson, J. Q. and Kelling, G. L. (1982). 'Broken windows', *The Atlantic Monthly*, March.

27 Bratton, W. (with Nobler, P.) (1998), *Turnaround, How America's Top Cop Reversed the Crime Epidemic*, New York: Random House, p. 152.

28 Bratton, W. (1998), *Turnaround, How America's Top Cop Reversed the Crime Epidemic,* New York: Random House, p. 229.

29 Giuliani, R. W. with Kurson, K. (2002), *Leadership,* London: Little, Brown. p. 74.

30 Mazerolle, L., Rombouts, S. and McBroom, J. (2007), 'The impact of CompStat on reported crime in Queensland', *Policing,* 30(2):237–256.

31 Levitt, S. D. and Dubner, S. J. (2005), *Freakonomics: A Rogue Economist Explores the Hidden Side of Everything*, New York: William Morrow.

32 Kelling, G. L, and Souse, W. H. (2001), 'Do police matter? An analysis of the Impact of New York City's police reforms', *Civic Report*, 22, December.

33 Bratton, W. J. and Malinowski, S. W. (2008). 'Police performance management in practice: taking CompStat to the next level', *Policing*, 2(3):259–265; Patusky, C., Shelley, M. and Botwinik, L. (2007). *The Philadelphia SchoolStat Model*, report, IBM Centre for the Business of Government, University of Pennsylvania; Behn, R. (2006). 'The varieties of CitiStat', *Public Administration Review*, May-June, 332–340.

34 Behn, R. (2008). 'The seven big errors of PerformanceStat', *Policy Briefs*, John F. Kennedy School of Government, Harvard University, February.

35 Behn, R. (2008). 'The seven big errors of PerformanceStat', *Policy Briefs,* John F. Kennedy School of Government, Harvard University, February. p. 6.

36 Wilson, J. Q. and Kelling, G. L. (1982), 'Broken windows', *The Atlantic Monthly,* March.

37 Giuliani, R. W. with Kurson, K. (2002), *Leadership,* London: Little, Brown.

38 Bratton, W. (with Nobler, P.) (1998), *Turnaround, How America's Top Cop Reversed the Crime Epidemic,* New York: Random House, p. 229.

39 Barber, M. (2008), *Instruction to Deliver: Fighting to Transform Britain's Public Services*, (revised paperback edn), London: Methuen.

40 Blair, T. (2010), *Tony Blair, A Journey*, London: Hutchinson, p. 339.

41 Barber, M. (2008), *Instruction to Deliver: Fighting to Transform Britain's Public Services,* (revised paperback edn), London: Methuen. p. 151.

42 Jenkins, M. S. (2006), *Thatcher & Sons: A Revolution in Three Parts,* London: Allen Lane.

43 Blair, T. (2010), *Tony Blair, A Journey,* Hutchinson: London.

44 Kelman, S. (2007), 'Improving service delivery performance in the United Kingdom: organization theory perspectives on central intervention strategies', *Journal of Comparative Policy Analysis*, 8(4):393–419.

45 Merton, R. K. (1968), *Social Theory and Social Structure* (enlarged edn), New York: Free Press.

46 Deming, W. E. (1986), *Out of the Crisis: Quality, Productivity and Competitive Position,* Cambridge: Cambridge University Press, p. 69.

47 Hood, C. (2006), 'Gaming in targetworld: the targets approach to managing British public services', *Public Administration Review,* July-August, 515–521.

48 Seddon, J. (2008), *Systems Thinking in the Public Sector: The Failure of the Reform Regime and a Manifesto for a Better Way,* London: Triarchy.

49 Barber, M. (2007). Examination of Michael Barber, *The Governance of Britain*, Public Administration Select Committee, London: House of Commons, July 19.

50 Lindquist, E. (2006). 'Organizing for policy implementation: the emergence and role of implementation units in policy design and oversight', *Journal of Comparative Policy Analysis*, 8(4):311–324; Wanna, J. (2006), 'From afterthought to afterburner: Australia's cabinet implementation unit', *Journal of Comparative Policy Analysis*, 8(4):347–369.

51 Simons, R. (1995), *Levers of Control: How Managers Use Innovative Control Systems to Drive Strategic Renewal,* Boston: Harvard Business School Press, p. 4.

52 Adapted from Simon, R. (1995), *Levers of Control: How Managers Use Innovative Control Systems to Drive Strategic Renewal,* Boston: Harvard Business School Press.

53 Anthony, R. N. (1965), *Planning and Control Systems: A Framework for Analysis*, teaching note, Division of Research, Graduate School of Business, Harvard Business School.

54 Simons, R. (1995), *Levers of Control: How Managers Use Innovative Control Systems to Drive Strategic Renewal,* Boston: Harvard Business School Press.

55 Lorange, P., Scott Morton, M. F. and Ghoshal, S. (1986), *Strategic Control Systems,* St. Paul: West Publishing.

56 Goold, M. and Quinn, J. J. (1990), *Strategic Control: Milestones for Long-Term Performance,* London: Hutchinson.

57 Kaplan, R. S. and Norton, D. P. (2001), *The Strategy-Focused Organization: How Balanced Scorecard Companies Thrive in the New Business Environment,* Boston MA: Harvard Business School Press.

58 Simons, R (1990), *Rethinking the Role of Systems in Controlling Strategy*, Internal Note, No. 9-191-091, Harvard Business School.

CASE 10.1 FAIR hoshin kanri for services at Xerox[1]

Hoshin kanri (policy management)

This case considers how *hoshin kanri*, in the form of the FAIR framework, was managed at Xerox. Xerox (UK) is the sales, marketing and support subsidiary of Xerox (Limited). It is structured as four business development units based on office document systems, office document products, document production systems, and printing systems. It uses a FAIR phase approach for its *hoshin kanri* (see Exhibit 10.1).

Focus

The American parent, Xerox Corporation, sets the Vision, Business Goals and Direction. These are passed to the companies in the Group. Vision is a statement, which shows a desired state – 'The Document Company', and reads, 'Xerox will be the leader in the Global Document Market, by providing Document Solutions that enhance Business Productivity.'

To progress this vision, Xerox uses four types of Business Goals: customer satisfaction; employee motivation and satisfaction; market share, and return on assets. As 'goals' Xerox see their purpose as a means to measure progress in the key areas which determine the company's longer term success, an overall Direction is used to align the goals; for example, for 1997 it was Profitable Revenue Growth. Xerox requires its companies develop Vital Few Programmes (*hoshins*) which are consistent with the direction.

Xerox (UK) starts to determine its vital few programmes after the board conducts a two-day planning session in July. This meeting produces an outline business plan as well as an outline of the vital few. The business plan is primarily made up of financials, which are worked out in terms of targets and measures of revenue, profit and so on, in collaboration with the business units. The vital few programmes are considered by the organization separately and are developed by central staff working with senior

executives to produce more detail with the aim to specific the vital few by year end for their introduction at Start Year meetings in the business units in January.

An individual senior executive acts as a sponsor for each of the vital few. They are chosen for their potential impact. A lot of this activity is spent in informal discussions between senior directors, with staff putting the information up, rewriting and getting the information into a usable format. The vital few are specified around each of the business goals to ensure they are linked: for example, the customer satisfaction goal was given its own vital few programme, which was documented as 'Only when we can demonstrate our loyalty to our customers can we expect to have their loyalty in return'. This programme aimed to reduce customer dissatisfaction and minimize revenue losses for existing customers. It also called for the introduction of new forms of customer care that would facilitate monitoring and the management of customer contacts during the period customers are with Xerox.

Over the years there is a degree of continuity in the subjects of vital few programmes. The programmes are put together on an annual basis, but they run

EXHIBIT 10.1 The FAIR phases of hoshin kanri at Xerox

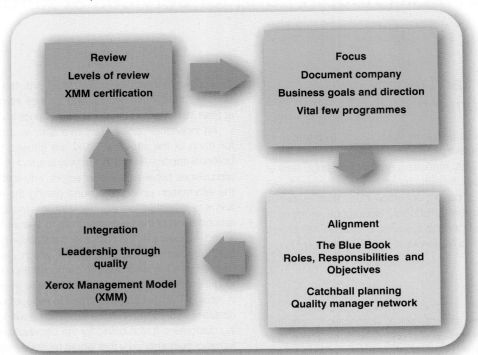

along a theme that last perhaps up to five years to implement, with each year being slightly different.

Alignment

The alignment of the vital few programmes at local level in the business units and teams begins with the distribution of documentation known as the *Blue Book* and the *Employee Guide to Policy Deployment*. This goes to the unit quality managers in time for the start-up meetings. This 'book' is intended for managers, since they have the responsibility for cascading its information about the vital few programmes to their teams. The 1997 edition listed the details of each programme, sponsor, and the scope. It also had a section that covered the key business activities and policies of each of the major business units. There was a section that clarified the role of managers in communicating the programmes. Unit and team managers are expected to produce a local translation of the book, to identify local objectives, and for individuals to keep close by in their work.

The *Blue Book* is translated for every employee as the *Employee Guide to Policy Deployment*. This is designed as a folder, explaining hoshin kanri and the programmes; it also has a pocket where an individual may attach their Role, Responsibilities and Objectives (RRO). This is a one-page sheet of paper that summarizes an individual's role in contributing to the vital few, and a summary of their primary job function (or that of their team). It thus contains those key activities and projects for which an individual is accountable, and the standards, targets and measures, which determine the criteria for successful progression and completion of work. All employees are expected to have a RRO, including senior managers and executives. Because the RRO is used for appraisals, it provides a direct link between an individual's performance and the progress of the programmes.

The RROs are updated annually as a part of the deployment process and linked to employee development. Self-managed teams do their own appraisals. Appraisals address the needs of the vital few by ensuring that staff can plan to develop any required new skills. Appraisals are done again towards the end of the year, and a formal review of the individual's development is carried out.

The Start Year presentations go through the *Blue Book* and *Employees' Guide*, and then they go into detail on the vital few. Basically, each unit decides its focus on one or more of the vital few. Managers then take the information away and develop more detail with their own teams. It goes through several strands of deployment. It begins at a large Start Year meeting, and then deploys through line managers through their teams.

Some of the programmes are more relevant to some staff than others. So while some concentrate on one particular programme, others address them all in different ways, depending upon the nature of their work and circumstances. It is difficult to generalize about how the vital few will be taken up and translated. For example:

One of the things that we're going to do across the board is customer first training, so everybody will need to know that is there. We are also doing digital skills, which will hit a very small community, so that will be different. It will all go through the various networks that we have got, to get it out to the field. For the individual, say the engineer, they probably won't have much of a clear idea about what is in the document; they will know that 'accelerate skills up' is one of the vital few programmes, they may translate that into say learning about PCs as an individual skills gap. Some of it will be a conceptual translation, which isn't a detailed plan. Others will be – well here is the detailed plan that is part of your job role so go away and implement it. These are all change initiatives so they may evolve over the year.

It is essential to be realistic about what can be achieved. If there are too many deployed secondary programmes and the cascade is very wide, then things can get quickly out of control and people lose focus. However, if teams are working to total quality management (TQM) then they will have the skills to prioritize so that deployment is manageable. The Customer Satisfaction Management Group provides an instance of problem solving priorities. This unit is in charge of the company's total satisfaction guarantee; it also tracks customer satisfaction and is the custodian for customer satisfaction company-wide.

At its Start Year meeting this unit focused on the customer satisfaction and loyalty vital few programme,

and worked first on a situation analysis of the present position of the unit's performance. This involved everyone in a series of brainstorming meetings where SWOT analysis was used to determine the unit's existing strengths and weaknesses, opportunities and threats, in a relation to a contribution to the programme, and to think up actions. One of these included the use of the voice of the customer in distribution channels; another on how to improve customer retention, and others concerned communications and query resolution. These were assessed for their impact and relation to each other by root cause analysis; actions were then prioritized using Pareto analysis. In this way four actions were selected and each one was ascribed a desired state with a set of means.

The full implications of actions worked out in this way must then be checked with affected third parties. This sometimes leads to conflict on means but, in the end, units and teams have to agree priorities against what is possible with existing budgets. This iterative deployment of plans is a catchball form of planning. The discussions are not about the correctness of the purpose of the corporate vital few programmes, but centre on the practical issues about how to achieve them. The activity is not a formal process and is influenced by the normal working elations people have in daily management.

Every unit within the company has a quality specialist or manager, and these are coordinated through an informal network. This has a pivotal role in that it facilitates deployment by offering advice about how to translate the priorities into local actions. They have an active role at Start Year meetings and informally oversee the progress of vital few programmes through the year. Quality managers do not own the planning process but they are regarded by the centre as the conscience of the organization for the hoshin kanri process. They inspect without people realizing what is happening, and assess understanding at the operational level. They also play an important role in organizing and following up reviews of progress on the vital few.

Integration

The essence of hoshin kanri is that people should work on those activities in their daily work, which are vital to strategic success. This is not just about how the vital few are deployed, but it is also about how they are managed day-to-day. It means that daily processes must be managed in such a way as to ensure that they are under control. Thus TQM is fundamental. Called Leadership through Quality, at the heart of TQM at Xerox is the Xerox Quality Policy. This is regarded within the Group as Xerox's Values Statement, which aims to create and maintain a competitive advantage through customer-focused quality.

Xerox is a quality company. Quality is the basic business principle for Xerox. Quality means providing our external and internal customers with innovative products and services that fully satisfy their requirements. Quality improvement is the job of every Xerox employee.

TQM began with a sheep-dip approach when everyone was trained in its ideas. In practice, after the training was done, the ideas were forgotten and people continued in the same way, so that there was a loss of morale and frustration among those who realized TQM could provide the tools to make change happen. It really began to work when managers switched from thinking about the management

of quality as such to the quality of the way Xerox manages. A key element was the introduction of the Xerox Management Model (XMM) that clarified and defined the way Xerox manages.

The XMM is a methodology used to deploy Xerox's vision and goals. Introduced in 1994 in a corporate-wide update of TQM, its aim then was to make quality Xerox's general approach to management. It provides a framework for managers to identify the key processes used to manage the business. It is comprised of five categories: leadership, human resource management, business process management, customer and market focus, and information utilization and quality tools (see Exhibit 10.2). Good management practice in all these areas leads to the achievement of its four business goals, in the business results part of the model.

In order to achieve the business Xerox has to have good leadership across the whole organization to manage people so that they can work effectively with the right processes, with the right information and tools, which are focused on what the customer expects and wants. If the five enablers are managed correctly that should drive out the results. The double

EXHIBIT 10.2 The Xerox management model

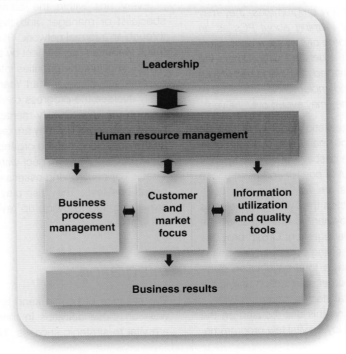

arrows in the figure emphasize the need for a continuing dialogue between management and other employees.

Xerox specifies elements of good practice for each of the categories: for example, the elements for Customer and Market Focus are:

- *Customer First*
- *Customer Requirements*
- *Customer Database*
- *Market Segment*
- *Customer Communications*
- *Customer Query and Complaint Management*
- *Customer Satisfaction and Loyalty*
- *Customer Relationship Management*
- *Customer Commitment*

Review

There are three levels of management review. The first two are similar to management meetings anywhere and apply at the business unit and the higher company level. Each business unit uses a management team to conduct a monthly review to sanction short-term action. The quality managers own these to ensure they are carried out and that the right things are reviewed. There is a similar meeting at company level when the Managing Director and his or her team (units and network heads) review progress overall. Both these reviews concern general matters and are not solely about the vital few programmes. There is also an operations review and this is entirely centred on the status of the vital few, when senior managers review performance every quarter with each unit's general manager and their staff. The agenda is a standard one that aims to achieve consistency in strategic direction. Unit representatives present current status against plan, and make an assessment of progress of their action plans, so that amendments and additions to local plans can be agreed if necessary.

More generally, progress is reported through the specialist networks, when the company's communications media are used to relay information about best practice and success stories. Through this way the networks, such as the quality managers, play an important learning role in dissembling the lessons

from what is happening across the organization Additionally, Xerox's TQM uses a Deming (PDCA) cycle to manage its business processes, when work is constantly monitored and checked: the aim is to translate the needs of the vital few into process targets that will be monitored and managed daily.

In the final months of the yearly cycle, Xerox conducts an annual audit of its business units, which provides feedback on the overall organizational effectiveness of how people are managing, and to provide information to use to change the vital few for the next annual cycle. This activity is called XMM Certification because the model is used as a framework to audit the units. Units self-appraise, but the company uses a senior director and senior line managers from other units to validate appraisals and approve Certification. This flags up to the rest of the company that the unit has demonstrated a high level of operational command of the XMM enablers, and has produced good business results. The XMM Certification represents a major event for the unit concerned.

Managing hoshin kanri

Hoshin kanri is organic and varies across the years in its nature and outcomes depending upon how senior management use it to enable the participation of others. For example, the 1996 hoshin kanri programme turned out badly at Xerox (UK) and failed to have an impact. This was a result of too many vital few programmes. Eight had been set for 1996 and these programmes had in turn been split into 24 'critical elements.' These 24 were designed to make the relevance of the vital few clearer to a maximum number of employees, and to help prompt staff to think in a more focused way about how a programme might be carried out. As a result the *Blue Book* was very complex. It gave descriptive detail of the XMM; templates for quality tools and deployment procedures; detail of the vital few; and listed the RROs of the major business units. All this meant a document of 35 pages (compared to its equivalent in the previous year of 15 pages). One of Xerox' quality managers summarized the problems:

> We struggled so much with the vital few. I think with other companies they tend not to do so much with

the how. We have objectives where the focus is *broader (because of the marketing nature of the work) and so we will give you a few more of the hows, and what you do in support of that is for you to decide. The previous MD could not agree to less than eight and would not countenance two or three. Problem was that by the time you get to 24 critical elements you are beginning to lose focus. My argument is that we do not have hoshin kanri, we have something, which is well recognized and used for communication, but what we actually communicate with – it would be debatable. We introduced elements because we used to have eight vital few programmes but they were then so broad that to try and get anything out of it at an individual level was difficult.*

Many units simply failed to consider the vital few distinctly enough from the things they were doing anyway, and the units designed their programmes more to suit local rather than corporate centre priorities. A new Managing Director came in who reduced the number to only four vital few programmes, and simplified the documentation, so that a renewed purpose improved results markedly for the following year.

Discussion questions

1 Outline specifically the components of the four distinct stages of the FAIR hoshin kanri process at Xerox.

2 How is the Xerox Management Model similar to, or different from, the European Excellence Model and the Baldrige criteria?

3 What are the salient lessons from the hoshin kanri experience at Xerox?

Case end-note

1 This case is adapted from Witcher, B. J. and Butterworth, R. (1999), 'Hoshin kanri: how Xerox manages' *Long Range Planning*, 32(3):323–332.

Chapter 11
STRATEGIC LEADERSHIP

Leaders

he prime responsibility for strategic management and making sure that it works lies at the top of the organization. The executive and other senior managers must lead the organization so it will achieve its purpose. Effective strategic leadership is the foundation for successfully using the strategic management process.

🔑 KEY TERMS

charismatic
  or visionary
  leadership

domain
  knowledge

eight-stage
  framework
  for managing
  change

emotional
  intelligence

entrepreneurial
  leadership

four
  competences
  of leadership

leader

leadership

participative
  or backroom
  leadership

strategic
  leaders

strategic
  leadership

transactional
  leadership

transformational
  leadership

LEARNING OBJECTIVES

This chapter provides you with an understanding of the following:

1 The nature of leadership and strategic leadership

2 The four competences of leadership

3 The four styles of leadership:
   - transformational
   - transactional
   - charismatic and visionary
   - participative and backroom

4 How leadership may be different to management

5 The consequences of the idea of management as a profession

6 How leadership issues may change with organizational size and growth

7 Leading strategic change

Business vignette Wise leadership and the ancients

The *Tao Te Ching* is an ancient Chinese book; regarded as a classic Taoist text it probably dates back many hundreds of years before it was written down at the start of the 1st century BC in a biography of Lao Tzu, by the historian, Ssu-ma Ch'ien.

The highest form of government
Is what people hardly even realize is there.
Next is that of the sage
Who is seen, and loved, and respected.
Next down is the dictatorship
That thrives on oppression and terror –
And the last is that of those who lie

And end up despised and rejected.
The sage says little –
And does not tie the people down;
And the people stay happy
Believing that what happens
Happens, naturally.[1]

The meaning of a 'sage' is often translated in Western circles today to mean a wise leader who makes it possible after the work is done for people to say 'we did it ourselves'. Peter Wickens, the founder-CEO of Nissan Motors UK, puts it his way: 'leadership is about getting people to do what you want them to do because they want to do it for you'.[2]

Consistency and constancy of purpose, objectives and strategies, at every level and part of the organization, require forms of strategic leadership that will build and sustain a team effort across the whole organization. **Leadership** is the ability of an individual or a group of individuals to influence others to achieve an organization's purpose and objectives. The nature of leadership varies for different stages of an organization's development, especially its size, when senior levels of management become more distant from daily management. Also, leadership styles vary according to the personalities and group dynamics of senior managers, and the importance they place on their own personal goals and motivations; this is especially true of chief executives. However, whatever the form and style, strategic leadership should work to promote organization-wide synergy and harmony.

The popular notion of a leader is of a person who is followed by others. There may be any number of reasons for following, but it is usually because they exercise a power to influence events. In the context of strategic management, a **leader** is one who by influencing others has an ability to take the organization forward to a common purpose. The most powerful people in an organization in this sense are, of course, the executives and other senior managers, who make the most important decisions for moving an organization towards its goals. While the basis for such decisions may emerge and be worked out involving many people throughout the organization, perhaps after conflict and many compromises, it is only the top managers that, in the end, make the decisions for the organization as a whole.

No bosses, but plenty of leaders

W.L. Gore & Associates is a privately-owned international industrial chemical company. Anyone among its 8000 'associates' can become a leader.

It is a happy company – in polls it is regularly voted one of the best companies to work for. Gary Hamel in his book, *The Future of Management*, uses Gore as a case to illustrate what leadership could be like in the future:[3]

Walk around the halls at Gore, or sit in on meetings, and you won't hear anyone use word like 'boss', 'executive', 'manager', or 'vice president'. These terms are so contrary to Gore's egalitarian ideals that they are effectively banned from conversation.

Although there are no ranks or titles at Gore, some associates have earned the simple appellation 'leader'. At Gore, senior leaders do not appoint junior leaders. Rather, associates become leaders when their peers judge them to be such. A leader garners influence by demonstrating a capacity to get things done and excelling as a team leader. At Gore, those who make a disproportionate contribution to team success, and do it more than once, attract followers.

'We vote with our feet', says Rich Buckingham, a manufacturing leader in Gore's techno-fabrics group. 'If you call a meeting, and people show up, you're a leader'.

Individuals who've been repeatedly asked to serve and tribal chiefs are free to put the word 'leader' on their business card. About 10 per cent of Gore's associates carry such a designation.

The company explains its approach as a 'Team-Based, Flat Lattice Organization':[4]

How we work at Gore sets us apart. Since Bill Gore founded the company in 1958, Gore has been a team-based, flat lattice organization that fosters personal initiative. There are no traditional organizational charts, no chains of command, nor predetermined channels of communications.

Instead, we communicate directly with each other and are accountable to fellow members of our multi-disciplined teams. We encourage hands-on innovation, involving those closest to a project in decision-making. Teams organize around opportunities and leaders emerge. This unique kind of corporate structure has proven to be the key significant contributor to associate satisfaction and retention.

… How does all this happen? Associates (not employees) are hired for general work areas. With the guidance of their sponsors (not bosses) and a growing understanding of opportunities and team objectives, associates commit to projects that match their skills. All of this takes place in an environment that combines freedom with cooperation and autonomy with synergy.

Everyone can quickly earn the credibility to define and drive projects. Sponsors help associates chart a course in the organization that will offer personal fulfilment while maximizing their contribution to the enterprise. Leaders may be appointed, but are defined by 'followership'. More often leaders emerge naturally by demonstrating special knowledge, skill, or experience that advances a business objective.

Question: How is it possible to manage strategically a latticed network like Gore's?

Strategic leadership

Strategic leadership is the style and general approach used by a senior management to articulate purpose, objectives and strategy, to influence implementation and execution of these through the organization. However, at every organizational level there are people with leadership qualities and abilities: for example, individuals who lead units, sections, teams, and those who are specialists in important areas of knowledge and competency. Many of these are **strategic leaders** in the sense that they are located in different parts of the organization but they use the strategic management process to help achieve the organization's purpose by influencing and empowering others to create strategic change as necessary. The ability to manage people is central, especially to develop core competences.

Peter Senge, in an influential book about the learning organization, argues for dispersed leadership; this is when it is important to enhance the strategic skills and decision-making for managers and employees generally.[5] The word, leader, in Senge's view is not a synonym for senior management, but a more complex concept that applies to anybody in an organization who is able to carry out three roles. The first is as a designer of living systems, or in other words, how a leader conditions working behaviour so people will say, 'We did it ourselves?' The second is a teacher role, when the leader enables people to self-develop within a space that is a priority for the organization. The third role is to be a steward for the larger purpose of the organization, which a leader uses to bring a depth of meaning to an individual's aspirations. The required skills for strategic leadership involve building shared visions for everybody; this is an ability to bring to the surface and test the mental models people have, or, in other words, the beliefs that people have which underlie their work. Finally, it is also an ability to use systems thinking to see and understand the important organizational inter-dependencies that condition action and relations.

Senge places an emphasis on the reflective nature of good enabling leadership to enhance inter-personal relations. This is present in the work of Goleman and others; they argue that an effective leader must skilfully switch between different leadership styles depending upon the situation they are faced with.[6] This ability is (at least in part) dependent upon a leader's **emotional intelligence**, the ability to recognize and understand their own emotions and the emotions of others. The attributes that comprise this quality are:

- self-awareness (the ability to articulate openly about feelings);
- self-management (the ability to control and use emotions to good effect);
- social awareness (the ability to empathize with others).

Executive leadership, however, is by its nature remote in the sense that only a small part of a large organization's staff will have regular contact with top managers. In this case, the appearance of leadership is also important. The political philosopher, Niccolo Machiavelli, writing in the early 16th century, observed that 'men in general judge by their eyes rather than by their hands; because everyone is in a position to watch, few are in a position to come in close touch with you. Everyone sees what you appear to be, few experience what you really are'.[7]

Statue of Machiavelli, Uffizi Gallery, Italy

> Men in general judge by their eyes rather than by their hands; because everyone is in a position to watch, few are in a position to come in close touch with you. Everyone sees what you appear to be, few experience what you really are.

The representation of what leaders do, especially in the symbols and artefacts that are associated with them, such as strategic plans, reports, purpose statements, public relations, and so on, can be as important in themselves as signifiers of credibility and legitimacy, as much as they are in practical terms to help a strategic decision or action.

The four competences of leadership

Warren Bennis maintains that leaders display **four competences of leadership**.[8] The first is management of attention: this is the ability to attract and draw people to them, and hold their attention and inspire them. This is typically associated with charismatic leadership (see below), but in fact the leader can be ordinary and the attraction of the intensity arises from the vision of the leader itself. There is a sense of conviction about what should happen next and that it will happen.

The second is the management of meaning: this is the sense of understanding the underlying patterns that make apparently unrelated elements form a coherent and understandable whole. Followers see the way forward and respond with organized energy and focus. It is not enough to be informed, but it is necessary to use language and visual slogans that communicate clarity. In other words, keep it simple and abstract simply from a complex and messy reality.

The third competency is the management of trust: it means that a leader can be trusted to keep to a constant theme or motif. Leaders, while periodically

changing direction as events unfold, must be true to their underlying principles. These may not be articulated, but perhaps conveyed in similar phrases and slogans over again. A constancy of purpose must be felt by others if loyalty is to be maintained over time, or else they will feel betrayed.

The fourth competency is the management of self: leaders know that their abilities are and will not worry about taking decisions and agonizing over progress and results. They will reflect just long enough on mistakes to learn from experience, but will move ahead again quickly. This gives confidence to others – it is not the confidence of leaders as such, but the sureness of their bearing and actions.

Transformational and transactional leadership

James McGregor Burns, a political scientist, in his book, *Leadership*, distinguishes between **transformational leadership** and **transactional leadership**.[9] Transformational leadership is charismatic and inspirational in a way that exploits the motives and higher needs of the follower, so that the 'full person of the follower is engaged'. He suggests that the relations between most leaders and followers are transactional, when leaders approach followers to exchange one thing for another, such as jobs for votes, and bargaining is central to most of the relationships between leaders and the groups and parties that follow them.

Burns' ideas have been used to explain the role of leadership in organization management in general (notably in Bass[10]). Transformational leadership is charismatic, and aims to associate individual self-interest with the larger vision of the organization, by inspiring people with a sense of collective vision. Good transformational leadership creates excitement, raises enthusiasm for challenges that bring about change. Transactional leaders, on the other hand, is more centred on mission and explicit management systems that clarify expectations, agreements, and which provide constructive feedback about performance. Burns was active in American politics and argued for strong leadership, and he favoured a visionary style of leadership.

Henry Ford in a Model-T

Charismatic or visionary leadership

Charismatic or **visionary leadership** is a personalized form of strategic leadership based on a leader's vision about purpose and behaviour of the organization that helps condition an organization's culture and strategic management. One of the most renowned examples is that of Henry Ford, who had a clear idea about why he founded his car company. In 1907, two years after the Ford Motor Company was incorporated, he wrote in the company prospectus:

> *I will build a car for the great multitude. It will be large enough for the family but small enough for the individual to run and care for. It will be constructed of the best materials, by the best men to be hired, after the simplest designs that modern engineering can devise. But it will be low in price so that no man making a good salary will be unable to own one and enjoy with his family the blessing of hours of pleasure in God's great open spaces.[11]*

It would be a few years before this vision produced the Model-T car, and the development of a modern mass production assembly line that made Ford's vision possible.

Sometimes a leader's vision has more to do with values. Richard Branson is never seen wearing a tie and his hair is long; he embodies an unconventionality that is used to colour the Virgin Group's identity. Many

of the industries that Virgin has invested in are long-established and the aim of Virgin has been to do things differently, or to challenge the existing rules, to give customers a choice, to be entertaining and 'put a thumb in the eye of complacent incumbents'. The culture is one of 'why not' rather than 'why' – an essence that Branson himself seems to personify and which suggests that Virgin competes very differently from its competitors.

For example, when the Virgin record label was competing with EMI:

> *Virgin's studios were more than twice as profitable as those of EMI's, and the reason was not hard to see.*

Sir Richard Branson, Founder and Chairman of Virgin Group

At EMI, there was an elaborate system of incentives, with managers setting targets and receiving salaries at the end of the year that reflected how well they had performed against these. At Virgin there was no formal system at all. Yet Virgin was managed more aggressively, and with more concern for the pennies, while at EMI the managers had simply set themselves targets that were low enough to be easily beaten.[20]

KEY DEBATE 11.1

Inspirational leaders and micromanagement

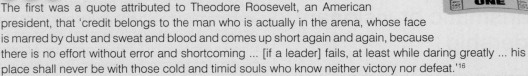

Michael Barber, writing about his time managing the delivery of government strategic priorities, observes that two things, one inspirational and the other analytical, had struck him as central to his job. The first was a quote attributed to Theodore Roosevelt, an American president, that 'credit belongs to the man who is actually in the arena, whose face is marred by dust and sweat and blood and comes up short again and again, because there is no effort without error and shortcoming ... [if a leader] fails, at least while daring greatly ... his place shall never be with those cold and timid souls who know neither victory nor defeat.'[16]

The second was about implementation: 'The neglect of implementation issues is more than a simple intellectual mistake: it may be a rational response to the fact that our political system confers more rewards for the shrewd deployment of symbols and generalized arguments than it does for detailed realistic analysis and forecasting.'[17]

Some leaders are very sure of themselves. This was certainly true of Margaret Thatcher, a charismatic leader who was very clear about what she wanted, and certainly used symbols and generalized arguments to great effect to leave no one in doubt about what she wanted. Michael Portillo, a minister in her government, has said that when given three options for action, there was never any doubt about which one to take, because you always knew what Margaret wanted.[18] As time went on, some of her senior ministers resigned because of her interference in their departments.

In 2011 Rupert Murdoch was called to public hearings at the British parliament to explain the reasons for illegal practices at one of his newspapers, *The News of the World*.[19] As chairman of a very large media empire, his defence was that he could not be expected to know about the detail of management practices in a part of his company that formed a only a fraction (about 1 per cent of global revenues) of his company, News Corporation. His time was normally full managing the larger parts of his global group. He believed that other senior managers who were responsible at the newspaper had broken his trust in allowing such activities to happen. His response was to close the newspaper down.

Trust is central to accountability. If people are put in charge then it should be their responsibility to manage the work given them. The extent to which a superior should oversee, and sometimes intervene, must rest with the judgement of the superior. However, there is a danger of over-management from micromanagement. This is a style of management when a superior closely observes or controls what subordinates do. This may lead to an excessive obsession with detail that leads to a superior's failure to focus on the most important strategic issues.

Questions: Taking into account trust, how can leaders really know what is going on in their organizations?

Jack Ma – China's Internet Godfather[12]

Jack Ma is from Hangzhou, China, and he started working life as an English teacher; he is now one of China's leading entrepreneurs. He is chairman of the Alibaba Group, which is a collection of Internet-based businesses. The mission of the group is to 'make it easy to do business anywhere'.[13] The group has become the world's largest online trading platform for businesses and employs 24 000 people in about 70 cities in Greater China, India, Japan, Korea, the United Kingdom and the United States. Alibaba was founded in 1999 and Jack Ma has ever since preached the importance of the Internet to convince companies that they should pay to offer their products on Alibaba's website.

His leadership style has been described by the *Financial Times* as energetic and stubborn. If one of his executives makes a decision he does not like, he says 'I will see if I can tolerate it. And if it's wrong, well, I think it is stupid and change it again.'

Mr Ma wants to be the 'guard' of the group's values and vision, and spends most of his time trying to make sure they are deeply rooted in the minds of each employee. New employees must attend an extensive orientation and team-building programme, which includes a strong focus on the company's mission, vision and values. This training is reinforced in by further regular training, team-building exercises and company events. 'Strong shared values have enabled us to maintain a common company culture and community, no matter how large we grow.'[14]

When Mr Ma, a slight gaunt man, birdlike in appearance, tried to sell online advertising space on China's nascent Internet in 1994, people viewed him with scepticism and suspicion. 'They would think I was crazy', he says, gesturing with his bony hands.

In 1995 he established the China Yellow Pages, an online directory for Chinese businesses. Alibaba was set up four years later to focus on small- and medium-sized businesses. For a fixed payment, Alibaba offers Chinese suppliers a place on its website. Ma believes that small- and medium-sized businesses can benefit most from the Internet because it gives them access to buyers they would otherwise only meet at trade shows. With access to a wider pool of customers, it also reduces their dependency on market-dominated clients.

Jack Ma, Executive Chairman of Alibaba Group

'Companies like Walmart, these big time buyers, killed a lot of SME buyers', says Mr Ma. 'But now most of the SME buyers and sellers started to do business throughout the world because of the Internet. So I think the world has moved. I strongly believe small is beautiful.'[15]

Question: What is Mr Ma's leadership style?

A similar form of leadership is **entrepreneurial leadership**, a style that is associated with small- and medium-sized businesses. This is characterized by the personality, usually of a single owner-manager, or sometimes of a few collaborating individuals, who impose their view on the business in ways that are characteristically innovative. However, it can also be used to describe an innovative leader, often a visionary one, in a large organization. Both entrepreneurial and visionary leadership have been cited as examples of transformational leadership. Over recent years, these types of leadership have been popularly favoured as the sort of leadership that reflects the pace of change a modern economy requires. However, these styles can encourage a dominating form of managing This is classically so with smaller enterprises: as businesses grow entrepreneurs need to recruit specialist managers as their lieutenants, but it is often hard for the chief executive to let them get on and do their jobs. A natural entrepreneur typically wants to do everything.

The Hopper brothers lament the passing of what they call the 'Golden Age of American management', when the chief executive had been a thoughtful listener, who had shared responsibility with the members of his or her team, and was paid only moderately more than them.[21] Now, they argue, this collegiate style of leadership has given way to the imperial chief executive. Michael O'Leary, the charismatic chief executive of Ryanair, thinks he can spot the trappings of empire:

> The more successful you are, the more likely you are to lose sight of the things that made you successful … Someone wrote a book in the States twenty years ago and said the three things you can always use to tell the time when a company turns from being a success to a failure are when they build a headquarters – the glass palace headquarters office – helicopter outside of it, and the chief executive writes a book. So I think as long as we stay away from all those things, we're fine.[22]

History is full of examples where belief appears to have achieved the impossible. However, there are also (probably many more) examples to show that the power of will and optimism may be less important than the reality of the adequacy of resources for the task envisaged. All leaders require good subordinates and it seems wise to involve them as much as possible.

Participative or backroom leadership

Participative or backroom leadership is low profile and self-effacing, and aims to involve colleagues in taking and forming decisions on purpose, objectives and strategy; they lead quietly from the backroom, rather than publicly and loudly from the front. In research that paired above and average performing companies, Bill Collins found that the above average performer was associated with leaders who do not force change nor try to directly motivate people, but that instead they stress the importance of understanding an organization's core values (see Chapter 2). In this they work to build up a disciplined culture that sustains results over the long term. This does not mean command and control, but it does require people to adhere to a consistent working system:

> … it gives people freedom and responsibility within the framework of that system … [a disciplined culture] is not just about action. It is about getting disciplined people who

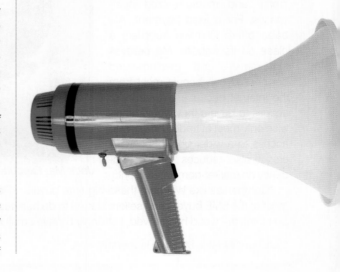

engage in disciplined thought and who then take disciplined action.[23]

This kind of leadership style is low key and does not require great efforts to raise motivation and commitment, particularly if the right thinking people have been put in place.

Clearly, the good-to-great companies did get incredible commitment and alignment – they artfully managed change – but they never really spend much time thinking about it. It was utterly transparent to them. We learned that under the right conditions, the problems of commitment, alignment, motivation, and change just melt away. They largely take care of themselves ... CEOs who personally discipline through sheer force of personality usually fail to produce sustained results ... [leadership is a] quiet, deliberate process of figuring out what needs to be done and simply doing it.[24]

> We learned that under the right conditions, the problems of commitment, alignment, motivation, and change just melt away. They largely take care of themselves ... CEOs who personally discipline through sheer force of personality usually fail to produce sustained results ... [leadership is a] quiet, deliberate process of figuring out what needs to be done and simply doing it.

TABLE 11.1 Leadership styles and their characteristics	
Transformational leadership	Leaders have a clear view of purpose as a desired future state. They are more concerned with objectives that indicate a broad direction rather than its detail, which is left to others to determine.
Transactional leadership	Leaders have a view of purpose as mission. They are more concerned with objectives linked to a clear programme of change that ensures staff know what is expected of them.
Charismatic or visionary leadership	Leaders embody a strong (often personalized brand) image that is distinctive. They scan opportunities in the external environment and sense purpose, sometimes as entrepreneurial action.
Participative or backroom leadership	Leaders involve others in understanding purpose as core values to share common ways of working (core competences) and participate in setting objectives so that they are more committed to executing them.

Leadership and management are different

A distinction is often drawn between leadership and strategy, which are understood as proactive concerns of senior levels of management, and management and control, which are understood as diagnostic concerns for managers who must ensure the organization remains fit for purpose. When the British politician John Reid was asked to sort out a dysfunctional government department (the Home Office), he was very clear about his role as a senior executive, and the role of his officials as managers. He maintained that the department was not fit for purpose in terms of its information technology, leadership, management, systems and processes. It needed to be managed properly, but it was not his task as a leader to do so. While he would provide leadership, strategy and direction, he made it clear that he expected the officials to run it properly.[25]

This divide between strategy and management at root rests with the classical notion that strategy implementation follows formulation (see Chapter 1). The view that leadership is different from management is very strongly represented in the general business and management literature. Abraham Zaleznik, writing in the *Harvard Business Review* in the 1970s, was one of the first to argue that leadership and management are different roles: a leader is proactive and shapes ideas, whereas a manager is focused on processes, teamwork, and working within the existing organization.[26] A leader is a change shaper and mover.

Zaleznik's ideas were developed by John Kotter, a professor of organizational behaviour and human resource management, who stressed that although leadership and management are different, they complement and need each other.[27] In practical terms a leader has to articulate the organization's vision so that it clarifies and reinforces the values of the organization's people. Everybody, however, ought to be involved in deciding how to achieve the vision so that they have a sense of control. This requires support from leaders through feedback, coaching and role-modelling, to help people develop professionally and to enhance their self-esteem through recognizing and rewarding their success. This is important, not just to build people's sense of achievement, but to show them that the organization cares about them.

With these things in place, Kotter argues that work itself becomes intrinsically motivating.[28] For organizations to develop leaders, young employees should be given challenging opportunities by increasing decentralization, and organizational cultures must be developed to institutionalize a leadership-centred culture. Whether or not the qualities associated with leadership can be learned is another matter.

Warren Bennis has listed the differences between management and leadership activities (Table 11.2). Leading is about influencing people to go in a certain direction, and embark on a certain course of action.

TABLE 11.2 The different qualities of leadership and management according to Bennis[29]

Leaders	Managers
• Innovate	• Administer
• Develop	• Maintain
• Investigate	• Accept reality
• Focus on people	• Focus on systems and structures
• Inspire trust	• Rely on control
• Take the long view	• Take a short-range view
• Ask what and why	• Ask how and why
• Eye the horizon	• Eye the bottom-line
• Originate	• Imitate
• Challenge the status quo	• Accept the status quo
• Are their own person	• Are the classic 'good soldier'

Managing is about having responsibility to accomplish the action.

Management is more inside-out in orientation than leadership which is outside-in. Doing the right things rather than deciding the right things. Henri Fayol, a pioneer of management thinking, described management functions as planning, organizing, to command and direct, co-coordinating and controlling.[30] However, research carried out by Henry Mintzberg found that managers' activities are characterized by 'brevity, variety and discontinuity and that they are strongly oriented towards action and dislike reflective activities'. The contrast between these two views of management's work are summarized in Table 11.3.[31] Mintzberg's work was published over a quarter of a century ago and times have probably changed significantly; when he was asked if things had changed over the years, he said he thought the pace of activity had increased, but that things had not really changed.[32]

An implication of Mintzberg's work is that senior managers are predisposed to action and activity rather than reflection and planning, and at its worst, micro-management. If so, this will favour a bias at strategic review in favour of operational rather strategic concerns.[33] However, the really substantive point from the leadership versus management debate, is that the management of strategic change is likely to need more in the way of leadership qualities than the management of a stable strategy and business model. Of course, for effective strategic management it is necessary to understand how the organization manages, especially in those core business areas or processes that are vital and critical to competitive advantage and organizational fitness for purpose.

Domain knowledge is important. This involves knowledge and experience of how the organization works and what it works on. It may be difficult for leaders who are external appointments. While these are generally well qualified with successful experience at other companies, it is likely they will have to depend on others in the organization for understanding the content and context of their new organization's work. This is a particular short-coming, if the new appointment has to be able to understand those organization-specific strategic resources that constitute the organization's competitive advantage.

Japan is a special case and stands out from most other countries. Japanese senior managers generally have a high level of domain knowledge and more importance is attached to customer-facing processes and engineering. So there is less reliance on professional management and the financial function. Leadership is less based on individual achievement and more on a sense of a commitment to be part of a greater whole. Traditionally, promotion has depended on the long-term commitment a manager has to the organization, so that one-company work experience is important. There is no equivalent separation in Japan of leadership from management. Leaders expect to be managers.

TABLE 11.3 The nature of managerial work

Managers should	Managers really
• Plan, organize, coordinate, control	• Work at an unrelenting pace, oriented to action and variety, dislike reflection
• Be reflective, systematic, concentrate on strategic rather than routine duties	• Use soft information on many routine duties
• Rely on formal information systems	• Work with verbal media, telephones, meetings, work on 'odds and ends of tangible detail'
• See management as a scientific and professional discipline	• Keep things inside their heads, judgement based on experience and intuition

KEY DEBATE 11.2

Transformational leadership or managerialism?

Columnist, Stefan Stern, writing in the *Financial Times,* in early February 2008, attacked the idea that management is boring and leadership will take us to the Promised Land, and argued the White House needs a competent manager.[34]

During the Democratic primaries, Senator Hillary Clinton was criticized as a policy and detail-obsessed manager, while Senator Barack Obama was presented as an exciting visionary leader. When criticized that his stirring speeches were long on aspirations but short on specifics, Mr Obama retorted that what his leadership would offer is more important.

Clinton argued that the role of the President is not only to provide visionary leadership, but also to control the federal administration downward to ensure that policies are carried out effectively. Clinton had the experience as head of the health-care reform initiative during her husbands' first term of office. This involved putting together a detailed and complex plan of reform. However, it created deep dissatisfaction among the relevant stakeholders, whose support was necessary to enact the proposed legislation, and the plans foundered.

Obama argued that the job of the President should be focused completely on providing leadership vision, judgement and inspiration. The federal agencies would report to him and he would delegate responsibility to them. He would hold himself aloof, but he would make the agency heads fully accountable for their performance and of the public servants in their charge.

Senator Hillary Clinton with US President Barack Obama

Question: Was Stefan Stern right?

Management as a profession

The professionalization of management is a pervasive move in business, academia, and in wider society, to regard management as a specialized set of knowledge skills and tasks that requires specialists to carry them out effectively. This view has become prevalent, especially so in Western companies, since about 1970. It is associated with the idea that it is possible to educate and train managers to manage any sort of business. However, because the content of knowledge is general rather than domain, the style of leadership involved involves control the medium of the finance department, and the tedious task of acquiring and using domain knowledge is delegated to lower level management. According to some, 'the outcome has been managerial incompetence on a scale inconceivable in earlier generations and extending over much of society'.[35]

This observation is a harsh one, but it is certainly true that leadership and how it manages has grow more complex as organizations have grown in size, and the administrative tasks more difficult to coordinate. A useful framework for understanding this is Greiner's growth phase model.

Leadership, size and growth of organizations

The growth phase model of Greiner suggests that organizations go through five stages of growth and need appropriate strategies to match each (see Figure 11.1). Each of these stages is brought to

FIGURE 11.1 Five states of leadership and organizing[36]

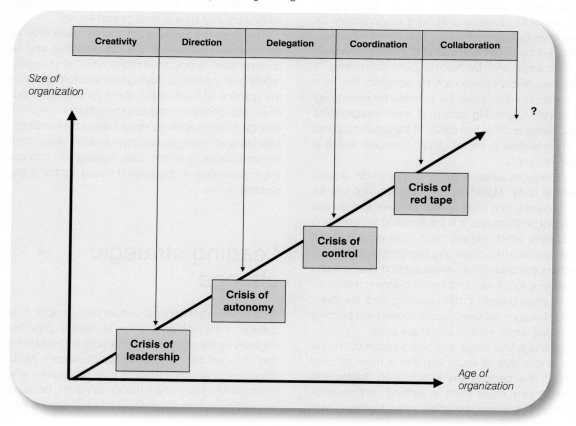

an end by a leadership crisis, which is solved by a new form of leadership, until eventually increasing size brings another crisis in leadership. The style of leadership in small organizations is typically informal, personal and entrepreneurial, and growth is achieved through creativity. As the organization grows the original owner manager becomes over-worked and partial, finding it too difficult to manage, so that a crisis of leadership occurs.

This ends as some power is ceded to functional management, when leadership becomes formal and introduces more detailed procedures and standard processes, involving bigger roles for marketing, accounting and finance. Growth is now achieved through directional leadership. Strains appear as senior management's chain of decision-making becomes over-stretched, and managers at operational and market levels find themselves disconnected from decisions at the centre. This results in a crisis of autonomy about who can effectively make the best decisions.

The solution that arises is a new delegating form of leadership, which decentralizes the organization into separate divisions that take responsibility for their own business strategy. The centre effectively manages by distance: monitoring (typically financial) performance, and by holding periodic reviews. It becomes directly involved only by exception. This form of leadership downplays the potential for economies of scale. A growing group of semi-independent businesses is difficult to control if the organization as a whole wishes to exploit group synergies: this is a crisis of control.

Synergy requires a closer contact with organizational parts. Monitoring is necessary not just for performance, but also of the activities that enable effective performance. It is the enabling activities and processes which benefit most from organizational synergy. Leadership takes on a coordinating role, which involves the creation of central support systems and consulting functions, and formal planning. However, with further growth, cross-reporting and the many formal linkages between organizational units become confused, which ends in a red tape crisis.

Greiner's final stage is growth through collaboration, and a style of leadership that is more defused through the parts of the organization. Teams and projects play major parts in forming and developing major decisions, especially cross-functional task teams, which are facilitated by decentralized support functions. Greiner later added a sixth stage to his original model, which was about by an internal growth crisis, and which calls for extra-organizational and networked leadership.

Much of the general literature about the management of people suggests that autocratic or command-and-control forms of leadership have given way to more devolved and networked forms of organizing. Gary Hamel, for example, advocates a latticed and networked style of organization.[37] Using Greiner's terminology, a new crisis of information is facing large organizations, which must adapt to new global drivers, notably the Internet and what it implies for leadership and coordination. The boundaries of an organization have become less clear in the modern world of business. The role for leadership is to stimulate and facilitate staff creativity and innovation and a different kind of entrepreneurial leadership, even, to follow Hamel (and the example of Gore, see Principles in Practice 11.1) a new form of entrepreneurial leadership through employees. To do this effectively, Hamel argues, we need to reinvent management. Or perhaps, more likely, wait for it to emerge and evolve.

The Greiner scheme is, of course, used only as an organizing framework. It is not predictive and its purpose here is only to illustrate how the changing nature of any strategic management task means that the practice of leadership cannot remain static but must evolve to accommodate the different needs for change. Chief executives should adapt their strategic agenda and management style to take account of circumstances. It is less easy, however, to change the organization in the ways it needs as the organization grows.

Leading strategic change

Broadly, an organizational culture (see Chapter 2) is a result of the kind of strategic leadership provided originally by the organization's founder, and sustained and changed over time by its top managers. As an organization grows it attracts new employees who are inspired by and share the same values; because organizations normally prefer and recruit those who share similar values, the organization's culture becomes more distinct as its members become similar. The advantages are that a similarly thinking management and workforce are strategically distinct from rivals, and more easily integrated and coordinated.

The core values laid down in the early days of an organization's life, and their role in the successful evolution of the organization's purpose and its subsequent activities imprint a distinctiveness that may last beyond the departure of the original founders and executives. IKEA is the world's largest furniture retailer, with over 300 stores, and it employs close to 140 000 people. Its overall goal is to increase sales by about 10 per cent each year. However, if this involves continuing a strong growth in the number of new stores across the world (it is present in 37 countries)

the challenge will be to hold on to and sustain its strategy and identity. The present chief executive, Mikael Ohlsson, has had to meet publicly aired criticism by IKEA's 86-year-old founder, Invar Kamprad (the 'IK' part of IKEA); for attempting to open too many new stores and risking the organization's culture.[38] In the past the group has run into trouble when it has tried to expand too quickly: for example, when the Swedish company in the United States offered mattresses that were too hard, and glasses too small for American tastes. At the time of writing it seems likely that Ohlsson will now open fewer stores.

John Kotter has devised an **eight-stage framework for managing change**.[39] It is the failure, in Kotter's view, to carry these out that constitute the most common errors in change programmes. All of them should be carried out for success.

KEY DEBATE 11.3

Leaders and the Icarus paradox

Miller[40] suggests the presence of an Icarus paradox. Icarus, escaping from King Minos of Crete and ignoring the advice of his father, flew too high and close to the sun, which melted the wax holding his feathers and he fell into the sea. The lesson is that successful organizations are likely, in the end, to over-reach themselves, because they continue to follow past prescriptions, thinking that success will breed success. They behave subconsciously, thinking they know the rules for success. They build control, measurement, and rewards systems, to enforce and encourage the existing recipes for success, so that eventually an organization becomes blind to the need for change and alternatives.

The possibility that pride comes before a fall or, in other words, success makes leaders too self-confident, an attribute of hubris, was true of many long-established companies when faced with new competition from start-up dot.com companies.

When fresh evidence appears that does not fit ... we filter it out, but welcome information that confirms our preconceptions ... Executives of all kinds are particularly susceptible, because they have to take decisions quickly, and because previous success reinforces their self-confidence and dislike of criticism. The more successful they have been in the past, the greater the danger ... Supermen without a restraining voice to remind them that they are mortal are not good at facing uncomfortable truths.[41]

The role of court jesters was to make emperors and kings look foolish to provide a check on their ambition. While arrogance may actually be advantageous to entrepreneurs, it can lead to important mistakes for successfully established organizations.

Question: Is there a case for bringing back jesters and 'fools'?

1 Establish a sense of urgency: this makes others aware of the need for change, and works to action them quickly while motivation is strong; it counters complacency.

2 Create a guiding coalition: put together a group that has enough power to drive the change and can work as a team.

3 Develop a change vision: this gives change a direction and is used to develop strategies for achieving the vision.

4 Communicate the vision for others to buy-into: as many as possible should understand and accept the vision and the associated strategies. A vision should be communicated by a factor of 10, a 100, even 1000.

5 Empower action across the organization: to remove obstacles to change, to change systems and structures that seriously undermine the vision; encourage risk-taking and non-traditional ideas, activities, and actions.

6 Generate short-term wins: plan for achievements that can easily be made visible and follow-through with these to recognize and reward those employees who were involved.

7 Never let up: continually sustain and reinforce the increasing credibility of the change; recruit, promote champions, develop these and other employees who can implement the vision; reinvigorate the change process with new projects, themes, and change agents.

8 Incorporate changes into the culture: change culture last in that the new ways of doing things must be seen to compare favourably with traditional ways; articulate the connections between the new behaviours and organizational success; develop the means to ensure leadership development and succession.

Organizations may not be perfect, but it is still necessary to manage

People in any organization will differ, and it is necessary for a leader to remember that most organizations are everyday affairs, and the people in them (including customers) are human beings! It is sometimes difficult to remember this. As British media personality Stephen Fry has written:

> Anyone who has lived and worked within a large organization, whether it be the BBC, the army, a school or a large hospital, will know that cream and scum alike rise to the top; that blundering, hopeless, blinkered, purblind and ignorant incompetence inform the actions and governance of such places at all times. That bitchery, cattery and rivalry frustrate co-operation, good fellowship and trust.[42]

True, organizations and people are rarely perfect. Leaders have to recognize this and be both tough-skinned and open-minded. Above all, they also have to lead and manage their organizations no matter what. The overwhelming importance of this to the economy at large should never be forgotten, for example: 'Improved management at Walmart probably played a bigger role in America's productivity miracle of the late 1990s than all the expensive investment in high speed computers and fibre-optic cable by businesses', observe Baker and Abrahams, reporting on a report of an analysis by the McKinsey Global Institute.[43] The report suggests it is not business opportunities themselves, but rather how they are managed that counts. This means that the core business process of strategic management must be understood and the process itself managed effectively to achieve and advance the organization's purpose.

For strategic management to be effective leaders need to be able to see and understand the big picture of the organization in terms of both its external and internal environment. Different, and often contrasting and conflicting strands of information must be considered against a broad array of possibilities and outcomes. Somehow leaders have to be both definite and yet at the same time be pragmatic. This involves thinking and acting dynamically in a consistent and clear way, which is yet flexible enough both to initiate and to manage change. Above all they must use strategic management as a framework to review external and internal activities in ways that enable others in the organization to manage change.

> *Improved management at Walmart probably played a bigger role in America's productivity miracle of the late 1990s than all the expensive investment in high speed computers and fibre-optic cable by businesses.*

PRINCIPLES IN PRACTICE 11.3
Leadership for New York

Rudolph Giuliani was a successful mayor of New York. In his book, *Leadership*, he introduced his view of leadership.[44]

Leadership does not simply happen. It can be taught, learned, developed. Those who influenced me ... all contributed valuable elements to my philosophy.

There are many ways to lead. Some people like Franklin Roosevelt, inspired with stirring speeches. Others, like Joe DiMaggio, led by example. Winston Churchill and Douglas MacArthur were both exceptionally brave and excellent speakers. Ronald Reagan led through the strength and consistency of his character – people followed him because they believed in him.

Ultimately you'll know what techniques and approaches work best – those you hope to lead will tell you. Much of your ability to get people to do what they have to do is going to depend on what they perceive when they look at you and listen to you. They need to see someone who is stronger than they are, but human too.

Leaders have to control their emotions under pressure. While I was mayor, on the few occasions someone who worked for me used 'panic' to describe their state of being during some crisis in their bailiwick, I made it clear that it would be the last time they'd employ that word ... You can't let yourself be paralyzed by any situation. It's about balance.

I tried to run the city as a business, using business principles to impose accountability on government. Objective, measurable indicators of success allow governments to be accountable, and I relentlessly pursued that idea.

Question: Are the principles for running a major city the same as for running a large commercial business?

SUMMARY OF PRINCIPLES

1   Strategic leaders are found across an organization, but strategic leadership is a responsibility of the executive and senior managers.

2   There are two kinds of leadership: transformational and transactional.

3 Visionary leadership is transformational and dependent upon the personal style of a single individual.

4 Participative and backroom leadership is transactional and dependent upon a collective discipline.

5 The management of strategic (big) change is likely to need more leadership qualities than the management of a stable strategy (business model), which is likely to need more management qualities.

6 Strategic leadership requires an integrated understanding for managing both longer-term strategy and feedback from short-term action.

7 The success of strategic management depends upon the people who lead and how they manage their organizations.

GUIDED FURTHER READING

Leadership is a subject in its own right and forms an important part of other subjects such as human resource management and organizational behaviour. There are tens of dozens of definitions. The classic text in the context of strategic management is Senge, which has recently been revised, see Senge, P. (2006), *The Fifth Discipline: The Art and Practice of the Learning Organization* (revised edn), New York: Doubleday.

For a general and in-depth critical account of the development of large companies and multi-nationals, see Hopper, K. and Hopper, W. (2009), *The Puritan Gift; Reclaiming the American Dream Amidst Global Financial Chaos,* London: I. B. Tauris & Co.

REVIEW QUESTIONS

1 What are strategic leaders?

2 Can charismatic/visionary leaders and participative/backroom leaders also be transformational and transactional leaders?

3 What is emotional intelligence?

4 Are leaders different to managers?

5 Are leaders born rather than made?

6 What is the relationship of size and growth of organizations to the style of leadership?

7 What are Kotter's eight stages for managing strategic change?

8 Is strategic management too difficult to do for ordinary organizations?

SEMINAR AND ASSIGNMENT QUESTIONS

1 Produce a list of ten leaders and list them in order of how well known you think they are. Why are they so well known? Ask 'why' five times. When you have a deep-rooted reason for their celebrity, redo your list according to how you think they are good managers. Explain any discrepancies between the before and after lists.

2 Compare and contrast the differences in leadership required for organizations in the hotel and catering business, the army, airline, and household appliances industries, and a small computer software firm. Does the strategy used in such organizations require different leadership styles at different stages in the industry life cycle?

3 Explore websites about well-known scandals and corporate failures. Evaluate these cases to see how 'leadership' might have played a part in the stories. Consider if a well managed organization can ever fail.

CHAPTER END-NOTES

1 Translation by Kwok, M-H., Palmer, M. and Ramsey, J. (1993), *Tao Te Ching,* Shaftesbury: Element Books.

2 Wickens, P. D. (1995), *The Ascendant Organization,* London: Macmillan Press.

3 Hamel, G. with Breen, B. (2007), *The Future of Management,* Boston: Harvard Business School Press.

4 Gore (2009), 'Our culture', *About Gore,* www.gore.com.

5 Senge, P. (1990) (2006: revised edn), *The Fifth Discipline: The Art and Practice of the Learning Organization*, New York: Doubleday.

6 Goleman, D., Boyatzis, R. and McKee, A. (2002), *Primal Leadership: Realising the Power of Emotional Intelligence,* London.

7 Machiavelli, N. (1950), *The Price and the Discourses,* New York: Random House, p. 165.

8 Bennis, W. (1993), *An Invented Life: Reflections on Leadership and Change,* Reading MA: Addison-Wesley.

9 Burns, J. M. (1978), *Leadership*, New York: Harper & Row.

10 Bass, B. M. (1985), *Leadership and Performance Beyond Expectations*, London: Collier Macmillan.

11 Ford, H. (1922), *My Life and Work,* Chapter IV.

12 Hille, K. (2009), 'The godfather of small enterprise', *Financial Times,* 19 January, p. 14.

13 Alibaba Group (2013), 'Culture and values', Alibaba.com.

14 Alibaba Group (2013), 'Culture and values', Alibaba.com.

15 Hille (2009), 'The godfather of small enterprise', *Financial Times,* 19 January, p. 14.

16 Taken from Olivier, R. (2001), *Inspirational Leadership: Henry V and the Muse of Fire – Timeless Insights from Shakespeare's Greatest Leader,* London: Industrial Society. The full quote is from Roosevelt's address at the Sorbonne, April 1910. See Barber, M. (2007), *Instruction to Deliver: Fighting to Transform Britain's Public Services,* London: Methuen, p. 74.

17 Barber, M. (2007), *Instruction to Deliver: Fighting to Transform Britain's Public Services,* London: Methuen.

18 Portillo, M. (2012), Daily Politics, BBC Two Television, 16 November.

19 Murdoch, R. (2011), oral evidence given to the House of Commons Culture, Media and Sport Select Committee, 19 July.

20 Jackson, T. (1995), *Virgin King: Inside Richard Branson's Business Empire,* paperback edn, London: HarperCollins Publishers, p. 295.

21 Hopper, K. and Hopper, W. (2009), *The Puritan Gift; Reclaiming the American Dream Amidst Global Financial Chaos,* London: I. B. Tauris & Co.

22 Quoted in Ruddock, A. (2007), *Michael O'Leary: A Life in Full Flight,* Dublin: Penguin, p. 267.

23 Collins, J. (2001), *Good to Great: Why Some Companies Make the Leap ... and Others Don't,* London: HarperCollins, p. 146.

24 Collins, J. (2001), *Good to Great: Why Some Companies Make the Leap ... and Others Don't,* London: HarperCollins, p. 178.

25 Johnston, P. (2006), 'Reid blasts management failures at Home Office', *Daily Telegraph,* 24 May, p. 1.

26 Zaleznik, A. (1977), 'Managers and leaders: are they different?' *Harvard Business Review,* 55(5).

27 Kotter, J. P. (1990), 'What leaders really do', *Harvard Business Review,* 68 (May-June), 103–111.

28 Kotter, J. P. (1996), *Leading Change,* Boston MA: Harvard Business School Press.

29 Bennis, W. (1997), *Learning to Lead: A Workbook on Becoming a Leader,* London: Addison Wesley.

30 Fayol, H. (1949), *General and Industrial Management,* translated by Storrs, C., London: Pitman.

31 Mintzberg, H. (1973), *The Nature of Managerial Work,* New York: Harper and Row.

32 de Holan, P. M. and Mintzberg, H. (2004), 'Management as life's essence: 30 years of the Nature of Managerial Work', *Strategic Organization,* 2(2):205–212.

33 Kaplan, R. S. and Norton, D. P. (2008), *The Execution Premium: Linking Strategy to Operations for Competitive Advantage,* Boston MA: Harvard Business School Press.

34 Stern, S. (2008), 'Whitehouse needs a competent manager', *Financial Times,* 4 February.

35 Hopper, K. and Hopper, W. (2009), *The Puritan Gift; Reclaiming the American Dream Amidst Global Financial Chaos,* London: I. B. Tauris & Co.

36 Adapted from Greiner, L. E. (1972), 'Growing organizations', *Harvard Business Review.* 50(4).

37 Hamel, G. with Breen, B. (2007), *The Future of Management,* Boston: Harvard Business School Press. Hamel seems to have taken over Tom Peter's role as management's iconoclast: See Hamel, G. and Breen, B. (2009), *The End of Management,* Boston MA: The Harvard Business School Press.

38 Milne, R. (2013), 'Ikea spat puts role of founder into focus', *Financial Times,* January 30, 17.

39 Kotter, J. P. (1996), *Leading Change,* Boston MA: Harvard Business School Press.

40 Miller, D. (1991), *The Icarus Paradox,* London: Harper Business Books.

41 Levis, K. (2009), *Winners and Losers: Creators and Casualties of the Age of the Internet,* London: Atlantic Books.

42 Fry, S. (1993), *Paperweight,* London: Mandarin.

43 Baker, G. and Abrahams, P. (2001), 'Forget IT, it was Walmart behind that US miracle', *Financial Times,* 17 October, p. 15.

44 Giuliani, R. W. with Kurson, K. (2002), *Leadership,* London: Little, Brown, pp. xii–xiii.

Steve Jobs and Apple

Steve Jobs, chief executive of Apple Inc., died in October 2011. Probably no other business leader of recent times has created so much debate. The company was very successful and its ethos, which emerged from its counter culture beginnings, seemed to reflect his personality. What are the leadership lessons of Steve Jobs?

I knew Steve Jobs well for more than 30 years ... The essence of Steve's approach to leadership is contained in Apples' two-word tagline, 'Think Different' ... [What he meant was that this] is the source of all wisdom in Eastern traditions – mindfulness. Mindfulness means paying attention to your present-moment experience ... Drop all your theories and preconceived ideas. Pay attention to the raw reality coming in through your five senses and your mind. This is where you will find insight and wisdom.[1]

Steve Jobs strove for perfection in design. He made others try for the impossible. When it came off it made people very loyal. The controversy comes over how he did things. His leadership style was bullying and abusive. He may have found personal relations difficult as he seems to have been overly impatient, stubborn, and hypercritical. While he attracted loyalty he was not always so loyal to his colleagues and friends.

Steve Jobs took risks; he was a man of courage and with persistence got through multiple failures. His visionary products certainly changed the way many of us live, and the course of many industries

including computing, publishing, movies, music and mobile telephony.

He co-founded and built Apple up into one of the world's largest companies. However, as the company grew he became more impossible to work with and was fired by the Apple board and his role was given to the more professional John Scully. However, Scully was later also fired for investing too heavily in the innovative Newton and the company refocused its attention on the Macintosh. The result of these decisions was to nearly bankrupt Apple. In the meantime, Steve Jobs had helped shape NeXT and Pixar (which was later acquired by the Walt Disney Company – when Jobs became its largest shareholder). After ten years away Jobs was brought back to Apple. He cut back on the number of project teams and focused his design teams on what became the iPod.

However, if you needed encouragement, you should not expect any help from Steve Jobs, and only a few very strong people at Apple became his 'A' players. Jobs was known for his 'distortion of reality' – a sense of unreality that drove design teams on regardless of common sense. He challenged and abused teams to achieve the impossible.

Very few top leaders pay as much attention to product and design detail as Jobs did. He always considered simplicity, functionality, and consumer appeal before cost efficiency, sales volume, or even profit. That attention was integral to the strategic and marketing capabilities of his companies. In these respects, Jobs was an entrepreneurial leader in mode of Walt Disney and Edwin Land, both of whom he admired.[2]

He was technology-push rather than market-pull; feeling that 'customers don't know what they want until we've shown them'. Control was important to Jobs. His strategy was to design closed systems that integrated operating systems with its hardware rather than take an open platform approach to allow independents to develop applications. In the 1980s Apple had not licensed out its Macintosh operating system. Eventually Microsoft gained a dominant market share by licensing its system to hardware makers. However, Jobs never wanted Apple to lose its power to differentiate its products from rivals: 'I like being responsible for the whole user experience. We do it not to make money. We do it because we want to make great products, not crap like Android'.[3]

However, Apple may now be more innovative than radical: 'its latest iPhones and iPads looking little different to their predecessors. That puts pressure on Apple's accompanying services to dazzle and differentiate from its many copycats.'[4] Of course, right at the end of his life, Jobs was looking for the next big opportunity, and he saw the iCloud, a services ecosystem, as 'our next big insight ... we are going to demote the PC and the Mac to be just a device to move the digital hub into the cloud'.[5]

The quality that made Jobs visionary was personal. At the very end he observed:

What drove me? ... a lot of us want to contribute something back to our species and to add something to the flow. It's about trying to express something in the only way that most of us know – because we can't write Bob Dylan songs or Tom Stoppard plays. We try to use the talents we did have to express our deeper feelings, to show our appreciation of all the contributions that came before us, and to add something to that flow. That's what has driven me.

... I really want to believe that something survives, that maybe your consciousness endures. ... But on the other hand, perhaps it's like an on-off switch. Click! And you're gone ... Maybe that's why I never liked to put on-off switches on Apple devices.[6]

Discussion questions

1 Steve Jobs was not a people person: as a leader was he an anomaly? Is the leadership story at Google, Facebook, Twitter and Linked-in, any different?

2 Sony, once the leader in using advances in technology to develop radically new products, such as the Walkman and the Discman, has now failed to make a profit for the last four years. Without the influence of its co-founder, Akio Morita, the company seems to have lost its entrepreneurial fervour. Is this likely to happen now with Apple?

3 It is not always the best product that wins, but the one that is most robust and even average in its performance? Is the perfection demanded by inventors sensible, or is it merely a creator's conceit?

Case end-notes

1 Rotenberg, J. (2012), letter to the *Harvard Business Review* by Jonathan Rotenberg, president, Centriq Advisors, 18 June.

2 Katzenbach, J. (2012), 'The Steve Jobs way', *strategy+business,* 23 April, www.strategy-business.com.

3 Isaacson, W. (2011), *Steve Jobs,* London: Little, Brown, p. 514.

4 Bradshaw, T. (2012), 'Innovator's dilemma', analysis, *Financial Times,* 21 December, p. 9.

5 Bradshaw, T. (2012), 'Innovator's dilemma', analysis, *Financial Times,* 21 December, p. 9.

6 Isaacson, W. (2011), *Steve Jobs,* London: Little, Brown, pp. 570–571.

Glossary of key concepts

Acquisition is when one organization buys a controlling interest in another, with the aim of creating a larger entity, or with a view to restructuring the acquired organization to resell at a profit.

Agency theory is the view that owners (principals) and managers (agents) of an organization form a 'principal-agent relationship' and try to work towards achieving a common goal, but have different (or even conflicting) motivations, therefore resulting in a divergence of actions to try to reconcile those differences.

Analyzer organizations are organizations that are a combination of prospector and defender organizations, while minimizing risk and maximizing opportunity for profit.

Balanced scorecard is a documented set of objectives and measures grouped into (typically) four perspectives.

Benchmarking is a comparison of an organization's practices with those of other organizations, in order to identify ideas for improvement and the adoption of useful practices, and sometimes to compare relative standards of performance.

Best-cost differentiation hybrid generic strategy offers superior value to customers by meeting their expectations on key product and service attributes, while also exceeding their expectations on price.

Black swan symbolizes a special form of structural break in the industry that is characterized by the enormity of its impact, low probability of it occurring, and the obviousness of its occurrence after the incident.

Blue ocean strategy is a focus on those parts of an industry where competition is weak and involves ways of competing that contrast to those of existing players.

Board (of directors) is the governing committee of an organization.

Bounded rationality is the extent to which making a fully rational decision is limited by complexity, lack of time, and absent information.

Brand is a name or label that incorporates a visual design or image, which differentiates a product, service, or an organization, from others.

BRICS is an acronym for Brazil, Russia, India, China and South Africa.

Business audit is an organization-wide capabilities review of the organization's critical business areas and areas of management, such as strategy, leadership and so on.

Business ethics are the ethical systems, typically based on prevailing professional and community morals, which an organization adopts and abides by.

Business-level strategy is an organization's fundamental approach for enabling a single business to sustain a competitive advantage within a given industry.

Business model is a theory of how an individual business integrates its critical areas responsible for the creation of value for its stakeholders (typically its customers) in a unique way. A generic business model applies to an industry and those ways in which the industry's organizations typically create value.

Business process is a sequence of tasks or stages to deliver a business objective.

Business process re-engineering (BPR) is the redesigning of business processes.

Capability review is a business audit of the effectiveness of the organization's core business and management areas.

Catchball is a process of iterative planning when draft plans are passed to and fro between affected parties until an agreement is reached.

CEO (chief executive officer) holds the formal position of the executive head of an organization.

Charismatic or visionary leadership is a personalized form of strategic leadership based on a leader's vision about purpose and behaviour of the organization that helps condition an organization's culture and strategic management.

Cooperatives and partnerships are organizations are owned by members (e.g. customers) and employees.

Co-opetition is a word collapsed from cooperation and competition and describes a state when they occur together.

Commoditization is the transfer of unsophisticated production and service units from advanced economies to developing countries where the cost of labour is low, while retaining more value-added products services at home.

Competitive advantage is an advantage an organization has over its rivals that enables it to compete effectively over time.

Competitive strategy is a strategy to sustain a competitive advantage over rivals and potential rivals.

Complementarities are activities where doing more of them, increases the returns to other activities.

CompStat is short for computer statistics or comparative statistics.

Coordinated market economy is where the spheres are coordinated around collaborative institutional relations, which act to reduce uncertainty on stakeholder longer term purpose.

Core capability is a key organizational ability of business area that is essential to the creation of value to customers.

Core competences are the organization-specific abilities people have, which they use in common to work together, to learn and apply knowledge, to be able to manage strategic priorities in ways that will create and sustain competitive advantage.

Core values (following Jim Collins) are an organization's basic strategic understanding on which it operates.

Corporate governance is the governing of the organization by a board or committee made up of executives who lead and manage the organization, and non-executives who are outsiders appointed or elected to advise and oversee the work of the executives.

Corporate identity is an organization's managed self-image, which is a communicable expression of an organization's purpose.

Corporate image is a general perception of an organization held by the public and its stakeholders, especially its customers.

Corporate-level strategy is a corporate centre's strategy for strategically managing a multi-business organization.

Corporate parenting is when a corporate centre acts as a corporate parent to nurture its corporate children (the corporate businesses) to create a unique fit between the corporation's capabilities and the critical success factors of the individual businesses.

Corporate social responsibility (CSR) is the view that large (especially international) organizations should fulfil a corporate (and world) citizen role.

Corporate sustainability is an emphasis on the longer term and the need to take into account the implications of an organization's activities for the welfare of future generations.

Corporate synergy is a strategic performance (such as in terms of value creation) that is achieved by a corporation that is greater than performance of the corporate businesses would be were they to exist independently. (The whole is greater than the sum of its parts.)

Cost-leadership generic strategy is a cost-based strategy that involves having a lead in terms of lower costs per unit produced than the other participants in the industry can achieve, and which enables the organization to earn above average profits for the industry.

Critical success factors (CSFs) are the factors that primarily account for an organization's success in achieving its strategic purpose.

Cross-functional is a horizontal level of management or structure that involves working across the functional areas of an organization.

Cultural fit is a term used in M&A to describe if the organizational culture of an acquired organization is compatible with the acquiring organization.

Cultural web is the manifestation of those things that indicate an underlying culture (or paradigm).

Customer is a person or organization that pays for receiving a product and service.

Customer value is the satisfaction from the benefits a customer receives from buying and using a product or service.

Daily management is the management of organizational routines, typically at an operational level.

Defender organizations are organizations that target a narrow market and concentrate on value delivery, mainly in core technologies.

Deliberate strategy is a planned strategy designed at a senior level of management for implementation at other organizational levels.

Delivery chain maps out the interactions of cause-and-effects of those individuals and organizations that affect the delivery of a policy.

Deutero learning is when an organization learns how to learn, which involves monitoring and reviewing how people learn and use ways to manage things.

Diamond model is Porter's framework for identifying the four forces for the competitive advantage of nations.

Diagnostic objectives and measures are those that monitor the health of the organization to ensure it remains fit for purpose, and they indicate whether the organization remains in control and can be used to signal up any unusual events that require managerial attention.

Differentiation industry-wide generic strategy is a strategy that offers unique value for an industry's customers in a way that more than offsets the costs of differentiation to enable the organization to earn above average profits for the industry.

Disruptive innovation is a revolutionary product that replaces existing ways of competing.

Diversification is when an organization is active in different types of business areas.

Domain knowledge is the knowledge individuals have based their experience and understanding of how their organization works and what it works on.

Double loop learning involves a double feedback loop, which connects the detection of errors not only to strategies and assumptions, but to the questioning of the norms that define effective performance.

Downscoping is a divesture, demerger, spin-off, or some other means of eliminating businesses, which are unrelated or are not core to an organization's corporate strategy.

Downsizing is reducing the size of an organization.

Dynamic capability is an organization's ability to integrate, build, and reconfigure core competencies to meet change. More widely, it is an organization's ability to renew and re-create its strategic capabilities (including core competences) to meet the needs of a changing environment.

Eight-stage framework for managing change is Kotter's framework for leadership in managing strategic change.

Emergent strategy is strategy not foreseen by a senior level that arises during the implementation of deliberate strategy.

Emotional intelligence is an individual's ability to recognize their own emotions and those of others, and act to take these into account in relationships.

Entrepreneurial leadership is characterized by the personality, usually of a single owner-manager, or sometimes of a few collaborating individuals, who impose their view on the business in ways that are characteristically innovative.

Evaluation is the management of feedback and learning to review, improve, and control the strategic management process.

Execution is the management of delivery of strategy in daily management and operations.

(an) Executive is an active member of a top management team of an organization.

Exploitative learning occurs within an organization's routine processes and is based on experience and existing knowledge.

Exploratory learning occurs as a result of new and unfamiliar information, which is obtained from outside the experiences of existing organizational routines.

External environment consists of the conditions outside the organization, including people and organizations, which influence the external changes in the organization's industry, especially those that influence the intensity of competition.

FAIR is an acronym for focus, alignment, integration, and review, which are parts of the annual strategic performance management cycle, especially for *hoshin kanri*.

First mover is an organization that is more successful than its rivals because it was to market a new product or service.

Five competitive forces are the primary influences in an organization's position within an industry that effect competitive advantage and profitability.

Focus generic strategy is narrowly based on a particular part of the industry, such as a market segment or niche, where an organization can design its strategy to meet the needs of customers more closely than its competitors.

Four competences of leadership are management of attention; management of meaning; management of trust and management of self.

Franchising is a contractual relationship between a parent organization (the franchisor) and its partners (franchisees) that specifies the control, sharing, and use, of the franchisor's strategic resources.

Functional management is the division of management into specialist areas of work; in a large organizations these are organized into departments, such as design, purchasing, operations, marketing, finance, human resources, IT, and so on.

General Electric–McKinsey matrix is a framework for managing a portfolio of corporate businesses that was designed by McKinsey for GE; businesses are grouped according to industry attractiveness and business strength.

Generic strategy is a type of strategy used to compete in a single industry, which is based on a competitive advantage and scope: the four types are cost leadership, differentiation, cost focus, and differentiation focus.

Global-level strategy is an organization's strategic management of its operations across multi-national borders.

Global strategy is one of four types of international strategy, and involves the use of a standardized product and service range for all of an organization's international markets.

Globalization is the phenomenon of changing commonalties and differences associated with a worldwide perception that the world is becoming smaller, similar, and more inter-connected.

Glocalization is a transnational strategy that involves a combination of globalization and localization.

Groupthink is a phenomenon that occurs when a team or group avoids disagreement amongst itself and seeks consensus that is tendentious, biased or superficial, which acts to exclude any real discussion of alternatives.

Growth–share matrix is the Boston Consulting Group's framework for managing a portfolio of corporate businesses that are grouped according to market share and market growth.

Guanxi means connections, where 'guan' and 'xi' approximate to 'a closed up door' and 'a joined-up chain' respectively. It is the practice of building a network of inter-personal relationships and connections through a process of reciprocal manners or favours.

Horizontal integration is the growth of an organization by expanding its operations to offer complementary products and services, or to acquire a competitor with similar products and services.

Hoshin is a policy that includes a breakthrough strategic objective, the context for it, and guidelines as to the means.

Hoshin kanri translates as policy (= *hoshin*) management (= *kanri*), it is an organization-wide methodology for the deployment and management of *hoshins* (or policies).

Hybrid strategy is a mixture of generic strategy.

Hypercompetition is a dynamic state of constant disequilibrium and change in an industry.

Implementation is putting in place the appropriate organizational structure to carry out an organization's strategy.

Improvement change is incremental and is typically driven by the need to sustain and improve productivity and customer value in daily management.

Industry life cycle likens the life of an industry to a living organism, which goes through stages of introduction, growth, maturity and decline, with each stage exhibiting distinct characteristics.

Inside-out is the direction of influence of internal firm-specific strategic resources on the development of strategy.

Internal environment consists of the conditions inside an organization, including its strategic resources, abilities and management capabilities.

International strategy is a type of global-level strategy that uses central direction to effect a common way of working across all of an organization's subsidiaries.

Joined-up management is bringing together government departments, agencies, and a range of private and voluntary bodies, working across organizational boundaries in the public sector.

Just-in-time management is the management of a process so that it responds to the needs of the next customer in line as and when the customer requires.

Key performance indicator (KPI) is a strategically related incremental objective.

Lagged measures are indicators of past performance.

Lead measures are indicators of the enablers of future performance.

Leader is a person, who by influencing others, has an ability to take the organization forward to serve a common purpose.

Leadership is the ability of an individual or a group of individuals to influence others to achieve an organization's purpose and objectives.

Lean working (or lean production as it is known in manufacturing) is a management system for ensuring any non-value creating activity is removed.

Leveraged buyout is a group of private investors who buy a publicly quoted company in order to take the company private.

Liberal market economy is where the five spheres are coordinated through competitive market arrangements and hierarchies.

Logical incrementalism is when strategy is formed as a result of small steps implemented by managers at lower levels as a logical response to local circumstances, and which add up for the organization as a whole as a substantial change to the strategy introduced originally by a senior level.

Loosely coupled systems are ways of working where there are opportunities of different means or pathways loosely linked to a common end.

M&As stands for mergers and acquisitions.

M-form organization is a multi-divisional organization.

Management by objectives (MbO) is the cascading of objectives through an organization's hierarchy via superiors to subordinates.

Matrix structure is organizational structure where units/projects report to more one than one division/unit.

McKinsey 7S framework is a framework of seven inter-related organizational variables for managing change.

Measures are quantified indicators of progress on an objective.

Medium and mid-term plans are statements of three to five year objectives (and sometimes with guidelines about means).

Merger is the agreement of two organizations to integrate their operations as a combined organization under common ownership.

Micro multinational is a small to midsize manufacturer that maintains a hub in a domestic economy, while its industrial customers are spread out, and who are typically carrying out production in low-wage regions of the world.

Middle management is the level of management placed between senior and operational levels.

Mission is the purpose of an organization in terms of its main products and services and the value they create for its stakeholders.

Monitoring is a process of scanning progress of work to ensure it is on track to achieve a plan or objective.

Multi-domestic strategy is one of four types of global-level strategy, and involves using different products and services to suit different markets in different countries.

Multinational corporations (MNCs), sometimes referred to as multinational enterprises or transnational corporations, are enterprises that are active in more than one country.

NGOs (non-government organizations) are community organizations that are active at a local level involving small groups that reply on unpaid effort, and voluntary organizational that involve formally constituted organizations.

Nemawashi is the Japanese activity for preparing a decision and building up a consensus for action.

Network is an informal group of individuals, who are typically distributed and found across (and sometimes outside) the organization.

Non-profit organizations are non-commercial organizations where the profit motive is not a primary goal.

Non-executives are members of a board of directors or trust who do not participate in the routine management of the organization.

Objectives are strategically desired outcomes that must be managed effectively if the organization is to continue to fulfil its purpose.

Organizational culture is comprised of basic assumptions and beliefs learned from experience that are shared by organizational members.

Outside-in is the direction of influence of external factors on the development of strategy.

Participative or backroom leadership is low-profile, self-effacing, and aims to involve colleagues in taking and forming decisions on purpose, objectives and strategy; they lead quietly from the backroom to build up a disciplined sense of core values.

PDCA (plan–do–check–act) cycle is a principle for managing a process of work – there must be a Plan for how the work is to be Done, its progress Checked and Acted upon, including any changes to Plan which will start the cycle over again.

Performance excellence models are assessment frameworks that are used to audit good practice and performance in the key areas of the business.

Performance measurement (management) is the quantification of objectives, progress, and results, in work (traditionally a human resource concern).

Periodic strategic reviews are held every two or three months to oversee the progress on the annual objectives.

Perspectives (of the balanced scorecard) are objectives and measures grouped according to their relevance to four areas (normally financial, customer, processes, and people).

PESTEL is a mnemonic framework to understand factors that are Political, Economic, Social, Technological, Environmental, and Legal.

Policy delivery units enable an organization's executive level to track the progress of its strategic objectives or targets.

POSIES model of strategic management is composed of long-term purpose, objectives and strategy, and of the shorter-term implementation, execution, and strategic leadership.

Project is a short to medium-term organized and finite series of activities that is finite, and is managed by a team (strategic projects are typically cross-functional).

Prospector organizations are organizations that emphasize new opportunities and seek growth through the development of new markets.

Public relations (PR) is a functional area used to explain organizational purpose to external stakeholder groups and to influence corporate image so it can be aligned to corporate identity. Purpose is the basic reason or reasons for why an organization is in existence.

Purpose the primary and basic reason for the existence of an organization.

QCDE stands for Quality, Cost, Delivery, and Education, which are roughly equivalent to the four perspectives of the balanced scorecard, and are used to group objectives in a similar way.

Quality is a standard of satisfaction customers expect of the products and services they buy.

Reactor organizations are organizations that tend to respond to change in inconsistent and inappropriate ways, typically due to inadequate response mechanisms in place.

Regulation is the control of an organization or industry by government or publically sponsored agencies, to guard the public interest against restrictive practices and monopolistic abuse, and/or to ensure environmental and legal requirements are maintained.

Related diversification involves different products and services in distinct but related business areas or industries.

Resource-based view of strategy (RBV) is a school of strategy that believes competitive advantage is based on strategic resources; those internal resources (or assets) that are unique to a particular organization, and are important to its competitive advantage.

Review is a considered check on work to understand how a plan or objectives are being achieved (it is different to monitoring, although data from monitoring will be used in some form) and if necessary to consider further action and follow-up.

Review wheel is an organization-wide integrated system of review.

Satisificing is making a satisfactory decision that is sufficient to give a good enough result.

Scenario planning involves the evaluation of critical success factors for varying contexts and the possible outcomes.

Shared value is policies and operating practices which enhance the competitiveness of a company, while simultaneously advancing the economic and social conditions in the communities in which it operates.

Single loop learning is when organizational members respond to and correct errors and resolve issues to maintain the present way of working.

SMART objectives are Specific, Measurable, Action-oriented, Realistic, Time-bound: these often used as criteria to evaluate the quality of objectives.

Social entrepreneurs lead organizations (social enterprises) that trade for social and environmental purposes, when surpluses are reinvested rather than used to maximize returns to owners and shareholders.

Stakeholders are individuals and groups who benefit directly by receiving value from what an organization does and provides.

State capitalism is a form of a commercial and profit-making activity undertaken by the state.

Straddler is an organization that competes using a hybrid strategy that is based on both sources of competitive advantage: cost and differentiation.

Strategic alliances and partnerships are formal and informal associations and collaborations between independent organizations.

Strategic architecture is a blueprint for an organizing framework that conditions how people work.

Strategic balanced scorecard is designed to achieve a vision.

Strategic business units (SBUs) are autonomous single businesses within a corporate structure, with perhaps their own generic strategy, ditinctive organizational cultures and competences.

Strategic change is a step or transformational change that moves an organization to a new and sustainable position in its environment. This is likely to require change in its existing business model.

Strategic control is the monitoring and review of the organization's strategic management of purpose, objectives and strategy, and if necessary, to adapt and manage follow-up action.

Strategic fit is the process of matching the opportunities of the external environment with an organization's internal capabilities.

Strategic groups are clusters of organizations in an industry that share similar competitive characteristics.

Strategic intent is a very ambitious and seemingly unrealistic long-term organizational goal (and slogan) used by Japanese firms to beat more powerful rivals.

Strategic leaders are leaders who are dispersed across the organization, who influence and empower others to participate in strategic management.

Strategic leadership is the style and general approach used by a senior management to articulate purpose, objectives and strategy, to influence implementation and execution of these through the organization.

Strategic levers are four information-based systems that senior managers can use to lever an organization into a desired strategic position.

Strategic lock-in is brought about when core competences (and other strategic resources) are sticky and difficult to change quickly.

Strategic management is the direction and management of an organization in its entirety subject to the strategic requirements of long-term purpose, overall objectives, and strategy.

Strategic map is a pictorial representation of the relative positions of strategic groups. It is used to assess and predict the possible strategic moves of competitors and for the identification of strategic space.

Strategic objectives and measures are objectives and measures used to sustain and progress an organization's purpose (see strategic balanced scorecard).

Strategic performance management is a strategically managed system that enables a senior level to execute and manage strategic priorities in daily management.

Strategic performance systems are systems for the implementation of strategy to achieve specific performance targets that link daily management to top level strategy making.

Strategic planning is a management process of sequencing activities in terms of responsibilities and resources within a given time frame to progress the organization's purpose, objectives and strategy.

Strategic platform is a basic product design or technological system that provides opportunities for the provision of adapted and complementary products and services.

Strategic portfolio analysis is used at a corporate level by executives and central management to appraise the performance of a portfolio of the corporate businesses.

Strategic reviews are periodic reviews of progress of the strategically-linked objectives.

Strategic resources are combinations or bundles of tangible resources (which are economic and tradable) and intangible ones (such as organizational culture and the way people work, which are idiosyncratic and have little external value). An organization's strategic resources are difficult for competitors to understand and imitate.

Strategic restructuring is when an organization substantially changes the composition of its portfolio of businesses.

Strategic risk management is a systematic and overall approach for managing those external events and trends that could seriously harm an organization's effectiveness for achieving its longer-term purpose.

Strategic space is a gap identified in strategic group analysis of apotential gain for an organization to move into.

Strategizing is an activity such as thinking about, formulating, and crafting, strategy to take account of reality and possibilities.

Strategy is an approach for directing an organization's operations over time. It is a long-term approach or policy for accomplishing an organization's purpose and objectives. "Strategies" may be used at any level, but these are typically sub-strategies, which are either derived from the overall strategy, or local strategies that must be in alignment.

Strategy implementation is putting in place an organization's strategy.

Strategy map is a reference framework drawn out to help strategists think about a scorecard's perspectives, objectives and measures – to explore possible cause-and-effect relationships and pressing issues.

Strategy review is a review of an organization's purpose, strategic objectives and overall strategy.

Structural break is a fundamental and unpredictable event in the general environment, which is likely to require organizations to suddenly rethink their purpose and strategy.

Structure is the organization of routine effort into a coherent and working entity.

Supply chain is the chain of external organizations that supply materials and services from primary source to the organization.

Sustainability (see corporate sustainability)

SWOT is a mnemonic used to analyze an organization's Strengths, Weaknesses, Opportunities and Threats.

Systems are formal and documented codes, policies and procedures, which organizations prescribe as normal or best ways of working.

Systems thinking likens organizations to organisms when problems must be considered within the whole rather treated as separate parts.

Takeover is an acquisition that is made when the target organization has not sought the acquiring organization's bid.

Target is a short-term objective that refers to a tactical or operational outcome.

Technology-based strategic platform is a standardized technical system over which an organization may have ownership, which can be used by other organizations as a platform to develop their own products and services.

Thresholds, in generic strategy, a variant of a hybrid strategy, are when basic factors provide a foundation for a separate and distinct competitive strategy.

Top executive audit (TEA) is a senior level business-wide audit of an organization's core competences.

Total quality management (TQM) is an organization-wide philosophy and set of management principles for improving continuously the quality of a product/service to meet customer needs.

Trade-off is choosing to do an activity that involves a reduced ability to do another activity.

Transactional leadership is centred on mission and explicit management systems, which clarify expectations, agreements, and utilize constructive feedback about performance.

Transformational leadership is charismatic leadership which works to associate individual self-interest with the larger vision of the organization by inspiring people with a sense of collective vision.

Transnational strategy is a type of global-level strategy used to exploit markets in different countries by using a mixture of multi-domestic and global strategies.

Unrelated diversification involves contrasting products and services in different markets and industries that have little or no connection with each other.

Value is the satisfaction and benefits customers (and other stakeholders) receive in return for buying and using products and services (and making a contribution to the organization).

Value chain is an organizational framework for disaggregating and showing an organization's strategically relevant activities in order to understand the behaviour of costs and the existing and potential sources of differentiation. An organization sustains its competitive advantage by performing these strategically important activities more cheaply or better than its competitors.

Value curve is used with blue ocean strategy and it depicts how rivals compete with other on relative value creating attributes, such as price, quality etc.

Values are the expected collective norms and behaviour of everybody in the organization: this can include the business methodologies and management philosophies that the organization requires as core competencies to manage vision and mission as an integrated management system.

Varieties of capitalism are generic types of market economy, with a liberal market economy at one end of the spectrum, and a coordinated market economy at the other.

Vertical integration is the growth of an organization by expanding its operations downstream along the distribution chain towards the ultimate customer, and/or upstream along the supply chain towards the primary sources of supply.

Vision is a view of some desired future state or ideal for the organization.

VRIO framework is an acronym meaning Valuable, Rare, Inimitable and Organizable. A resource is strategic if it has these qualities.

Index

CREDITS

Images

Alamy – 31b (Frances Roberts), 49bl (Rolf Adlercreutz), 44bl (Ian Dagnall), 57t (MTP), 63b (David Cole), 118b (Jeff Morgan 02), 157b (Iain Masterton), 170bl (Realimage), 183b (Peter Stroh), 204br (Art Directors & TRIP), 209bl (Philip Scalia), 213bl (Michael Ventura), 232b (Dorling Kindersley), 284b (Frances Roberts), 307tr (Mary Evans Picture Library), 307br (jim forrest), 314b (White House Photo), 323b (incamerastock); **AP** – 265b (AP Photo/Paul Sakuma); **HB Press** – 68tr (Harvard Business Press); **Press Association Images** – 21tr (J. Scott Applewhite/AP), 123b (Eugenie Absalom / Demotix/Demotix), 257m (AP); **Reuters** – 226b (David Moir); **Rex Features** – 177bl (United National Photographers), 309br (Kristin Callahan); **Shutterstock** – vibr (EDHAR), viitr (Kasia Bialasiewicz), viiibr (OPOLJA), vmr (TRINACRIA PHOTO), viiitl (Studio DMM Photography, Designs & Art), 2 (daseaford), 4tr (S.Borisov), 5b (brinkstock), 13tr (Viktoria), 27ml (Darrenp), 30tr (Tatiana Popova), 33b (Piotr Marcinski), 34br (pandapaw), 60 (Margo Harrison), 62tr (Perig), 67tr (Jorge Salcedo), 85b (Grobler du Preez), 90tr (Christian Draghici), 91tl (Mark Schwettmann), 91tr (vvoe), 91ml (saiko3p), 91mr (Yuri Yavnik), 91b (Denis Mironov), 93tr (William Perugini), 97bl (Vladimira), 102tl (scyther5), 105t (Luis Louro), 122tr (Francesco Dazzi), 127tl (Alexandra Lande), 127tr (ixpert), 130tr (ketsu), 132br (Aleksey Klints), 138br (ronfromyork), 143bl (wellphoto), 150b (Rainer Plendl), 154 (Katrina Brown), 156tr (Christian Mueller), 159bl (Sven Hoppe), 160b (Lichtmeister), 162bl (Aleksandra Zaitseva), 182tr (Chris Jenner), 190tr (Dragon Images), 195t (Rafal Cichawa), 195b (Erik Lam), 198bl (Sebastian Knight), 199tl (William Silver), 201tl (Neil Wigmore), 203tr (Pavel L Photo and Video), 212tr (joyfull), 213br (James Steidl), 214tr (Anton Balazh), 217bl (Worldpics), 229 (El Greco), 224ml (crystalfoto), 231bl (Pakhnyushcha), 246 (Rob Byron), 248tr (S.Borisov), 249bl (Federico Rostagno), 249br (Corepics VOF), 251br (Carlos Caetano), 255tl (TDHster), 259tl (Alex Staroseltsev), 270tr (S.Borisov), 279mr (Stuart Jenner), 280br (Neale Cousland), 288tl (Essl), 289tr (carroteater), 295br (Yuri Arcurs), 302tr (Laszlo Halasi), 303br (xstockerx), 305br (wjarek), 310br (Art Allianz); **WED Institute** – 137tl

Text and figures

'**Principles in Practice 2.2:** Two examples of purpose statements', screenshot reproduced courtesy of Alibaba Group. All rights reserved.

'**Figure 3.3:** The Tesco steering wheel' is reproduced courtesy of Tesco. © Tesco Plc. All rights reserved.

'**Principles in Practice 3.3:** A balanced scorecard at the non-profit making University of Virginia Library' includes a figure that is reproduced courtesy of the University of Virginia. © 2009 University of Virginia. All rights reserved.

'**Figure 5.4:** The European Excellence Model' © EFQM (European Foundation for Quality Management) (2013), *The EFQM Excellence Model*, Brussels: EFQM, www.efqm.org. Reproduced with kind permission.

'**Figure 7.8:** The GE-McKinsey matrix' Adapted from Coyne K. (2008), *Enduring Ideas: The GE–McKinsey Nine-Box Matrix*, McKinsey & Company, September. www.mckinsey.com. Courtesy of McKinsey & Company.

'**Exhibit 8.1:** Vision, 2002-2007' from © Tata Steel (2002), Vision 2007, Annual Report 2002-2003; 'Exhibit 8.2: The strategic management process' is adapted from Tata Chemicals (2008), www.tatachemicals.com. Both exhibits are reproduced with kind permission of Tata Steel.

'**Exhibit 9.1:** Toyota's organizing pyramid' from Toyota (1999), 'Ensuring the achievement of the second action plan (FY2000) and taking actions for the 21st century', *Toyota Environment Management*, company document. Courtesy of Toyota (GB) Plc.